Readings in Local Government Management and Development — A Southern African Perspective

Readings in Local Government Management and Development — A Southern African Perspective

P S Reddy
(editor)

Juta & Co, Ltd

First published 1996
© Juta & Co, Ltd
PO Box 14373, Kenwyn 7790

ISBN 0 7021 3612 3

Subediting by Mike Golby, Cape Town
Cover design by Inspiration Sandwich, Cape Town
Book design, computer graphics and typesetting by Jo Goodwill, Cape Town
Set in 10 on 12 pt Palatino

Printed and bound by Creda Press, Eliot Avenue, Eppindust II

To my wife Vimla, my son Vishad and daughter Yetika,
for all the time I spent away from home

— Foreword —

The winds of change have swept across the African continent and, more particularly, the southern African region. This has demanded that the public sector change its leadership and management style. Local government, affecting the quality of every citizen's life through service delivery, is at the cutting-edge of this change. The Community Elections of November 1995 ushered in new, non-racial and democratic local authorities that have a crucial role to play in our country's transition to democracy and beyond. Consequently, local government management and development will have to respond to the needs of South Africans while addressing the challenges of the Government of National Unity's Reconstruction and Development Programme (RDP).

There is a dearth of literature on the peculiarities of South African local government management and development, especially as they apply to our current situation. This publication will begin to fill this void, encouraging critical debate and discussion on the subject. Its content indicates a comprehensive and in-depth coverage of the field. Although it has a theoretical bias, it will be a valuable source of practical information for students, practitioners and politicians interested and involved in local government.

The Democracy Development Programme (DDP) has worked closely with the School of Public Policy and Development Management at the University of Durban-Westville in the field of local government. Many workshops and conferences have been held to develop capacity among elected representatives and officials in the Kwazulu Natal region. The DDP is proud to be associated with this publication. We hope that it will reach its target audience and make a significant contribution to good practices in local government, now and in the future.

Dr R A Naidu
Executive Director
Democracy Development Programme

— Preface —

Significant and far-reaching changes have taken place throughout southern Africa. South Africa and its neighbours are undergoing a process of fundamental political, economic and social restructuring. The decisive strategic and even paradigmatic shifts in the governance of these countries have impacted very strongly on local government management and development in the region.

Part One of this text provides an overview of local government management and development in the southern African region. It reviews the theory of local government in developing countries, emphasising the African and South African experiences. An overview of urban development and local government in South Africa, Mozambique, Angola, Zimbabwe and Namibia is provided. Liberalisation, democratisation, economic restructuring and increasing urbanisation have redefined local government throughout southern Africa. Liberalisation has encouraged local action, and democratisation has countered the dominance of the central state by, *inter alia*, creating and strengthening sub-national government. Economic restructuring has resulted in increased autonomy for local economies now fending for themselves against a globalising international economy; and urbanisation has resulted in urban centres attempting to address socio-economic needs with limited assistance from central government. To meet the challenges of these dynamic forces, local government will have to be appropriately structured and resourced.

The South African local government elections of November 1995 ushered in new, democratic local authorities which will face tremendous political, economic and social challenges. It is an opportune time to review strategy and capacity, and to introduce systems capable of developing, managing and delivering programmes of reconstruction and development. Part Two focuses on the constitutional, structural and organisational development of local government. The notion of intergovernmental relations assumes importance when a division of powers exists at both the administrative and legislative levels of different tiers of government. A creative mechanism is needed to maintain cooperative relationships and coordination among and between vertical and horizontal sites of power within a polity. The need to establish formal and informal institutions to facilitate intergovernmental relations is addressed. Additionally, the possibilities and limitations created by institutional arrangements are examined.

The functions of organising, structuring and designing are prerequisites to meeting the various challenges facing the new, democratic, non-racial local authorities of South Africa. Structuring is centred on the principles of specialisation, departmentalisation, delegation, coordination and relationships. Designing is based on the matrix contingency and strategic approaches. The process of organisational structuring and designing needs to take cognisance of and absorb the impact of different scales of institutional change, including fine-tuning, incremental adjustment, modular and corporate transformation.

'Strategic management' has become a buzzword in local government. The increasing literature on the subject bears ample testimony to it topping the management agenda of local authorities worldwide. The need to adopt a strategic focus to the management of South African local authorities has been given added impetus by the Government of National Unity's Reconstruction and Development Programme (RDP). Local authorities as implementation vehicles are critical to the success of the RDP. For South African local authorities, strategic management holds enormous potential for community empowerment and social and economic development now and in the future.

Part Three focuses on human resource management and affirmative action. Local authorities require human resources to, *inter alia*, implement policy, render services and manage their delivery. Human resource management is manifest in the process used by a local authority to employ or deploy its labour. In the context of local government, human resource management refers to the provisioning, use, training, development and maintenance of human resources. With the restructuring and transformation of local government, the profiles of local authorities need to reflect regional demographics. So, to address racial and gender inequities in employment, every local authority needs to formulate, as a priority, a human resource development policy intrinsic to its overall resource plan.

A case study of affirmative action in the Durban metropolitan area is reviewed in Part Three. Methodologically, the chapter is based on two evaluation studies by the Training and Development Scheme (TDS), currently carried out by the Centre for Community and Labour Studies and the School of Public Policy and Development Management at the University of Durban-Westville. The chapter assesses strategies used to qualitatively improve the work experience, the effect of exposure to decision making on interns, planning, project management, and the development and improvement of interpersonal skills and leadership qualities. It analyses the programme's monitoring components, the strengths, weaknesses and qualities of mentorship, and the ingredients of an appropriate teaching programme. It also highlights internal obstacles to affirmative action strategies and the forms this resistance takes.

The 1990s were heralded as the decade of opportunity for women, a time when they would be recognised as a vital resource capable of filling the skills gap in the labour market. Yet, in South African local authorities, women remain in menial, lowly paid jobs without status and are under-represented in decision-making structures. To maximise the potential of women in local government management and development, various strategic initiatives need to be initiated and developed by the new, democratic and non-racial local authorities.

Part Four focuses on developmental aspects critical to local government and its financing. The planning functions of local authorities have substantial impact on local development. In the RDP, there is strong emphasis on planning and implementation by local authorities. Provided all other conditions are equal, there is a huge potential for benefits accruing to local authorities involved in development planning. Planning has, in common with all other activities in South

Africa, a legacy of constrained development. Consequently, the process has to be transformed to focus on development rather than on control.

To meet the justifiable expectations of South Africans beyond the apartheid era, current local government financing systems are expected to undergo fundamental changes. A new and adequate financing system will have to be formulated to pay for essential services local authorities will be compelled to provide in future. However, at this stage, there can be no 'absolute' measures for financing. Many approaches, systems and processes from a pot-pourri of financing options are expected to be tried and tested over the next few years. In the long term, both experiential learning and changing local government dynamics will determine how local authorities should be financed.

International experience of local economic development has some telling lessons for the reconstruction of South Africa's cities. Locally driven and community oriented economic development programmes present unique opportunities and possibilities for empowerment. Socially and economically sustainable local economic development initiatives revolve around local government harnessing, shaping and encouraging the growth of a productive sector. An approach driven by a centralised state in partnership with communities complemented by the investment of the private sector is needed. This developmental role incorporates traditional functions of local government, including, *inter alia*, infrastructural and land use planning, but it may also extend into more novel forms of activity such as the laying out and operation of science parks; the underwriting of venture capital activities; the organisation of worker training programmes, and the formation of public–private and public–public development corporations.

The restructuring of local government in South Africa's rural areas is high on the political agenda. The shortcomings of the centralised local government transition process in the run-up to South Africa's first democratic elections highlighted the need for postulating solutions to local government issues in rural areas. At this juncture South Africa has to make a deliberate choice. In following a centrist route, the requisite commitment to strong, rural local government is lost. The alternative is not only imperative for local democracy; it is also a precondition for rural development. However, given that the country will be governed by the interim constitution until 1999, it is not too late to pursue lasting solutions.

The past two decades have been characterised by the rapid growth of NGOs, especially in developing countries. While they do not fulfil the role of formal governance, NGOs have articulated and responded to the development needs of poor communities. NGOs, functioning at grass roots, support a strong civil society, beyond the state authorities. It is expected that NGOs will contribute to a stronger civil society and promote 'people orientated' development. But, to increase their significance and to be influential in reproducing their activities on a massive scale, NGOs need to influence government at local, regional and national levels. South African NGOs, which failed to form a uniform community, reflect a rich diversity. Some have mass-based constituencies, others are restricted to limited membership. They comprise, *inter alia*, unions, lobby groups, self-help organisations, service organisations and charitable associations.

There is ample justification to claim that, by and large, South African NGOs kept the tradition of democratic governance by civic institutions alive and acted as a bulwark against political and civil oppression. The emergence of a political democracy based on popular will has opened new opportunities for NGOs to make a meaningful contribution to South African society, particularly at a local government level.

It has become imperative that South African local authorities adopt an urban environmental planning and management approach focusing on sustainable development while recognising the links between environmental quality, poverty, and quality of life. A planning process including, *inter alia*, community participation, the identification of key environmental issues, the establishment of environmental priorities, the development of environmental strategies and action plans and the institution of appropriate evaluation and feedback mechanisms should be adopted. This approach is consistent with the directives implicit in the Local Agenda mandate emanating from the United Nations' Earth Summit in 1992 and the Global Plan of Action that will be endorsed at the forthcoming United Nations City Summit in Istanbul.

Finally, and on a personal note, I thank the contributors to this text for the cooperation and enthusiasm needed to make its publication a reality. Dr R A Naidu has always been supportive of us and the sponsorship of the Democracy Development Programme is deeply appreciated.

Professor P S Reddy
February 1996
Durban

Note

For easy reading, the male gender is used wherever the text demands specificity. Its use reflects the inadequacies of language — not the views of contributors.

— List of Contributors —

T Botha is Director-General of the Eastern Cape Regional Administration.

S Jaggernath is Director of the Chatsworth Child and Family Welfare Society.

F Khan is Senior Researcher at the Centre for Community and Labour Studies at the University of Durban-Westville.

N Levy is Director of the Training and Development Scheme at the University of Durban-Westville.

B Maharaj is Senior Lecturer in Geography at the University of Durban-Westville.

P Maharaj is a lecturer in Public Administration at the University of Durban-Westville.

S Maharaj is Research Associate at the Centre for Community and Labour Studies at the University of Durban-Westville.

A McIntosh is a researcher at the Institute for Social and Economic Research at the University of Durban-Westville.

S Moodley is Senior Lecturer in Public Administration at the University of Durban-Westville.

Y Penceliah is a lecturer in Public Administration at the University of Durban-Westville.

P S Reddy is Associate Professor in Public Administration at the University of Durban-Westville.

D Roberts is the Environmental Manager of the Durban Transitional Metropolitan Council.

T Sabela is Senior Lecturer in Political Science at the University of Zululand.

D Sing is Associate Professor in Public Administration at the University of Durban-Westville.

M Swilling is Director of the Graduate School of Public and Development Management at the University of the Witwatersrand

M Wallis is Professor and Head of Public Administration at the University of Durban-Westville.

— Contents —

— PART 1 —

Overview of Local Government Management and Development in the Southern African Region

The Philosophy of Local Government in Developing Countries with Particular Reference to South Africa

T Sabela & P S Reddy

1 INTRODUCTION

Globally, local government is the second or third tier of government deliberately created to bring government to the grass roots, as well as give its members a sense of involvement in the political processes that control their daily lives. Democracy denotes a political system in which the eligible people in a polity participate not only in determining who governs them, but also participate in shaping their government's policies. Determining the composition of a government is done in free and fair elections supervised by an impartial electoral body.

South Africa is a country of almost forty million people, constituted of heterogeneous cultural and political groups. The need for effective, democratic local government as a vehicle for development and national integration is imperative. The first non-racial, democratic local elections were held in November 1995. A dual electoral system applied for the elections — 60% of the councillors were elected on a ward basis and the other 40% were elected on a system of proportional representation.

This chapter reviews the philosophy underlying local government in developing countries and the trend towards democratisation and decentralisation on the African continent. It also focuses on South Africa's quest for democracy.

2 LOCAL GOVERNMENT DEMOCRACY

Local government is a peculiar theme, always recognised in developing countries as important, yet seldom comprehensively written about or understood. Unlike some aspects of national politics, the local government environment needs close personal observation for an understanding unobtainable from secondary sources (Mahwood 1983:v). The importance of local as the basis of all structures of governance, and its role in the quest for a stable democratic society, cannot be overemphasised. Local government is created deliberately to bring government to the grass roots, giving people a sense of involvement in the political processes controlling their lives. The essence of good local government, ie stable government, has therefore been advocated throughout the democratic world.

A major crisis experienced in local government is one of ill-adjusted functions in terms of meeting the demands of citizens. According to Leemans (1970:17–27), the crisis manifests itself in various ways:

☐ Local government does not meet the material and cultural needs of its communities;

☐ Services that should be functionally consolidated or placed in the hands of the authority are fragmented among several bodies, thereby increasing the difficulty of meeting the needs of communities; and

☐ Many local authorities are too small in size and revenue and, consequently, fall short of adequately qualified personnel and technology to execute their activities to an acceptable standard.

The above deficiencies often hamper the development of satisfactory local government. Mahwood (1993:x–xii) shares this view when he states that the problems of public management and rural development in developing countries are intractable and that many difficulties remain unresolved despite the efforts of government.

2.1   Meaning of local government democracy

The notions discussed below are hallmarks of the classical, representative local government democracy practised in many countries.

2.1.1   Popular consultation

The implication of the above is that government requires the consent of the citizens whose rights it is bound to respect and protect. The dignity of a man is best manifested when he determines and controls his affairs. Therefore, that form of government which best projects the dignity of the individual, protects and fosters it, is what this paper proposes to call democracy. Democracy pursues a policy of self-determination. Self-government is a natural outcome of self-direction which means that one is not imposed upon by unwanted rulers, and that one is not compelled to live under rules to which one has not contributed (Ayoade Mni, Nwabuzor & Sambo 1992:9–10).

Democracy cannot be said to exist where the majority of the people in a political system are denied a say in the process of governance. Ranney (1990:109) argues that it is impossible in a modern polity to have 'direct democracy', as it was realised by classical Athens that full participation in every aspect of decision making was physically and managerially impossible. This task should be entrusted to a class of democratically elected politicians. In a truly democratic setting, it is the reconciliation and processing of these views into popular policy that should be the main function of those who hold political power in trust for the people. A situation in which politicians turn to the people only during elections, and rule according to their whims and caprices afterwards, is undemocratic (Ayoade Mni et al 1992:8). There must be constant dialogue between the governors and the governed. Only then can people's views and aspirations be ascertained and taken into account in the policy-making process (Ayoade Mni et al 1992:8; Ranney 1990:114).

2.1.2   Popular participation

Full individual participation in making societal choices and decisions is a natural outcome of the endowment of individual dignity because it contributes to individual self-development. Responsibility for the governing of one's own conduct develops one's dignity. What is more, full individual participation within the local government context contributes to the creation of community solidarity, because citizens feel involved in matters relavent to their welfare.

Full individual participation boils down to popular participation where citizens are invited and expected to express their wishes on issues of governance. On every issue, the views of the majority should prevail. This popular participation may be achieved through meetings of ratepayers' associations, vigilante groups, and other social and political associations in small and large communities. Public or popular participation in decision making is an imperative tenet for democratic local government (Gildenhuys, Fox & Wissink 1991:124). But, in order not to deny the minority its right of self-assertion, it is also a democratic imperative that while the majority should have its way, the minority must have its say. In return, the minority must accept the majority decision once that decision has been freely arrived at.

In recent years, 'participation' has become something of a political catch-phrase and many people with a serious interest in politics have become suspicious of it. According to Derbyshire (1984:226), this scepticism is perhaps best summed up in the words printed on a poster displayed by French students during the 1968 disturbances in Paris. Translated into English, it read:

> 'I participate
> Thou participatest
> He participates
> We participate
> You participate
> THEY PROFIT'

Whether it is political or local government participation, the one thing that sceptics ask is: how real is it? In other words, to participate effectively must mean to be able, as a consequence of the participation, to have some influence over any resultant decisions (Derbyshire 1984:227).

2.1.3   Competition

People with different political views or ideological standpoints must be allowed to articulate these views and canvass support for them from the platform of the political party of their choice. It is absurd to talk of democracy when individuals with particular political interests or views are denied the opportunity to compete for popular support when such views and interests are not inimical to the survival of the political community.

Within the context of democracy, elections are viewed as an important vehicle for a free exchange of views in which the voter can make a choice. Elections should not be seen as warfare. In a democracy the winner must allow the loser to exist and continue to express his views until the next election. It is undemocratic to ban or destroy opposing parties. It is also, after a fair election, undemocratic for the losing parties to behave in a manner that prevents the will of the majority being implemented (Derbyshire & Derbyshire 1989:87–88; Ayoade Mni et al 1992:10).

2.1.4 Freedom of expression

Another consequence of the right to self-determination and popular participation is the need for free expression. Individuals must be free to express themselves on the issues of the day. They cannot fully influence the course of events, especially governmental policies, without this freedom. Indeed, there is no way to ascertain the popular will if the individual is not free to express his opinion. The availability of wide-ranging views provides vital information and assists in the popular control of government by a well-informed citizenry (Ranney 1990:125–137).

2.1.5 Equality

Since all men are created equal, they should also be treated equally before the law, irrespective of gender, ethnicity, religion, economic class or social stratification. Equality before the law extends to political equality. All citizens should have equal access to political power and influence in shaping policy (Ranney 1990:113–114).

Ayoade Mni et al (1992:11–12) state that in modern times the notion of equality has been expanded to include equality of opportunity in many important aspects of life. This is the aim of the egalitarian society. Equality aims at equality of opportunity in education, employment and social justice for the oppressed, neglected and disadvantaged. This expansion of the notion of equality is to ensure that each person has equal opportunity to develop his naturally endowed potential to the utmost. It is important for developing countries to note that democracy does not seek to level every citizen, but accepts inequalities resulting from individual merit and hard work in order not to enthrone mediocrity.

3 DECENTRALISATION AND DEMOCRATISATION — THE AFRICAN EXPERIENCE

In the flow of new ideas emerging from the continent as it experiences change on virtually all fronts, terms like democracy and decentralisation regularly surface. It is hoped that these ideas and strategies will shape the contours and form the legal basis for established African states or countries presently in transition.

3.1 Defining terms: decentralisation

The word 'decentralisation' indicates something at the centre, from which it may be dispersed. Most people and governments favour the concept of decentralisation as it implies opening the blockages of an inert central bureaucracy, curing managerial constipation, giving more direct access to government by the people, and stimulating the whole nation to participate in national development plans (Mahwood 1993:1).

According to a study by the United Nations (1962:8) there are two distinct uses for the term, namely:

> 'Deconcentration of decisionmaking authority to dependent field units of the same department or level of government, that is the delegation to civil servants working in the field of power to make decisions in the execution of central policies (also referred to as administrative or bureaucratic decentralization);
>
> Devolution of decisionmaking authority to relatively autonomous regional or local governments, or to special statutory bodies, that is the cession to power to make decisions (including restricted policy making power) to representative (usually elected) authorities, or to more or less autonomous public or voluntary enterprises (also referred to as political or administrative decentralization).'

However, according to Allen (1990:4), deconcentration and devolution may be territorial (ie to units geographically separated from the centre); or functional (ie assigning responsibility for specific kinds of governmental activity). Moreover, both types of decentralisation may be general-purpose, with responsibility over a range of governmental activities (eg the functions of an elected city or county council or an appointed regional or provincial governor), or they may be special-purpose, (eg appointed income tax commissioners or the post office, or an elected local education authority or water board). A body enjoying devolved power may itself deconcentrate or devolve those powers, for example when a city council delegates authority to a representative district committee (Allen 1990:4).

Many writers (Mahwood 1993:4; Nzouankeu 1994:213; Meenakshisundaram 1994:11) still believe there is a need for some working definition of decentralised or local government in developing countries to distinguish it from bodies which are representative but have minimal or only specialised responsibility. It is assumed that a local government has its own budget and a separate legal existence, with authority granted to it by the central government to allocate substantial material resources on a range of different functions (Mahwood 1990:4).

3.2 Reasons for decentralisation

According to the World Bank (1989:71) there are four arguments in favour of decentralisation, namely:

☐ the demand for local public services varies from place to place. Only the decentralised provision of local services will meet multifaceted demands;

☐ efficiency. It can be argued that locally financed and produced services will cost less;

☐ political. Local government is an important training ground for democracy. Stronger regional or local governments can control the tendency of central government to become all-powerful; and

☐   institutional. Coordination of local public services is necessary. They cannot and should not be treated independently. Local government can coordinate these services more easily than could a national government.

3.3 Role of local government in democratic decentralisation

Decentralisation is a natural, indispensable counterpart to pluralistic democracy, ie it extends the work of democracy and fulfils democratic aspirations. Consequently, any political reform aimed at democratising institutions, particularly in founding a pluralistic democracy, will only be fully effective insofar as it is accompanied by far-reaching administrative reforms which effectively redistribute power (Nzouankeu 1994:215). The term 'decentralisation' does not necessarily contain any democratic connotation; however, the adjective 'democratic' is indicative of a special meaning attached to the term. According to Meenakshisundaram (1994:16), democratic decentralisation possesses two virtues, namely:

☐   it is consistent with the democratic trend and is also technically the most efficient method of formulating and executing local projects. It is democratic in the sense that the source from which power is decentralised has a democratic base, and the body to which power flows is also democratically organised. In this context, 'democratic decentralisation' is a political ideal and local self-government is its institutional form; and

☐   the administrative orientation must shift from making decisions and issuing orders to helping people make decisions through cooperatives and other traditional structures. Consequently, decentralisation facilitates the combination of, and cooperation between, the official machinery of administration and non-official leadership and control through the mechanism of local governments.

The existence of democratic local government can prevent the emergence of alternative power centres at the local level that are not subject to the influence and authority of the state. In addition, it can be used as a vehicle to decongest the government at higher level(s), thereby freeing national and provincial leaders from direct involvement in local issues. Local government provides an opportunity and a channel for a government to hold a dialogue with the masses, to influence them and to get necessary feedback from them (Meenakshisundaram 1994:16).

3.4 The African experience reviewed

A major characteristic of governance on the African continent following political independence was the overt centralisation of governmental authority. This was due partly to historical legacies inherited from colonial administration, with its rigid emphasis on control from the centre. On achieving self-government, many countries retained rigid, centralised structures (United Nations 1992:xv). This resulted in considerable reliance on centralised institutions and agencies and the de-emphasising of decentralised institutions, including local government. This has often meant the neglect or suppression of local self-government or the absence of any meaningful grass-roots involvement in governance. The consequence of overcentralisation has been, *inter alia*, a distortion of the development process owing to insufficient dynamising of the rural population; the stifling of local initiative and of the contribution that local talent can make in development, and an under-mobilisation of local resources or a failure to use them to their best advantage (United Nations 1992:xvi).

Recent trends on the continent have brought the role of the state in social and economic development into question. This has been significantly influenced by severe resource constraints and deteriorating social and economic situations in many African countries. In addition, the adoption by many countries of structural adjustment programmes involving assistance from external agencies has resulted in market systems that imply significant reductions in the economic role of the state. This has resulted in a need to develop alternative service systems and structures catering to all sections of the community in small and large areas.

That there is need for decentralisation in African countries is undeniable. The reasons for this can be summarised as follows:

☐ At a political level, decentralisation enables people to participate in a real and effective way in the management of public affairs. Consequently, decentralisation is conducive to local democracy, which is the real or tangible form of democracy, very different to the theoretical and quasi-mythical democracy of electoral campaigns and speeches;

☐ At an economic and social level, economic decentralisation is now considered to be a sine qua non for development and democratisation. In this respect, there can be no doubt as to the value of proper regional development plans which are qualitatively different from the regional components of national plans and which, within the context of effective decentralisation, mobilise valuable local energies and resources around integrated projects (Nzouankeu 1994:215).

Economic decentralisation will certainly add a human dimension to any development policies implemented.

At a recent 'Commonwealth Roundtable on Democratisation and Decentralisation for Senior Local Government Policymakers in Africa', the following programme, relating to governance and the promotion of democratic local government, was endorsed:

☐ adherence to the Commonwealth principles of democratisation and decentralisation including a commitment to democracy, fundamental human rights, the rule of law, the independence of the judiciary and just and honest government, including the empowerment of people at the local level, unrestricted political activity, and organising of fair and free elections at local level;

☐ allocation of the necessary resources and technical expertise by central governments as well as the international donor community to ensure the successful preparation and implementation of the democratic agenda, including support for civic education programmes;

☐ recognition of the role that participatory local government can play in consolidating democracy and development objectives;

☐ the promotion of a cooperative policy and institutional framework for intergovernmental relations in the area of local government;

☐ an adequate, enabling environment for local government, including the necessary constitutional, legislative and financial safeguards and allocations;

☐ effective devolution of power to ensure that local government is recognised by central government as a distinct sphere of government and a partner in development;

☐ restructuring of ministerial organisations, and decentralisation of the national administrative machinery in response to public sector reform and support for good governance;

☐ consolidation of the democratic process by support for post-election capacity building and induction/training programmes for elected local representatives;

☐ recognition of the need for close links between local democracy and parliamentary democracy at national level;

☐ effective implementation of the International Union of Local Authorities (IULA) Toronto Declaration on the Worldwide Declaration of Local Self-Government as a valuable guideline for the promotion and strengthening of local government;

☐ recognition that traditional leadership is afforded considerable credibility and functions in many local communities and that, with the creation of appropriate mechanisms for their involvement, such leadership can assist in the realisation of development goals;

☐ full and active participation of women in local government;

☐ full participation of local communities in the decision-making process, especially with regard to project identification and implementation; and

☐ democratisation and decentralisation strategies must not compromise the integrity of the countries concerned (Commonwealth Local Government Forum 1995:3–4).

4 LOCAL GOVERNMENT DEMOCRACY IN THE SOUTH AFRICAN CONTEXT

The new South Africa has to go beyond purely representative democracy to address the inequalities of the apartheid era. The new South Africa must bequeath to its citizens a local government democracy giving the majority the fullest opportunity to participate in shaping the country's political destiny. It must try to correct the ills of apartheid by making it mandatory for any political aspirant to obtain a genuine mandate from the people at a local government level. By so doing, the new government in South Africa would be dealing a nasty blow to the elitist politics of men and women of means who monopolised politics without the genuine consent of the masses, pursuing their own interests to the detriment of the majority. What then are the functions local government democracy has to fulfil in the political lives of South Africans, now and in the future?

4.1 Representation

The notion of representation is a fundamental tenet of democracy. Therefore, local government democracy has to grapple with:

☐   Who is represented?
☐   How many are represented?; and
☐   How do representatives represent?

The last two questions shall be at the base of local government in the new South Africa. Since all citizens cannot congregate to make day-to-day decisions, some people must be chosen to perform such functions. Every decision is a fulfilment of a wish or desire. Whose wish or desire, therefore, should the representatives carry out? Purely representative democracy would be satisfied if after one has been elected, one is given a free hand to act and vote in local government according to one's conscience. Venter & Johnston (1991:154–156) are quick to point out that the complete independence of representatives is inconsistent with the concept of democracy, which requires a local government response to citizens' desires. On the other hand, complete mandatory democracy is impossible because the electorate lacks clear views on many issues that have to be addressed (Ball 1991:114–117; Ranney 1990:281). Burke (1854:446–447) argued appropriately when he stated that elected representatives should be independent of their constituents' wishes when those wishes conflict with the representative's best judgement on an issue. This chapter suggests that a mixture of the two theories, the mandate and independence theories, should be accepted, with the proportion adjusted by each representative according to his judgement of what is needed in particular circumstances. Local government democracy further demands that it is not just the representative who goes to the higher level, but also the citizens' decisions.

4.2 Self-determination

Self-determination at local government level in the new South Africa must demand more stringent conditions for the behaviour of elected officials vis-à-vis the electorate. Self-determination demands that decision making takes place at the level where one can truly participate. This raises the question of the optimally feasible size of the ward from which the councillor is chosen. The ward must be reduced to a manageable community where opinion can be realistically sounded. It must not be a large unit where the citizen is anonymous. Realising that the local government councillor is not elected by only his party members but by the larger ward electorate, the councillor cannot afford to limit his search for views to those of party members, but must constantly interact with as many constituents as possible.

Councillors must devise ways to ascertain the wishes of the wards' electorates. Councillors must be given allowances for running offices in their local constituencies. These allowances must be used to establish effective monitoring offices from which to obtain the views of the electorate. Allowances must not be converted into personal emoluments.

4.3 Constant dialogue

Councillors at local government level must be fully-fledged members of their constituencies. Consequently, they have the opportunity to listen to the views of constituents and also have the opportunity to express their views. In dialogue, there is learning and either the councillor's views will be modified by the community or he will change the opinion of the constituency. Dialogue must be regular and frequent. The councillor can never be so busy as to not attend ward or party meetings. He has to maintain regular contact with his constituents.

4.4 Openness of policy making

Local government democrats in developing countries must ensure that there is openness in government's decision-making processes. Local government democrats in developing countries must accept that every human is an intelligent and good-natured being. The average citizen knows best where the shoe pinches and, if enough information is placed at his disposal, is likely to come up with the best solution to the problem.

4.5 Accountability

The discussion so far of the purposes of local government democracy has touched on the issues of representation, full participation and constant dialogue. The last directive purpose is that of accountability. Accountability means being put in a position to give account of one's stewardship. Stewardship includes financial accountability and representational accountability. Financial accountability requires that all public resources entrusted to the local authority be judiciously used for the projects they were intended, and that public funds should not be diverted for private use.

The second aspect of accountability concerns the council legislator as a representative of his party in government and the constituency of voters that put him in office. As such the councillor cannot claim to have been elected purely on his personal merit or resources. He is fully accountable to the party membership.

4.6 Financial management process

To function, an organisation needs money. Local government without money would merely be a talk-shop. The viability of local government, the level at which services are rendered, and the quality of those services are inextricably linked to the financial resources available to it. The assumption here is that if funds are available, local government will be able to procure other resources such as staff, materials and equipment to enable it to perform its assigned responsibilities.

Local governments in the new South Africa need to recognise that, as the third tier of government and the one closest to the people, whatever happens or does not happen at their level is easily noticed and has a significant impact on the people. In a developing country like South Africa with a very large illiterate population, to many people the concept of government terminates at the level of local government because other, higher levels are too remote for them to appreciate (Nwabuzor & Mueller 1989:61–62). This is why it is incumbent on councillors to act responsibly and to feel accountable to the public.

5 THE 1995 LOCAL GOVERNMENT ELECTIONS

The first chapter in the democratisation of South Africa was brought to a satisfactory conclusion with local government elections being held in eight provinces in November 1995. The run-up to the local government elections started on 27 January 1995 with a ninety-day campaign resulting in twenty-three million potential voters being registered (Fray 1995:2). The registration process, which started officially in January 1995, was a completely new concept to most voters as they had little or no experience of democratic local government. A local government task team was established to facilitate registration, ensuring that the process was coordinated and standardised at a national level. The objective was to ensure that the elections in November were free, fair and efficiently managed. Other functions included, *inter alia*, ensuring uniform election regulations, assisting where problems arose, ensuring adherence to time-frames set, mobilising resources of whatever nature whenever necessary, and organising and overseeing voter education (*Sunday Tribune* 26 March 1995).

The task group introduced a communication plan to promote participation in the elections. The overall aim of the communication plan was to encourage all adult South Africans to participate in the elections by:

□ emphasising the impact local government has on their lives;
□ explaining the composition and functions of the new local authorities; and
□ explaining the electoral process from voter registration to polling day (Institute of Multi-Party Democracy 1995).

The target group comprised metropolitan/urban voters, rural voters, community leaders and organisations, news media executives, women's organisations, school and tertiary institutions, youth organisations, churches and other religious institutions, the business community and agricultural organisations.

The campaign was planned and executed in support of the overall government communication strategy, reflecting progress made in transforming the lives of South Africans. The campaign, which was non-partisan, objective and credible, was allocated R42 million (Institute of Multi-Party Democracy 1995).

In terms of results, the local government elections reflected national trends set in the April 1994 elections, but with less enthusiasm and lower polls (Streek 1995:25). It was generally accepted that the resources, finance and organisational skills of the different political parties also influenced the results. In the April 1994 elections, all the political parties received substantial funding from the taxpayer through the Independent Electoral Commission. Consequently, this enabled them to launch massive advertising campaigns, hire staff and offices and, generally, maintain a high profile. The local government elections were, however, organised by the nine provincial governments, none of which had the resources to subsidise the costs of political campaigning (Streek 1995:26). Well-resourced political parties able to raise funds consequently had greater organisational strengths. This impacted on voter registration as well-organised parties ensured that more of their than the opposition parties' supporters were registered to vote.

The elections also gave South Africans an opportunity to call their parties to account. In addition, the elections decided the future of many political parties.

Given these developments, local government elections were indeed an important event in the country's political history.

6 CONCLUSION

This chapter has reviewed the needs of local government in and during the transition to a post-apartheid South Africa, and it has explored how it can contribute to the search for local democracy. In a country such as South Africa, ravaged by apartheid, the need is for local government to serve as a breeding ground for the democratic ethos. Based on the premise that if genuine democracy is not only established but is seen to be established at a local level, the fundamental concerns of the country's constitutional elements would have been addressed, and its people would be carried along in the democratic train.

It was further stated that social equality demands the support of well-known tenets of true democracy. The objective of local government democracy is to create conditions under which each individual may achieve the greatest measure of welfare and prosperity. It should be noted that, in order to attain the objective of local government democracy, the machinery of local government should be organised in a manner allowing mutual deliberation and consultation. It could be said that democracy is that form of government seeking to unite its citizenry as a community which constantly pursues the happiness of the largest number of its people. This form of government is based on two fundamental assumptions, ie the dignity of a person, and the natural endowment of man with freedom, a freedom he has an overpowering impulse to preserve. Democracy ensures self-determination and self-government through popular consultation, popular participation, competition of ideas and policies, basic individual freedoms, equality before the law and access to opportunity to influence policy.

Democratisation and decentralisation have taken on considerable significance on the African continent. Many countries have undertaken major political and constitutional reforms, involving participatory democracy and greater pluralism, including the holding of representative elections at local level. Democratisation and decentralisation in Africa can be seen as the means towards an end, namely the development of communities and the improved provision of services, rather than ends in themselves. Both strategies are mutually reinforcing.

With the local government elections of November 1995, the democratisation of South Africa was complete. Voter registration was considered an integral part of the process and party politics were the order of the day. For the smaller parties, poor performances could signal their demise. Undoubtedly, the November local government elections were always going to be a watershed in South African political history.

7 REFERENCES

Allen HJB. 1990. *Cultivating the Grassroots: Why Local Matters*. Bombay: All-India Institute of Local Self-Government.

Ayoade Mni JAA, EJ Nwabuzor & A Sambo. 1992. *Democracy and the New Local Government System in Nigeria*. Abuja: Centre for Democratic Studies.

Ball AR. 1988. *Modern Politics and Government*. London: Macmillan.

Burke E. 1955 Address to the electors of Bristol. In *The Works of Edmund Burke*. New York: Harper and Row.

Commonwealth Local Government Forum. 1995. *Commonwealth Roundtable on Democratisation for Senior Local Government Policymakers*. (Africa) Harare: June 27–29.

Derbyshire JJD. 1984. *An Introduction to Public Administration*. London: McGraw-Hill Inc.

Derbyshire JD & I Derbyshire. 1989. *Political Systems of the Third World*. Edinburgh: W and R Chambers Limited.

Fray P. 1995. The tasks of the task group. *Towards Democracy — Journal of the Institute for Multi-Party Democracy*. First Quarter.

Gildenhuys H, W Fox & H Wissink. 1991. *Public Macro Organisation*. Kenwyn: Juta & Co Ltd.

Institute for Multi-Party Democracy. 1995. *Local Government Elections '95*. Focus Seminar Durban: March.

Leemans AF (ed). 1976. *Management of Change in Government*. The Hague: Martinus Nijhoff.

Mahwood P. 1993. *Local Government in the Third World — The Experience of Decentralization in Tropical Africa*. 2nd ed. Pretoria: Africa Institute.

Meenakshisundaram SS. 1994. *Decentralisation in Developing Countries*. Bombay: Concept Publishing.

Nwabuzor EJ & M Mueller. 1989. *An Introduction to Political Science for African Students*. London: Macmillan.

Nzouankeu JM. 1994. Decentralisation and democratisation in Africa. *International Review of Administrative Sciences*. Vol 60 no 2 June.

Ranney A. 1990. *Governing: An Introduction to Political Science*. Englewood Cliffs, New Jersey: Prentice Hall Inc.

Streek B. 1995. Do or die elections. *Towards Democracy — Journal of the Institute for Multi-Party Democracy*.

Sunday Tribune. 26 March 1995.

United Nations. 1962. *Decentralization for National and Local Development*. New York: United Nations.

United Nations. 1992. *Decentralization in African Countries*. Conference proceedings, Department of Economic and Social Development 27 July. New York: United Nations.

Venter A & A Johnson (eds). 1991. *Politics: An Introduction for South African Students*. Cape Town: Oxford University Press.

World Bank. 1989. *Strengthening Local Governments in Sub-Saharan Africa*. New York, 5–17 March.

CHAPTER 2

A Review of Local Government and Development in the Southern African Region

M Swilling

1   INTRODUCTION

An exploration of the meaning and modalities of local urban governance in southern Africa in the mid-1990s comes at an opportune time in the region's history. The reason is that the notion of local urban governance refers to a complex set of vertical and horizontal relations that are changing rapidly because of the fundamental transformations taking place across southern Africa at the political, socio-economic, spatial and subcontinental levels. Southern Africa in the 1990s is a remarkable subcontinent. Its countries are undergoing decisive strategic — indeed even paradigmatic — shifts in their respective modes of governance. Although world attention is focused on the South African democratisation process as this new nation attempts to break from its apartheid past, no less dramatic transformations are taking place in neighbouring Mozambique, Angola, Zimbabwe and Namibia. The older, more established (albeit very small), southern African polities of Botswana, Swaziland and Lesotho are also going through changes in their systems of local governance as they adjust to the changing southern African regional context.

   As the southern African polities look forward to a post-apartheid, post-war era, there are five factors shaping the public policy choices of the above-mentioned countries, namely:

☐   the post-Cold War consensus that some sort of democratic mode of governance is the most appropriate way to structure intra-state and state–society relations in developing countries;

☐   the very serious economic crisis that the region as a whole faces that will, by virtue of the power of the international economy, need to be addressed according to market principles straitjacketed into international economic regulations set by GATT, LOME and other agreements;

☐   the high average regional urbanisation rate that is rapidly pushing the average regional population over the critical 50% urbanisation level (Mozambique: 40–50%; Zimbabwe: 30–40%; Namibia: 30–40%; South Africa: 60–70%; Angola: 35%; Botswana: 10–20%; Lesotho: 0–10%; Swaziland: 10–20%.);

☐ the severe negative pressures that are being placed on natural environmental resources (for fuel, building material, food and water) and on the capacity of the environment to absorb liquid, aerated and solid waste; and

☐ the increase in demands for sustainable livelihoods, services and goods that will emanate from enfranchised populations created by liberalisation and democratisation.

Taken together, these five macro processes will directly affect the way policy makers in the state system, civil society and business will imagine, articulate and implement new governance approaches and strategies. The significance of these combined processes is that policy makers concede (at least in principle) that they cannot be managed by a centralised political system that disempowers both lower levels of the state system and non-state actors. Decentralisation is assumed to be a necessary condition for successful democratisation (Pickard et al 1995); market-oriented economic policy frameworks often refer now to the importance of local economic development (Tomlinson 1995) and the informal sector (Preston-White & Rogerson 1991); urbanisation is now seen to be best managed where it is manifest at town and city level (Burgman 129–146; Davidson & Nientied 82–150; Onibukun & Faniran 1995; Wekwete 1994); the establishment of environmentally sustainable planning and development systems are now believed to be viable only if local communities play a central role (Rogerson 163–167); and it is now an article of faith (although often contradicted in practice) that without strong local government, effective delivery will be impossible (Cheema & Ward 1993; Goetz & Clarke 1993; African National Congress 1994: chapter 5).

What follows is a review of the changing nature of local governance in four southern African countries. This is done by analysing changes taking place in the urban development process in each country, followed by a discussion of the respective local government frameworks beginning to emerge. This provides the background for an analysis of the dynamics and trends shaping the evolution of governance at the local level. After reviewing the four countries, a section is developed that describes cross-subcontinental trends that will directly shape the challenges that will face policy makers in future.

Local governance essentially refers to the structures, dynamics and processes that shape and determine the nature of urban development at the local level. It is the realm of relations between and within organisations operating at the local level in urban areas, with local governments playing some role in governing and managing the urban development process in conjunction with an array of formations in civil society that are involved in one way or another in promoting and/or defending civic interests within the civic public realm. If this definition is turned into a normative statement, it would be that democratic local urban governance in our towns and cities will develop if accountable and democratically managed local governments are developed that, in partnership with well-managed formations in civil society who are committed to the principles of trust and reciprocity in the promotion and defence of citizen interests, have the capacity to formulate and implement policies that deal effectively and efficiently with urban development problems.[1]

2 SOUTH AFRICA

2.1 Urban development

The graphic images of the apartheid city are now world-famous. On the one hand opulent white suburbs with commercial services and municipal service standards on a par with societies that have GDPs several times higher than South Africa's. On the other hand, the sprawling black townships on the peripheries of the towns and cities with their uniform housing units, poor services and ever-widening bands of informal housing erected by the increasing number of homeless people.

South Africa's 1990 population of 38 million is expected to double over the next three decades. The Urban Foundation estimates a population of 46,5 million by the year 2000 and 59,7 million by 2010. The black population alone is expected to increase by 130% between 1980 and 2010, from 21,1 million to 48,5 million (Coetzee & De Coning 1992). It is expected that by 2000, 69% of the black population will be living in urban areas.

South Africa has five major metropolitan agglomerations: the Pretoria–Witwatersrand–Vaal (PWV) region (which has been renamed Gauteng and is now one of the nine provinces), Greater Cape Town, the Durban Functional Region (DFR), Port Elizabeth–Uitenhage and East London–Mdantsane. By 2010, 75% of the population are expected to be living in these five metropoles which, in turn, will be responsible for 75% of the GDP. The PWV is the primary metropole with an expected population of 12 million by 2010 and responsible for the production of up to 50% of GDP by this time. However, there are indications that the PWV's economic performance is weakening relative to other centres such as the DFR.

Although apartheid did little to affect the process of urbanisation, it created a settlement pattern that can be summed up as follows:

- □   concentrations of people in the five metropolitan areas which are, in turn, dispersed and sprawling conurbations characterised by extremely inefficient land use, long travel times, highly unequal access to services between richer and poorer areas and the distribution of the urban poor on the peripheries in both formal townships and increasingly in sprawling squatter settlements that provide shelter for at least 7 million people;
- □   the distribution of the non-metropolitan population in some 300 settlements outside the homelands;
- □   growing urban populations in 293 towns inside the former homelands, many of whom had economic bases supported by the government's industrial decentralisation policies;
- □   the proliferation of semi and peri-urban informal settlements located inside homeland boundaries, but located on the peripheries of metropolitan economies from where they derive some of their incomes;
- □   the survival of a rural population that is expected to increase from 11,4 million to 15,3 million between 1985–2010 (Coetzee & De Coning 1992:16).

Underlying the division of the cities along racial grounds, however, there was also an integrative urban economic and ecological logic that worked in favour of the white urban classes. In other words, whereas the ideology of racial division was justified in terms of the need for the separate development of the different race groups, in reality the economic relationship between the white and the black (African, coloured and Indian) halves of the city was similar to a colonial relationship of exploitation and unequal exchange. This was most evident in the way the local government finance system was structured.

Because of apartheid zoning, all the major commercial and industrial areas were located in the white areas and fell under the jurisdiction of the white local authorities (WLA). The central business districts (CBD) around which most South African cities developed were where economic activities were concentrated, although suburbanisation and deconcentration in the metropolitan urban areas has been taking place since the 1970s. Calculations have shown that between 50% and 70% of all revenue to WLAs came from the commercial and industrial areas in the form of property rates and service charges. This was the revenue that was used to cross-subsidise the development of high-level services in the white suburbs. None of the revenue that accrued to the WLAs was expended in the black areas (Swilling, Coetzee, Cobbet & Hunter 1991).

As far as the black townships were concerned, they had virtually no commercial or industrial base. They were residential areas populated by people who worked in the white areas. Revenue for their services came from service charges on the services they paid and from rentals paid on the largely state-owned housing that they lived in. Some intergovernmental grants from the national government subsidised up to 30% of the costs of running the townships. This meant, therefore, that the labour from the townships that worked in the white areas, plus the consumer spending in white areas that was necessary because of the absence of commercial services in black areas, built up the economic base of the white areas. This economic base, in turn, created a viable tax base for the WLAs which enabled the cross-subsidisation of white suburbia. The end result was the systematic underdevelopment of the black townships as a result of the net financial drain of resources from the poor black to richer white areas. This was the exploitative logic that held the apartheid city together as a single, interdependent urban system. It needs to be pointed out that, given the high rate of urbanisation and the high number of South Africans living in the urban areas as a proportion of the total, it is no surprise that urban reconstruction and development is seen as the highest development priority of the post-April 1994 Government of National Unity (GNU).

2.2 Urban government

The transformation of South Africa's local government system has taken place in a way that is probably unique. Of all the political systems that have gone through a non-revolutionary regime transition from authoritarianism to democracy, South Africa is the only one where this transition occurred simultaneously at a national and sub-national level. The reasons for this relate to the structure of South Africa's towns and cities and to the nature of the urban social movements that resisted, challenged and overthrew urban apartheid during the decade of defiance, the 1980s, that led to the decade of transition, the 1990s (Swilling & Boya 1995).

The form and function of the apartheid city was resisted and challenged in numerous ways during the 1980s. While one-off demonstrations, stayaways, strikes and collective violent crowd action against specific targets were commonplace, it was sustained mass action that tended to have a more decisive effect. Consumer boycotts and rent boycotts were mounted by communities across the country. Although success depended on the strength of grass-roots organisation and the capabilities of leadership, these localised collective actions created localised stalemates that neither the targets of these actions (white shopkeepers, black local authorities) nor the social movements behind them could tolerate for very long. The targets were deprived of money, and the constituencies of the social movements were deprived of services. The result was frequently so-called local level negotiations. By the early 1990s, hundreds of local level negotiations had broken out across the country. Inevitably, the parties involved were representatives of the various local government structures, business, municipal service providers, civic associations and residents' organisations, political parties, trade unions and numerous community organisations. These interactions resulted in the creation of local negotiating forums.

Local forums became the schools of the new South African democracy. This is where networks and relationships were built, mutual learning took place and a new culture of governance and consensus building developed. It was also to support social movements involved in the these forums that a network of technical assistance non-governmental organisations (NGO) emerged across the country that provided these movements with information, technical advice, training and policy options. Although imperfect and fraught with tensions and instabilities, these local forums became the model for similar structures that emerged at regional level and, eventually, at national level in the form of the Negotiating Council that finally negotiated the national constitutional settlement of 1993–94. The first and most well known of these local forums was the Central Witwatersrand Metropolitan Chamber (Swilling & Boya 1995).

In 1992–93 the national negotiators realised that a national framework was needed to guide the local government transition via the local forums. The result was the establishment of the national Local Government Negotiating Forum (LGNF) early in 1993. The main players in this forum were the national government, organised associations of local governments, political parties, and the alliance led by the African National Congress (ANC), including trade unions and the South African National Civics Organisation (SANCO) which represented local civic associations.

The LGNF very rapidly negotiated a framework for guiding the local government transition. This was embodied in a Bill that was eventually enacted as the Local Government Transition Act late in 1993. The Act made provision for democratic municipal elections to take place in November 1995. The Local Government Transition Act provides a framework for negotiated transition of local governance that runs parallel to the finalisation of the national constitution by the Constitutional Assembly (CA). Both processes then converge in the final constitution that will be the basis for the next general election in 1999.

What is most significant about the South African interim constitution and the Local Government Transition Act is the provision of a framework for negotiation at local level that compels political and civil society stakeholders to negotiate. This process of mandatory negotiation has been relatively successful. For example, statistics released on 23 November 1994 by the government revealed that approximately 70% of local negotiation forums had been established and that by the end of the first quarter of 1995, most forums had reached agreement on the establishment of Transitional Metropolitan Councils (TMC) or Transitional Local Councils (TLC) for their areas. Given that this amounts to about 400 different agreements, this represents a groundswell of consensus-building around non-racial modes of governance at society's grass roots. The forums allow for inclusiveness, representation and legitimacy, and depending on the capacity of the technical assistance NGOs, access for civil society to the policy process.

It would be naive, however, to assume that the local transition process outlined above would be without its problems. The lack of sustainable and economically viable local authorities, the absence of local administrations in certain areas, the appalling level of service provision in townships, the continued non-payment for rent and services as the so-called 'culture of boycott' persisted into the new era, violence, the lack of private sector investment, the insolvency of black local authorities, widespread poverty and unemployment are factors that will inevitably impact on local governments' capacity to govern urban areas. How well government manages this transitional process and development initiatives will determine the extent to which the locally managed transition in local urban governance succeeds.

The government has recently embarked on two programmes to promote development and governance. First, the Reconstruction and Development Programme (RDP) aims to eradicate apartheid and poverty and promote sustainable growth through a people-driven process (Republic of South Africa 1994) for specific programmes. R175 million was allocated for the local government projects for the 1994/95 fiscal year, and a further R350 million has been allocated for the 1995/1996 fiscal year from the RDP Fund (Department of Constitutional Development and Provincial Affairs). There are three basic local government programmes:

☐ The rehabilitation of collapsed infrastructure, systems and facilities to ensure the provision of basic municipal services;

☐ The extension of infrastructure, systems and facilities for the provision of basic municipal services to new areas — thus, close interaction between the provision of housing and other basic services and infrastructure is essential in this regard; and

☐ The creation of institutional and financial capacity to operate and maintain new and restored services.

The second programme which the government has implemented is Operation Masakhane which aims to accelerate the delivery of services and stimulate economic development. In order to achieve an enabling environment, and sustainable growth and investment, the programme will focus on:

☐ the mobilisation of public and private resources;

☐ enhancing the administrative capacity of TMCs/TLCs;

☐ maximising community participation and responsibility by convincing people to resume payment for services;

☐ the integration of RDP programmes; and

☐ assistance in the process of democratising local government.

However promising these programmes appear, the one shortcoming is that both the RDP and Operation Masakhane are policy frameworks and the real task is to implement them as programmes. There remain three fundamental issues at local government level that need to be addressed in very concrete and practical ways. First, the implementation of the Local Government Transition Act encountered a number of problems such as difficulties in the negotiation process and the establishment of forums. There are also costs associated with the transformation at local level. Conducting the elections in 1995 would require the demarcation of substructures, the preparation of voters' rolls, voter education, and the actual running of the elections. The amalgamation of administrations would require parity in pay and service conditions. This process had to be done in conjunction with a complete redefinition of personnel requirements and job descriptions. Issues such as harmonising pension benefits, redundancy costs, retraining and affirmative action will have an enormous impact on local authorities. Billing, auditing, computing and budgeting systems will also have to be harmonised. Thus, the process of change will have to be managed in a coherent manner to ensure staff morale and productivity is maintained, and that services and systems do not collapse.

Before looking more closely at the dynamics of local urban governance, it is worth dwelling for a moment on the problem of local government administrations. Besides being racially structured, they were also built up over decades to be extremely hierarchical, technocratic, multilayered, inward-looking bureaucracies that may be incapable of being developmental and citizen-friendly. However, certain TMCs/TLCs have identified this as a problem and have mounted 'change management' strategies to transform their administrations. One example is the Greater Johannesburg Transitional Metropolitan Council. The prescribed change management approach that was built into the agreement reached by the forum that created this structure (namely the Central Witwatersrand Metropolitan Chamber) was probably the most innovative aspect of the agreement because it demonstrated an understanding of the critical connection between newly established constitutional structures on the one hand, and the need to create results-oriented, citizen-friendly developmental administrations on the other. The change management approach was premised on the assumption that organisational change should be a process managed in accordance with the following principles:

□ organisational change should be strategy-led, ie structures and systems should flow from an agreed strategy;

□ strategic vision must be collectively generated by groups that comprise senior and middle management as well as front-line workers rather than determined from the top through a conventional strategic planning approach;

□ the knowledge base for organisational change should be derived from expertise located within the organisation at all levels rather than from outside management consultants operating in accordance with predetermined expert models; and

□ the quality and sustainability of organisational change is dependent on the degree to which leadership at all levels is developed and empowered to understand and guide the change process.

It has been agreed that the change management process will be driven jointly by management (which is still largely white) and the municipal trade unions (which are largely black). This approach to the type of change management process outlined above will fundamentally challenge the rigid, hierarchical, bureaucratic and user-unfriendly administrations that have developed over the decades to service (in the main) white citizens. Instead, as evidence from the implementation of the process has already begun to reveal, the process generates a vision of governance that is results rather than rule-driven, citizen-led rather than citizen oppressive, outward rather than inward-oriented, empowering rather than domineering, flexible rather than rigid, market responsive rather than monopolistic, and, above all else, developmental rather than exploitative. The social movements mentioned earlier are themselves transforming as their environment undergoes fundamental changes. These movements persist into the new era as fairly powerful forces within civil society. How they are changing and how civil society is evolving during the post-apartheid era has far-reaching implications for the future of urban governance (Swilling 1993).

2.3 Conclusion

There is no doubt that the nature of the South African local government transitional framework has to now promoted the development of trust through consensus-building at the local level and reciprocity through stakeholder-based negotiations in forums. The result is the constitution and institutionalisation of TLCs and TMCs that are formally accountable. South Africa's first local government elections in November 1995 tested these accountability mechanisms. However, as the new urban political elites consolidate their hold on these instruments, there is less certainty about whether the space for far-reaching reciprocity will survive. Ironically, however, the fiscal, technical and administrative incapacities of the new local governments to meet basic needs on their own, create a new rationale for the retention of reciprocal relations between local governments and their respective civil societies. Whether or not incapacity translates into sustained reciprocity will, in turn, depend on the management culture of local government managers and the degree to which political leaders remain committed to a culture of political tolerance. It will also, of course, depend on how the Development Facilitation Act (DFA) gets implemented and whether the idea of local development forums succeeds in promoting inclusiveness around development planning, or whether they will simply institutionalise the control of the new urban elites over both local government power and civil society. The converse could also occur: local development forums could become the power bases for elites that feel excluded from the urban political coalition that succeeded in capturing the TMCs/TLCs. In both scenarios, the presumed rationality of participatory development planning could degenerate into unmanageable politicisation — and even paralysis — of decision making.

When these dynamics of local urban governance are comprehended within the context of the crisis of South Africa's urban development, then the linkage between local urban governance and the overall success of the South African democratic project becomes clear. As pointed out earlier, the level of urbanisation — and the concentration of the urban population in the five major metropolitan areas — makes urban development problems particularly important for the new government. However, given the inequalities in wealth distribution, the skewed public and private sector investment patterns that will still take time to reverse, the spatial form of the urban economy that confines the urban poor to areas where employment opportunities are scarce, the institutional weaknesses of the informal sector and small, micro and medium enterprises (SMME), the inherited planning legislation that the DFA will take time to override, and the fiscal limits imposed on local governments by central and provincial governments who are worried about the fiscal autonomy of local governments, then it becomes clear that the restructuring and transformation of the urban systems will be fraught with ongoing conflict, tension and power struggles. It would be a mistake to assume that local governments have sufficient control over these dynamics to make a direct impact. Changes in the global and national economies, the policies of national and provincial governments, the lending policies of the commercial and developmental banks, and the increasing mobilisation of independent CBOs against the new transitional councils (in the form, for example, of the numerous ongoing land invasions), are just some of the major macro forces that will shape urban development outside the policies and strategies of the transitional councils and — where they exist — their local development forums. Nevertheless, the transitional councils remain the only truly representative bodies of the major urban stakeholders. Their perception of how to build democratic modes of local urban governance will directly determine the extent to which these transitional councils manage to respond positively to the urban development challenges. Either they can lead through facilitating trust, reciprocity and participatory governing in order to maximise resource mobilisation to address urban poverty, or they can insulate themselves from civil society and risk becoming impotent political coalitions who prop up the illusion of developmental local government by encasing themselves in the trappings of political pomp, legitimised by a rabid populist discourse that depicts their actions as direct expressions of the will of the people.

3 NAMIBIA

3.1 Urban development

Although Namibia is largely a poor rural society with a total population of 1,6 million, the share of the nation's population living in urban areas increased from 25% to 33% over the period 1981–91 period. During this time, the urban population grew by 5,8% per annum nationally and 3,89% per annum in Windhoek for the same period. These urban population growth rates are considerably higher than the annual population growth rate of 3,1%. The total population is expected to double over the next 17 years. In some primary cities, urban growth rates have reached dramatic levels — 21% in six months in Walvis Bay after its reintegration into Namibia on 1 March 1994, and from 150 000 in 1991 to 250 000 people in 1994 in Windhoek according to some estimates.

The multiple causes of rapid urban growth in Namibia include drought, poor land-use management, mass evictions from farms, the illegal fencing of communal lands, resettlement programmes, and inheritance laws that have forced many women-headed households off their rural lands.

Urbanisation and urban population growth after independence have not resulted in fundamental changes in the form and function of the urban centres. Although former white suburbs are deracialising, the towns and cities are now divided by class rather than race and therefore the old correspondence between wealth and high quality service infrastructures persists. Added to this is the fact that recent migrants cannot be seen as permanent urban dwellers. Temporary urban migration by poor people looking to earn money for rural investment is a process that has already caused government site-and-service projects, premised on the assumption that people were permanent urban dwellers, to fail.

The emerging urban crisis is a function of Namibia's economic inequities. According to the World Bank, 5% of the population control 70% of GDP while the poorest 55% control only 3% of GDP. Furthermore, it has been conservatively estimated that 75% of all black Namibians live in absolute poverty. The averages are worse for women-headed households. These levels of inequality are refracted through the form and function of the urban systems.

Given this fairly classic African economic malady, it is not surprising that the informal sector has grown to accommodate the unemployed (estimated at between 20–40%). However, the formal sector is highly dependent on imported goods from South Africa and has very few linkages with the informal sector. This imposes a constraint on this largely urban-based economic sector. Unfortunately, local governments do not have capital resources to construct markets to stimulate informal economic activities and the formal private sector remains insensitive to the potential benefits of support for this sector. Local governments also do not have resources to plan and make available serviced land to attract investments in commercial, industrial and residential developments.

In short, in addition to the increased urban population growth rates in towns and cities that have retained intact their pre-independence form and functions, the combined impact of the nature of the urbanisation process, low economic growth rates, inadequate measures to encourage the informal sector, skewed investment patterns and an inappropriately structured public administration is such that a resolution of the urban crisis will be extremely difficult. These problems are exacerbated by the way the local government system is structured and operated.

3.2 Urban government

Namibia inherited a divided local government system with autonomous, fully developed local governments in the former white areas, and highly dependent local government bodies in communal towns, villages and townships. The basic legislative framework for local government is provided for in the Local Authorities Act and the Regional Councils Act, both of 1992. The Ministry of Regional and Local Government and Housing is responsible for the management of this framework. In essence, Namibian local government structures are, at least on paper, quite standard and conventional: elected councils, an executive committee with a chairman, town clerk as CEO, own administration, and a set of legislative and executive powers including revenue raising and the right to make by-laws. There are fifty-two local governments in Namibia. The local authorities are, however, subordinate to the regional councils, of which there are thirteen. The regional councils are, at this stage, the most active in lobbying for an appropriate allocation of powers, functions and resources to sub-national levels of government.

Since independence, private investment in urban development has been heavily concentrated in the capital city, Windhoek. This means local governments outside Windhoek are suffering from dwindling revenue bases and increased financial dependence on central government at a time of increased demands for urban services. Central government capital allocations for urban infrastructure, however, are dwindling. This is forcing many local authorities to increase the costs to the consumer of water and electricity and they are trying to raise additional revenue by speculating on the sale of serviced land. These measures effectively marginalise the urbanising poor to informal settlements on the urban peripheries — a process that ensures the ongoing replication of the pre-independence urban forms and functions.

Regional councils get a proportion of the urban property rates raised by local authorities plus they get block grants from the Ministry of Regional and Local Government and Housing. These block grants are calculated on a flat-rate basis and are not tied to the incidence of poverty in the region or the amount of money regional councils raise from local governments. This means, for example, that the Khomas Regional Council gets several million Namibian dollars from Windhoek (the main city in its region) plus its block grant that creates a fund that it has not been able to spend, while the Okavango Regional Council has received nothing from the local authorities in its area and yet faces the greatest demand for service provision.

The newly created regional councils and local governments that have been established in terms of the 1992 legislation are only just beginning to operate as viable governing bodies. Virtually all suffer from a lack of qualified personnel and many officials from the pre-independence era have resisted affirmative action. Newly elected politicians with little or no experience in the business of government are slowly beginning to come to terms with their roles and the constraints they face in meeting the urban challenges in their respective areas.

The real problems, however, derive from an inappropriate allocation of functions and powers along the vertical axis. As the newly established local authorities come to tackle both urban service provision and the severe problems of very low levels of economic development at the local level, they come up against the legal constraints on their horizontal relationship with the citizens. Some local authorities and regional councils have begun to lobby the ministry for changes in the legislative framework — efforts that seem in some cases to be assisted by NGOs. Many ordinances, such as zoning and planning regulations, building standards, health regulations, licensing rules, land pricing criteria and tendering procedures remain intact in their pre-independence form. Collectively, they undermine local control of economic development and limit NGO and parastatal effectiveness in urban development projects and programmes. On the whole, local governments are not taking responsibility for the implementation of the national housing policy because their role has not been clearly stipulated. Only Windhoek and Otjiwarongo have begun to realise that they need to get more involved in the management of informal settlements. Very few have even begun to think about the environmental impact of rapid urban growth in a country that is exceptionally fragile in ecological terms.

On the positive side, the National Planning Commission has initiated efforts to strengthen regional planning capacities and the Ministry of Regional and Local Government and Housing has implemented training programmes aimed at regional and local government officials. New partnerships between local governments and parastatals and NGOs have begun to emerge with respect to various projects. For example, there is cooperation with respect to housing and business loans and various community development initiatives. At a policy level, the ministry allows the Association of Local Authorities of Namibia (ALAN) to review national budget allocations for urban infrastructure. And from an affirmative action point of view, the first black CEO has been appointed in Windhoek and 40% of all mayors in Namibia are women.

In short, of the three forms of decentralisation, Namibia's local governments are caught in the classic African dilemma of formal legal devolution without substantive financial and institutional resources. This attests to their de facto dependence on central government for finance in particular, but also for policy changes with respect to constraining regulatory measures. These factors, plus their institutional weaknesses, severely undermine their formal legislative structure and gives central government significant power to control local government. Nevertheless, at least there is a commitment to devolution and there is no evidence that local governments are seen exclusively as the local administrative agents of central government as has been the case in Angola to now and as existed in Tanzania at times. Instead, the future trend may well be the continuation of formal devolution, but due to resource constraints a shift towards increasing central control over local government in the name of administrative decentralisation to ensure the implementation of central government policies. The only real pressures against this trend could come from ALAN with the requisite political will supported by networks of NGOs and CBOs committed to greater autonomy for local government. This kind of alliance, however, will probably only emerge around a specific issue rather than around a general demand for political decentralisation due to the rather deep-seated hostility in southern Africa towards anything that smacks of federalism.

It is probably too early in the process of transforming Namibia's local government system to make definitive judgments. Nevertheless, some trends are already apparent and are worth highlighting. On the one hand, the newly established and struggling local authorities are facing an urbanisation process that is reinforced by macro-economic policies that do not prioritise the needs of the urban areas and that are taking place within an exceptionally fragile ecological context. The urban development processes, in turn, are impacting negatively on rural areas as able-bodied labour gets drawn into the urban areas. On the other hand, local authorities cannot respond appropriately to these urban development problems because of dwindling financial resources (outside Windhoek), legal constraints on what they can and cannot do, poor institutional capacity and an over-centralised planning system. Nevertheless, there is an emerging consensus that local authorities are best placed to deal with the urban crisis. It is clear that if this recognition of local power in urban governance is to become meaningful in any way, local governments will need much greater policy influence over macro-economic policies, urban infrastructure investment decisions, environmental regulatory frameworks, and development planning. However, before this can happen they will need capacity at both the political and administrative levels. This, however, will require resources that, in turn, will only be committed to develop capacity if it is accepted that local governments should have a greater policy role than they have now. The result, then, is a vicious circle. How this is overcome will depend to a large extent on the dynamics of the governance realm.

Namibia also has a fairly well-developed non-governmental sector that is actively involved in policy formulation and capacity building. However, this is manifested largely at a national level because this is the locus of policy making — centralised systems concentrated in a capital primate city tend to have this effect. The relative weakness and newness of local governments as loci of urban development policies that NGOs and CBOs can relate to, means that governance at the local level is still embryonic.

3.3 Conclusion

In conclusion, it is possible to argue that local urban governance in Namibia is relatively weak. Poor urban management policies, centralised policy making, the underdeveloped nature of sub-national government, the legacy of strict urban regulation and the nature of intergovernmental fiscal relations combine to under-mine the salience of locally constituted urban dynamics in the shaping of urban development policies and processes. The emergence of NGO and CBO lobbies at policy level are indicative of trends that are beginning to counter state domination of urban policy. However, until they develop strategies for empowering local governments to attain greater control over urban policy and urban development resources, and until local urban civil society is focused on local governance, it will not be possible to build democratic forms of local urban governance in Namibia.

4 MOZAMBIQUE

In Mozambique's case, the state system that was constructed after independence was premised on a Marxist–Leninist, one-party framework coupled to (initial) attempts to mobilise grass-roots energies for regime-driven development and reconstruction programmes. The economic system was centrally planned, includ-ing attempts to collectivise the agricultural sector, with about 90% of the population of 11 million (1980) living in rural areas at independence. Superimposed on this general strategy was the state's commitment to support the guerrilla struggle against the then 'Rhodesian' regime which, after Zimbabwean independence in 1980, turned into a vicious civil war inside Mozambique. South African security forces became the primary backers of Renamo, the party that coordinated resources for the insurgent forces.

After a decade of 'socialist' experiments and gathering violent disruption, the governing party (Frelimo) concluded that a different approach was needed. In the name of 'turning to the free market' and democratisation, Mozambique opened itself up to World Bank/International Monetary Fund (IMF) programmes, massive bilateral-aid agency support and multinational corporate investment, especially South African based capital. By the turn of the decade, the commencement of transition in South Africa began to make possible the ending of the civil war which, in turn, was coupled to a regime-driven 'structural adjustment' programme. There is considerable debate about how effective such a programme can be in a country which is now officially designated by the World Bank as the poorest in the world.

4.1 Urban development

In a United Nations report, *The Emergency Situation in Mozambique — Priority Requirements for the Period 1988–89*, it was pointed out that Mozambique had 1,1 million displaced persons, 2,2 million people affected by severe shortages of food and essential items, 2,6 million people affected by commercial food shortages and about 700 000 people living as refugees in neighbouring countries. Mozambican researchers now operate on the assumption that the population is 16 million and that one-third of the population is displaced by war, drought and economic collapse.[2] Although it was assumed in 1980 that there was a 13% urbanisation rate, the impact of the displacement of 5 million people and fundamental societal dislocation had placed perhaps half the population either within the urban areas or directly dependent on the urban economies as massive numbers of people moved towards urban settlements and as the rural economies collapsed.

In 1980, Maputo was the largest city with 770 000 people relative to Beira's 228 000 and Nampula's 158 000. It was assumed then that Mozambique only had twelve areas that could be regarded as urban. In little over a decade, however, Maputo had grown to 2,2 million people as it absorbed many of the displaced people and the number of areas regarded nationally as urban increased to 23 'cities' and 68 'towns' due to a new classification undertaken in 1987.

Despite the destabilisation-driven urbanisation of up to half of Mozambique's population and the rapid increase in the size of its largest city and in the number of new 'urban areas', the Mozambique government and its multilateral and bilateral aid partners still operate on the assumption that Mozambique is primarily a rural society. It was asserted with little supporting evidence that the people would return voluntarily to the rural areas after the civil war. This assumption ignored the fact that the fairly extensive land grabbing that took place will ensure permanent urbanisation for those that are alienated from their land. It also ignores the fact that economic opportunity will remain concentrated in the urban areas as long as there is insufficient investment in rural development programmes. Consequently, a clear and coherent urban development policy premised on an understanding of new internal realities does not exist. Problems the urban research community in Mozambique need to address can be summarised as follows (Mozambique Delegation 1992):

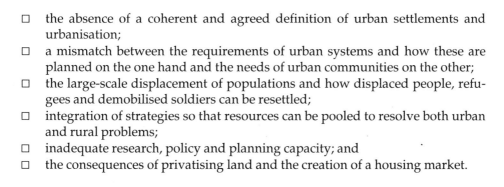

- □ the absence of a coherent and agreed definition of urban settlements and urbanisation;
- □ a mismatch between the requirements of urban systems and how these are planned on the one hand and the needs of urban communities on the other;
- □ the large-scale displacement of populations and how displaced people, refugees and demobilised soldiers can be resettled;
- □ integration of strategies so that resources can be pooled to resolve both urban and rural problems;
- □ inadequate research, policy and planning capacity; and
- □ the consequences of privatising land and the creation of a housing market.

In addition, researchers raised the following problems:

☐   the absence of organised community-based organisations and community-linked support organisations;

☐   the impact of externally designed development programmes funded by multi- and bilateral aid agencies such as the World Bank;

☐   insufficient trained and skilled management personnel at all levels; and

☐   impact of South African based investment in Mozambique's energy, transport-ation, tourist, agricultural and construction sectors.

4.2 Urban government

Urban governance in Mozambique must be seen in the context of the Portuguese colonial administrative heritage, despite almost twenty years having elapsed. Important changes were proposed in the first three years of independence. However, the immediate priority that the confrontation with the Rhodesian regime and later the apartheid system came to represent, reduced the chances of success for these early changes. Later on, the spread of permanent conflict and the emergency situation led to a void in policy formulation. This ended only with the adoption of a new set of constitutional guidelines for local government when a new multi-party constitution was adopted in 1990. It is significant that it was only in September 1994 that it was possible to adopt a new law on local government both for urban and rural areas incorporating the principles set up in the constitution. However, before this is examined, the historical legacy needs to be described.

Portuguese administration in Mozambique made a distinction between admin-istration in the urban and rural areas. Rural areas were administered by officials appointed by the central government in Lisbon. In the urban areas, the system was formally based on local autonomy as it had developed historically in Portugal during the fight against feudal domination. But its transplant to the colonies was for the benefit of the settler population only. Urban areas were administered by bodies elected by the white residents of the area of the city, which in practice meant the formally planned urbanised area. The surrounding areas inhabited by the African population were excluded from the local government system and were administered, instead, by appointed officials very much like in the rural areas.

The first period after independence brought some changes to the system. The underlying concept was that the cities should represent and encompass all state functions in the territory of the city, ie a shift away from the functional definition of local government in accordance with the Westminster tradition, to a more territorial definition of local government in accordance with the European tradi-tion. The functions of the city administration were therefore not limited to tradi-tional functional matters.

In a way this allowed more participation of lower levels of government in policy making, but within a deconcentrated rather than a devolved framework. However, it meant that there were no own powers vested in the local bodies, as most activities fell in line with the directives of central ministries through the principle of dual subordination, with the exception of classical urban affairs. Widening of powers of the municipalities therefore meant a limitation of autonomy.

Organisation of the cities was based on a city assembly, a Presidente do Conselho Executivo, an executive council, the city administration and grass-roots organisations called Grupos Dinamizadores e Comissões de Moradores (dynamising groups).

The main functions of the cities were formulated as being production, education, culture and sports, health, social services, urban sanitation, transport and transit, housing, public order.[3]

The urban assemblies also had the power to appoint three to five members (according to the size of the city) of the executive council who would supervise the departments in the city administration. This power conferred upon them by the law was never used. In fact the practice prevailed of the heads of departments assuming the position of members of the executive council.

The real power of the urban assemblies rested mainly with their political influence and popular pressure. Their relation with the administrative machine was made through the president of the executive council, who, being at the time the local party leader, had to yield to the political pressures of the population. The heads of departments were not appointed by the municipality.

It must be remembered that the one-party system was in force until 1990, which meant that the nominations for members of the city assembly had to originate from the party. This did not mean that all members were party members, but it had a bearing in the sense that many matters were simultaneously discussed in the city committees thus entailing a certain duplication in roles and discussions.

The city administration varied according to the classification of the city but had many common features in order to facilitate understanding and training. It consisted of the office of the president and the administrative departments.[4] Of these, the Department of Urban Services absorbed most of the services dealing previously with urban matters. The others corresponded broadly to central ministries, eg health and education, some of them blending activities performed centrally by two ministries (eg housing and urbanisation, transport and traffic).

The most important innovation was the institutionalisation of grass-roots participation. At community level, in every Bairro, the Reunio Geral dos Moradores (residents' meetings) elected the Grupos Dinamizadores (literally translated as dynamiser groups) and were supported at a lower level by a Comissão de Moradores (residents' committee) for every cluster of houses with special responsibilities for the management of state-owned buildings and urban amenities in their area (gardens, sidewalks, etc).

The tasks of the Grupo Dinamizador concerned promotion of household production, consumer cooperatives, local transport, social affairs (elderly people, etc), solution of neighbourhood conflicts, health and sanitation, cultural affairs, self-help for housing. They were formed by up to six members performing their duties on a voluntary basis and became an important force in the life of the neighbourhoods. In order to make them more operative, in some cities one paid officer was delegated by the Conselho Executivo to work under the Grupo Dinamizador.

The model was adopted for all areas of the cities but was clearly inspired by its most dynamic component — the semi-urban areas — and worked far better there where the tradition of African participation was more alive than in urbanised areas with a more colonial middle-class style of life. It happened often that the same people who were active in their previous semi-urban neighbourhoods lost part of their vigour in different surroundings when they moved to the urban area.

With independence, the urban system was extended and transformed in the following ways:

☐ as the demand and expectations increased, municipal service provision was extended to far larger areas, without enough attention being paid to how these extensions were to be financed; and

☐ in line with a particularly radical conception of political decentralisation through grass-roots participation in centralised policy making that resulted in deconcentration rather then substantive devolution, local governments were defined as the local representatives of the state and therefore all state activities within the borders of a town or city were defined as the responsibility of the city. For example, education at the pre-primary and primary level as well as primary health care became the responsibilities of local authorities. Unfortunately, this kind of deconcentration was not coupled to programmes to build up the capacity of local authorities to take on these new functions.

Housing became a major area of city management. Private property abandoned by the Portuguese was nationalised and the management was initially handled by a specially created central body with local delegations. However, these assets were progressively handed out to the cities. Because this involved more than 80% of the total formal housing stock of the country, this resulted in the transfer of fairly substantial powers to local authorities, but again, without complementing this with the necessary capacity building to ensure proper management.

In 1992, a decision was taken to proceed with the sale of state-owned houses to the present occupants, but only from 1994–95 did this movement gain momentum and, by the end of 1994, houses were being sold at the rate of a thousand a month. This should be followed by the sale of commercial property. The income generated is earmarked to launch a housing programme that will help to finance other urban development programmes.

One of the more effective service expansion programmes took place in the fields of education and health, areas where popular demand was high. It was also consistent with the political ideology and the management experience of the new leadership, developed in the schools and health centres created in liberated areas and neighbouring countries during the war of liberation. Primary schools and primary health care centres were transferred to the local governments and later the same occurred with respect to secondary schools in Maputo.

The promotion of the small-scale agricultural producers along the green belts that traversed the cities, was one of the more creative and relatively successful initiatives of local governments after independence. This took the form of both private and cooperative production of vegetables for the supply of the city. Some of these cooperatives where women's participation was dominant have become particularly effective as well as politically very influential.

In the field of urbanisation, soon after independence planning was transformed into a grass-roots process involving high levels of participation by the residents. Residents' groups (Grupos Dinamizadores) played an active role in the process and were given an important role in allocating land for housing which they still perform, either by allocating land directly (in the suburban, traditionally African areas) or by providing advice when the urban administration allocates land in the 'modern' areas.

The activities of urban local authorities were complemented by the activities of the Grupos Dinamizadores in the Bairros. Some of the Grupos were effective in the search for solutions for daily problems like providing basic supplies through the setting up of cooperatives, supporting and, in a few cases, even building schools and participating in the improvement of sanitary conditions.

This resulted to a certain extent from the needs of local authority administrations that did not have the capacity to execute their functions or meet the developmental expectations of their constituencies. Popular participation was a way of generating capacity for activities that local government administrations were responsible for, but could not handle.

Therefore the crisis of managerial and technical capacity in the cities was more pronounced than at other levels. Most staff positions were assigned to people holding third or fourth level positions in the hierarchy. Some of them had responsibilities far beyond their capacity. It is a tribute to their dedication that they were able to keep the services running. But effectiveness was hindered when they were expected to handle more and more functions as deconcentration measures were implemented. This eventually led to the breakdown of capacity thus forcing reconcentration or, if capacity did not exist at higher levels, service collapse.

The situation began to change in the 1990s, but new factors such as financial constraints derived from structural adjustment programmes affecting conditions of pay and the development of the private sector, began draining most of the newly qualified staff. Traditionally, all urban services had been managed by the local administrations, with very few activities contracted out to external contractors. Not only was contracting out contrary to the prevailing ideology of the post-independence period, but also no private sector really existed to undertake such contracts.

Following worldwide reassessments and trends, the debate about public versus private participation in the management of urban services has been taking place in Mozambique since 1986. Present policy favours the privatisation of services currently managed by public entities. It is assumed that either private ownership or contracting out the management to the private sector could improve service delivery, reduce costs and improve management.

Under colonialism, the cities had resources from local taxes and fees, building tax, revenues from services of water and electricity supply, sale of land, special levies imposed on certain public enterprises and state subsidies. These resources were reduced after independence as a result of:

- □ immediate economic crisis following the change in the nature and economic status of the inhabitants of the cities;
- □ inability to collect most of the local taxes;
- □ centralisation of all central and local resources in a national budget which resulted in a resource allocation to the benefit of sectors such as education, health and defence to the detriment of urban areas, as part of central planning procedures;

- ☐ inability of the urban administrations in general to set up a coherent budgetary strategy to defend their interests in the budget bargaining process;
- ☐ land nationalisation and the cessation of construction and property development;
- ☐ loss of income from water and electricity services because of the way these services were integrated into national enterprises. Water enterprises have begun to be handed back to local authorities in the 1990s, but electricity will remain centralised. Due to the loss of cheap Cahora Bassa energy power, the service runs at a loss; and
- ☐ nationalisation of buildings and non-payment by the state of the building tax to local governments. To take an example of one city, this represented 10,7% of the city budget but meant actually only about 23 000 thousand contos in 1992[5] which, at the time, corresponded to about ten thousand dollars, rents being little more than symbolic.

Transfers from the state to the larger cities were in the order of 40%–60% of the budget of the cities in 1989 and 4%–17% to smaller cities. In terms of the central budget, these transfers were reduced from 34% to 13% in 1988.[6]

The process has contributed to a culture of local government dependence on state subsidies and a corresponding decline in attempts to find locally generated revenues. Very few local governments even bothered to update taxes and fees until 1987. The state budget covers the deficits by paying the wages of local government staff and in so doing the central state has gained increasing control of local government personnel and hence their loyalties. The search for local resources is nevertheless gaining rapid ground as the value of national currency improves.

The city of Maputo negotiates its budget directly with the Ministry of Finance while class B and C cities negotiate with the provincial governments, and the class D cities negotiate with the district administrations. The demarcation of the areas of the cities was guided by two major principles:

- ☐ the inclusion of all areas linked to the life of the city (services, industrial as well as residential areas, irrespective of the material used, where people lived who related to the city on a continuous basis); and
- ☐ the inclusion of a greenbelt area whose production served mainly city inhabitants, in order to use management capacity in the cities to support peasant urban production.

Later on, it was decided to subdivide the major cities into administrative units, working as delegations of the city administration without representative bodies. Maputo was divided into eight urban districts and some of the other major cities into postos administrativos which are smaller administrative entities.

One may characterise the situation as an heterogeneous blend of centralising and decentralising factors. On one hand the political system expressed integration with state bodies but left openings in terms of political participation at two levels: appointment of members of the executive council by the city assembly that were never fully exploited, and grass-roots participation. The latter was dominant during the first six years, but should have been consolidated by the transfer of more powers and, especially, resources to these community-based bodies. This never happened, and so this fairly unique aspect of Mozambique's local governance system disintegrated.

During the early years after independence, frequent meetings took place between the dynamising groups and the local government administration. Requests and complaints were voiced at these meetings and the administration informed these groups of the problems or took note of the proposals that were put forward. Unfortunately, local government officials tended to agree on the spot to recommendations that could hardly be implemented given their resources and capacity. Ultimately, lack of results and the difficulties involved explain why limited delivery led to a decline in participation and the eventual collapse of the dynamising groups.

On the other hand, the central administration was not a reliable supporter of local government administrations. It was erratic and randomly intervened in local affairs. This affected the freedom and initiative of local leaders who did not always know what they could or could not do. However, it was the absence of a sustainable and sufficient source of finance that really impaired the effectiveness of local authorities.

By 1986 it was becoming clear that a new political organisation for the cities was required, granting them more autonomy and freeing them from the centralising trend that pervaded the dominant political and administrative model. The main principles were discussed during the debate on the new constitution and were enshrined in the constitution adopted at the end of 1990. The main principles that were adopted were as follows:

- □ local governments should be statutorily autonomous;
- □ representative bodies should be elected by the residents of a given territory;
- □ executive bodies should be accountable to the elected representative bodies; and
- □ exclusive powers should be granted to local governments to empower them to decide on their own affairs.

A law was passed in 1994 establishing the new local governments for both the urban and rural areas. The boundaries of these new structures corresponded to the former cities and districts, the latter being the immediate subdivision of the provinces.

The political balance between central and local in the new constitution and the subsequent 1994 law was premised for the first time on the recognition of the principle of autonomy. This was expressed by the granting of legal personality to local bodies, the creation of elected legislatures, the devolution of powers to the local level (at least in theory), the granting of the right to own property, and the fact that local governments will have their own budgets and access to resources that are still to be defined by a further law. Decisions taken by municipal bodies can only be challenged *ex post facto* by central state bodies on the basis of violation of legality.

The 1990 constitution in combination with the 1994 law, however, stops short of being a fully federal constitutional and legal arrangement. The following principles are embedded in the new arrangement:

- □ The principle of national unity and the constitutional competence of central bodies (the usual state prerogatives) were retained and protected with respect to the sovereignty of national legislation and the concomitant denial to local governments of the right to pass laws outside of the scope of their devolved powers.

☐ From the organisational point of view, the principle of simplicity and economy meant adoption of a standard, one-tier system for all municipalities with the same powers and functions. Maputo is an exception and will benefit from a special status to be adopted.

☐ The principles of political pluralism and popular participation, including access for all citizens to public sittings of the municipal bodies.

☐ Democratic legitimacy through the election of municipal bodies.

☐ Separation of powers, as expressed in the way ample powers are conferred upon the head of the executive body, the mayor, under the supervision of the municipal assembly.

☐ The principle of responsibility establishes that municipal bodies are answerable to the state and the citizens, allowing for both administrative recourse and judicial process against its decisions and acts.

☐ Implementation of the law, while being guided by the principle of gradualism, taking place in a phased way, starting on 1 October 1994 in Maputo and all provincial capitals and in all other cities on dates to be defined by the council of ministers. First elections for the new bodies will take place before October 1996.

The 1990–94 local government dispensation has fundamentally redefined the intergovernmental relations between central and local levels with respect to the allocation of powers and functions. Some functions have been defined in very broad terms, eg promotion of development; while others are defined in more specific terms. General formulations can be interpreted as a way to accommodate and benefit from experiences gained in the past.

Specific areas include urban sanitation, environment, land management, public supplies (fairs, slaughterhouses, consumer protection), public transport, physical planning, urban regulation, housing, parks and gardens, urban equipment, roads and traffic, education and professional training, culture, leisure and sports, health, cemeteries, fire services and civil protection, water and energy supply, registrar of citizens, social assistance. Their powers include passing by-laws, the right to self-organisation and planning, the right to take executive decisions, to levy taxes and own property, to contract and to litigate.

Taken in combination and given that devolution on paper hardly ever translates into substantive devolution in practice, this distribution of functions and powers makes the Mozambican local government system the most decentralised system in southern Africa. It remains to be seen how this translates into reality when strategies are devised to overcome the three classic obstacles to implementing this kind of approach, namely institutional capacity and financial resources. As far as the main structures of the new local authorities are concerned, these are as follows:

☐ the municipal assembly, which is directly elected by the citizens and acts as the local legislature — a separate law that will define the electoral system is still being devised;

- the mayor of the city who is chairperson of the executive and as such is an executive mayor — significantly, he is directly elected by the voters on the same day as they vote for the assembly and he also appoints the municipal council;
- the municipal council which is the executive and is appointed by the mayor with half the members drawn from the assembly; and
- an administration with staff employed by the local government and not by central government.

The law does not address the issue of community-based organisations and their relationship to the local authorities.

The assembly is composed of a number of members proportional to the number of residents (one councillor to 1 500 residents), with a minimum of 35 and a maximum of 61 councillors. The assembly meets a minimum of two and a maximum of five times annually. The main powers of the assembly, beside passing by-laws and regulations and approving the municipal plan, consist of approving the budget, imposing taxes and special contributions, determining fees for services, delegating of powers for the purchase of buildings in amounts to be established by the assembly, adopting the development plan, approving loans of a certain amount as well the participation of municipal capital in private enterprises of local interest, creating bodies like municipal police and voluntary firemen and approving the staff list.

The municipal assemblies were given special tasks in the field of protection of the environment ranging from penalising polluting activities to establishing incentives and programmes to protect the environment (promoting alternative sources of energy, encouraging the use of non-pollutant means of transport).

The municipal council is composed of a number of councillors, determined by the assembly, between one-sixth and one-quarter of the members of the assembly appointed and dismissed by the mayor, at his own discretion, half of them chosen among the members of the assembly. The main function of the municipal council is to assist and work as an advisory body to the mayor, to limit his executive powers. Certain decisions or proposals have to emanate from this body. These include major decisions to be submitted to the municipal assembly such as by-laws and regulations and all plans and programmes. It has the right to grant land concessions, sell municipal property, appoint heads of departments and municipal agencies, initiate the process of expropriation, deliver building permits, and order demolition.

The mayor assumes all executive powers with the assistance of the council. He is the head of the municipal administration, but can delegate his functions to the councillors. In matters of urgency the mayor can exercise the powers of the council, but must submit his decisions to the council for ratification within fifteen days. The personnel will be part of an own municipal staff list and will abide by the General Statute of the Public Service.

As far as fiscal arrangements are concerned, the new law establishes the principle of financial autonomy. This is practically expressed in the existence of a separate budget and own revenue sources for each local government. These may include municipal taxes, actual national taxes to be transferred to the municipalities, a percentage of certain other national taxes collected by the state, fees for licenses and tariffs for services rendered and penalties.

However, a law on local finance is yet to be approved and a study of the economic and fiscal situation in five cities is currently being carried out with World Bank assistance.

4.3 Conclusion

The Mozambican local government system has evolved through three phases: the colonial phase of racially segregated local government; the post-independence phase of racially integrated, politically centralised and administratively deconcentrated local government; and the third phase of politically decentralised local government that has yet to be implemented. It is still too early to predict what the substance of this third phase will be. In theory, it could result in high levels of decentralised policy making around local issues. However, Mozambique's political culture, very serious capacity weaknesses and inadequate local tax bases, could combine to undermine the purported intentions of constitutional and institutional decentralisation. There are enough examples in Africa of systems that were formally decentralised, but substantively highly centralised. Mozambique will only break this trend if it invests heavily in a capacity-building programme to support local governance.

5 ZIMBABWE

5.1 Urban development

After attaining independence in 1980, the Zimbabwean government committed itself to a political and economic philosophy that, rhetorically, was openly socialist. However, during the first decade of independence the state did little to fundamentally transform the inherited white-controlled agricultural and industrial economy. The desire to 'plan' an economic future, reflected in the 1982 Transitional National Development Plan, contradicted the reality that this was an economy that Zimbabweans had virtually no control over. With up to 70% of the formal economy controlled by South African and other foreign-based capital, and with a combination of drought and world recession diminishing internally generated economic resources, the entire Zimbabwean economy went into serious crisis by the late 1980s. This drove it into adopting and implementing a harsh IMF/World Bank structural adjustment programme for the 1990s.

Zimbabwe had a population of 10,4 million in 1992, growing at 3,2% per annum. Given the 1982 census definition of urban settlements as being 2 500 people or more, then 27,3% (or 2,84 million) of the population was urbanised in 1992. The United Nations estimated that by 2025, Zimbabwe's population will be 54,1% urbanised (Mlalazi 1994). The largest cities/towns in 1992 were: Harare with 1,1 million people, nearly twice the size it was in 1982; Bulawayo with 620 000 people compared to 414 000 in 1982; Chitungwiza (which is a dormitory city 25 kilometres outside Harare but was never integrated into it) with 274 000 compared to 172 000 in 1982; Gweru with 124 000 compared to 79 000 in 1982; and Mutare with 131 000 compared to 70 000 in 1982. These figures are indicative of high urbanisation rates.

Andrew Mlalazi (1994:8) summarises the problems that the ZANU government tried to address in various ad hoc ways during the 1980s as follows:

' (a) How to spread the urban network and consequently employment, infrastructure and services to areas that have hitherto been denied this service;

(b) How to restructure the colonial city in the light of the present socio-economic circumstances; and

(c) How to cope with the demand and provision of urban services when other sectors of the economy are demanding the same amount of resources and when the national economy is not expanding as expected.' (Mlalazi 1994)

Whereas the first two national development plans — the Transitional National Development Plan (1983–86) and the First National Development Plan (1986–1990) — were focused on rural development, it was only in the Second National Development Plan (1991–95) that public investment in urban areas was regarded as a significant priority. Despite this, it is difficult to argue that by the mid-1990s Zimbabwe had a coherent urban development policy with its own identity and goals. Whereas urban policy in the Transitional National Development Plan was 'to minimise the rate of rural-to-urban migration', this resulted in what Mlalazi called rural urbanisation, ie urbanisation outside the main cities in the smaller towns. By the late 1980s/early 1990s, the growth point approach was challenged and it began to be replaced by the notion that public investment should build on existing centres, rather than attempting to create new ones. This was one of the spatial consequences of increasingly severe fiscal constraints as the Zimbabwean economy failed to pull out of the recession. But, equally importantly, planned regional development to rectify spatial imbalances was replaced by the notion that urban economies must compete for investment, people and resources. For Mlalazi, this, together with structural adjustment measures to reduce public spending on social infrastructure, could lead to the gradual return to an economy dominated by Harare as the primary city (Mlalazi 1992:12).

The rising level of urbanisation and the centrality of Harare in the Zimbabwean political economy would suggest that the future of this city, together with the fifteen or so secondary cities, will fundamentally shape Zimbabwe's future. Furthermore, the importance of Harare in southern Africa's transportation, industrial and migratory networks suggests that regional changes will profoundly impact on this city. In short, Zimbabwe's search for a transition path determined by a new vision for the 1990s, will be heavily influenced by the urban development policy framework that emerges from its main cities.

5.2 Urban government

In May 1980, soon after independence, President Banana stated his government's policy on local government:

'In the field of local government, it will be my Government's intention to democratise all municipalities and to create a unified local government administration to replace the different local government systems for blacks and whites.... The introduction of a unified system of local government will also do away with the present structure which divides the rural regions of the country into commercial and subsistence farming areas.' (Appalraju 1995:14)

This statement reflected the new Zimbabwe government's two main priorities with respect to local government, namely racially divided systems of local governance and access to land. The language and focus, however, was primarily rural. There was no real understanding of urban governance in the first five years of independence in central government policy thinking. The result was that most of the policy and institutional work on changing local governance in Zimbabwe has been focused on the transformation of rural local government (Hammar 1994).

At independence, Zimbabwe had a tripartite system of local government, namely Urban Councils for white urban areas with urban Africans only entitled to advisory-type Area Boards, Rural Councils for white rural areas, and District Councils for rural communal areas. Central government policy since independence has been premised on a separation of rural and urban local government, with an initial period lasting until the mid-1980s when the old structures were merely renamed, retained and deracialised. In the urban areas, urban councils were extended to include the former black townships (including the advisory area boards which were either downgraded, transformed or scrapped). In the rural areas, after an initial period where rural councils (for white farming areas) and district councils (for black communal areas) were retained, they were eventually merged in 1988 to create Rural District Councils including former white commercial and African communal lands.

As far as the urban areas are concerned, the Urban Councils Act that was enacted soon after independence in 1980 effectively provided for the continuation of the British colonial mode of local governance, but with the proviso that it was deracialised. The latter was achieved by scrapping the 'twin city' concept and replacing it with the 'one city' concept while retaining the institutional structures and functions provided for the pre-independence version of the Urban Councils Act. Local governments retained their powers to raise local revenue, deliver services in fifty-three different areas, make by-laws with respect to over one hundred local matters, employ their own personnel, and formulate policies and plans in a fairly autonomous manner. The Act also provided for a hierarchy of non-racial local governments according to size and importance in the sub-regional economy. Hence there are four city councils, seven municipal councils, four town councils, and town boards for small towns which are normally subsumed under the rural district councils, but there is one that is autonomous (Jordan 1984).

Despite the acceptance of the 'one city' concept, the two interlinked cities of Harare (the capital) and Chitungwiza (its dormitory township) were never integrated into a single metropolitan city. Instead, these two 'cities' were defined as two different city councils despite the latter's dependence on the urban economy of the former. The reasons for not integrating Chitungwiza and Harare have more to do with the jealously guarded autonomous power base of Chitungwiza's local political elite than with the outcome of a rational policy process — in fact, technical advisors and urban planners actively advised against the separation of Chitungwiza from Harare.

Significantly, unlike in South Africa, the post-independence urban councils retained the 'committee system'. Given that the committee system is by nature designed merely to ensure that elected councillors are there to keep a watching brief on administrators rather than be active in the policy-making process, and given the retention of an array of sector-specific national legislation that allocated powers and functions to the administrative heads of local governments rather than to the political structures (ie the council), this effectively meant that the town clerk and his departmental heads became the primary policy-making force in local government and not the newly elected political leadership. It was only in the mid-1990s that this began to be questioned and there are now moves to change the legislation to provide for directly elected Executive Mayors in the four city councils — this being a presidential model found most commonly in certain United States cities and which has already been established in the 1994 Mozambican system. Whereas the committee system was consistent with a very narrow definition of the role of local governments as mere service providers and enforcers of land-use plans through legal and administrative procedures that were technocratically rather than politically defined, the move towards elected executive mayors is a reflection of a much larger rethink of the role that urban governments can play in resolving urban problems at the local level. This relates back to the changes taking place in the urban economy, as well as to the dynamics within civil society that are referred to in the next section.

There is a strong consensus in the Zimbabwean literature that the poor administrative, technical and managerial capacity in rural local governments was one reason for the relatively poor performance of these local governments. This, however, does not seem to apply to the urban local governments. Instead, the pressures for change in urban local government come less from capacity problems, and more from fiscal constraints and the consequences of a participatory planning system that never worked.

The planning system within which urban councils were supposed to operate is a combination of participatory development planning for all three levels of government (local, provincial, national) linked to the national budget, and conventional spatially-based town planning which produces statutory plans for enforcing adherence to the determinations laid down in the master plan. These two forms of planning are closely linked to the structure of Zimbabwe's intergovernmental fiscal relations. In general, most urban councils derive sufficient funds from locally generated revenue to maintain the existing service provision systems and infrastructure. However, they are dependent on grants and loans from central government for investment in new development, particularly urban infrastructure and housing. Whereas the national planning legislation (Regional, Town and Country Planning Act and related sector Acts) empowers urban councils to generate their own statutory plans that are used for spatially-based development control consistent with local fiscal resources, the national development planning framework allows urban councils to feed their development plans and corresponding financial requirements upwards to provincial councils and to national government.

Zimbabwe's development planning system was created in the mid-1980s through three measures: the 1984 Prime Minister's Directive on Provincial Governors and Local Authorities; the 1985 Provincial Councils and Administration Act that established the provincial councils as intermediate bodies between national and local government; and the 1985 Prime Minister's Directive on the Structure of Village Development Committees and Extension Services. Together, these measures created a framework for bottom-up integrated development planning through many levels. In theory, every local area was supposed to form a Village Development Committee (VIDCO) and groups of local areas were supposed to form Ward Development Committees (WADCO). These structures were supposed to facilitate community participation in planning at the grass roots. Their proposals were then supposed to be fed upwards to the local government level through District Development Committees who would then formulate a district/urban plan that would then go upwards to the provincial development committee that would, together with the provincial council, integrate the local plans into Provincial Plans. The provincial plans were then to be fed upwards to generate the National Development Plan which, in turn, was to be the basis for annual budgeting.

Both the legalistic town planning system and the development planning system have failed to create the kind of planning environment that urban councils need to respond to the urban challenges. As far as the participatory development planning system was concerned, there is consensus in the literature that it failed to be genuinely participatory because the VIDCOs, WADCOs and upper level planning structures did not have the capacity to effectively organise genuine development planning.[7] Instead, lists of demands came up from below that were not very useful for effective development planning. In addition, the participatory development planning system was mainly set up with the rural areas in mind and in a context where investment in urban infrastructure was not a priority at national level. This meant that urban councils may have put in their plans for infrastructure and housing development, but with little or no response given the rural development bias. Although this has begun to change, this change comes at a time when the enthusiasm for participatory planning has all but drained away.

As far as legalistic spatial planning is concerned, this reinforces the view that local government's role is merely to provide a land-use framework for development. Now that urban development is receiving a higher priority and urban councils are being seen as key actors in the stimulation of development, the limitations of spatial planning are becoming apparent. In particular, quite a few urban councils are asking how they become active participants in poverty alleviation, urban economic development and the control of environmental degradation (Ndlovu 1995:45).

As far as fiscal pressures are concerned, urban councils have been caught in a double bind. As already mentioned, the rural bias in public sector investment to retard urbanisation effectively meant that urban councils only really had their own locally generated revenues to keep the existing urban infrastructure and system going. This meant they were unable to respond to the new needs created by urbanisation and natural growth of the urban population to any meaningful extent. However, as this overall policy trend changed and urban development came to be recognised as important, this came at a time when the Structural Adjustment Programme was steadily cutting back public sector resources. According to Mlalazi

(1992:18) whereas \$20 billion is required to upgrade the urban infrastructure, the public sector will probably only be able to raise 10% of this over a ten-year period.[8] This means that urban councils will have to find ways of raising capital through borrowing on the capital market and through innovative developmental measures aimed at extending the local tax base. This, in turn, is dependent on the urban councils becoming involved in workable participatory development planning and changing their administrative and managerial culture to become more involved with civil society.

5.3 Conclusion

Urban councils in Zimbabwe have enjoyed a high level of policy and implementation autonomy with respect to their existing urban infrastructure. However, the participatory development planning system forced them to become highly dependent on provincial and national governments for extra finances for new development. This planning system effectively defined local governments as implementors of the national development plan. However, because urban investment was not seen as a priority, urban councils were not subject to pressures to implement national policies, but rather to pressures that came from the absence of urban development policies. With structural adjustment and the new policy significance of urban development, urban councils are expected to increase their autonomy with respect to managing urban development, but without the requisite resources for new development from higher levels of government. This will get worse as decentralisation policies start taking effect and things like local clinics and other public services (previously run by national departments at local level on a deconcentrated basis) get transferred to urban councils. This, in turn, may lead from a fiscal crisis as development needs fail to be met by urban councils, to a capacity crisis as operating budgets get pruned down to finance newly acquired responsibilities that will initially be regarded by politicians as priorities. If all this leads to a serious failure in the urban local government system, then this may, in turn, result in a reversion to provincial or national control of local service provision and development.

   In summary, the transformation of Zimbabwe's local government structures to meet the social and economic challenges of urban development may well be constrained by three factors: (i) the continuation of a colonial, institutional form into the post-independence era that has hitherto limited the definition of the role of local government to being mere service providers and not development agencies; (ii) a political culture (and low skills base) that has militated against the effective political and developmental leadership of elected politicians and favoured the initiating role that officials have played in public policy formation; (iii) the planning and fiscal system that has hitherto led to the low prioritisation of urban development needs. Unless these constraints are overcome, Zimbabwe's local governments will find it difficult to become the leading institutional force in local urban governance.

6 CONCLUSION

6.1 Urban development challenges for southern Africa during the 1990s

As southern African societies rapidly approach the point where most of their citizens live in urban areas, they will be forced to acknowledge the importance of urban development. Unfortunately, there is as yet no evidence of a coherent urban development policy framework that can be the basis for sustained development programmes and projects aimed at resolving the key urban problems in the region's towns and cities. There are great statements of policy intention in some countries, and a few successful urban development programmes in others, but an integrated urban development policy and programme has yet to emerge. This is probably the single greatest legacy of the colonial order. This was an order that made racially-based spatial planning the primary basis of development and governance. The only way this underlying spatial order can be dismantled is through a combination of public investment, creative planning, interventions in the land market and economic development strategies that are labour and community-based. Without this, the inefficiencies, cultural divisions and political consequences of a divided urban spatial order will continue.

While urban form is a central policy issue in urban development in post-colonial societies, this review of urban development in southern Africa has also revealed the need to focus on four key issues within the context of an urban development policy aimed at building a non-racial integrated urban system. These are:

☐   the need for a carefully planned multi-year urban infrastructure investment programme that deploys both public and private sector resources and is aimed at creating the water, sanitation, drainage, transport and communications systems that are required by viable towns and cities;

☐   the complexities involved in building local economies, in particular the mobilisation and organisation of local economic stakeholders around an agreed set of local economic development strategies aimed at generating sustainable urban economies;

☐   the crisis of unsustainable use of environmental resources by the urban poor who need free land, building materials and fuel and by industries and urban systems that require 'cheap' (or preferably 'free' if environmental costs are excluded from the definition of 'cost') means of waste disposal that only the environment can provide;

☐   the search for an approach to planning that combines effective popular participation in the setting of policy goals, with mechanisms for controlling development in ways that are affordable, efficient, effective and responsive; and

☐   the formulation and implementation of a managerial style and capacity that complements rather than undermines a developmental approach to urban problems — this will effectively mean transforming urban government administrations, business organisations, NGOs and CBOs into organisations that can work in partnerships because they have the necessary capacity and information base to exploit the opportunities and overcome the constraints of the new urban order.

6.2 Problems and challenges for urban governments in southern Africa

Liberalisation and democratisation, economic restructuring and rising levels of urbanisation have, in combination, fundamentally redefined the problem of urban government across southern Africa. Liberalisation opens up space for local action; democratisation reduces the dominance of the central state by, *inter alia*, creating and strengthening sub-national government; economic restructuring has led to the increased autonomy of local economies that must now fend for themselves or sink under the pressures of a globalising world economy; and urbanisation is relocating the population into a hierarchy of urban centres that must now find ways of meeting socio-economic needs without too much assistance from national governments. If urban governments are inappropriately structured and resourced to meet these challenges, the results across the southern African subcontinent could be disastrous.

Widely divergent responses to the new significance of urban government are evident across southern Africa. There is the introduction of a completely new constitutional and statutory framework in Mozambique using the traditional approach of agreeing at central level on a model, and imposing it uniformly across all localities through legislation. This differs substantially from the South African approach where a uniform national approach was imposed through legislation. However, this approach was not a single model, but rather a uniform process that local stakeholders had to participate in to reach agreement on a model that is suitable to the local conditions. Whereas urban government was reconstituted in Mozambique and South Africa as part of the overall reconstitution of the state system as a whole, the same does not apply to the cases of Namibia and Zimbabwe where pre-existing post-independence state systems have been retained. As far as Zimbabwe is concerned, the problem is not seen as constitutional or institutional, but rather about the new roles urban governments must play, and how they will find the fiscal resources and institutional/human capacity to perform these new roles. In Namibia, much of the focus is on capacity and legal constraints rather than on the redefinition of roles.

What is common across the subcontinent, however, is the search for institutionalised participatory modes of governance in response to the generally accepted incapacity of urban governments to meet the urban challenges on their own. In other words, probably more so than at any other level of government, urban governments are searching for modes of governance that will meet the new governing needs emerging in rapidly urbanising societies in a context where these urban governments do not have the combined fiscal, institutional and human capacity to meet these needs on their own.

If, however, urban governments are allowed the space to deepen and extend participatory modes of governance, two aspects of the history of urban government in southern Africa will re-emerge. The first will be the popular participation experiments that Mozambique and Zimbabwe initiated after independence, namely the Dynamising Groups in Mozambique and the VIDCOs/WADCOs in Zimbabwe. South Africa seems to be going down the same route with its proposed Local Development Forums. In general, these state-driven participatory processes have failed largely because of unfounded Roussean assumptions about the desire amongst citizens for permanent participation and lack of capacity. This raises questions as to how participatory modes of governance will be structured so as to avoid the disappointments that follow populist attempts to bring the people into governance.

The second aspect from the past is the degree of autonomy that urban governments will enjoy. In general, increased participation has often been coupled with tighter central control and centralisation. This happened in Mozambique and Zimbabwe, and there are signs that this is the trend in South Africa. However, there is also the opposite trend gathering momentum in the mid-1990s, with the Mozambican and South African systems laying down in law the key principle of local government autonomy. Similar principles underlie the Namibian and Zimbabwean urban government systems. All four, therefore, face the challenge of finding some way of ensuring that urban governments have the capacity and resources to give substance to local autonomy, without compromising the unitary nature of the political system as a whole. This very delicate balance will not be easy to create and sustain.

In the final analysis, there is no doubt that without some sort of shared southern African vision about the structure, role, capacity and rights of urban governments, a powerful strategic approach to the issues referred to above will not emerge.

Local governance in southern African cities will be shaped by the socio-economic dynamics of urban development, and the political dynamics of democratisation. There is significant evidence that the trends referred to in the preceding two sections are already stimulating and creating the space for emerging networks and coalitions within civil society that can and want to participate in organised modes of local urban governance. However, the relative strengths, coherence and interactions with urban governments differ from country to country.

Local urban governance is being shaped in different ways and is going in different directions in each of the countries studied. However, the common denominator is that as urban governments develop to the point where they come to take on the urban challenges directly, they will find themselves needing allies in the community and private sectors to mobilise the necessary resources for sustained urban development. How they do this will directly affect the quality and durability of local urban governance. If they fail, civil society formations may well emerge to take up urban development problems, but as direct challengers to urban governments, rather than as development partners.

7 REFERENCES

African National Congress. 1994. *The Reconstruction and Development Programme: A Policy Framework.* Johannesburg: Umanyano Publications.

Appalraju J. 1995. Urban and rural development in Zimbabwe. In Reddy PS (ed) *Perspectives on Local Government Management and Development in Africa.* Durban: Department of Public Administration, University of Durban-Westville.

Burgman J. Who can deliver sustainability? Municipal reform and the sustainable development debate. *Third World Planning Review.* Vol 16 no 2.

Cheema GS & E Ward (eds). 1993. *Urban Management: Policies and Innovations in Developing Countries*. London: Praeger.

Coetzee M, W Cobbet & R Hunter. 1991. Electricity costs and rent boycott. In Swilling M et al *The Apartheid City in Transition*. Cape Town: Oxford University Press.

Coetzee SF & C de Coning. 1992. *An Agenda for Urban Research: South Africa in the 1990s*. Paper presented at workshop on Urban Research Agenda for Southern Africa, University of the Witwatersrand, Johannesburg.

Davidson F & P Nientied. Urban management in the Third World: developing the capacity. *Cities*. Vol 8 no 2.

Frayne B & K Gowaseb. 1992. *Urban Research in the Developing World: Towards an Agenda for the 1990s*. Paper presented at workshop on Urban Research Agenda for Southern Africa, University of Witwatersrand, Johannesburg.

Goetz EG & S Clarke (eds). 1993. *The New Localism: Comparative Urban Politics in a Global Era*. London: Sage.

Hammar A. 1994. *Amalgamation of Rural and District Councils in Zimbabwe: Institutional Strategies for Policy, Planning and Implementation*. Paper presented at workshop on Metropolitan and Local Government Issues in Zimbabwe and South Africa, Harare.

Helmsing AHJ et al. 1991. *Limits to Decentralisation in Zimbabwe: Essays on the Decentralisation of Government and Planning in the 1980s*. The Hague: Institute of Social Studies.

Hyden G & M Bratton (eds). 1992. *Governance and Politics in Africa*. Boulder, Colorado: Lynne Rienner.

Jordan JD. 1984. *Local Government in Zimbabwe*. Harare: Mambo Press.

Mdiba B. 1992. District level planning in Zimbabwe: manpower and administrative deficiencies of district development committees, Mashonaland Central Province. *Journal of Rural Development*. Vol 11 no 1.

Mlalazi A. 1992. *Urban Planning, Development and Research in Zimbabwe*. Paper presented at workshop on Urban Research Agenda for Southern Africa, University of Witwatersrand, Johannesburg.

Mlalazi A. 1994. *Reflections on Some Aspects of Urban Development and Policy in Zimbabwe*. Paper presented at workshop on Metropolitan and Local Government Issues in Zimbabwe and South Africa, Harare.

Mozambique Delegation. 1992. *Strategic Overview of the Key Themes in Mozambican Urban Research for the Last Three Decades*. Paper presented at workshop on Urban Research Agenda for Southern Africa, University of Witwatersrand, Johannesburg.

Namoya-Jacobs R & J Hokans. 1994. *Urban Governance in Namibia*. Paper presented at workshop on Urban Governance in Southern Africa, University of Witwatersrand, Johannesburg.

Ndlovu MN. 1995. Local government financing and economic development: an overview. In Reddy PS (ed) *Perspectives on Local Government Management and Development in Africa*. Durban: Department of Public Administration, University of Durban-Westville.

Onibukun P & A Faniran. 1995. *Governance and Urban Poverty in Anglophone West Africa*. Ibadan: Centre for African Studies and Development.

Packard L et al. 1995. Politics, the bureaucracy and the local state. In Packard L & M Garrity (eds) *Local Government in Southern Africa*. Boulder, Colorado: Lynne Rienner.

Preston-White E & C Rogerson (ed). 1991. *South Africa's Informal Economy*. Cape Town.

Rogerson C. Sustainable urban development in South Africa. *Regional Development Dialogue*. Vol 13 no 4.

Swilling M. 1993. Civic associations in South Africa. *Urban Forum*. Vol 2 no 3.

Swilling M & L Boya. 1995. Local transition and the challenge of sustainable urban development: the greater Johannesburg case. In Fitzgerald P & B Munslow (eds) *Managing Sustainable Development in South Africa*. Cape Town: Oxford University Press.

Swilling M, Coetzee M, W Cobbet & R Hunter. 1991. *The Apartheid City in Transition*. Cape Town: Oxford University Press.

Swilling M, O Monteiro & K Johnson. 1995. *Building Democratic Urban Governance in Southern Africa: A Review of Key Trends*. Paper presented at the World Congress of the Global Urban Research Initiative, Mexico City.

Tomlinson R. 1995. *Urban Poverty and Local Development Planning in Southern Africa*. Johannesburg: University of Witwatersrand Press.

Wekwete K. 1994. *Urban Poverty in Southern and Eastern Africa: An Overview*. Paper presented at Urban Poverty and Governance Workshop, UNCH, Nairobi.

NOTES

1. I am aware that we have used some of Hyden's concepts, but this definition is much less 'state-centric' than his definition of governance. He focuses on the management of 'regime structures' only, and not on the wider set of relations that mesh at the local level in urban areas to create each city or town's unique patterns of governance. The notion of regime in a southern African context is much too restrictive to be used profitably. See Hyden G. Governance and the study of politics. In Hyden G & M Bratton (eds). 1992. *Governance and Politics in Africa*. Boulder, Colorado: Lynne Rienner.

2. Swilling M. *Towards an Urban Research Agenda for Southern Africa* op cit 287.

3. Law n¼ ⅟₇₇ for the Assemblies, Law n¼ ⅟₇₈ for the Executive Councils. Production as a function of the cities was a consequence of large state ownership of the economy, namely enterprises abandoned by their former owners at independence.

4. Reunio Nacional sobre Cidades e Bairros Comunais, Imprensa Nacional de Mocambique, Maputo 1979.

5. One conto = 1 000 Meticais (MT). 1$ US = 6 400 MT.

6. Guambe. 1994. 12–13.

7. This is a dominant theme in various articles in Helmsing AHJ, op cit. See also Mdiba B, 1992, District level planning in Zimbabwe: manpower and administrative deficiencies of district development committees, *Mashonaland Central Province. Journal of Rural Development*. Vol 11 no 1, 101–12.

— CHAPTER 3 —

Local Government Restructuring in South Africa

P S Reddy

1 INTRODUCTION

South Africa is undergoing a process of rapid transformation. The whole question of making local government structures more democratic, ie the creation of unitary and non-racial cities, towns and villages has now come under close scrutiny. Local government usually provides a wide range of services including, *inter alia*, water, sewerage, electricity, transport, libraries, parks, sportsgrounds, housing and health. The issues of representation and democracy in local government are directly linked to this as they affect the daily activities of the local populace. Democratic local government would obviously reflect people's needs more satisfactorily and would result in the improvement of the local citizenry's quality of life. This chapter critiques the political development of local government in urban areas in South Africa from 1948 to date. More specifically, it reviews the transitional arrangements for local government restructuring and developments up to the local government elections in November 1995.

2 WHY LOCAL GOVERNMENT?

Local authorities are created to render services in defined geographical areas, primarily because of the inability of central governments to attend to all the detailed aspects of government.

It is important to conceptualise the difference between 'local authority' and 'local government' as they are frequently used or misused when municipal topics are discussed. In this regard Meyer (1978:10) defines local government as

> '...local democratic units within the unitary democratic system, ... which are subordinate members of the government vested with prescribed, controlled governmental powers and sources of income to render specific local services and to develop, control and regulate the geographic, social and economic development of defined local areas' (Meyer 1978:10).

Given the above definition, the following characteristics of local authorities can be identified:

☐ the direct participation of the people of the locality in their governance. This should be accomplished by the election of their representatives to the local government;

☐ Locality — the relationships of the local authority to a particular geographical area, of a particular size. The area over which a local authority has jurisdiction should not be too big and the population should not be too large;

☐ they have the power to raise money from the occupiers of land within their jurisdiction, with a view to the execution of particular activities;

☐ Legal personality, meaning that the local government system should owe its existence to laws and not be simply a structure of administrative convenience;

☐ Autonomy, meaning that the local government should be able to make legally binding decisions on its own within a specified legal framework; and

☐ Governmental authority. The local authority should be able to exercise formal governmental powers (Meyer 1978:10; United Nations 1993:152–153).

It is generally accepted that local authorities are largely free to take decisions on the management of their areas provided that they act within the parameters laid down by the regional and national governments. The criteria for a viable local authority in a democratic context are, *inter alia*:

☐ the size of the population in the given area;

☐ an electorate;

☐ legitimate leaders and the feasibility of means to identify those leaders;

☐ clear areas of jurisdiction; and

☐ the availability of financial resources (World Bank 1989:89).

The range of urban services provided by local authorities in developing countries, more particularly in Africa are, *inter alia*, parks, street cleaning, sanitation, refuse collection, road construction and maintenance, housing, water and sewerage, primary education, clinics, estates-residential and industrial, planning and zoning, fire and ambulance services, camping sites and recreational services. It is imperative that these services become the responsibility of democratically elected and representative local authorities if the delivery of these urban services is going to be efficiently and effectively discharged.

The division of responsibilities for urban services between the national and local government is a political or policy issue. There are several preconditions which determine successful relationships between the central and local government. They can be summarised as follows:

☐ the need and urge for a strong system of local government in a democratic environment;

☐ that local government be allowed to play a vital role as a full partner in regional and national development;

☐ a fair division of financial resources between central, regional and local bodies;

☐   a fair division of human resources between central and local government, and the need for a non-restrictive remuneration system;

☐   formal and strong checks and balances between the central and local government;

☐   full and adequate consultation, and a regular flow of accurate information at and between all levels;

☐   the full participation of each citizen, irrespective of race or gender at all levels of administration and government — thus, the extension of democracy to all levels of government;

☐   political and social harmony;

☐   defined legal relations between the different levels of government and the ability for local pressure on central government to change legislation;

☐   trust and honesty as basic principles of government; and

☐   openness for innovation (World Bank 1989:88; Tötemeyer 1988:6).

The roles of local government in establishing a prosperous, orderly and enlightened society can be summarised as follows:

☐   they are essential links in the relationship between the government and citizenry, especially because they are bound to particular geographical areas, and to the people who are affected by the problems which are peculiar to those areas. This enables them to better understand and address these problems;

☐   they are also instruments for greater community participation, because they have jurisdiction over fewer people than do higher levels of government. Consequently, they provide more channels and opportunities to utilise the talents, insights and creative abilities of individual citizens;

☐   they are cornerstones in the structure of a democratic political system, because they serve as vehicles for intelligent and responsible citizenship on this particular level. Through allowing initiative and discretion at the local level, well-developed local government serves the cause of democracy;

☐   they are important training grounds for future leaders in government and could also serve to educate voters in the execution of their civic duties;

☐   they are potential bulwarks against uniformity, conformity, bureaucratic regimentation and dictatorship. They promote individualism and diversity, thereby ensuring that they are energetic and active growth points for the idea of self-government; and

☐   their suppleness and adaptability, and the room they provide for variety and enterprise make them important socio-political areas for experimenting with new ideas, policies and methods (Hanekom 1988:18–19).

3 RELATIONSHIP BETWEEN LOCAL GOVERNMENT AND DEMOCRACY

Local government is the second or third tier of government deliberately created to bring government to the grass-roots population, giving them a sense of involvement in the political processes that control their daily lives. Democracy denotes a political system in which the eligible people in a polity participate actively not only in determining who governs them, but also participate in shaping the policy output of their government. Determining the composition of a government is done in free and fair elections supervised by an impartial body.

3.1 Local government and democratic values

Gildenhuys et al (1991:124) are of the opinion that there are certain democratic values that can serve as guiding principles for local government management and development. The reconciliation of conflict through local policy and decision making identifies common collective needs and the equitable allocation and application of scarce public resources among the competing needs. According to Gildenhuys et al (1991:124), these values can be summarised as follows:

☐ the application of resources must satisfy the collective needs of individuals. The object of local government is to serve the individuals in their communities. In democratic theory, local government exists for the sake of the individual and not the other way around;

☐ direct participation in decision making by citizens. This could be achieved through town meetings in small communities and through ratepayer associations, vigilante groups and social/political associations in larger communities. Direct or indirect public participation in decision making is an imperative for democratic local government;

☐ value of responsibility and accountability arising from the tenets of democracy. Councillors must be sensitive to public problems and needs, feel responsible for satisfying those needs and problems and realise their accountability to the public. This calls for frequent interaction between councillors and the electorate;

☐ responsibility for management of programme effectiveness in order to ensure that needs are satisfied efficiently and effectively; and

☐ social equity emanating from the tenets of democracy. The conventional and classical philosophy of local government and management revolve around the following: Do municipal services rendered by local authorities enhance social equity? One of the main principles of social equity is the maintenance of high ethical and moral standards.

Consequently, this requires councillors and officials with integrity which in turn demands fairness, reasonableness and honesty. Social equity may also demand that local government management and development should take place in such a manner that the rule of law will prevail (Cloete 1988:24–25). In the context of local government this means that:

☐ local authorities should not be allowed to exercise discretionary powers that are too wide and unrestrained. Nor should they be allowed to act in an arbitrary manner;

☐ all citizens should be equal under local law and should be treated equally in terms of such law;

☐ the judiciary should function independently of the local authorities and judges; and

☐ magistrates should act as independent guardians to ensure that the rights and freedom of the individual are respected (Gildenhuys et al 1991:125).

Social equity requires the support of the well-known tenets of democracy. The objective of democracy is to create conditions under which each individual may achieve his greatest welfare and prosperity. Consequently, the machinery of local government should be organised in such a way that will allow mutual deliberation and consultation to attain the objectives of democracy. Caution should be exercised at all times to ensure that the interests of one group are not unfairly prejudiced or those of another not unjustly favoured (Cloete 1988: 25). Furthermore, there should be no secrecy in local government administration. The citizenry observing or investigating the particular activity should have the right and freedom to express their views on the matter (Cloete 1988:25).

4 LOCAL GOVERNMENT AND THE POLICY OF APARTHEID

4.1 Introduction

The former government regarded 'urban blacks' as appendices to the homelands and as temporary sojourners in 'white South Africa' who had to exercise their political rights in the homelands (Heymans & White 1991:4). Blacks were not regarded as permanent citizens of South Africa and their presence in the urban areas was linked to their contribution to the urban economy (Johnson 1994:1). Consequently, South Africa's town and cities have been, for the most part, divided along racial lines. The graphic images of the apartheid city/town have been well documented and publicised locally and internationally. On the one hand, the wealthy white suburbs with commercial and municipal services comparable to those of established democracies and, on the other hand, the sprawling black townships on the peripheries of these towns and cities, with their stereotypical dwelling units, poor services and the ever-increasing shacks erected by the increasing number of people desperate for housing of some sort. Black townships were developed as dormitory 'towns' without central business districts (CBDs) or industrial areas, leaving them with no income base.

4.2 Segregated local authorities

4.2.1 Black local authorities

The Native (Urban Areas) Act of 1923, as amended in 1945, provided for segregated urban areas and enabled white local authorities to manage the black townships within the so called 'white' urban areas. The residents were also required to finance the expenditure of the townships based on a principle of self-sufficiency through sorghum beer production and retailing, liquor sales, rent and other service charges (Cameron 1991:153). Blacks at that stage could not own property and consequently could not be taxed for property ownership. According to Cameron (1991:153), there was a deliberate attempt by the then government to restrict commercial and industrial activity in the townships, thereby forcing black businesses to move to the homelands. Despite oppression and hardships experienced in the townships, most residents remained in the urban areas. It was generally accepted that conditions in the rural areas were much worse.

The reality of blacks in the urban areas resulted in a number of measures being introduced to address the issue. The legislation and resultant effects can be summarised as follows (Heymans & White 1991:4–5; Cloete 1993:17):

Table 1: Legislative and Administrative Provisions for Urban Blacks (1923 – 1982)

Acts	Institutions and their Functions
Black (Urban Areas) Act 21 of 1923.	Black advisory boards to advise white local authorities on the administration of black townships.
Black (Urban Areas) Consolidation Act 25 of 1945 (repealing Act 21 of 1923).	Black advisory boards to serve the same functions as those stipulated by Act 21 of 1923.
Urban Black Councils Act 79 of 1961.	Urban black councils to which white local authorities could assign powers to perform functions of a local authority.
Black Affairs Administration Act 45 of 1971 (amended to Black Communities Development Act 4 of 1984).	Black affairs administration boards (later renamed development boards) established for fourteen (14) regions. Took over the administration of black urban areas from the white local authorities. Continued to create urban black councils for urban areas. Development boards abolished in terms of the Abolition of Development Bodies Act 75 of 1986. Personnel and functions transferred to the then four (4) provincial administrations.
Community Councils Act 125 of 1977 (repealing Act 79 of 1961).	Community councils could be established for the urban areas by the administration boards.
Black Local Authorities Act 102 of 1982.	Black local authorities, the equivalent of white local authorities, could be established.

From 1982, fully-fledged local authorities could be established in the black urban areas. Consequently, it could be said that the government and administration of black urban areas was brought in line with the urban areas for the whites, Indians and coloureds. The day-to-day control over black local authorities was assigned to the then provincial administrators of the four provinces. The overall policy direction relative to local government matters was provided by Acts of parliament.

Black local authorities have been plagued with difficulties since their inception. Even though they received more formal powers over the years, the fiscal inadequacies and political illegitimacy of these bodies had left them as ill-functioning and controversial institutions (Heymans & White 1991).

4.2.2 Indian and coloured local authorities

The urban areas populated by Indians and coloureds previously formed part of the municipal areas governed by white local authorities. The genesis of separate coloured and Indian local government structures can be traced to the repealed Group Areas Act 41 of 1950, which made provision for separate residential areas and local structures in these areas. The Group Areas Amendment Act of 1962 made provision for three phases in the evolution of coloured and Indian local government:

□ the first stage would be a Consultative Committee with nominated members having advisory powers only;

□ the second stage was to be a Management Committee which would be partly elected and partly nominated and was intended to have slightly wider powers. In Kwazulu Natal, the equivalent were Local Affairs Committees (LACs);

□ the third stage was fully-fledged municipal status (Cameron 1991:29).

Although the national ministry of local government was ultimately responsible for the development of local government, the practical implementation of the legislation was the responsibility of the provinces, which introduced ordinances and regulations in this regard.

Since 1962, very few Indian or coloured urban areas progressed to fully-fledged local authorities. Four Indian designated areas, namely Marburg, Umzinto North, Verulam and Isipingo were granted Indian autonomy. No coloured management/local affairs committee has evolved into an autonomous local authority. However, the Indian local authorities have, since their inception, always remained financially and administratively weak and politically controversial due to a lack of revenue, management expertise and a weak political base.

The introduction of Regional Services Councils (RSCs) in the then Orange Free State, Cape and Transvaal, and Joint Service Boards (JSBs) in Natal saw a reversal of the self-sufficiency principle. These bodies, instead of providing a sound basis for urban financing merely attempted to make black local authorities viable (Centre for Development Studies, 1990:122). They were also seen as symbols of apartheid as they were directly linked to the ethnic local authorities established for the different race groups. It could be said that local government management and development during this era, with the exception of white local authorities was one of oppression, illegitimacy, inefficiency and fragmentation (Johnson 1994:3).

4.3 The disintegration of segregated local authorities

The then government introduced the Free Settlement Areas Act of 1988 which acknowledged for the first time the infiltration of blacks into the towns and cities. This created limited open spaces where people could live, regardless of race. In addition, the government introduced the Local Government Affairs in Free Settlement Areas Act of 1988, which made provision for mixed or non-racial local government. The management committees envisaged in the Act were subordinate and intended to act in an advisory capacity to the white local authorities, unless specifically allocated certain powers in this regard. Despite these measures being transitional, they were rejected by the black communities and the legislation was repealed without ever being used (Mackay 1993:7).

In 1986, the Council for the Coordinating of Local Government Affairs appointed a technical committee under the chairmanship of Dr Thornhill to investigate a new local government dispensation for South Africa. The committee released its report on 28 May 1990 and the government considered this as a framework for local negotiations. The report proposed negotiations by leaders of all races in each city/town for a new local government dispensation and towards this end, five options were put forward:

☐ racially separate local authorities for the different population groups;
☐ local services councils, where autonomous local authorities would constitute a joint administration;
☐ community government, which entailed a joint local authority for a town or city with an option to establish neighbourhood management committees on a non-racial geographic basis, with a non-racial voters' roll on a ward system;
☐ a single, non-racial municipality elected on a common voters' roll; and
☐ any other system which resulted from negotiations among the residents themselves (Council for the Coordinating of Local Government Affairs 1990:23-34).

These proposals were rejected by the ANC, the United Democratic Front (UDF) and civic organisations throughout the country, as they were seen as still trying to maintain apartheid through cooption (Botha 1990:17).

The government repealed the Group Areas Act of 1966 and the Reservation of Separate Amenities Act of 1953 in June 1991 and this made it increasingly impractical to have separate local government structures for different race groups in mixed areas. It also introduced the Interim Measures for Local Government Act of 1991 for integrated local government. This Act was rejected by the ANC on the grounds that it would not result in the creation of a non-racial, democratic, non-sexist, open and united local government in South Africa.

4.3.1 Principles

The democratic movement put forward several key principles for the restructuring of towns and cities to make them democratic and non-racial. These included, *inter alia*, the following:

☐ a definite, legitimate and fully constituted system of local government can only be created in the context of a unitary and democratic South Africa, in which the powers of local government are conferred on it by a constituent assembly or other democratically delegated legislative body;
☐ the creation of a national and democratic tradition of local government remains a priority and interim structures of local government should be created that will lay the basis for a smooth transition to a definitive future system;
☐ local authorities should be delimited, taking into account the principles of non-racism and the redistribution of resources;
☐ these interim structures should strive to overcome some of the limitations imposed by the apartheid and homelands systems and they should reflect as

closely as possible the structure of a future democratic system. These structures will be subject to review at a later stage;

☐ local government needs to be built on an optimal combination of democratic accountability to the community and efficient and rational planning that maximises a community's development potential;

☐ the establishment of interim structures must involve a process of local level consultation that draws in all significant interest and pressure groups in the area under discussion, including the relevant regional formations. The process must be designed to empower residents and community activists at the local level and equip them for tasks of local government;

☐ affirmative action programmes must be introduced and implemented to address the historical, racial and gender imbalances resulting from the apartheid era;

☐ metropolitan government structures must be created for cities and big towns and unified local authorities for small towns and other areas;

☐ elections for local government structures must be held on the basis of universal suffrage as the ratepayer voting system discriminates against the poor and entrenches their powerlessness; and

☐ the need for local autonomy on certain community issues must be balanced with the need for a coordinated national policy that will seek to overcome the inequalities of the apartheid era. The balance between local and central control of various policy issues must be determined for each issue (Olver 1990:169–170).

5 CONSTITUTIONAL REFORM AND LOCAL GOVERNMENT RESTRUCTURING

Although negotiations for new local government structures began some time before national negotiations, it was very disjointed and depended to a large extent on the initiatives of some of the stakeholders, namely individual local authorities, political parties and civic organisations. The address to parliament by the former state president, Mr FW de Klerk, acted as an impetus to negotiations and many local government negotiating forums were established throughout the country within the ambit of the Interim Measures for Local Government Act, 1991. The ANC argued that the government was attempting to manipulate local government initiatives by unilaterally introducing this legislation which put too many powers in the hands of the then administrator. The government believed that the legislation was aimed at giving legal effect to agreements arising from local government negotiations. However, the ANC and the government did eventually agree that a framework for local government would have to be negotiated at national level, which would not contradict the constitution emerging from the multi-party talks.

5.1 Local Government Negotiating Forum (LGNF)

5.1.1 Introduction

The deliberations of the Local Government Negotiating Forum (LGNF) took place while the main constitutional negotiations were taking place. There was ongoing consultation between the LGNF and the Multi-Party Negotiating Council (MPNC) on matters of a common interest. This ensured that what was acceptable to the negotiators at the local level was also acceptable at the national level.

The establishment of the LGNF was a major breakthrough for local government in South Africa. The mission of the LGNF was to contribute to the democratisation of local government and to bring about a democratic, non-racial, non-sexist and financially viable local government system (*Sunday Times* 1 August 1993). Despite the criticism levelled at it, its establishment was a significant development in local government. This was the first time that statutory and non-statutory organisations were making a joint effort to solve the problems of local government.

The LGNF was a non-statutory, voluntary body. It did not replace any existing statutory body and did not have legal status. Its objective was to explore, research and recommend options for local government structures to the MPNC (*Sunday Times* 1 August 1993).

5.1.2 Establishment and composition

The LGNF was launched on 22 March 1993 after four months of negotiations. It was made up of two delegations — statutory and non-statutory. The statutory side consisted of representatives of central, provincial and local government; representatives of the United Municipal Executive (UME) and its four provincial affiliates; National Committee for Local Government Associations representing United Municipalities of South Africa (UMSA) and Urban Councils of South Africa (UCASA). The non-statutory side stood under the banner of the South African National Civics Organisation (SANCO). There were two chairpersons, one from each side. There were long and detailed discussions in the MPNC, resulting in the introduction of the Local Government Transition Act 209 of 1993. In addition, chapter 10 of the Republic of South Africa Constitution Act 200 of 1993, focusing on local government and the Agreement on Finances, Services and Service Rendering was also negotiated.

5.2 Statutory framework

The constitution established the status of local government, its powers and functions and related aspects. It requires local government to be autonomous and to regulate its affairs within the limits prescribed by law. In addition, parliament and the provincial legislatures must not encroach on the powers, functions and structures of local government to such an extent as to comprise its fundamental status, purpose and character. Chapter 10 also provides for a code of conduct for local government members and officials.

5.2.1 Phases in local and metropolitan government reform

The Local Government Transition Act 209 of 1993 has to be read in conjunction with chapter 10 of the Republic of South Africa Constitution Act 200 of 1993. Consequently, this gives considerable protection to local government against interference by higher levels of government.

The Act makes provision for:

- □ the pre-interim and interim phases for the restructuring of local government;
- □ the establishment of provincial committees for local government;
- □ the establishment of local forums for negotiating the restructured form of local government in each area for the pre-interim period; and
- □ provincial demarcation boards to set the boundaries of local authorities and delimit the electoral wards within them (LGNF 1993:6).

In addition, the Act also determines the powers of the provincial premiers in ensuring and controlling progress relative to the restructuring. It also repeals certain local government laws that will become redundant when the transitional arrangements come into effect.

5.2.1.1 Pre-interim Phase

The pre-interim phase ran from the promulgation of the Act (February 1994) until the elections in November 1995. The steps involved can be summarised as follows (NADEL 1995:2–23):

(a) *Step one: abolish the old apartheid structures*

The Act made provision for the establishment of forums resulting from negotiations. The minister of local government in the provincial legislature concerned must approve such a forum in accordance with principles and procedures contained in schedule 1 of the Act. An important consideration in this regard is the principle of inclusiveness and representation resulting in negotiating forums in 'economically and historically bound areas' bringing together communities that have been artificially separated by apartheid. Half the forum's members must be from the statutory component and half from the non-statutory component. The former comprises those from the former establishment side and the latter from those that were previously excluded from structures of local government. The statutory functions of a forum are negotiations on and the determination of the following issues:

- □ recommendations to the provincial premiers on the boundaries, the size and composition of the forum (statutory and non-statutory members, observers and advisors);
- □ the name of the new transitional council and the number of seats on it, taking the existing number of seats in the various local bodies in its area as departure points;
- □ which transitional model will be applied, and its functions, ie whether the newly appointed transitional council will replace all existing government bodies or only supplement them by taking over some of their functions in the form of a local government coordinating committee; and
- □ which existing councillors are to be re-nominated and which are not, and which new councillors are to be nominated (Cloete 1994:51).

(b)   *Step two: establishment of transitional structures*
The local negotiating forums may choose one of two options for restructuring local government within their areas for the pre-interim phase:

☐   Option A: Appointed local or metropolitan councils, nominated by the forum on the basis that at least half of the persons nominated should be acceptable to the 'statutory' component and at least half to the 'non-statu-tory' component. These councils will become the Transitional Local Council (TLC) for a primary local authority; or the Transitional Metropolitan Council (TMC) for a metropolitan area.

☐   Option B: Leaving the existing councils in the forum area as they are and having them appoint members to a local government coordinating com-mittee for the area (LGNF 1993:7).

An important clause in the Act is that the administrator may exempt certain local authorities from certain provisions of the Act during the pre-interim period if he is satisfied that they are non-racial, inclusive and achieve local stability through effective government and orderly financial management.

Any negotiating forum established for a metropolitan area must function simi-larly to a local negotiating forum. The only difference is that a negotiating forum established for a metropolitan area must negotiate on the establishment of a transitional metropolitan council with transitional metropolitan substructures. The metropolitan council will have certain defined powers and duties with the sub-structures having all other local government powers and duties. The provincial minister establishes these bodies by proclamation.

(c)   *Step three: operation of transitional structures*

The provincial minister:

☐   delimits the area of jurisdiction of the transitional councils and transi-tional metropolitan substructures;

☐   determines the powers and duties of any transitional metropolitan council and transitional metropolitan substructure;

☐   determines the number of seats; and

☐   delimits the area into wards.

The transitional councils' representations and the advice and recommenda-tions of the Local Government Demarcation Board (LGDB) are considered in this regard. Existing laws applying to local authorities are to apply to transi-tional local/metropolitan councils unless a proclamation is issued to the contrary. The transitional authority is to elect an executive committee by proportional representation. It must try to reach decisions on the basis of consensus. However, if this fails, a two-thirds majority is required or the matter must be referred to the transitional authority for a decision if this is agreed by a majority in the committee.

(d) *Step four: establish voting systems*

In terms of section 9(2) of the Act, the provincial minister is required to make regulations relative to:

- □   determination of wards and polling districts;
- □   voters and voters' lists and qualifications of voters;
- □   members of transitional councils and metropolitan substructures, including qualifications and terms of office;
- □   conducting of election and election procedures;
- □   election expenses;
- □   corrupt and illegal practices and other offences; and
- □   other matters deemed to be necessary or expedient.

In addition, the Act specifically provides that the ministers for the various provinces must strive for substantial uniformity in the content of these regulations.

(e) *Step five: mechanism for resolving conflicts*

The Act makes provision for a Provincial Committee of Local Government (PCLG) in each province. It consists of six members representing the different local government stakeholders in the province. Decisions are taken on the basis of a two-thirds majority vote. The provincial minister, in the exercise of his functions and duties, must act with the concurrence of the PCLG. Should there be a disagreement, the matter is referred to a Special Electoral Court. These committees will exist until local elections are held.

The LGDB investigates demarcations of local government areas and delimitation of wards on the request of the provincial minister. The following criteria are used for the demarcation of boundaries:

- □   the topographical and physical characteristics of the area;
- □   population distribution;
- □   existing administrative boundaries;
- □   existing and potential land use;
- □   economic functionality, efficiency and financial viability of service provision;
- □   development potential of the area;
- □   the degree of integration of the urban economy indicated by commercial, industrial and residential linkages; and
- □   the degree of common interest among residents on the basis of residency, work, commuting and recreation (schedule 6 of the Local Government Transition Act, 1993).

5.3 Local government elections

The interim constitution requires that local authorities be elected democratically, at intervals of three to five years The electoral system should include both proportional and ward representation. A person eligible to vote is:

- ☐ either a South African citizen or he or she has the right to vote in terms of an Act of Parliament;
- ☐ ordinarily resident in the jurisdiction of that local government, or under law liable to that local government for payment of property rates, rent, service charges or levies;
- ☐ is registered as a voter on the voters' roll of that local government.

Section 245(3) of the interim constitution provides that:

- ☐ 40% of the councillors shall be elected by proportional representation; and
- ☐ 60% on a single member ward basis.

In addition:

- ☐ half of the ward representatives (30% of the councillors) shall represent traditional white, coloured and Indian areas in the jurisdiction of the new local authority; and
- ☐ the other half (30%) shall represent current black local authorities and other areas traditionally outside municipal boundaries, but now falling in the jurisdiction of the new local authorities (farms, as well as rural or informal villages in local or peri-urban areas).

5.3.1 Review of the local government elections of 1 November 1995

The recent local government elections across most of the country were, in many ways, a repeat of 1994's combined national and provincial elections. Kwazulu Natal and metropolitan Cape Town did not vote as a result of problems including, *inter alia*, demarcation/ward disputes, the inclusion of tribal areas, and the absence of a model for rural local government (*Daily News* 1 November 1995). It is anticipated that elections in these areas will take place in May 1996. However, the third tier of elected government is now in place across most of the country and South Africans can once again congratulate themselves on their good sense and pragmatism in completing the structure of democracy. According to Dr van Zyl Slabbert, co-chairperson of the Election Task Group, the poll augured well for a spirit of democratic tolerance in South Africa (*Daily News* 3 November 1995).

The national percentage of party votes cast for the African National Congress was 57,74%, 21,18% for the National Party, 0,62% for the Inkatha Freedom Party, 1,24% for the Democratic Party 1,65% for the Conservative Party, 1,04% for the Pan Africanist Congress, 0,3% for the African Christian Democratic Party, 5,06% for ratepayer groups and 4,36% for smaller parties. A comprehensive analysis of the results of the 686 local elections would only be available in 1996 (*Daily News* 4 November 1995).

6 CONCLUSION

South Africa is presently in transition and will shortly have a democratic local government dispensation in place. It is generally accepted that the restructuring of political and administrative systems per se at the local government level are unlikely to provide final solutions. Any future local government dispensation will have to address the historical and socio-economic imbalances that have resulted from the apartheid era. In addition, the establishment of workable transitional arrangements must include all key stakeholders, in order to ensure an effective sustainable and democratic local government system.

The Local Government Transition Act 209 of 1993 was negotiated at Kempton Park by relevant stakeholders and passed by parliament in December 1993. This piece of legislation set out to create a framework for the orderly transition to a full democracy. It sets out the steps by which the change from exclusive, apartheid local government structures will take place. It also seeks to address inequalities, structural deficiencies and financial and legitimacy problems at the local government level. It also paves the way for the ushering in of a new local government dispensation in terms of the final constitution.

The November 1995 local government elections were an integral part of the transitional process. The new, democratic local authorities arising from negotiation and compromise have been created through a combination of the new dispensation and the apartheid era. The elections were the last chapter in the democratisation of the South African state. However, the structure of local democracy is only the start. The act of voting democratically does not itself produce the fruits of democracy. Only a commitment to creating conditions for political stability, order and respect for the law will make economic and social growth possible.

7 REFERENCES

Cameron R. 1991. An analysis of the structure and functioning of coloured and Indian local authorities since the introduction of the tricameral parliament. *Politikon.* Vol 18 no 1.

Centre for Development Studies. 1990. Municipal finance. In *Local Government and Planning for a Democratic South Africa.* Cape Town: University of the Western Cape.

Cloete F. 1994. Local government restructuring. *Politikon.* Vol 21 no 1.

Cloete JJN. 1993. *Towns and Cities: Their Government and Administration.* Pretoria: JL van Schaik.

Constitution of the Republic of South Africa Act 200 of 1993 (as amended by Act 2 and 3 of 1994).

Craythorne DL. 1994. *Municipal Administration: A Handbook.* Kenwyn: Juta & Co Ltd.

Daily News. 1 November 1995.

Daily News. 3 November 1995.

Daily News. 4 November 1995.

Fray P. 1995. The tasks of the task group. *Towards Democracy — Journal of the Institute for Multi-Party Democracy* . First Quarter.

Hanekom SX. 1989. Why local government matters. In Heymans C &
    G Tötemeyer (eds) *Government by the People? The Politics of Local Government
    in South Africa*. Kenwyn: Juta & Co Ltd.

Heymans C & G Tötemeyer. 1988. *Government by the People? The Politics of Local
    Government in South Africa*. Kenwyn: Juta & Co Ltd.

Heymans C & R White. 1991. Playing politics without the power: the state of
    black local government in the South Africa of the 1980/90s. *Politikon*. Vol 18
    no 1.

Institute for Multi-Party Democracy. 1995. Local Government Elections '95 Focus
    Seminar, Durban: March.

Johnson K. 1994. *Urban Governance: The South African Experience*. Cape Town:
    Inlogov.

Local Government Transition Act 209 of 1993.

Mackay S. 1993. *Towards Deracialising Local Government*. Johannesburg: South
    African Institute of Race Relations.

Mahwood P. 1993. *Local Government in the Third World: The Experience of
    Decentralisation in Tropical Africa*. Pretoria: Africa Institute of South Africa.

National Association of Democratic Lawyers (NADEL) (1995). Workshop on the
    Transformation of Local Government, Durban.

Olver C. 1991. Rural local government in South Africa. In *Local Government and
    Planning for a Democratic South Africa* . Bellville: Centre for Development
    Studies, University of the Western Cape.

Schmidt D. 1990. Shaping a new future in our towns and cities. *Democracy in
    Action*. August/September.

Streek B. 1995. Do or die elections. *Towards Democracy — Journal of the Institute for
    Multi-Party Democracy*.

Sunday Times. 14 September 1993.

United Nations. 1992. Seminar on Decentralisation in African Countries,
    Department of Economic and Social Development, New York.

World Bank. 1989. *Strengthening Local Governments in Sub-Saharan Africa*.
    Washington DC: Economic Development Institute.

— PART 2 —

Constitutional, Structural and Organisational Development

— CHAPTER 4 —

Intergovernmental Relations — the South African Experience

T Botha

1 INTRODUCTION

The concept of intergovernmental relations assumes importance where there is division of powers at both administrative and legislative levels among different tiers of government. Put differently, it is a creative mechanism to maintain cooperative relationships and coordination among and between vertical and horizontal sites of power within a polity.

Division of power as opposed to separation of powers is an integral feature of a federal form of state. In a federal form of state, power is divided among the first, second and third tiers of government. In contrast, in a unitary system of government, parliament is sovereign. The only division of power is between parliament and the electorate in a horizontal sense. The doctrine of separation of powers between the legislature, the executive and the judiciary applies horizontally and not vertically as is the case with the division of powers.

Whereas under a unitary system of government authority is delegated, within a federal context power is devolved or constitutionally assigned and protected. The manner in which powers and functions are assigned to the different levels of government differs from constitution to constitution. Power can be assigned exclusively to the first and second tiers or even the third tier of government and the residual powers become a preserve of the other tier. Alternatively, only concurrent powers can be listed and the remaining powers are allocated to the centre as is the case in South Africa.

In assigning powers and functions the drafters of the constitution are unable to predict all problems which might arise between the different sites of power. Such problems are resolved through dialogue between and among the different stakeholders.

A system of government where the sub-units of a federal form of state are assigned powers differentially is referred to as an asymmetry. Such powers can be assigned through state/provincial constitutions or by administrative arrangements. Although the Constitution of the Republic of South Africa Act 200 of 1993 assigns the same powers and functions to all provinces, it also allows for institutional and administrative asymmetry.

In terms of section 160(1) the provincial legislature shall be entitled to pass a constitution for its province by a resolution of at least two-thirds of all its members. Such a constitution shall not be inconsistent with a provision of the national constitution (see section 160(3)).

But, in recognition of the unique features of the provinces, section 160(3)(a) of the constitution allows provincial legislatures to pass a constitution providing for legislative and executive structures and procedures different to those provided for in the national constitution. For instance, Kwazulu Natal is free to make provision in its provincial constitution for the Zulu monarch.

However, in regard to schedule 6 functional areas, a province may indicate to the centre that it does not have administrative competence to administer a particular law/s in which case the centre may administer the law until the province is ready. For example, national ministries such as Health and Education entered into arrangements with the provincial MECs whereby the national departments would continue to render services until the transfer of all the relevant powers and functions had been effected. It should be noted that not all provinces would be ready to administer their laws at the same time because of the varying degrees of institutional capacity among them.

This arrangement makes it possible for a province which has not developed its administrative capacity to approach the centre to administer such laws on its behalf. This can be referred to as an administrative asymmetry rather than a constitutional asymmetry. The principle of administrative asymmetry can also be described in the same way as agency agreements are entered into between two levels of government.

The only difference in what is described above is that delegation is upwards from the provinces to the national government. Such agency agreements are symptomatic of cooperative arrangements aimed at promoting good government. The doctrine of asymmetry, whether constitutional or administrative, should always be balanced by the principles of accountability and fiscal equalisation.

The following are some of the factors contributing to the way in which powers are divided among the different tiers of government:

☐ to limit the power of central government;
☐ to cater for ethnic diversity;
☐ reflects the degree of trust or mistrust among the constitution drafters;
☐ the historical factors which influence the political constitution;
☐ political environment at the time of drafting;
☐ the desire to bring decision making closer to the consumers of those policies and thereby strengthen accountability;
☐ make government accessible to the grass roots;
☐ interpretation of the constitution by the constitutional court;
☐ who sits in the constitutional court; and
☐ what political clients perceive as the necessary powers of their government.

The operational principle is that powers and functions should be assigned to the level of government best suited to efficiently and effectively administer implementation. Experience tells us that whatever the views of the constitution drafters, division of powers cannot be construed to mean absolute autonomy of one tier of government from the other. The notion of the paramountcy of legislative competency is hollow if the competent authority is unable to finance its functions.

For example, if a province passes legislation which requires national government money to implement its policy and the former refuses to advance the necessary funds, then paramountcy becomes hollow. In this case it may not always be easy for the Constitutional Court (CC) to interpret this as an encroachment into the area of competency of the provinces. And yet, if informal, cooperative institutional arrangements exist, such disagreements can be addressed politically without referring them to the constitutional court.

It is against this background that the process of constitution implementation should allow for the evolution of informal institutions in order to promote smooth and dynamic intergovernmental relations. It should also be noted that a constitution is not a fixed set of administrative rules but is a set of principles and values upheld by a particular society at a particular historical moment.

This chapter addresses itself to the conditions which give rise to the need for the establishment of formal and informal institutional intergovernmental arrangements. It also examines the possibilities and limitations created by some of those institutional arrangements.

2 THE CONSTITUTIONAL FRAMEWORK

The history of the new South African dispensation is a history of struggle for power between central government and provincial governments. The basis of the relationship among the three tiers of government (central, provincial and local) is primarily enshrined in the Constitutional Principles as well as in section 126 of the Constitution Act 200 of 1993 as amended by Act 2 of 1994 and Act 3 of 1995.

Constitutional principle XVI states that government shall be structured at national, provincial and local levels. In terms of principle XIX the national and provincial government shall have powers and functions which shall include exclusive and concurrent powers as well as the right to perform functions for other levels of government on an agency or delegation basis. The meaning of principle XVI is further clarified by principle XXVII which provides that each level of government shall have a constitutional right to an equitable share of revenue collected nationally, to ensure that provinces and local government are able to provide basic services and execute the functions allocated to them.

Furthermore, principle XXII prevents central government exercising exclusive or concurrent powers in a manner that encroaches on the geographical, functional or institutional integrity of the provinces.

In order to monitor and regulate the relationship among the three tiers of government, the competency of each has to be clarified either in the constitution or in legislation. Towards this end, schedule 6 lists the functional areas which exhibit elements of both concurrency and exclusivity.

It is not easy to find functional areas or competencies relating exclusively to a particular level of government, but only powers within a functional area or competency can be defined exclusively. For instance, aspects of primary and secondary education that require national standards, such as matric examinations, core curricula and teacher qualification requirements, for purposes of ensuring uniformity, ease of transferability from one province to the other and even development, shall have to be regulated nationally, even though these competencies fall under the provincial level of government.

To illustrate this point further, the implementation and administration of national competencies often takes place at provincial level. Sometimes, while the competency may be vested in national government, aspects of the powers relating to such competency may be delegated to the sub-national levels of government. Put differently, the province may ask for the exercise of a particular power from national government without the transfer of the actual competency. This could only happen if it is deemed that the exercise of such power would be most effective if it is done at provincial level and/or local level. In this case the responsibility remains with the level of government in which the competency is vested. Therefore it retains the right to withdraw such delegated authority if it is not satisfied that it is being effectively and efficiently exercised. It is interesting that, while this framework seems to be relatively clear between national and provincial governments, the same cannot be said of the relationship between provincial and local governments.

Hence the need to revisit the constitution with a view to creating checks and balances to protect local government from erosion of its powers by provincial government and to create mechanisms to avoid and/or limit its impact on the communities.

This is so for two reasons:

☐ Although local government remains linked to both the national and provincial governments, its employees are not part of or regulated by the Public Service Act.

☐ Local governments are not homogeneous entities and their competencies and scope of operation differ. For example, a metropolitan government cannot be compared with a small municipality.

In terms of the South African constitution, section 126(3) outlines the conditions under which the centre can intervene in the functional areas which appear to be an exclusive competence of provincial governments, but the same is not true when it comes to the competencies of local government vis-à-vis the provincial government. One of the observable shortcomings of section 126(3) is that it does not explain who determines national standards and uniformity. Should it be national government? Should it be provincial government? Should it be both sitting together?

Drawing from the experience in the exercise of these powers and the emergent relationship between the three tiers, it is becoming apparent that the constitution may not be exhaustive in spelling out the powers and functions and the nature of the relationship between the different levels of government. Often the depth of the relationship between the different tiers finds expression in both formal and informal institutional arrangements.

3 FORMAL INSTITUTIONAL ARRANGEMENTS

Formal institutions are those bodies which are established in terms of the constitution or in accordance with parliamentary statutes. It must be stated from the outset that the relationship between the constitutional bodies is both complementary and competitive. To the extent that the functional areas and lines of authority of each institution are clearly delineated, either in statutes or in the constitution, means they can complement one another. However, in reality the functional areas of these institutions, insofar as they are responsible for intergovernmental relations, tend to overlap.

In order to illustrate these relationships, it is necessary to identify the most critical institutions responsible for managing intergovernmental relations in South Africa. They include the Department of Constitutional Development and Provincial Affairs, the Commission on Provincial Government (CPG), the Public Service Commission (PSC), the Financial and Fiscal Commission (FFC), and the Constitutional Court (CC). Also, the senate is supposed to provide a link between the provincial legislatures and the national parliament. But this link is missing.

3.1 Department of Constitutional Development and Provincial Affairs

The Department of Constitutional Development and Provincial Affairs is responsible for coordinating policy between national, provincial and local governments. For example, it convenes meetings between the premiers of the nine provinces and ministers of various national departments to coordinate and reach agreements on crucial policy issues.

Furthermore, the department also assists in managing horizontal relationships between provinces such as facilitating dialogue where there are border disputes. It is also responsible for intergovernmental grants to local governments and for creating legislative frameworks for local government elections as well as for those of traditional leaders. Local government training and disaster management are coordinated by this department.

However, the department may not intervene or be construed to be interfering in areas of competency of other line functions ministries. Its role is more to coordinate and assist to create the necessary conditions for cooperation. In order to ensure fruitful discussions in the Intergovernmental Forum (IGF) meetings, the Director-General of the Department of Constitutional Development convenes meetings of the Technical Intergovernmental Committee (TIC) comprising provincial directors-general and some national directors-general. The work of the department is complemented by the Commission on Provincial Government (CPG). Hence the CPG is also invited to attend those meetings to share information.

3.2 Commission on Provincial Government (CPG)

This commission was primarily created to facilitate the establishment of provincial government under the new constitutional dispensation. Towards this end, in terms of section 164(1)(a) of the Constitution of the Republic of South Africa Act 200 of 1993, the commission advises the constitutional assembly (CA) on the development of a constitutional dispensation with regard to systems of provincial government. It:

☐   advises national government or a provincial government on the establishment and consolidation of administrative institutions and structures in a province; and

☐   makes recommendations to the national government or provincial government on the rationalisation of statutory enactments or public sector resources directed at the introduction and maintenance of an effective system of provincial government.

Section 164(2) provides that the recommendations referred to in subsection (1)(a) shall include recommendations in the form of draft constitutional provisions regarding:

☐   the finalisation of the number and the boundaries of the provinces of the Republic;

☐   the constitutional dispensation of such provinces, including the constitutional structures within such provinces as well the method of the election and their authority, functions and procedures;

☐   measures, including transitional measures that provide for the phasing in of new provincial constitutional dispensations;

☐   the final delimitation of powers and functions between national and provincial institutions of government, with due regard to the criteria set out in subsection 3;

☐   fiscal arrangements between the institutions of national government and those of the provincial governments;

☐   the powers and functions of local governments; and

☐   any matter that the commission considers to be relevant or ancillary to its functions.

Furthermore, in terms of section 239(1)(d) the commission's advice is almost decisive in the event of a dispute between two or more governments on the division of assets. It might be interesting to note that section 237(2)(a) places the responsibility for the rationalisation of provincial institutions on national government but not exclusively. National government exercises this responsibility in cooperation with the provincial governments and the CPG, with due regard to the advice of the PSC.

At the constitutional level, the work of the CPG overlapped with the theme committees of the CA.

The major political parties at national level began to see the CPG as creating an opportunity for division between party positions at national level and party structures at provincial level. As a consequence of these concerns, a proposal was placed before the IGF (meeting of premiers with national ministers) for its dissolution.

If it is dissolved, its work will be divided between the Department of Constitutional Development and the Department of Public Service and Administration, including the PSC.

3.3 Public Service Commission (PSC)

The Public Service Commission (PSC) is established in terms of section 209(1) and is accountable to parliament (subsection (2)).

The PSC is responsible for (section 210(1)(a)), *inter alia*, giving direction and conduct enquiries with regard to:

- ☐ the organisation and administration of departments and the public service;
- ☐ the conditions of service of members of the public service and matters related thereto;
- ☐ personnel practices in the public service, appointments, promotions, transfers, discharge, and other career incidents of members of the public service;
- ☐ the promotion of efficiency and effectiveness in departments and the public service; and
- ☐ a code of conduct applicable.

Any of these powers can be delegated to a member of the commission or an official in the public service subject only to limitations imposed by law. Furthermore, the commission advises the President, a minister or a member of the executive council of a province in regard to any matter relating to the public service, or the employment, remuneration or other conditions of service of functionaries employed by any institution or body which receives funds wholly or partly appropriated by parliament or a provincial legislature (section 210(b)).

Although the national PSC is charged in terms of the constitution with these responsibilities the implementation of these policies at provincial level is delegated to the provincial service commission. The policies which are either expressed through legislation or the staff codes sometimes are derived from decisions and agreements reached in the national collective bargaining chamber.

The provincial service commissions, although they enjoy some autonomy from the national PSC, may not initiate policy which could have personnel implications beyond their provincial boundaries. Their role is more to implement national norms and standards within the province at the level of procedures. The process for implementation of decisions can be taken at the level of the provincial bargaining chambers. Since there is only one public service in South Africa, the provincial chambers may not negotiate new policies save for purposes of recommendation to the central bargaining chamber. The decisions should be both administratively and financially sound.

3.4 Financial and Fiscal Commission (FFC)

The section of the constitution dealing with financial and fiscal arrangements among the three tiers of government is extremely important because it determines not only the measure of autonomy but also the effectiveness of each of these governments in the execution of their powers and functions. According to section 155(1) of the constitution, a province shall be entitled to an equitable share of revenue collected nationally to enable it to provide services and to exercise and perform its powers and functions. The equitable share of revenue referred to is, in terms of section 155(2):

- ☐ a percentage, as fixed by an Act of parliament, of income tax on individuals which is collected within the province;

- ☐ a percentage, as fixed by an Act of parliament, on value tax or other sales tax which is collected within the province; and

- ☐ other conditional or unconditional allocations out of national revenue to a province.

In addition to the above revenue sharing arrangements, section 156(1) entitles provinces to levy taxes, surcharges or levies other than of a kind referred to in section 155(a) or (b). However, a provincial legislature shall not be entitled, in terms of the constitution, to levy taxes detrimentally affecting national economic policies, interprovincial commerce or the national mobility of goods, services, capital and labour.

The sharing of revenue and the taxation powers of the provincial legislatures shall have to be conducted with due regard to the provision of constitutional principle XXVII wherein national interest, economic disparities between provinces as well as the population and developmental needs, administrative and other legitimate interests of each province are the primary guides.

However, investigations conducted by the FFC and the CPG indicate that, in view of the inequalities existing among provinces, only limited taxing powers can be devolved. The revenue raised from these taxes will not be adequate to finance the expenditure of the provincial governments based on their powers and functions.

In order to enable the provinces and local governments to meet their expenditure needs, the constitution allows them to raise bridging finance through loans only for capital expenditure. In terms of section 157(a) a province is not competent to raise loans for current expenditure.

The reason national parliament is given powers to regulate borrowing on the part of lower levels of government is both in the interest of national economy, and to dispel any expectations that the national government will bail out lower levels of government unable to service their debt commitments.

Because of the crucial role of the FFC in formulating and influencing national parliament on a revenue sharing formula and the borrowing limits of the sub-national governments, it is important that each level of government be adequately represented.

4 INFORMAL INSTITUTIONS

Where it has been found that the formal intergovernmental institutional arrangements are inadequate to address policy issues, and to ensure coordination between tiers of government, informal structures have been established.

For example, in a meeting between the national government and provincial premiers held at Tuynhuis on 12 August 1994, a set of resolutions was adopted after noting delays in the assignment of powers from national to provincial government.

This meeting resolved that political functionaries at the national and provincial level entrusted with matters referred to in schedule 6 of the constitution should establish joint technical committees within ten days to propose an appropriate distribution of powers and responsibilities in terms of section 126 of the constitution.

Recommendations from such technical committees were to be submitted to the IGF for approval. More importantly, the premiers and the national ministers at the meeting, noting the importance of intergovernmental relations to ensure and encourage the development of a cooperative relationship and spirit between the provinces and the national government, established:

☐ the Intergovernmental Forum (IGF) — comprising the premiers of the nine provinces and central government. The IGF meets monthly and is attended at least twice annually by the President of the Republic of South Africa as well as the deputy executive presidents; and

☐ ministerial forums (Min-MECs) — between line function ministers at central government level and their respective counterparts in provincial government. They are to meet on an ad hoc basis.

These forums supported by technical committees of administrative staff guided by the national and provincial directors-general.

One of the observations of the IGF was that, although provinces may have common interests, it is unlikely that they will develop administrative capacity simultaneously or that their eventual administrative capacities will be the same. It was therefore felt that schedule 6 competencies could be assigned to those provinces which have demonstrated administrative competency and readiness to exercise this authority. The initial agenda of these informal intergovernmental and inter-ministerial meetings (Min-MECs) was dominated by demands for the transfer of schedule 6 functions to provinces.

Other dominant matters were disagreements between the provincial premiers and the national ministers and the PSC over the interpretation of administrative capacity and the provisions of chapter J of the Public Service Regulations. However, it was relatively easy to reach agreements on many of these matters through the IGF.

Administrative capacity became an issue because the provinces demanded their powers soon after provincial governments assumed power in May 1994. The national ministers expressed concern about the provinces inability to demonstrate sufficient administrative capacity to exercise their powers. The argument of national departments was that provinces were not ready to govern because administrative structures were not in place and the provincial legislatures were not fully capacitated to carry the legislative work load.

The provinces, in their defence, argued that national departments were trying to play a 'big daddy' role and that they were still bent on centralisation in violation of the constitution. The provinces also accused the centre of not having the capacity to deliver on the schedule 6 competencies, despite the claims and the pretence to this end at national level. Therefore there was no rationale for national government to control legislation which belonged to provinces if it was not better able to exercise those powers.

Another problem which confronted national government was the interpretation of section 126(3). Out of frustration, and realising that nothing in the constitution prevented them from legislating on schedule 6 functional areas, the provinces wanted to pass legislation in any of the defined areas.

Yet, if they decided to legislate without consulting their national counterparts, they stood a chance of violating provisos stipulated in section 126(3), relating to national standards, uniformity and interprovincial commerce.

The Min-MECs meetings between provincial members of the executive councils and national ministers were therefore held to discuss the delineation of powers within schedule 6 functional areas. In short, the Min-MECs meetings took place out of necessity rather than as a result of constitutional or statutory requirements. Similarly, the premiers' IGF was prompted by premiers needing a platform from which they could exert pressure on national government in pursuance of their powers.

When they arrived at the IGF meetings the premiers soon realised they would have to caucus their positions. At times their arguments were weakened by disagreement among themselves. Consequently, the premiers formed their own forum, attended only by premiers, without attendant advisers and minute takers. Minutes are taken and kept by the premiers themselves.

The IGF became more important than constitutional structures because it served as a platform for exchanging political ideas and an arena for venting frustration by provincial premiers. The importance of this forum is underscored by the Min-MECs, after a few months, being requested to give regular reports on progress achieved in the transfer of powers to the provinces.

This was because premiers attended IGF meetings without being properly briefed by their MECs. To further empower the premiers it was deemed necessary that their provincial directors-general attend IGF meetings to give technical support. This led to the establishment of the Technical Intergovernmental Committee (TIC), a structure convened by the Director-General of the Department of Constitutional Development, and attended by all provincial directors-general or their proxies as well as by national directors-general. This committee meets in preparation for IGF meetings.

The TIC was born of necessity. Premiers were increasingly hamstrung by detail and had little time to discuss policy. In other words, the TIC took away from the premiers' agenda many detailed administrative matters. This process was not without its problems. The bureaucrats tended to dominate discussions in IGF meetings. The directors-general and their staff members tended to influence decisions of the forum. This frustrated and angered some politicians who perceived the civil servants as powerful and sometimes arrogant because of their control of and access to information. Consequently, in the meetings of the premiers and some of the Min-MECs, civil servants are asked for advice when needed and do not take part in debate except when asked to do so.

This led to the civil servants using their own forums more effectively. For example, in addition to the TIC meetings, the PSC established a forum of all provincial service commissions to discuss personnel and administrative matters. It would be fair to say this forum, too, was established out of need rather than constitutional requirements. The relationship between the PSC and the provincial service commissions is more complex in practice than as explained in the constitution.

As stated, the PSC sets national norms and standards, and the provincial service commissions are compelled to follow these guidelines. This relationship is crucial when one considers that section 237 places the responsibility for the nationalisation of a provincial administration with the relevant provincial government. In this regard, it becomes clear that a direct relationship exists between the provincial executive and the PSC. The dilemma here, however, is in the role of the provincial service commissions in relation to the PSC and the provincial executives.

This dilemma exists because, while the provincial service commission could be perceived as a provincial employer, it does so as an extension of the national PSC. It is not always the case that the position of the PSC enjoys the support of either the provincial service commission and the provincial executive councils owing to implementation problems. The real questions are, what platform does a provincial service commission have, or what recourse does it have, should it disagree with centrally determined policies or find itself incapable of implementing them?

Some of the problems which have occurred could not have been foreseen. Hence it was not deemed necessary to provide constitutional structures to deal with these relationships. Therefore the forum of service commissions is an informal structure designed to iron out whatever differences might arise between the national PSC and its provincial counterparts. There is a view which argues for the constitutionalisation of these various bodies, or at least argues that they should become statutory bodies with legal status and powers.

It should be noted, however, that these informal, intergovernmental structures are perceived by some political parties as being attempts by national government to erode the powers of the provinces. They are seen as ploys to centralise even constitutionally devolved powers.

An area which has not been fully addressed is the relationship between national competencies and provincial administrations in the exercise of relevant powers. Some national departments have been reluctant to delegate powers to the provincial administrations. This has given rise to problems for the provincial governments as the recipients of services vent their frustrations against the provincial governments. Yet the provincial governments are neither competent nor authorised to direct national government to act in particular ways on these matters. But when people wish to express their frustration against the government, they do not travel to or disrupt services at national offices. They do so within the province.

Furthermore, the staff of these departments were drawn from previously adequately coordinated structures adept at dealing with national departments and relating to local government structures. They now find themselves having to create provincial intergovernmental structures to coordinate vertical and horizontal intergovernmental relations. This coordination is in the interest of the provincial governments and the national government. Having noted the value of cooperative institutional arrangements, the speakers of the provincial legislatures also established a forum to deal with matters such as the separation of powers between the executive and the legislature.

4.1 Speakers' forum

The nine speakers' meetings have assisted in developing uniform conditions of service for their staff. The guidelines in this regard were drawn up by the commission on provincial government after consulting with the national parliamentary staff. The provincial speakers occasionally meet the speaker of the national assembly to deal with matters of mutual interest such as parliamentary rules. An issue which has been addressed is the principle of the separation of powers between provincial legislatures and their executive councils.

Although this principle is crucial to keeping the executive under constant check it could, if exaggerated, lead to serious conflict between the executives and members of the provincial legislatures. The exercise of this principle could easily degenerate into a power struggle between the two institutions.

Members of the provincial legislature from the same party sometimes articulate conflicting views. While this may have its advantages, a lack of unity on crucial policy issues could paralyse government. This problem is exacerbated by weak links between the national parliament and the provincial legislatures. It is generally accepted that the senate could strengthen this vital link.

4.2 The Senate

The constitution establishes a ninety-member senate, comprising ten senators from each province. Each province's senators are nominated in proportion to the size of their party in the provincial legislature. In terms of section 48(2)(a), the number of senators each party is entitled to nominate is determined by multiplying the number of seats such party holds in the provincial legislature tenfold, and dividing the result by the total number of seats in the legislature plus one. A member of a provincial legislature or local government nominated as a senator has to vacate his seat in the provincial legislature or local government upon accepting his nomination.

The senate was designed to voice provincial interests in the national parliament. However, the proportion of the senators to party seats in the provincial legislature tends to duplicate the composition of the national assembly. Furthermore, a distancing between the senators and their respective provincial legislatures takes effect soon after their nomination. It is not bridged by any formal arrangements. Consequently, the views of the provincial legislatures are only filtering through to the national assembly through the Min-MECs and the IGF.

The senate enjoys delaying powers on parliamentary bills affecting provinces. For example, in terms of section 61, bills affecting the boundaries or the exercise or performance of the powers and functions of the provinces shall be deemed not to have been passed by parliament until they have been passed by both Houses. Bills amending the constitution shall, to be passed by parliament, have to be adopted at a joint sitting of the national assembly and the senate by at least two-thirds of the members of both Houses. Bills other than those referred to in section 62 of the constitution (such as those affecting boundaries or the exercise or performance of powers or functions by a province or provinces), shall not be passed by parliament unless approved by a majority of senators of the province or provinces in question.

This arrangement presupposes adequate consultation between the senators and their provincial legislatures. Currently, where the senators have no structured relationship with their provincial legislatures, it is doubtful who they represent in the national assembly. This anomaly has prompted the CA and the CPG to explore ways in which relations between the senate and the provincial legislatures can be strengthened. This can be achieved either through a completely restructured senate where senators represent provincial legislatures, or a senate of directly elected representatives. Although the latter is favoured by some political parties, it has shortcomings in that it does not link the senator to the provincial legislature. In the case of the former option, the senate is made up of representatives of the provincial legislature. For example, when an issue affecting a particular line function is being discussed, the relevant MECs and representatives of the select committee would represent the provinces in the senate. This makes it possible for the voice of the provinces to be heard nationally throughout the legislative process. The interests of local governments would have to be included in this form of representation.

4.3 Local and provincial governments

Constitutional principle XVI provides that government shall be structured at national, provincial and local levels and, according to principle XVII, at each level of government there should be democratic representation. However, although constitutional principle XVI creates three apparently equal levels of government, the powers of national and provincial governments are defined in the constitution while only the framework of local government's powers, functions and structures is provided. The comprehensive powers, functions and other features should be set out in parliamentary statutes or provincial legislation, or both. Constitutionally, neither provincial nor national governments can exercise powers encroaching on the geographical, functional or institutional integrity of local governments. Furthermore, even though section 158(b) indicates that funds from national to local government should be made available through the provincial government, the use of the words 'shall ordinarily be made through provincial government' suggests that a direct transfer of funds from national to local government is not constitutionally precluded. This formula protects local governments from provincial governments prejudicing their access to funds.

Although there are consultative forums for the provincial and national line function ministries, the same does not exist in a structured manner for provincial and local governments. As a result, the local government lobby is of the view that provincial associations of organised local government should be represented in the Min-MEC meetings.

The constitutional conflict between national and provincial governments on the one hand, and the fears of local government (that its future will be determined by the first and second tiers without its participation) on the other, implies a need for local government powers and functions to be detailed in the constitution. Although local government seems to be protected from an erosion of its geographical and institutional integrity by national and provincial governments, the extent of that protection is not obvious. Similarly the scope of provincial governmental powers in comparison to national government, especially with regard to traditional authority, is problematic. This uncertainty was illustrated by the legal dispute between the premier of the Western Cape and the President of the Republic of South Africa regarding Cape Town's metropolitan boundaries.

The basis of the dispute was a proclamation promulgated by the President taking away powers that appeared to some to be the right of the premier and/or the local government MEC to determine and finalise local government boundaries. A similar dispute occurred when the Council of Traditional Leaders of South Africa (Contralesa) challenged the constitutionality of amendments to the constitution and the Local Government Transition Act whereby provisions for rural ward demarcations created elected, representative rural councils based on proportional and group representation. The traditional leaders insisted that they should have been consulted in terms of section 183(1)(c), according to which traditional authorities resident in a province should, before the introduction of a draft legislation, be consulted in a manner determined by a resolution of the provincial legislature.

In this particular case, although consultation did take place, it was not done through the House of Traditional Leaders or through a resolution of the provincial legislature. However, the national Ministry of Constitutional Development had conducted the campaign for the amendment bill and had it approved in a Ministerial–Min-MEC Forum where all local government MECs are represented. The Forum was chaired by the Minister of Constitutional Development. This policy, coupled with that seeking to have traditional leaders' salaries paid by national government, illustrates that, even in the area of local government, national interests will always take precedence over provincial or local interests. But the conflict between the provincial government and traditional leaders on the one hand, and national on the other, illustrates that without sufficient consultation, suspicion is inevitable.

Secondly, narrow group interests cannot be adequately addressed by the constitution. Constitutional principle XXVI seeks to ensure the autonomy of each level of government by protecting its share of national revenue. The constitutional principle provides that each level of government shall have a constitutional right to an equitable share of revenue collected nationally, thereby ensuring that provinces and local governments are able to provide basic services and execute the functions allocated to them. The formula for revenue sharing and for the allocation of revenue raising power is, according to principle XXVI, a responsibility of the FFC, an independent commission in which all three levels of government have representation. This allows for dialogue within the FFC on the crucial issue of taxation powers. Such details could not be listed in the constitution.

Concern about a detailed constitution arises from a fear of people becoming enslaved by it. This enslavement might detract from the constitution's purpose of serving the country's interests at any time. It is not easy to amend an unworkable constitution. It is easy to amend or repeal legislation.

5 CONCLUSION

One of the reasons for intergovernmental institutional arrangements is a recognition that levels of government least responsible for policy implementation are often charged with legislative and executive powers covering a range of socio-economic and financial duties. While this is desirable for uniformity, national standards, keeping together a national economy, and interprovincial commerce, it does not always work well when it comes to implementation. National departments are able to introduce policies impossible to implement. Labour and other disputes emanating from such policies are likely to cause disruptions at a provincial level with little or no effect on the mother departments.

National government is able to initiate policies and rush into their implementation without necessary planning. In order to harmonise the policy development and implementation processes, the various tiers of government have to interact at different levels. For example, if a sub-national government felt it would be discredited through implementing unpopular policies it might become intransigent. Consequently, the national government, responsible for competency, could be discredited. The provincial government could even oppose an unpopular national policy and make it difficult to implement. To ensure smooth implementation, second and third tiers of government need to interact. National government needs its sub-national tiers to provide the stability necessary for policy implementation. Similarly, the provinces have no choice but to liaise with national government if they wish to inform policy development or lobby for revenue. For these reasons too, provinces need to bargain collectively if they wish to share the spoils.

This interdependence creates conditions conducive to establishing vertical and horizontal cooperation. The irony is that institutional arrangements emanating from the need to cooperate form the basis for some provinces criticising the centre for trying to centralise everything. Whatever the case, it is clear that formal and informal intergovernmental institutional arrangements are complementary rather then competitive.

6 REFERENCES

Constitution of the Republic of South Africa Act 200 of 1993 (as amended by Act 2 and 3 of 1994).

De Villiers B (ed). 1994. *Evaluating Federal Systems*. The Hague: Martinus Nijhoff.

De Villiers B (ed). 1994. *Birth of a Constitution*. Kenwyn: Juta & Co Ltd.

De Villiers B & J Sindane (eds). 1993. *Regionalism: Problems and Prospects*. Pretoria: HSRC Publishers.

Elaigwu JI, PC Logams & HS Galadima (eds). 1994. *Federalism and Nation Building in Nigeria: The Challenges of the 21st Century*. Abuja: Nigerian National Council of Intergovernmental Relations.

Franzsen RCD (ed). 1994. *Regional Taxation in the Future South Africa*. Centre for Human Rights, University of Pretoria.

Fletcher C. 1992. 'Altered states': federalism, sovereignty and self-government. *Australian National University Paper no 22*. Federalism Research Centre.

Intergovernmental Forum. 1994. *Intergovernmental Forum Report*. November.

Jeffrey C & P Savigear (eds). 1991. *German Federalism Today*. Leicester: Leicester University Press.

Kriek DJ, DJ Kotze, PA Labuschagne, P Mtimkulu & K O'Malley. 1992. *Federalism the Solution?* Pretoria: HSRC Publishers.

McRoberts K & P Monahan (eds). 1993. *The Charlotte Town Accord: The Referendum and the Future of Canada*. Toronto: University of Toronto Press.

Van Meerhaeghe MAG (ed). 1992. *Belgium and EC Membership Evaluated*. London, New York: Pinter Publishers, St Martin's Press.

CHAPTER 5

Organising for Local Government

D Sing & S Moodley

1 INTRODUCTION

The establishment of non-racial, democratically elected local authorities in South Africa in the form of transitional metropolitan councils (TMCs) and transitional local councils (TLCs) raises many challenges to councillors, civic organisations, managers, specialist professions, trade unions, front-line workers and service users. Concomitant to the overall challenges is the organising imperative for local government. Accordingly, in this chapter attention is focused on the following organisational imperatives:

☐ Organisational structure;
☐ Organisational design; and
☐ Organisational (institutional) change.

2 ORGANISING IMPERATIVE

Organising is an enabling activity and concerns, *inter alia*, concepts and practices relating to organisational structure, organisational design and organisational (institutional) change. Benington & Hartley (1994:15–22) discuss five organisational models namely:

☐ model A: traditional public administration;
☐ model B: corporate management;
☐ model C: the local authority as a commercial contractor;
☐ model D: strategic management; and
☐ model E: a new structure for South African local authorities.

According to Benington & Hartley (1994:17) current local authority structures in South Africa do not fall into any single model. Model E, depicted in figure 1, is regarded as a possible organisational model for the new, democratic South African local authorities. (This model is used to illustrate the concepts that follow.)

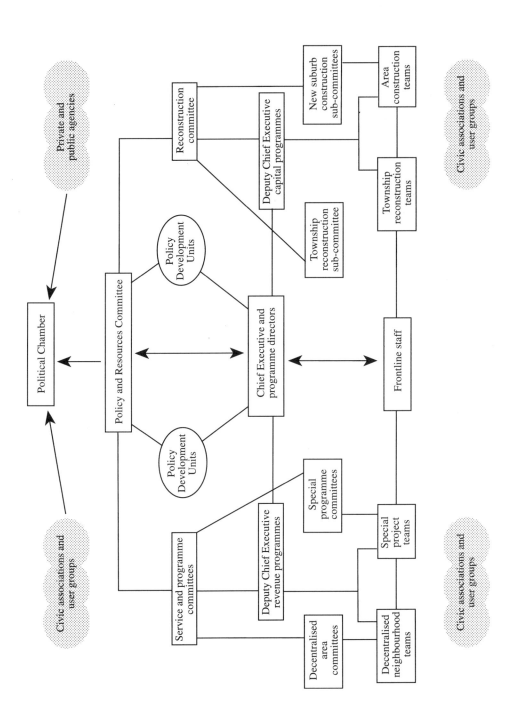

Figure 1:   A new structure for South African local authorities
(Source: Benington & Hartley 1994:22)

3 ORGANISATIONAL STRUCTURE

Griffin (1990:274–275) mentions that organisational structure can be regarded as the building blocks of an institution. A child, wanting to build a castle with a set of building blocks, selects small and large blocks. Some are square, some triangular and they vary in colour. When the castle is built, the child has his own castle, unlike any other. Just as the child can assemble the blocks in any number of ways, so too can a local government manager put his institution together (Griffin 1990:275). For example, the political chamber of a local authority may want to function through a central policy and resource committee with two subcommittees; a service committee and a reconstruction committee. The executive function in a local authority may be the responsibility of a chief and deputy director to whom teams and front-line staff are accountable. A reconstruction committee may divide itself into smaller, focus committees called township and new suburb construction committees with their own terms of reference. Front-line staff and team members may be given specific functions to perform.

Writers on the subject of organisational structure attribute the following aims and characteristics to this phenomenon (Smit & Cronjé 1992:176; Hanekom 1995:158):

☐ Aims at controlling, eliminating or reducing uncertainty in the behaviour of individual employees.
☐ Comprises relatively stable groups of tasks and implemental relationships and processes within an institution.
☐ Serves as a framework for the various activities of the institution.
☐ Entails the process of formulating rules and procedures pertaining to the behaviour of individuals and groups.

The building blocks (Griffin 1990:275), the basic principles (Smit & Cronjé 1992:180), and the dimensions (Pride, Hughes & Kapoor 1991:165–166) of organisational structure that must be considered include specialisation, departmentalisation, relationships, delegation, coordination and differentiation.

3.1 Specialisation

Specialisation is the degree to which the overall tasks of the institution are broken down and divided into smaller components to which positions are assigned (Griffin 1990:275; Pride et al 1991:165). According to Schermerhorn, Hunt & Osborn (1991:292–300) there are two types of specialisation, namely, vertical and horizontal. Vertical specialisation refers to a hierarchical division of labour that distributes formal authority and establishes where and when critical decisions will be made. This activity creates a hierarchy of authority consisting of work positions in order of increasing authority. The more levels that exist between, for example, directors and front-line staff, the more complex is the organisational structure (Schermerhorn et al 1991:292; Robbins 1993:399).

Horizontal specialisation involves grouping similar positions and resources together, resulting in horizontally different units such as branches, divisions or sections (Hanekom 1995:158). The more groups, the more horizontally complex the organisational structure becomes, because diverse orientations make communication and coordination difficult (Robbins 1993:398). For example, communication and coordination difficulties could arise if the chief director only is responsible for the functioning of the neighbourhood, special project, township reconstruction, and area construction teams.

3.2 Departmentalisation

Grouping various positions logically into branches, divisions and sections determines the nature and degree of departmentalisation of the institution (Pride et al 1991:165). There are various schemes or criteria by which grouping occur. These include departmentalisation according to function, service, location and client (Smit & Cronjé 1992:185).

3.2.1 Departmentalisation by function

A functional departmentalisation pattern is created through grouping by knowledge, skill and action (Schermerhorn et al 1991:300). For example, the township reconstruction and new suburb construction committees will have to possess the knowledge required to guide the reconstruction programme of the local authority. Front-line departments will be staffed by people who possess knowledge about township and area construction.

3.2.2 Departmentalisation by service

Service departmentalisation is the grouping of all activities related to a particular service (Pride et al 1991:170). For example, the deputy chief executive of revenue programmes and the deputy chief director of capital programmes will each have a human resources section and a financial section; or the local authority may have one human resources section and one financial section to contribute to all the programmes of the local authority.

3.2.3 Departmentalisation by location

Departmentalisation by location involves grouping of positions or units on the basis of defined geographic sites or areas (Griffin 1990:283). For example, engineers, town planners and supervisors who constitute the front-line staff of the town reconstruction team may be distributed in different areas of various townships.

3.2.4 Departmentalisation by client

Client departmentalisation is achieved by grouping together activities so as to respond to and interact with specific client groups (Smit & Cronjé 1992:188). For example, front-line staff involved in township reconstruction may advise clients of the money that is required of them in the form of monthly payments for new houses. Another set of staff may concern itself with advising clients on the economic usage of water and electricity.

3.3 Relationships

Establishing relationships among the various positions in the institution depend on issues such as chain of command, narrow versus wide spans, and tall versus flat structures (organisational height) (Griffin 1990:284; Pride et al 1991:174). The chain of command concept implies clear and distinct lines of authority need to be established between various divisions of the institution (Griffin 1990:286). A further component to the concept of unity of command is that each subordinate must have one supervisor or manager to whom he is accountable (Smit & Cronjé 1992:191). In a local government institution, this would mean that various programme directors must be accountable to the deputy chief executives, who are in turn accountable to the chief executive. Furthermore, distinct lines of authority will prevail between the service and programme committee, the reconstruction committee and the policy and resources committee. The policy and resource committee will account to the political chamber which is the political and governing authority.

Spanning concerns determining how many people or units will report to each manager or committee (Griffin 1992:191). A wide span exists when a manager or committee has a large number of subordinates or many subcommittees to supervise. A narrow span exists when, for example, deputy chief directors have only a few subordinates to manage (Pride et al 1991:173). Spanning has an impact on the height of the organisational structure. The concept of organisational height relates to the number of layers or levels of management in an institution. An organisational structure with many layers is considered tall, whereas one with few layers is flat (Pride et al 1991:176). The political chamber could be regarded as one level of management. The policy and resource committee could be regarded as another. At these two levels the functions are political and governmental in nature. The positions of chief directors and programme directors are other levels of management concerned with executive functions.

3.4 Delegation

In organisational structuring it is essential to consider the determination of how authority is to be delegated (Griffin 1990:289). Delegation, according to Basu (1992:102), involves entrusting authority to another person or body, usually to a subordinate level, to facilitate institutional functioning. The political chamber of a local authority may delegate some of its political and governing authority to a policy and resources committee. Similarly, chief executives may delegate a portion of their management authority to programme directors. This phenomenon, also referred to as decentralisation, is at one end of the continuum. At the other end is the phenomenon of centralisation. This is the systematic retention of authority at the higher levels of the institution (Smit & Cronjé 1992:196).

3.5 Coordination

According to Griffin (1990:294), the primary reason for coordinating is that departments, divisions, sections, units and individuals are interdependent. Coordination is the process whereby the objectives of the various departments and individuals are integrated so that the objectives of the institution can be achieved optimally (Smit & Cronjé 1992:199). Two types of coordination can be distinguished (Basu 1992:98):

☐ Internal or functional coordination; concerned with coordinating the activities of individuals in the institution. The chief executive director of a local authority is responsible for the coordination of the activities of deputy chief executive directors.

☐ External or structural coordination; concerned with coordinating the activities of the various organisational units in an institution. The policy and resources committee of a local authority will concern itself with coordinating the policy-making functions of the service and programme committee, as well as that of the reconstruction committee.

3.6 Differentiation

In organisational structuring, differentiating between line and staff positions is essential. A line position is concerned with direct responsibility for achieving an institution's goals. On the other hand, a staff position aims to provide expertise, advice and support for line positions (Griffin 1990:296; De Bruyn 1995:247). Chief executive directors of local authorities are regarded as holding line positions and are responsible for achieving the goals of the local authorities. Policy development units could be regarded as performing staff functions, in that they provide advice to chief executive directors in their policy functions.

A formal organisational structure is normally reflected in the organisational chart. The formal structure is established through deliberate management action (De Bruyn 1995:244). There is also an informal organisational element in an institution which revolves around informal personal contact and interaction at vertical and horizontal levels (Smit & Cronjé 1992:176). Fox & Meyer (1995:63) attribute the following characteristics to the informal organisation.

☐ Structured interpersonal relationships within the institution but outside the formal structure.

☐ Spontaneously formed groups of employees who interact regularly for some identifiable purpose, distinct from the formal organisation.

☐ Political, social and communication patterns that develop in an institution irrespective of the structures management put into place.

According to De Bruyn (1995:243–244), the informal organisation can have a positive and a negative effect on the institution. Resnick (1993:625) asserts that these informal associations often exert such strong restraining influences on changes initiated by management that, unless their power can be harnessed in support of change, no enduring change is likely to occur. Ingenuity, sensitivity and flexibility are required by management in involving the informal groups in planning changes (Resnick 1993:625).

4 ORGANISATIONAL DESIGN

According to Smit & Cronjé (1992:210) organisational design aims to construct and change the organisational structure so that the goals of an institution can be achieved in an optimal manner. It also implies the process of choosing and implementing the structural configuration of the institution to best meet the challenges faced at any time (Schermerhorn et al 1991:316). Organisational design implies conscious, proactive and prescriptive action by local government managers such as directors to ensure effective performance (Smit & Cronjé 1992:210; Kast & Rosenzweig 1986:243).

Questions associated with issues of organisational design are, *inter alia* (Griffin 1990:309):

☐   Should a high level of specialisation be matched with a higher degree of centralised authority?

☐   What scheme of departmentalisation will be appropriate to ensure effective coordination?

☐   How can differentiation be aligned to the various schemes of departmentalisation?

☐   What is the relationship between spanning and the different layers of management?

☐   How can the various schemes of departmentalisation be used in a combined manner?

☐   To what extent are specialisation, departmentalisation, relationship, delegation, coordination and differentiation responsive to legal, constitutional, technological, political, sociological, economic, demographic and cultural influences?

☐   In what ways can the design process enable external and internal participation, public accountability, sensitivity, equity and transparency?

Writers on the subject of organisational design state that there is no 'best' approach to it (Luthans 1988:573; Griffin 1990:309; Smit & Cronjé 1992:210). Some of the approaches include classical, bureaucratic, neoclassical, contingency, matrix and strategic (Smit & Cronjé 1992:210–233). Given the challenges facing local authorities, it is expected that local government managers will have to focus on and emphasise the contingency, matrix and strategic approaches.

4.1 Contingency

The basic principle of the contingency approach is that the prevailing situation should determine what approach should be used. Factors in the local authority environment determine the situation. These factors may be external or internal to the local authority (Smit & Cronjé 1992:219). Technology, size and organisational culture comprise the internal situational factors and the external factors include environment and information (Robbins 1993:407–413; Smit & Cronjé 1992:218–224; Griffin 1990:313–318). These factors are dynamic and local government managers should adapt and revise the organisational structure according to situational changes (De Bruyn 1995:236). According to the contingency approach there are two fundamental organisational designs namely, the stable–mechanistic and the adaptive–organic (Kast & Rosenzweig 1986: 264–265).

The stable–mechanistic design has the following features (Kast & Rosenzweig 1986:265; Griffin 1990:316).

- It is relatively closed and environmental influences are selected and minimised.
- Tasks are highly fractionated and little regard is given to clarifying relationships between tasks and institutional goals.
- Tasks tend to remain rigidly defined unless altered in a formal way by senior managers.
- Coordination is enabled through the hierarchy by defined rules and procedures.
- Source of authority is based on position and is concentrated.
- Responsibility is attached to roles and specific positions.
- Many and specific rules are formally written.
- Decision making is centralised and is concentrated at top management levels.
- Structural form tends to be relatively fixed.

The adaptive–organic design has the following features.

- It is relatively open and adaptive to environmental influences.
- Tasks are more independent. The focus is on their relationships with institutional goals.
- Tasks are redefined and adjusted continually through the interaction of institutional members.
- Coordination is facilitated through interpersonal interaction.
- Source of authority is based on knowledge and expertise, and is dispersed.
- Responsibility is shared by many members of the institution.
- Few and general rules, which are unwritten.
- Decision making is decentralised and is shared throughout the institution.
- Structural form adapts to changing situations.

4.2 Matrix

In the matrix approach to organisational design, specialist teams from organisational units are established to achieve specific objectives and are supported by other units which coordinate rather than supervise activities (Chandler & Plano 1988:210). The essence of the matrix design is the combination of functional and service departments in the same organisational structure (Koontz & Weihrich 1988:193). Members of the matrix design are simultaneously members of a specific function. For example, they can supervise capital programmes while being members of a specialist team charged with monitoring housing development.

4.3 Strategic

Organisational design assists managers achieve the objectives of their institution. Since objectives are derived from the institution's overall strategy it is logical that the strategy and structure should be closely linked. More specifically, structure should follow strategy (Robbins 1993:40). For every institutional strategy there should be an alternative organisational structure (Smit & Cronjé 1992:228). If management makes significant changes to the institution's strategy, structures will need to be designed to accommodate and support the changes (Robbins 1993:408–409). For example, the policy and resources committee of a local authority might resolve to improve recreation facilities in townships within the next five years with maximum participation from civic associations and user groups in the programme's design and implementation. This policy will require representatives to be integrated formally into the policy development units.

5 ORGANISATIONAL (INSTITUTIONAL) CHANGE

One method to understanding change is in terms of institutional scale and impact. Dumphy & Stace (1993:193) define the scale of change in four categories.

5.1 Fine-tuning

In this perspective, institutional change is regarded as an ongoing process characterised by matches between the institution's strategy, structure, people and processes. Such an effort is reflected at departmental, divisional or sectional levels in one or more of the following ways.

- ☐ Refining procedures and methods (the finance section of a local authority may clarify the discretionary powers of spending departments).
- ☐ Creating specialist units and linking mechanisms to permit increased attention to quality and cost (a local authority may create a work and methods study unit to investigate how the processing of housing plans can be reduced without incurring extra costs in terms of human resources).
- ☐ Fostering individual and group commitment to the mission of the institution and the excellence of one's own department (directors could arrange forums in which links between department goals and the local authority's mission are reinforced).
- ☐ Clarifying established roles (directors of a local authority, through regular meetings, may describe and explain the authority and power that front-line managers possess).

5.2 Incremental adjustment

Organisational change in this perspective is characterised by incremental adjustments to the changing environment. Such effort entails distinct but not radical changes to the institution's strategies, structures and management processes, for instance:

- ☐ expanding service areas (local authorities such as transitional local councils may extend rubbish removal services to rural areas);
- ☐ shifting the emphasis on services (the transitional metropolitan council may, for the first two years, concentrate only on public transport and roads rather than on museums and libraries);
- ☐ articulating a modified mission statement to the workforce (transitional substructure councils may authorise the executive directors to explain to the workforce that the mission now focuses on activities that directly affect citizens' health); and

☐ adjusting organisational components within or across boundaries to ensure better relationships in rendering services (organisational components of a local authority such as sanitation and road construction may be realigned so that they function so as to minimise disruption to transport activities in a township).

5.3 Modular transformation

Major realignment of one or more departments, divisions or sections characterises this type of organisational change. The process of radical change focuses on sub-parts rather than on the institution as a whole. For example:

☐ particular departments, divisions and sections are targeted for major restructuring (a local authority may require the environmental promotion department to redefine the relationships of its workforce and to shift authority from top to front-line management);

☐ changes in key management appointments in these organisational components (a local authority council may authorise its chief executive director to appoint staff from the housing and recreation departments to the top level management of the environmental promotion department);

☐ redefining departmental, divisional and section goals (the public transport department of a local authority may decide to provide free, special services to physically disabled persons); and

☐ significantly new technology is introduced, impacting on key departments, divisions or sections (a local authority's environmental protection department may install computer technology to provide information on pollution levels in industrial parks. This information may be used by the health department to monitor the impact of pollution on people living close to the industrial park).

5.4 Corporate transformation

Organisational change in terms of corporate transformation is 'institution-wide'. It requires radical shifts in strategy and revolutionary change throughout the institution, including:

☐ institutional mission and core values are reformed (a transitional substructure local authority may only want to focus on the development of services in disadvantaged communities for a certain time);

☐ distribution of power in the institution is affected through altered power and status (the various committees of the council of a local authority may be delegated full authority to approve funds for major capital works. No approval from council is necessary);

☐ major fundamental changes in organisational components throughout the institution (the community services and recreation departments of a local authority may be rationalised to form one single department. The centralised complaints offices of a local authority may be decentralised so as to function in various areas. Certain committees of the local authority may be regrouped with new terms of reference);

☐ interaction patterns in terms of work flow, communication networks and decision making are revised (transitional metropolitan councils and transitional councils may minimise decision routes and maximise communication networks in dealing with public protests against the quality of services being rendered); and

☐ management executive positions are filled from outside the institution (a transitional local council may authorise its human resources subcommittee to fill all directors posts from the private sector and the academic professions).

The expert-led and the change management approaches could be regarded as two different approaches to institutional change. The expert-led approach is characterised by management (who are backed by experts) designing a new organisational structure for the institution and imposing the structure through directives and instructions. The change management approach is regarded as an alternative to top-down, expert-led institutional reform. This approach has two points of departure, namely empowerment and internal expertise. In the empowerment thrust, managers at all levels and front-line workers need to be brought into all-inclusive processes that intersect existing hierarchical levels, before any changes are designed and implemented. The processes aim to empower managers and front-line workers with information, knowledge and skills to get to grips with external and internal change dynamics. The internal expertise thrust is premised on technical expertise required to design and implement institutional restructuring existing within the institution rather than in external experts. Those within the institution best know, understand and appreciate the dynamics of the institution (SAMWU Discussion Document 1994:1–3). The first approach could be regarded as a directive and coercive management style and the second approach as a collaborative and consultative management style (Dumphy & Stace 1993:195).

Implicit in the change management approach are concerns that are to be understood in terms of a macro perspective. These relate to (The Price Waterhouse Change Integration Team 1995:11–17):

☐ creating a powerful mandate for change;
☐ developing sound performance measures;
☐ building consensus for change at different levels of management and with different stakeholders;
☐ recognising diversity; and
☐ monitoring and measuring progress.

6 CONCLUSION

Fundamental to meeting the challenges facing the new local authorities in South Africa are the requirements of organisational structure and organisational design. Structuring revolves on the principles of specialisation, departmentalisation, relationships, delegation and coordination. Design is based on the matrix, contingency and strategic approaches. The processes of organisational structuring and organisational design need to take cognisance of the impact of different scales of institutional change such as fine-tuning, incremental adjustment, modular transformation and corporate transformation.

7 REFERENCES

Basu R. 1992. *Public Administration: Concepts and Practices*. New Delhi: SK Ghai.

Benington J & J Hartley. 1994. *From Transition to Transformation: The Strategic Management of Change in the Organisation and Culture of Local Government in South Africa*. Unpublished paper, Warwick Business School, Warwick, United Kingdom.

Chandler RC & JC Plano. 1988. *The Public Administration Dictionary ABC*. Santa Barbara, California: CLIO.

De Bruyn HEC. 1995. Organisation systems. In Kroon J (ed) *General Management*. Durban: Kagiso Tertiary.

Dumphy DC & DA Stace. 1993. Strategies for organisational transition. In Golembiewski RT (ed) *Handbook of Organisational Consultation*. New York: Marcel Dekker Inc.

Fox W & IH Meyer. 1995. *Public Administration Dictionary*. Kenwyn: Juta & Co Ltd.

Griffin RW. 1990. *Management*. Boston: Houghton Mifflin Company.

Hanekom SX. 1995. The organising and the designing of public sector institutions. In Thornhill C & SX Hanekom *The Public Sector Manager*. Durban: Butterworths.

Kast FE & JE Rosenzweig. 1986. *Organisation and Management*. New York: McGraw-Hill Inc.

Koontz H & H Weihrich. 1988. *Management*. New York: McGraw-Hill Inc.

Luthans F. 1988. *Organisational Behaviour*. New York: McGraw-Hill Inc.

Price Waterhouse Change Integration Team. 1995. *Better Change: Best Practices for Transforming Your Organisation*. New York: Irwin.

Pride WM, RJ Hughes & JR Kapoor. 1991. *Business*. Boston: Houghton Mifflin Company.

Resnick H. 1993. Managing organisational change: a primer for consultants and managers. In Golembiewski RT *Handbook of Organisational Consultation*. New York: Marcel Dekker Inc.

Robbins SP. 1993. *Organisational Behaviour*. New York: Prentice Hall Inc.

South African Municipal Workers Union. 1994. *Comments on the Change Management Proposal for Managing Institutional Change in the Central Witwatersrand*. SAMWU Discussion Document.

Schermerhorn JR, JG Hunt & RN Osborn. 1991. *Managing Organisational Behaviour*. New York: John Wiley and Sons Ltd.

Smit PJ & GJ de J Cronjé (eds). 1992. *Management Principles*. Kenwyn: Juta & Co Ltd.

— CHAPTER 6 —

The Theory and Practice of Strategic Management in Local Government*

P S Reddy

1 INTRODUCTION

Strategic management has become a 'buzz' term in local government. The substantial and increasing literature on the subject bears testimony to it being at the top of the management agenda of local authorities worldwide. However, despite all the attention this management technique has received, there is still confusion as to what the term actually means, particularly in a local government context. Despite this, most local authorities believe it is a powerful management system, capable of the most profound impact on corporate success. Strategic management has grown in popularity as other methodologies have been rejected (Chape & Davies 1993:3). Taylor & McKinlay (1990) are of the opinion that strategic management grew as a result of dissatisfaction with corporate planning in the 1960s and 1970s, particularly in the United Kingdom. It was seen as being capable of overcoming the shortcomings of corporate planning in three areas, namely, decentralised responsibility for performance, concern with outcomes as well as inputs, and focus on qualitative issues. The need to adopt a strategic focus to the management of South African local authorities has been given added impetus by the Reconstruction and Development Programme (RDP). Local authorities as implementation vehicles are critical to the success of the RDP. This chapter reviews the theory underpinning strategic management and its implementation process at the local government level.

2 WHAT IS STRATEGIC MANAGEMENT?

2.1 Strategic management: defining terms

A number of prominent thinkers have attempted to define this elusive term. David defines strategic management as follows:

---

* This chapter originally appeared as an article in the *SAIPA Journal of the South African Institute of Public Administration*. Vol 30 no 2 June 1995.

'Strategic management can be defined as the formulation, implementation and evaluation of actions that will enable an organisation to achieve its objectives. Strategy formulation includes identifying an organisation's internal strengths and weaknesses, determining a firm's external opportunities and threats, establishing a company mission, setting objectives, developing alternative strategies, analysing these alternatives and deciding which ones to execute. Strategy implementation requires that a firm establish goals, devise policies, motivate employees, and allocate resources in a manner that will formulate strategies to be pursued carefully. Strategy evaluation monitors the results of formulation and implementation of activities' (in Schwella 1990:222).

Wheeler & Hunger define strategic management as:

'... that set of managerial decisions and actions that determines the long-run performance of a corporation. It includes strategy formulation, strategy implementation, evaluation and control. The study of strategic management therefore emphasises the monitoring and evaluating of environmental opportunities and constraints in the light of the corporation's strengths and weaknesses' (in Schwella 1990:222).

Steiner (1979:47–48) is of the opinion that strategic management (or strategic planning) is vitally important to organisations for the following reasons:

☐ it improves decisions about future opportunities and threats faced by the organisation;
☐ it stimulates the development of appropriate aims which serve as powerful motivators of people;
☐ it enhances communication, coordination and participation in the organisation;
☐ it creates the ability to proactively initiate action and influence the organisational environment. It also provides an objective basis for management decisions leading to improved managerial decision making. Through improved management decisions, effective goal achievement, efficient resource utilisation and personnel morale is achieved; and
☐ there are research findings suggesting that organisations using it are more successful than those who do not.

The above definitions emphasise the importance of environmental scanning and organisational assessment for the purpose of formulating, implementing and evaluating strategies to enhance organisational effectiveness and efficiency. Schwella (1990:222) believes that although their idiom is that of the private sector firm, company or corporation, it is evident from the definitions that the approach could, with the necessary adaptations, be useful in public sector contexts. However, it is useful to explore the differences and similarities between a private and public sector approach to strategic management.

2.2 Private and public sector approaches: similarities and differences

There is no dearth of literature in public sector management exploring whether concepts in private sector management can be applied effectively to a public sector setting. However, to date, no attempts have been made to examine the differences and similarities between a private and public sector approach to strategic management. In the private sector, the term strategic management is used to refer to the entire scope of strategic decision making in an organisation and has three fundamental objectives, namely:

☐ to determine the strategic direction and long-term performance of the organisation;

☐ to provide a set of managerial decisions that relates the organisation to its environment; and

☐ to guide priority use of resources and internal management activities (Choo 1992:42).

It should be noted that there is no single, standard approach to strategic management in the private sector. Most approaches embrace some aspects of rational planning and analysis and share five fundamental tasks, namely:

☐ environmental analysis: monitoring the external and internal organisation's environment to identify both present and future strengths, weaknesses, threats and opportunities;

☐ developing a corporate vision: infusing the organisation with a sense of purpose, providing long-term direction and establishing a mission and objectives;

☐ strategy formulation: creating a strategy that leads to the attainment of organisational objectives;

☐ strategy implementation: executing the chosen strategy efficiently and effectively; and

☐ strategy control: evaluating performance, reviewing the situation and initiating corrective action (Choo 1992:42–43).

In practice, several of these tasks are performed simultaneously or in a different order. The effectiveness of the approach is partly contingent on how well the organisation manages and coordinates the five fundamental tasks. Historically, the process of these five fundamental tasks has been to help firms make better strategic decisions thereby improving financial performance (Rhyne 1986). This continues to be the major benefit of the rational approach, but research done recently (Greenly 1986) indicates that the process rather than the decision is the most important determinant of success in this approach.

According to Scholes (1992), there are certain assumptions underlying the private sector approach to strategic management:

☐ performance can be measured against a few quantifiable market and financial objectives;

☐ optimum performance results can be achieved;

☐ different level and types of strategic management can be clearly distinguished;

☐ strategy is the product of systematic analysis, search and evaluation; and

☐ strategic implementation can be carefully planned.

At this juncture it is necessary to examine the differences between a private sector and, more specifically, a local government approach to strategic management. It could be said that most approaches currently adopted by local authorities resemble some aspects of the private sector rational approach, eg various types of 'authority-wide' strategic planning are still used in many local authorities. They are unable to reconcile and consolidate the underlying assumptions of the private sector rational approach because of the constraints of, *inter alia*, an absence of profit measure, non-salient sources of revenue, community politics, central government intervention and control, and a less responsive bureaucracy. They do not have the same flexibility to act strategically. Consequently, many local authorities have developed their own approaches, embracing some distinctive practices, to suit their circumstances.

According to Choo (1992:43), the approaches currently adopted by local authorities can be classified into three types:

2.2.1 Rational action approach

This is the most common and comprehensive approach, and it is similar to the private sector planning model. A position statement is produced to identify where the authority is now, identify where it wants to go, identify problems that exist and identify the resources available to tackle them. These are set out in a documented strategic plan followed by some objectives based on issues prioritised for some services. The actions to achieve those objectives are then translated into budgets within the resources available and into operational action plans. Performance measurement as a basis of control is an important part of this approach. This approach also involves a high degree of analytical projection and most of the local authorities' strategic or long-range planning come under this category.

2.2.2 Political visionary approach

This approach embraces distinctive practices used by some local authorities in the United Kingdom. The type of organisation desired by the authority is set out in a mission statement. The political values, priorities and key issues of the authority are articulated clearly in the mission statement. These political dimensions form the main thrust of the strategic management approach. How to achieve those political dimensions and who will achieve them vary among authorities and are usually unclear. This approach is set to shape the longer-term political agendas of the entire authority.

2.2.3 Prioritising issues approach

This approach also embraces distinctive practices used by many local authorities in the United Kingdom. It places emphasis on selected initiatives or issues facing the authority. These issues are prioritised under various headings, eg community care, management of change, local management of schools, urban programmes, decentralisation of service, performance review and competitive tendering. The issues are dealt with strategically. However, some of the issues can be all-embracing and interrelated. Consequently, it can be difficult to distinguish between strategic and operational issues.

It is not yet clear how effective the implementation of these three general types of approach can be, as each type has relevance for particular circumstances. However, strategic management has recently been recognised by some authorities as an ongoing process integrating planning with other management systems or techniques, and the discipline has become a complicated, rich, and diverse field. Some of these integrative practices are evident in some local authorities, eg organisational development techniques and group-decision support systems have been widely used in the strategic management context (Choo 1992:44).

2.3 Strategic management or planning: the issue reconsidered

In most local authorities strategic management is synonymous with strategic planning. The latter is not a new phenomenon in local government as it was firmly on the agendas of local authorities in the 1970s. Caulfield & Schultz (1989:viii) observe that, in recent years, there have been some notable attempts by local authorities in Britain to revive their strategic planning systems. This has been influenced by the Audit Commission (1991 paras 2–16) in Britain who argued for a 'strategic planning process, the outcome of which is a strategy.' In addition, in the 1990s, strategic management has been advocated by a number of key public institutions in Britain. The Local Government Management Board encouraged local authorities

> 'to adopt a strategic approach, ...traditional structures, practices and procedures are being re-examined to find new ways of improving service to their communities' (LGMB 1991:3).

Strategic planning is characterised as a private sector, rational approach embracing detailed projections. In local government, it is set in the context of a political and changing environment with a recognition of the need to plan for uncertainty (Choo 1992:45). The end product is simply a long-term plan with little or no consideration given to the way the plan is to be implemented and controlled, ie the organisational and managerial aspects are often neglected.

However, it is widely accepted that strategic management is more than just strategic planning (Choo 1992:45). In the context of local government, it would be more appropriate to refer to it as a process by which top management determines ways of managing the authority's external environment strategically, ie it is concerned with an awareness of the external environment, threats and opportunities, as well as choosing and implementing the strategy that the authority follows (Choo 1992:45).

Caulfield & Schultz (1989:3–28) observe that despite some notable attempts by local authorities to restore the reputation of strategic planning, there are still some elements of doubt about its usefulness in practice. Of late, unitary authorities, fundamental political, economic, social and demographic changes and metropolisation have impacted on all South African local authorities. Many local authorities have found it necessary to formulate strategies to address, *inter alia*, structural reform, change management, affirmative action, gender sensitivity, local economic development, environmental issues, inner city revitalisation and community safety. Consequently, this has resulted in local authorities having to prioritise and target their resources far more precisely than they have to now (Chape & Davis 1993:4). The profound impact of these issues on local government corporate management is clearly visible and it is highly unlikely that it could be dealt with by the routine rational analysis inherent in strategic planning. Consequently, local authorities are increasingly adopting strategic management techniques geared towards systematically planning the total resources of the organisation in order to achieve certain goals within a specified time.

However, according to Choo (1992:45), local authorities' experience with strategic planning has shown a number of shortcomings, namely:

☐ it underscores the importance of the conceptual skills of managers, ie their ability to understand the complexities of the organisation and where one's own operation fits into the organisation;

☐ it underscores the need for managers to think strategically, to see things from different perspectives, and to think ahead, ie what the authority currently does and how it will be done in future;

☐ officers and councillors usually do not have sufficient time and knowledge to read and understand the plans drawn up by specialists; and

☐ the demands for local authorities' services are always likely to outstrip available resources. Moving the financial goalposts to meet unexpected demands tends to render plans redundant.

In the light of the above, local authorities may have to supplement strategic planning with an approach to strategic management that can provide officials and councillors with a forum for discussing key strategic issues. It should also assist them to cultivate strategic thinking and develop an awareness in their front-line management. In the final analysis, the aim is to avoid strategic plans around forecasts of unworkable futures. It is possible that such a rational approach will depend on some form of systemic planning, but it is certainly an insufficient condition for effective corporative management. Strategic planning is not an effective corporate tool on its own.

2.4 Characteristics of a strategic management approach in local government

There are certain characteristics critical to a strategic management approach at the local government level. Clarke & Stewart (1991:15–16) summarise them as follows:

☐ It should have a perspective beyond the normal way of working and should not be dominated by the requirements of existing activities. The rhythm of operational management is the rhythm of continuity and of moulding incremental change to maintain continuity. Strategic management must look beyond this and aim to break past patterns to achieve significant change.

☐ It identifies issues to be dealt with, choices to be made, values to be expressed or activities to be undertaken, which will not be beyond the existing organisation's capacity — they lie beyond present organisational capacity because of, *inter alia*, structure, processes, culture or the allocation of resources.

☐ It requires a close partnership of elected representatives and officials and an understanding of their respective roles, distinct and shared. The primary focus for the former will be direction, choice, monitoring and review while the latter will contribute to these activities, providing the base for sound judgement. They will, however, have to face the resulting organisational and management consequences.

☐ It should be concerned with organisational change designed to establish new ways of working. Strategic management builds an organisation capable of carrying out this strategy by:
 − changing organisational culture, although not assuming that this alone will suffice;
 − modifying the processes through which the organisation works;
 − building the culture through processes of socialisation;
 − giving leadership to certain themes;
 − altering the balance of all and not only financial resources.

In reviewing the characteristics, it is imperative that strategic management should be:

☐ selective in action: it focuses on the need for a particular organisational change;
☐ wide-ranging in review: it requires understanding of the environment, political values and organisational capacity;
☐ changing in focus: its rationale lies in changing the organisation to encompass new ways of working — once accomplished, this removes the need for strategic management's concern;
☐ linked to organisational development: this provides the mechanism for action;
☐ the expression of political purpose: this must guide organisational response to a changing environment;
☐ based on a close partnership between elected representatives and officials: there needs to be a shared understanding of roles;
☐ dependent on communication: organisational change gains meaning through communication. A strategic plan is an exercise in communication for strategic management, not an end in itself (Clarke & Stewart 1993:17).

2.5 Planning for change in the South African context

Local government is presently in the throes of fundamental structural and functional changes. The future role of local government is emerging as:

☐ the securer but not necessarily the provider of services;
☐ the enabler or facilitator; helping to make things happen. Many local authorities have been quick to seize the initiative through enterprising and entrepreneurial partnerships with the private and non-governmental sectors, as well as with

other public sector agencies. Such partnerships are the precursors of many more;

☐ the quality controller of services provided by the private or non-governmental sector (Caulfield & Schultz 1993:4).

In many parts of the world, there is a growing acceptance that, if a democratically elected local authority proactively harnesses and adopts three distinct roles, it will have both direct and indirect impact. These roles include:

☐ its traditional role in distributing, administering and 'delivering' services to users;

☐ a more active economic role in stimulating and developing the local and regional economy; and

☐ a political role in representing and giving voice to diverse needs and interests within the local community (Benington & Hartley 1994:8).

These three potentially strategic roles can be amplified and illustrated as follows (Benington & Hartley 1994:9–10):

2.5.1 Social reproduction and redistribution

The local authority's policies for setting local taxes and then allocating and delivering resources (both goods and services) can have the following major redistributive effects within the local community:

☐ social (between different classes of people and categories of need within the population);

☐ spatial (between different geographical areas and neighbourhoods within the locality);

☐ sectoral (between different services and functions, eg housing, education and economic development within the authority).

2.5.2 Economic agency and development

The local authority, as an economic actor, can impact on the local economy as a major:

☐ employer (whose recruitment, training and wage policies have a significant impact in the labour market);

☐ investor (whose capital building, repair and maintenance programmes represent important business for the construction industry and allied trades);

☐ purchaser (whose expenditure on goods and services creates business for many, often local, producers and suppliers);

☐ producer (whose production of goods and services meets local community needs, eg for example housing, horticulture and food can often produce surpluses, and/or generate local economic multiplier effects);

☐   land and property developer (whose role as a large landowner, planner, property developer, housing manager and estate manager has considerable impact on the locality).

2.5.3 Political representation and participation

The local authority, as a democratic political institution, can have a major impact on levels of political knowledge, consciousness, participation and cohesion within the locality as:

☐   councillors are supported in acting not just as the management committee but also as the elected representatives;
☐   the representative political process is harnessed to the participative political process, and councillors are enabled to act, not just as advocates of particular individuals or interest groups, but also as facilitators and channels for broad-based civic movements within the community;
☐   the council sees itself as the forum for the diverse and often competing interests and voices within its area, and tries to build coalitions of common interest; and
☐   the council recognises that, as a democratically elected body, it is the only organisation with a mandate to reflect and represent the common interests of the whole community.

2.6 Challenges facing South Africa's new local authorities

The new, democratic local authorities that have been established will face several challenges (PLANACT 1992:2).

2.6.1 Political

The new local authorities will have to craft strong and stable local political systems from the chaos and distrust of the past. They will have to reconcile conflicting local interests, taking due regard of national and regional policies and, within this context, develop their own strategic direction. Consequently, productive and positive relationships will have to be forged with, *inter alia*, the civic and non-governmental sectors, elected representatives, local authority managers, specialist professions, the trade union sector and local citizens.

2.6.2 Service provision

The urgent provision of basic infrastructure and services will constitute a major challenge for the new local authorities. They will have to develop management structures and systems capable of managing and delivering programmes of reconstruction and development while maintaining the continuity of service provision.

2.6.3 Financial

The new local authorities will have to identify sources of revenue and capital to finance programmes of economic and social development. Additionally, they will also have to devise new, fair and equitable systems of collecting, managing and redistributing funds.

2.7 Local government and the Reconstruction and Development Programme (RDP)

The government believes it can unlock the political and creative energies of the people and bring the concept of government closer to them. Consequently, local government will have an important role to play. The national government, working with the Commission on Provincial Government (CPG) and provincial governments, will ensure proper coordination of the development process, maintenance of standards and the coherence of change management strategies (RDP White Paper 1994:22). It is anticipated that the new, democratic local authorities in South Africa will be under considerable pressure as local communities will see them as vital to improving the quality of their lives. Local government is of critical importance to the Reconstruction and Development Programme (RDP) as it is the level of representative democracy closest to the people. It will be the delivery mechanism for the RDP. The new roles envisaged for local authorities can be summarised as follows (African National Congress 1994:120–130; RDP White Paper 1994:22–230):

☐ Local authority administrations should be structured to ensure maximum participation by civil society and communities in decision making and development initiatives;

☐ A development culture among local administrations should be encouraged. The actions of elected representatives and officials should be transparent;

☐ A women's portfolio should be established at the local government level to scrutinise local authority programmes and budgets for gender sensitivity. Local authorities can implement affirmative action with the private sector through special criteria for local government contracts;

☐ Local authorities are key institutions for delivering basic services, extending local control, managing local economic development and redistributing public resources. However, for the first time in South Africa's history, emerging democratic local authorities will have to work with community-based organisations (CBOs) and NGOs to establish minimum conditions of good governance;

☐ The RDP depends on democracy and social stability in local communities. Consequently, the management of institutional change and the delivery of municipal services must occur simultaneously. Restoring and upgrading services where they have collapsed, and extending services to new areas are vital preconditions for the continued legitimising of the new local authorities. Improved services must be implemented in a manner which enhances appropriate institutional change within local authorities;

☐ Local authorities must ensure that sufficient resources are made available for the extension and upgrading of municipal services, and for capacity-building to permit community-based structures to assist in the planning and implementation of local upgrading. Local authorities will need additional sources of revenue for operating, maintenance and subsidy expenses, as well as staff retraining and some new capital expenditure;

☐ Transitional local and metropolitan councils will gain access to increased resources only if they become developmental in their orientation, proactive in winning the trust of all residents, sensitive to issues of affordability, creative about financing and more efficient in delivery of services. Local authorities must demonstrate that they are already, in the transitional phase, shifting resources (staff, management, equipment, skills), switching their spending priorities, freezing clearly inappropriate projects and engaging in consultation with community groups; and

☐ With due recognition of indigence, administrative constraints and a need of equitable and fair default procedures, the principle of payment of services is fundamental to the implementation of the RDP.

In the light of local authorities' changing role, they will have to adopt a strategic focus to their management and performance. They will have to adopt appropriate management systems and structures. They will have to adopt a developmental approach, be responsive to community needs and have a reconstruction focus. Consequently, the strategic management model appears to hold the most potential.

According to PLANACT (1992:7), one of the features of the new administrations should be strategic centres. The challenges to be faced by each of the new local authorities requires that they operate effectively and with a clear, overriding mission. They will have to develop and provide the overall development vision for their areas, ie they will have to mobilise coalitions of interest groups around specific goals, and they will have to bring organisations and agencies together to implement particular programmes.

If local authorities are to fill the political role of providing leadership and bringing together the coalitions needed to put strategy into effect, they will need a strategic centre capable of developing their vision and strategy, and coordinating and implementing large-scale interdepartmental and inter-agency programmes (PLANACT 1992:8). The centre will also require staff with acute political and social instincts, as well as modern information systems. The strategic centre in South African local authorities will almost certainly be a reconstruction and development committee. It could consist of politicians and management staff and representatives from private, voluntary and community organisations. It could function directly under a chief executive or his deputy.

2.8 General guiding principles for local authorities adopting strategic management

Local authorities adopting strategic management:

☐ should avoid the side-effects of rational planning, ie they should not rely too heavily on routine planning. The bureaucracy is counterproductive and will get in the way of effective strategic management;

☐ should foster pervasive strategic thinking and awareness, ie it should help local authorities to integrate the behaviour of officers and councillors into total effort and allow for identification, prioritisation, and the exploitation of strategic environmental issues facing local authorities;

☐ should be capable of providing a flexible framework for responding to central government intervention and control and the demands of new legislation;

☐ should provide an environment that is conducive to introducing, debating and sharing political issues and values grounded in elected councillors, community agencies and central government. The aim is to assure everybody that strategic management is helping the authority attain its political goals;

☐ should provide a means for generating learning, ie allow officials and councillors to engage and share in institutional learning. If the strategic management approach does not result in any form of partnership or institutional learning between and by officials and politicians it is not worth having. Institutional learning maximises favourable attitudes, rewards cultural change and enhances organisational development; and

☐ should be formalised and clearly defined (Stewart 1991:64).

It is essential to separate the role of strategic management from ongoing operational management perspectives to ensure that it gets sufficient attention. This can only be achieved by giving strategic management a degree of discipline and formality:

☐ it should provide a framework for better coordination and strategic allocation of resources between committees to meet attainable objectives. It should also improve communication at all levels — a basic requirement for strategy implementation;

☐ it should provide a framework for introducing and coordinating political values and officials' concerns, ie strategic decisions should not be determined solely by officials' personal values and professionalism (Choo 1992:46).

3 THE STRATEGIC MANAGEMENT PROCESS — THEORETICAL CONSIDERATIONS AND IMPLEMENTATION OF PRINCIPLES

Choo (1992:47) has put forward the following supportive and structured arrangements for the management of the process at the local government level:

☐ A rolling agenda must be introduced, capable of responding to the strategic needs of the authority as they evolve, rather than a planning cycle that takes place at a time set each year.

☐ Strategic management working groups (SMWG) must be set up within the formal committee structure for dialogue on strategic issues as they emerge. The group must be made up of elected councillors, chief officers, and the leader of the council who will share the view of the strategic issues that reflects both political and managerial problems.

☐ Members of the SMWG are expected to monitor and raise, at any time with the chief executive, any strategic issues pertinent to the services for which they are responsible. Councillors are expected to play a more active role in identifying strategic issues than their officials. The reason for this is that councillors get their mandates from the electorate. In addition, it is a reflection of differing roles; unlike officials, elected councillors have formal responsibility for relating an organisation to its external environment.

☐ Agenda setting is a two-way process, ie every strategic issue raised should be vetted by the chief executive and the leader of the council before it is formally addressed and debated. This ensures that every strategic issue raised has a well-defined purpose and, furthermore, is strategic. In the final analysis, the process should help the chief executive to prioritise the authority's strategic issues. Distinguishing strategic issues from operational issues can be difficult. Choo (1992:47) has suggested that the following factors can serve as guidelines:

— Strategic issues deal with concerns grounded in the entire community and other agencies served by the authority and consume a large portion of the authority's resources;

— Strategic issues represent new areas of activity or concern and, typically, are peculiar to the authority, rather than lending themselves to routine decision making. The authority must also be capable of doing something about the issues. If the organisation cannot do anything about them, they are not strategic issues;

— Strategic issues have a profound impact on the political direction of the entire authority and have repercussions for the ways operational decisions are made in the authority; and

— Strategic issues entail significant shifts in corporate culture and can bring about fundamental change in organisational structures.

☐ All strategic issues to be formally addressed through the SMWG should be chaired by the chief executive. He should be responsible for providing political and strategic leadership. The importance of the active involvement of the chief executive in strategic management cannot be overstated (Steiner 1989:15). It is generally accepted that there will be no effective strategic management in a local authority in which the chief executive does not give support by ensuring that councillors and officials in the organisation understand their depth of commitment. In addition, personal involvement by a chief executive ensures that the formality of the strategic management process is recognised, leaving little room for doubt concerning its importance. When the chief executive does not have the time to coordinate the process, its success rests to a large extent on his delegatory abilities.

☐ Feedback is also a very important aspect of the process. After each meeting, all members of the SMWG should be given feedback on the level to which they agree with the strategic issues and their implementation plans. The feedback process should be carried out by the chief executive and the leader of the council immediately after the issues have been discussed to ensure they remain valid and members' enthusiasm and motivation are sustained. The contents must be concisely detailed in a memorandum to ensure it serves as a stimulus for action and does not become an academic exercise. A review meeting must be set up to enable group members to raise any issues of concern and any areas of the action plan they do not fully understand.

☐ Since the SMWG will continually be dealing with strategic issues having no fixed, formal plans, action learning and creativity are preserved, forming the basis of strategic management. The most important aspect of all is the creation of an environment conducive to open debate and dialogue on key strategic issues facing local authorities. This environment provides an opportunity to improve the communication of political direction and priorities within the authority.

It should be noted that, since the communities local authorities serve are becoming more complex and the speed of environmental and technological change is increasing, and with local authorities being compelled by central government to expose a wider range of services to market forces, it has become extremely difficult to develop a workable, longstanding and comprehensive strategic plan. Consequently, it has become imperative that local authorities alter the way in which they operate, ie supplement rational strategic planning with a system of strategic issues management where matters of strategic importance can be debated and dealt with rapidly.

4 REVIEWING THE IMPACT OF STRATEGIC MANAGEMENT ON LOCAL GOVERNMENT: SOME ADVANTAGES AND DISADVANTAGES

Strategic planning and management in their simplest forms require a local authority to exploit the inevitable. This new planning and management technique provides a mechanism for local government managers to shape their external environment, limit threats, take advantage of opportunities, and it enables civic leaders to respond to issues proactively rather than reactively. However, with these apparent advantages, the astute local government functionary should take cognisance of some of the disadvantages of undertaking a strategic planning and management exercise (Kemp 1992:168–169).

4.1 Advantages

- ☐ Imposes discipline on the organisation;
- ☐ Makes an organisation more proactive;
- ☐ Facilitates the use of forward planning among the governing body, top management and the employees of the local authority;
- ☐ Educates the governing body and top management in the methods of a new management technique;
- ☐ Provides 'agreed-on conditions' to cope with changing conditions — within and without the organisation;
- ☐ Helps establish organisational priorities and their funding requirements; and
- ☐ Helps establish and foster public credibility and confidence in a local authority and its leaders.

4.2 Disadvantages

- ☐ Lacks either governing body or top management support;
- ☐ Exceeds local authority financial capacity, particularly if consultants are used in the planning process;
- ☐ Exhausts the time resources of the local authority's employees involved in the programme;
- ☐ Magnifies politically sensitive issues that could have been swept under the carpet;
- ☐ Encounters the natural resistance to change inherent in the organisation at any level;

☐ Demands action that, in some cases, cannot be undertaken owing to a lack of commitment or improper implementation planning or capacity;

☐ Involves a gamble by forecasting factors not presently acknowledged by the organisation;

☐ Reveals organisational weaknesses and/or management deficiencies;

☐ Receives little or no support from the local authority's external stakeholders.

Furthermore, there is also the distinct possibility that all stakeholders, rightly or wrongly, perceive that there is no need for a strategic plan and prefer the status quo.

5 CONCLUSION

It has been argued that the practice of strategic planning and management in the public sector and, more particularly, local government will differ from the private sector. Fundamental differences in culture, governance, inbuilt constraints and unique features of local government make the practice of strategic management broad and diffuse. In the final analysis, the practice of strategic management (be it in the private sector or local government) will entail a process of linking policy making with the tactical management aspects of the institution.

Local authorities in South Africa have recently been placed under tremendous pressure as a result of increasing demands arising from fundamental political, economic and social changes, financial strictures, new legislation, environmental matters and socio-economic decline. Consequently, local government councillors and officials have to think strategically and be aware of strategic issues to meet the challenges of local government. The mammoth tasks that will confront the new, non-racial local authorities beyond transition necessitate major organisational and management changes if they are to be robust enough to ensure effective delivery of services and programmes. A major challenge facing them will be their need to harness the vitality of the political process generated by the civic movements and other organs of civil society to the crucial task of reconstructing and developing their localities.

6 REFERENCES

African National Congress. 1994. *The Reconstruction and Development Programme: A Policy Framework.* Johannesburg: Umanyano Publications.

Audit Commission. 1991. *Improving Economy, Effectiveness and Efficiency.* London: Audit Commission.

Benington J & J Hartley. 1994. *From Transition to Transformation: The Strategic Management of Change in the Organisation and Culture of Local Government in South Africa.* (Unpublished paper, Warwick Business School, Warwick, United Kingdom).

Caulfield I & J Schultz. 1989. *Planning for Change: Strategic Planning in Local Government.* London: Local Government Training Board/Longman Publishers.

Chape A & P Davies. 1993. Implementing strategic planning in local government: Liverpool City Council as a case study. *Local Government Policy-Making*. Vol 20 no 3 December.

Choo KL. 1992. Strategic planning in local government: guiding principles for effective practice. *Local Government Policy-Making*. Vol 19 no 3 December.

Clarke M & J Stewart. 1991. *Strategies for Success*. Luton: Local Government Management Board.

Greenley G. 1989. *Strategic Management*. New York: Prentice Hall Inc.

Kemp RL. 1992. *Strategic Planning in Local Government: A Case-Book*. Washington DC: American Planning Association.

Office of the President. 1994. *White Paper on the Reconstruction and Development Programme*. Pretoria: Government Printer.

PLANACT. 1992. *Transforming Local Authority Administrations*. Johannesburg.

Rhyne LC. 1986. The relationship of strategic planning to financial performance. *Strategic Management Journal*. No 7.

Schwella E et al. 1990. *Public Management*. Kenwyn: Juta & Co Ltd.

Scholes K. 1992. *Sheffield Business School*. New York: Prentice Hall Inc.

Steiner AL. 1979. *Strategic Planning*. New York: The Free Press.

Stewart J. 1991. Considerations in strategic management in local government. *Local Government Policymaking*. Vol 17 no 4 March.

Taylor W & A McKinlay. 1990. Quality drive. *Local Government Chronicle*. November.

— PART 3 —

Human Resource Management and Affirmative Action

— CHAPTER 7 —

Human Resource Management for Local Government

Y Penceliah

'In this age of wonders, no one will say that a thing or idea is worthless because it is new. To say it is impossible because it is difficult, is again not in consonance with the spirit of the age. Things undreamt of are daily being seen. The impossible is ever becoming possible.'

Mahatma Gandhi

1 INTRODUCTION

Local authorities are significant, not only as the mainstay of basic services, but also in the upliftment of communities. Since expectations usually exceed the capabilities of local authorities and the resources available, the cornerstone should be the effective and efficient use of resources to ensure that they enhance the quality of life of the communities they serve. In this regard, human resources are exigent for the effective functioning of local authorities. Consequently, the provision and use of human resources should be qualitatively and quantitatively adequate, to ensure that local government administration is maintained as cost-efficiently and cost-effectively as possible. Moreover, any institution which aims at productive and dynamic functioning has to give top priority to the management of its human resources.

Despite the high level of unemployment in the country, local authorities in South Africa are experiencing a critical shortage of skilled human resources. This situation could, however, be alleviated by effective and efficient human resource management. The importance of human resources is evident from the fact that, in South Africa, up to 70% of a local authority's operating budget is allocated for staff expenditure (Cloete 1978:30).

Over the last few years human resource management has become much more important in South Africa, both in management theory and as an applied management practice. The number of scientific articles and books being published globally, as well as the focus of many conferences and seminars in the field, has increased substantially. Moreover, the importance of human resource development has begun to be increasingly recognised in the last decade as social and economic empowerment may apparently be achieved.

The object of this chapter is to provide a theoretical overview of local government human resource management, focusing specifically on the normative guidelines of the process. Thereafter it proposes a normative human resource plan for local government during the transition.

2 DEFINING TERMS

To obtain a clear meaning of important terms in the domain of human resources, it is necessary to explain and clarify some key terms.

2.1 Human resource

The term 'human resource' is defined as 'the number of people needed or available for a job' (The New Collins Concise English Dictionary 1985:687).

According to the Oxford Dictionary (1976:523), although the term 'human resource' also refers to human beings, it is more specific, in that it bears upon employees active in organisations which would include business, public undertakings and the armed forces.

Therefore, in a broad sense, human resource can be understood to mean employees, staff, personnel or personpower.

2.2 Human resource management

According to Fisher, Schoenfeldt & Shaw (1990:6) human resource management involves all management decisions and practices that directly affect or influence the people who work for the organisation. Ivancevich & Glueck (1986:6) add that human resource management is the function performed in organisations facilitating the most effective use of people (employees) to achieve organisational and individual goals. Human resource management, therefore, refers comprehensively to the procurement, development and use of an institution's human resources.

2.3 Affirmative action

Affirmative action entails positive, remedial action taken to redress historic inequality and injustice. In a practical sense, this means, *inter alia*, reevaluating standards, attitudes and practices in respect of recruitment, training, development, qualifications, promotional practices and the corporate culture of the workplace (Albertyn 1993:24).

3 WHAT IS LOCAL GOVERNMENT HUMAN RESOURCE MANAGEMENT?

Local government human resource management is an essential activity of local government administration. Moreover, it is an important and necessary function to attain the objectives of a local authority. Public institutions, including local authorities, require human resources to, *inter alia*, implement policy, manage service delivery and render services. The process through which a local authority mobilises human labour manifests itself as human resource management. Therefore, in local government, human resource management refers broadly to the provisioning, use, training, development, and maintenance of human resources.

4 ACTIVITIES CONSTITUTING LOCAL GOVERNMENT HUMAN RESOURCE MANAGEMENT

Human resource management is a distinct field of activity comprising many functions executed by local government functionaries. The functional activities of human resource management include the provision, use, remuneration, training and development, and retention of personnel (Andrews 1988:6). Within each functional area of human resource management, many activities must be undertaken or accomplished so that the institution's human resources are managed optimally.

4.1 Provision of personnel

The provision of personnel is made possible through, *inter alia*, human resource planning, position determination and job classification, recruitment, selection and placement.

4.2 Personnel utilisation

The effective use of personnel is attainable through transfers and promotions, discipline and punishment, guidance and motivation.

4.3 Personnel training and development

Training is primarily directed at preparing an individual to do a job corresponding to his abilities (Gunter 1974:23), while development is concerned with the growth of the whole person (Craig & Bittel 1967:1). Personnel training can be either formal or informal. Different methods may be used to provide both types of training. Development entails a process whereby employees prepare themselves for higher positions. However, it is important that the local authority creates the requisite ambience and opportunities for employees to acquire skills and to develop holistically.

4.4 Personnel retention

Personnel retention is made possible through effective (Andrews 1988:22):

☐ personnel services;
☐ personnel evaluation;
☐ retirement arrangements;
☐ collective bargaining; and
☐ health and safety measures.

These measures not only aid the local authority to retain staff, but also improve their quality of work life.

4.5 Personnel remuneration

Personnel remuneration refers to the total compensation package; that is, the monetary as well as the non-monetary compensation an employee is offered in exchange for his labour (Andrews 1988:20).

5 THE RELATIONSHIP BETWEEN HUMAN RESOURCE MANAGEMENT AND STRATEGIC PLANNING

Within the organisational framework of an institution the relationship between human resource management and strategic planning is undoubtedly significant. Strategic planning is the process of setting institutional objectives, and deciding comprehensive programmes of action to achieve these objectives (Kochan & Barocci 1985:113). Human resource management involves all management decisions and practices that directly affect or influence the people who work for the institution (Fisher et al 1990:6). Therefore, human resource management is ostensibly the vehicle for bringing to reality the institution's strategic plans. In a local authority strategic planning may be seen as a proactive process where key decision makers decide what actions to take based on service needs. Moreover, objectives and goals are drawn up because of these decisions to implement the strategy. A strategic plan is exclusive to the institution that develops it and, therefore, will differ from local authority to local authority. However, the overall purpose of institutional strategies in the public sector will be to supply or render products or services.

6 ENVIRONMENT OF HUMAN RESOURCE MANAGEMENT

Human resource management in a local authority operates within a specific environment. An understanding of the environment is crucial as this has a decisive influence on the functioning of the local authority and on its human resources. The environmental factors are, *inter alia*, as follows:

6.1 Government legislation and regulations

Local authorities in South Africa derive their powers, functions and duties from Acts of parliament and provincial ordinances. They are, however, allowed considerable freedom to employ and to decide, for example, the conditions of service of their officials (Cloete 1993:81). However, legislation or other directives only prescribe general guidelines that must be adhered to in human resource management. The following Acts, *inter alia*, have a bearing on local government human resource management.

☐ Basic Conditions of Employment Act 3 of 1983;
☐ Labour Relations Act 28 of 1956;
☐ Labour Relations Amendment Act 9 of 1991;
☐ Local Government Training Act 41 of 1985;
☐ Local Government Transition Act 209 of 1993;
☐ Manpower Training Act 56 of 1981 (amended);

☐ Municipal Accountants Act 21 of 1988;
☐ Profession of Town Clerks Act 75 of 1988;
☐ Remuneration of Town Clerks Act 115 of 1984;
☐ Unemployment Insurance Act 30 of 1966; and
☐ Workmen's Compensation Act 30 of 1941.

Although the importance of black worker empowerment through affirmative action is of fundamental importance in South Africa, it is not yet enforced by law. However, under section 8 of the Constitution of the Republic of South Africa Act 200 of 1993

> 'there is a right to equality before the law, and 'unfair discrimination' on grounds of, *inter alia*, race, ethnicity, gender, religion or disability is forbidden'.

According to a labour survey, legislation to enforce affirmative action could be introduced by a new government within two years of taking office (*Business Times* 24 July 1994). This legislation may require institutions to set targets and time-frames for affirmative action policies, and could involve the establishment of a commission to monitor progress, and penalise those not complying with the law. However, at this stage it is premature to surmise what tone affirmative action legislation, if any, would take.

6.2 Development in technology and science

Technological changes have profound effects on a local authority's human resource management. Innovations in technology and science, in particular, tend to have a dramatic and often immediate impact on skill and talent needs. Obsolete equipment or work methods can lead to surpluses of skill in a relatively short time. Shortages of certain skills in the labour market may suggest the need to develop specialised internal training programmes, to redesign certain jobs, or to encourage educational institutions to offer programmes in certain skills (French 1987:168). In other words, new skills are needed to meet new technology demands. Moreover, as technological changes occur, certain skills are no longer required. A common example of this in many local authorities is where computer technology has replaced manual typewriters. Future technological changes will no doubt pose challenges to local authorities for further adaptation, especially in areas such as human resource management.

6.3 Labour market

It is commonly believed that the interface between human resource management and its environment is in the labour market. The labour market is particularly significant, especially where the local authority depends on it for quality human resources in quantity. Moreover, human resource planning, an important aspect of human resource management, will not succeed at institutional level unless the forecast of requirements is reconciled to the supply of human resources from within and without the local authority, namely, the labour market.

6.4 Economic changes

Economic conditions have a decisive influence on human resource management. According to Walker (1980:30), describing personnel as a 'human resource' bears the responsibility of managing personnel as an economic resource, with each expenditure viewed as an investment. As costs of interviewing, recruiting, relocating, training and compensating employees rise, local authorities are compelled to effectively manage their human resources. The impact of, *inter alia*, economic conditions on public and private sector conditions in South Africa is reflected by the country's astronomical rate of unemployment.

7 NORMATIVE FACTORS AND HUMAN RESOURCE MANAGEMENT

The philosophy of public administration prevailing in a country provides the normative guidelines or factors for the practice of public administration and, invariably, for local government management. It therefore goes without saying that the practice of human resource management should abide by, and give deference to, the guidelines. In the USA, for example, the Arlington county (1989:2) states in its guidelines that those holding public office should be mindful that, as officials of the public, they are not masters of authority but rather agents of public purpose. Public officials at all levels of government are expected at all times to abide by and respect the normative guidelines of public administration. On this point, the Local Government Transition Act 209 of 1993 states that

> 'an enforceable code of conduct for members and officials of local governments shall be provided for by law'.

According to the Collins Concise Dictionary (1984:767) the word 'normative' means to prescribe a norm or standard. Additionally, normative implies value-laden prescriptions 'which are based upon moral, ethical, or value judgements.' Therefore, in the context of local government management, the concept 'normative' suggests the prescription of an acceptable standard of conduct for public functionaries.

The normative factors that should guide public officials in the performance of the human resource management function are, *inter alia*, human rights, moral and ethical norms, democratic requirements, public accountability, efficiency and effectiveness, and transparency.

7.1 Human rights

Section 10 of the Constitution Act 200 of 1993 provides for respect for and the right to protection of a person's dignity. The issue of human rights, that is, the dignity and worth of the human being, should be of fundamental importance in the workplace. Men and women, irrespective of race, disability, colour or creed should not be discriminated against in terms of labour practices. In other words, the matter of human rights should be central to human resource management both in the public and private sectors, and at any level of government.

7.2 Moral and ethical norms

For the purpose of this chapter, moral or ethical norms refers to the standards that guide the behaviour and actions of personnel in public institutions. Experience indicates that the reputation and success of public institutions depend largely upon the conduct of public functionaries and their credibility in the public's opinion. Universally, it is an accepted principle that the actions of public officials in the performance of their duties should always be ethically justifiable (Andrews 1988:33).

Therefore, public officials should not only be committed to loyal and effective performance of their functions, but are obliged to carry out a public objective (Stahl 1976:269). For this reason, it is incumbent on each public functionary, on securing public employment, to keep in mind that he has a distinct calling to be fair and impartial in his dealings with the public. In an attempt to control unethical behaviour, viz to prevent corruption, institutions adopt codes of ethics. Most professions, eg personnel, medical, engineering, law, accounting and social work accept codes of conduct for their practitioners. Human resource or personnel practitioners are required to be registered with the South African Board for Personnel Practice. Registered members of the personnel profession are obliged to uphold certain standards in their practice, both in the interests of the public and of their calling. These include, *inter alia*, 'conducting themselves at all times in keeping with the dignity, standing and reputation of the profession' and 'doing their work to the best of their ability and so discharging their duties to employers, employees and clients' (SABPP 1994). Clearly therefore, human resource practitioners should at all times be cognisant of their conduct, so that they perform their functions impartially, to the best of their ability.

7.3 Democratic requirements

In a representative society or democracy, authority is obtained from the consent of the governed, or the community. Local government management, therefore, must serve the interests of the community. According to Stahl (1976:271) public administration at every level must serve the public in a manner strengthening the integrity and processes of democratic government. This fundamental principle has implications for public officials, viz (Stahl 1976:271):

☐ that all people must be served equally and impartially;
☐ that this must be achieved with full respect for and reliance on representative institutions; and
☐ that internal administration in public institutions must be consistent with these codes of behaviour.

Human resource management can only achieve success in local authorities if public functionaries display sound respect and commitment for democratic principles prevailing in the community.

7.4 Public accountability

It is an accepted principle that every political office bearer and every public official should display a sense of responsibility when performing his official duties (Cloete 1991:62). This suggests that elected political office bearers and public officials have an obligation to be answerable or accountable to the electorate. Public account-ability means that an official must be able to justify his actions or inactions to the public.

Therefore, it is important that public accountability is taken seriously in local government human resource management where all activities and inactivities are accounted for.

7.5 Efficiency and effectiveness

Efficiency evaluates the ratio of inputs consumed to outputs achieved, whilst effectiveness refers to goal accomplishment (Robbins 1982:317). Efficiency and effectiveness, from the perspective of human resource management, must be directed primarily at improving the productivity of employees. Human resource managers need not only be concerned with the numbers of employees but also with the output of each. The reason for this is that the needs of the community will inevitably be greater than the resources available to meet those needs.

Evidently, it is a given that the concepts of efficiency and effectiveness are at the core of public administration in the sense that the needs of the public almost always exceed scarce public resources. Therefore, efficiency and effectiveness in terms of local government human resource management can play a significant role in improving personnel productivity, thereby enhancing the quality of life of the community.

7.6 Transparency

Human resource management in local government should promote transparency in all its activities. This means ensuring that, *inter alia*, affirmative action, industrial relations, remuneration, and retrenchment should all be open and transparent. The modi operandi must be known, understood and accessible to all.

The adherence and deference to the above normative factors is critical for suc-cessful local government human resource management.

8 A NORMATIVE HUMAN RESOURCE PLAN

In local authorities, which are service and information-oriented, personnel tends to be the most significant resource. In general terms, a substantive amount of a local authority's budget is personnel related, so the need for the effective management of human resources is all-important. Moreover, with the transformation of local authorities, their profiles need to reflect the demographics of the region. Accord-ingly, human resource management in local authorities should focus on adequate staffing, both qualitatively and quantitatively, and address the imbalances caused by past discriminatory labour practices.

8.1 Developing a normative human resource plan

A human resource plan emanates from an institution's human resource requirements. This could be a short, medium or long-term requirement. The development
of a human resource plan in a local authority mays be summarised as the accomplishment of:

☐   determining institutional goals;
☐   setting human resource objectives;
☐   approximating future skill requirements by occupational category;
☐   estimating human resource shortage or surplus for each occupational category;
and establishing specific objectives, plans, and policies for recruitment, selection, placement, training, compensation, promotion and career paths.

8.1.1 Determining institutional goals

The first step in developing a human resource plan is to determine the local
authority's goals, which are derived from its mission statement. In any institution,
the goals serve as the foundation for estimating the forecast demand for human
resources.

8.1.2 Setting human resource objectives

The second step is embarked on once the local authority's goals are specified. The
human resource management department or section should then specify its objectives with regard to human resource utilisation. In developing these objectives,
specific human resource policies need to be formulated. According to Anthony &
Nicholson (1977:96), the policies should address the following questions:

☐   Should positions be filled from within or by employing individuals from
outside the local authority? More specifically:
    – What is hoped to be accomplished from promotions from within, and why?
    – What jobs will be filled by promotion?
    – Does the local authority have the requisite skills and, if not, can staff be
trained and developed for these jobs?
    – What types of skills exist in the relevant labour market, and, can potential
staff be recruited from this market?
    – What effect will bringing in people from the outside have on present
incumbents?
☐   Can the commitment of the local authority to affirmative action and equal
employment opportunity be adequately met?
☐   How does the training and development objectives of the local authority
interface with its human resource planning objectives?
☐   What trade union constraints does the local authority face in human resource
planning, and what policies should be developed to effectively handle these?
☐   What is the local authority's policy on providing personnel in the local authority with a meaningful, challenging job?

With the emergence of new, non-racial local authorities, it is imperative that policies for the measures outlined above be formulated, emphasising training, development, and affirmative action.

8.1.3 Estimating future skill requirements by occupational category

The third step in the human resource plan is to estimate the skills, and number of people, required by occupational category, in terms of the local authority's goals. It is important that local authorities have a complete, current listing of all occupational categories in their staff establishment. It is also important that the job descriptions should specify the duties, skills and qualifications required for each job, taking into consideration, that in the past, blacks have been denied exposure to senior public positions. Job descriptions should also attempt to forecast future changes in the duties, skills, and qualifications for these positions based on changes in technological requirements, the aspiration levels of individuals in the local authority and the external labour market.

8.1.4 Estimating human resource shortage or surplus for each occupational category

The fourth step in the human resource plan is the estimation of the human resource shortage or surplus in each occupational and job category (Anthony & Nicholson 1977:97). At this point, the local authority should determine what it plans to do about estimated surplus or shortage in view of human resource utilisation objectives. Figure 1 presents a procedure that may be useful to local authorities in estimating a given surplus or shortage for a particular occupation or job category.

Where a surplus is predicted for an occupational category, the local authority needs to determine if these individuals will be discharged, temporarily laid off, transferred without any training, provided with training and then transferred, or provided with a cash bonus for leaving (Anthony & Nicholson 1977:97). These decisions will be determined by the local authority's overall human resource objectives for training and development. If a shortage is predicted, then the local authority must look to the external labour market to fill the resulting job vacancies.

8.1.5 Establishing specific objectives, plans and policies for recruiting, selection, placement, training, compensation, promotion and career paths

The final step in the human resource plan is to establish specific recruiting, selection, placement, training, compensation, promotion objectives, plans, policies, and career paths to meet the estimated vacancies. It must be realised that people cannot be expected to compete equally when they have not received equal opportunities, *inter alia*, in education, quality of life and exposure to public office. Therefore, how this step of the human resource plan is defined will be decisive as it has to accommodate South African realities. It will challenge local authorities to examine their policies and establish new criteria where necessary.

Ostensibly, a human resource plan is an inherent part of the total planning process of a local authority. Further, it involves the specification of plans for more specific human resource areas. As local authorities are at the cutting-edge of change, the challenges confronting them are significant, especially in human resource development.

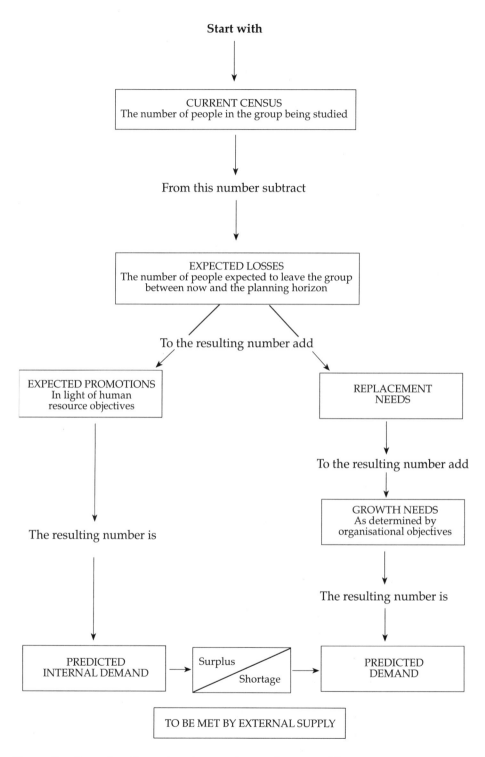

Figure 1: Procedure for estimating surplus or shortage of human resources
(Source: Nawas et al in Anthony & Nicholson 1977:97)

8.2 A human resource development policy as part of the human resource plan

The effects of discrimination in employment over the years have created momentous challenges for a competent and representative workforce in local authorities. To remedy the effects of labour discrimination in local government employment, there is an urgent need for a viable human resource development policy. Such a policy would help to identify, *inter alia*, the number, skills and occupational categories of personnel required in the future. Moreover, a framework that can serve as a guide in developing an affirmative action compliance strategy will be essential for rationalising human resource development training policies (Levy 1994:189). The development of existing and potential personnel should have a notable influence on human resource forecasting and rationalisation in the transformation phase. Moreover, training needs will be influenced by the political and economic transformation of local authorities. In this regard, precedence should be given to developing, *inter alia*, technical and development-oriented skills.

Every local authority needs urgently to develop a human resource development policy within its human resource plan, in order to address the racial and gender inequities in employment. Affirmative action, training and development should be integral parts of the policy.

8.2.1 Affirmative action

Affirmative action should enjoy high priority on the local government agenda. It is at a local level that the public meets personnel on a day-to-day basis. It is therefore imperative that the public is assured that goods and services are rendered by people reflecting the demographics of the local authority. It is important that local authorities should not confuse affirmative action with equal employment opportunities, although both are strategies for creating an integrated workforce. Affirmative action entails, not only ensuring equal opportunity, but implementing positive, corrective action to redress past inequalities and injustices by removing obstacles to black empowerment. For this reason, affirmative action not only requires removing obstacles to equal employment, it also requires the aggressive recruiting, selection, placement, training and development of blacks. It must inculcate leadership skills and provide opportunities for promotion (Luhabe 1993:26). In this regard, the top management of local authorities must be committed to empower and advance blacks to substantive positions. To aid this process, programmes to enhance skills and management development must be vigorously implemented. The training should include, *inter alia*, on-the-job training, workshops, short courses and intensive programmes. In addition, mentorship will play an important role in complementing formal training by providing skills-enhancing guidance.

On the question of gender, local authorities must recognise that women (particularly black women), were disadvantaged under the apartheid system and by male domination. These factors impacted severely on and handicapped their education and opportunities for advancement. In this regard, special programmes should be instituted. Black women's advancement and empowerment in local government and into mainstream society as a whole should be accelerated.

8.2.2 *Training and development*

The representation of black people in the middle and upper levels of management in local government in South Africa is minimal. For this reason, training and development are fundamental to equipping blacks with managerial skills. In the context of South African local government, management development is increasingly being seen as crucial in the transformation process to increase the effectiveness of existing management and to develop the potential of blacks.

To undertake this training, all available avenues should be explored. This could include universities, technikons (apart from their regular, structured management courses/degrees/diplomas), and private colleges, where short-term programmes and workshops are offered to in-service and potential employees. Management development could also include self-study courses, conferences, internal workshops and participation in modular or short-term programmes, simulation exercises and first hand comparative experience of local government processes (Levy 1994:6). In addition, Levy (1994:6) suggests that 'fast-track' courses will become increasingly important, as will the development of mentorship schemes, on-the-job training, workshops, field trips and role-playing methodologies.

It will be meaningless to adopt a human resource development policy, and then assume that this will automatically remedy the imbalances in local government. To address the under-representation of blacks in the management of local government, the policy will need to be aggressively implemented, and the results carefully monitored, preferably, by an affirmative action officer. Moreover, career paths for black employees, commensurate with their ability, motivation, potential, skills and preferences, need to be identified and detailed. In other words, opportunities should be opened up for those that have been denied access to substantive positions. Without doubt, an effective human resource development policy would begin to normalise society, and help create a competent and representative local government corps.

9 CONCLUSION

Human resource management is important in the transformation of South Africa as it is critical for effective institutional functioning. Every effort would be required to mobilise, organise and use resources within the local authority effectively and efficiently, resulting in the production of goods and services. Moreover, knowledge, skills and expertise can contribute greatly to the effective functioning of the local authority. In this regard, human resource development is a critical factor of human resource management as it involves upgrading the qualitative aspects of staff. The effects of discriminatory labour practices over the years have created momentous challenges for a competent and representative workforce in local authorities. As a priority, local authorities need to develop a human resource development policy within their human resource plans, and to address racial and gender inequities in employment.

10 REFERENCES

Albertyn C. 1993. Legislating for equality. *People Dynamics.* Vol 11 no 4.

Andrews Y. 1988. *The Personnel Function.* Pretoria: HAUM Educational Publishers.

Anthony WP & EA Nicholson. 1977. *Management of Human Resources: A Systems Approach to Personnel Management.* USA: Grid Inc.

Arlington County Code of Ethics 1989. Arlington, USA.

Armstrong M. 1988. *A Handbook of Personnel Management Practice.* 3rd ed. Bungay, Suffolk: Richard Clay Ltd.

Business Times. 24 July 1994.

Cloete JJN. 1978. *Local Government Administration.* Pretoria: JL van Schaik.

Cloete JJN. 1991. *Public Administration and Management.* 6th ed. Pretoria: JL van Schaik.

Constitution of the Republic of South Africa Act 200 of 1993.

Craig & Bittel eds. 1967. *Training and Development Handbook.* New York: McGraw-Hill Inc.

Fisher CD, LF Schoenfeldt & DB Shaw. 1990. *Human Resource Management.* Boston: Houghton Mifflin Company.

French WL. 1987. *The Personnel Management Process.* 6th ed. Boston: Houghton Mifflin Company.

Glueck WF. 1978. *Personnel: A Diagnostic Approach.* USA: Business Publications, Inc.

Ivancevich JM & WF Glueck. 1989. *Foundations of Personnel — Human Resource Management.* 4th ed. USA: Richard D Irwin, Inc.

Kochan TA & TA Barocci. 1985. *Human Resources Management and Industrial Relations.* Boston: Little Brown.

Levy N. 1994. Human resources development in South Africa: a framework for a democratic public sector. In Bayat MS & Meyer IH (eds) *Public Administration — Concepts, Theory and Practice.* Halfway House: Southern Book Publishers.

Local Government Transition Act 209 of 1993.

Luhabe W. 1993. Affirmative action: creating the reality. *People Dynamics.* Vol 11 no 8.

McLeod WT & P Hanks (eds). 1985. *The New Collins Dictionary of the English Language.* London: Guild Publishing.

Robbins SP. 1982. *Personnel — The Management of Human Resources.* 2nd ed. Englewood Cliffs, New Jersey: Prentice Hall Inc.

Schwella E. 1982. *Training as a Vehicle for Change.* Paper presented at Repositioning and Energising the Public Sector, Executive Seminars Conference, Midrand.

South African Board for Personnel Practice. 1994. *Code of Professional Conduct.* Pretoria.

Stahl G. 1976. *Public Personnel Administration.* 7th ed New York: Harper Row Publishers, Inc.

Sykes JB (ed). 1976. *The Concise Oxford Dictionary of Current English.* 6th ed. Oxford: Oxford University Press.

Walker JW. 1980. *Human Resource Planning.* New York: McGraw-Hill Inc.

CHAPTER 8

Affirmative Action in Local Government— A Case Study

N Levy & S Maharaj

1 THE SCENARIO

The Training and Development scheme (TDS) is an affirmative action programme located in the greater Durban metropolitan area in Kwazulu Natal. With an estimated population of around 4,2 million, the new metropolitan council presides over the second most densely populated and economically developed area in the country. In essence, the TDS, conceived in 1992, aimed to address the racial and gender disparities in the Durban Functional Region (DFR) which broadly forms the boundaries of the newly constituted 'metro'. The title 'public sector' is used to encompass both local and provincial government. The TDS was extended into the province during its second year of operation.

At the time the scheme was conceived, the transition from an apartheid city council to a non-racial council had yet to take place, and the uneven racial and gender employment patterns were all too evident. The persistent under-representation of black personnel is reflected in figures 1 and 2 (overleaf) which refer to the largest local authority in the province, the former Durban City Council (DCC).

The TDS anticipated the democratic transition in local government and the establishment of the metropolitan council: it was evident that the under-representation of black employees (African, Indian and coloured) in senior and middle management positions would need to be addressed rapidly if services were to be extended effectively. The TDS would be one of a number of mechanisms to do this while the Local Government Transition Act of 1993 would transform the council politically. It was clear that, while the dearth of black personnel in management positions had to be addressed by effective affirmative action employment policies at the macro level, the TDS would have to develop the management potential of young black graduates through internship and lateral entry at the micro level.

In the words of the scheme's first evaluator, 'the Training and Placement Scheme (TPS) [since renamed TDS] has been a pioneering programme in that it brought black people, albeit a relatively small number of young and usually inexperienced black people, into the council. As far as this evaluator is aware, that is the first time such a shift has taken place in the council, and the first time some of the prevailing attitudes and practices have been challenged' (Hemson, Naidu & Tapson 1994).

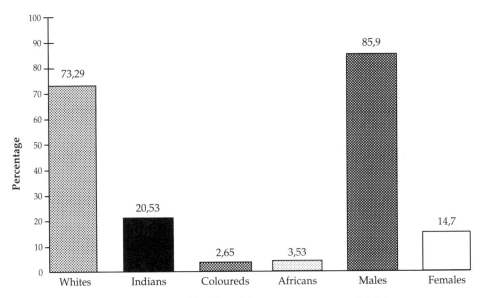

Figure 1: Race and gender profile of middle management — 1995

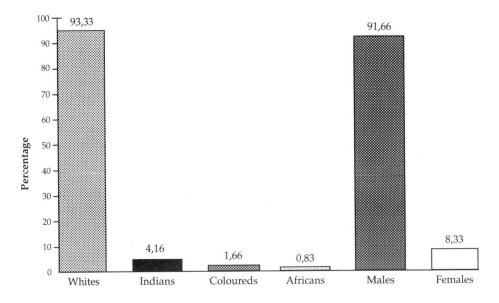

Figure 2: Race and gender profile of senior and top management — 1995

1.1 Internship

The internship component of the scheme was, in fact, only part of the strategy to train and equip black graduates with the necessary managerial skills to reach managerial positions. Training is an integrated process in which the various parts add incrementally to the total learning experience. In this instance, the internship element was at the centre of the programme, supported by two other components without which it was thought the participants would fail: these included mentorship and a campus-based course programme in development management. The TDS is therefore a three-part affirmative action-based strategy comprising internship, mentoring and training. The scheme was designed to enable trainees, through incremental experience, to develop their specialities and leadership qualities, encourage their sense of enquiry and help them develop a culture of accountability and transparency in their work relations. At the same time, it was hoped that the internship of twelve months would provide opportunities for exposure to management, to how management functioned and how significant decisions were taken.

While it was thought unrealistic to target graduate trainees without previous work experience for immediate employment in middle management positions, the year's internship and fast-track training programme would, it was felt, provide opportunities to acquire basic skills in local government management. The trainees would later build on these as their career paths widened.

1.1.1 Selection and recruitment

The selection criteria for participation in the scheme were based broadly on these assumptions and explored the applicants' management potential and skills, their capacity to plan and resolve problems, accept challenges, problematise situations and deal with people. Other selection criteria were related to governance and were designed to gauge the social concerns of applicants regarding the environment and their relative awareness of urban developmental criteria.

All applicants were treated on the same basis for selection, irrespective of population group or gender. The balance of the racial and gender proportions, relative to the total number of applicants, was borne in mind and all applicants were selected from the under-represented sections of the population. Recruitment reflected the multidisciplinary nature of local authority services and was open to personnel from the various departments of the local and provincial authorities as well as graduates from all the tertiary institutions in the greater Durban metropolitan region. Technical and social science disciplines ranging from public administration, industrial psychology and accounting, to engineering, law and social work, were regularly prioritised.

1.2 The course and impact of the TDS

The preparation, content and design of the course is undertaken by the core course team in the School of Public Policy and Development Management at the University of Durban-Westville (UDW). This is done in partnership with the Centre for Community and Labour Studies (CCLS) and a network of visiting, external lecturers. The course modules reflect an interactive and participative methodology chosen to develop critical thinking and problem solving. Trainees are allocated to syndicate groups which consider case studies and practitioners' exercises and then report to plenary, each trainee in turn using the mode to develop presentational skills and increase assertiveness. In all, seven course modules have been developed and taught over 162 hours of class contact time. Regular exposure to external lecturers has proved popular and stimulating (see the participants' evaluation below) and the aim is to increase the frequency of these. Saturday schools encourage participants to deal with issues in greater depth and help to develop communication skills.

The course modules include: the reorientation of local government; organisation and management systems; the management of human resources; administration, law, finance and public administration; issues in urban administration and development; an introduction to financial planning, and a module on project planning and management. Two field visits are undertaken each year as an integral part of the scheme.

The programme was designed for its wider view of the environment and insights into issues that are not immediately 'job-specific', although a number of trainees would have preferred the course content to be more directly job related. This tension continues to exist although there is increasing acknowledgement that the course material enlarges their vision of work and alerts them to the wider issues of public sector practice.

1.3 Mentorship

Mentorship support systems are seen by management specialists as indispensable for the achievement of an empowering environment. For an affirmative action programme they are unquestionably essential. Each of the participants has two mentors: an 'internal' senior employee is assigned to a trainee and is responsible for his development in the workplace, and an 'external' mentor is appointed from the university staff to address academic problems, mediate relations between the parties and oversee personal development.

The realisation that mentoring skills were not dormant attributes within the person of the mentor but techniques that had to be acquired through training, led CCLS to develop certificated courses in mentorship, facilitated by consultants whose courses extended through the programme. Indeed, a culture of mentorship has developed in the provincial and local authorities since the programme's inception.

1.3.1 Partnerships

Initially the programme was undertaken as a pilot project of the Development Bank of Southern Africa (DBSA). The scheme is currently run in partnership with the central transitional council of the metropolitan council where most of the graduate participants are placed, the former Pinetown Municipality (now the western transitional council of the metro), the Local Government and Housing Department of the Kwazulu Natal Provincial Administration (KZNPA), and the CCLS which devised the scheme and is part of the School of Public Policy and Development Management at the University of Durban-Westville.

A steering committee of the main stakeholders governs matters of policy and oversees the coordination of the programme. In a scheme straddling the worlds of work, the university and the local state bureaucracies, coordination is not easy. This was addressed in the 1994 evaluation report: 'Besides the internal coordination problems, the simple fact that three different organisations were involved in a common programme provided ample opportunity for breakdowns in communication. Despite this, my view is that the development of such cooperation is vital, that the different worlds of university and local government need to work together and that, in the process, coordination should be seen as an essential element and not an obstacle to success' (Hemson et al 1994).

1.4 Statistical profile

In the 1993/94 cycle 20 UDW graduates were chosen for internship of which six were permanently employed by the council and three managed to secure positions elsewhere. This cycle also comprised 11 employees from the former DCC.

The intake of graduate participants was increased to 40 in the 1994/95 cycle, including 11 employees of the KZNPA. A total of 63 participants were enrolled for the 1995/96 scheme. Eight of the 63 were placed at the KZNPA while three interns were attached to the former Pinetown Municipality.

Table 1 depicts the racial and gender breakdown for the TDS over the past three years.

Table 1

Gender	African	Indian	Coloured	White	Total
Male	47	23	2	1	73
Female	40	11	6	2	59
Total	87	34	8	3	132

Table 2 gives a numerical, gender and race profile of KZNPA trainees on the 1995/96 scheme.

Table 2

Gender	Total	Population group	Total
Male	6	African	7
Female	2	Indian	1
Total	8		8

Table 3 gives a numerical, gender and race profile of former DCC employees on the TDS from 1993–1996.

Table 3

Gender	African	Indian	Coloured	White	Total
Male	17	11	2	1	31
Female	2	1	1	1	5
Total	19	12	3	2	36

1.5 Evaluation of the scheme

Thus far two evaluations have been conducted on the scheme. One was commissioned by the DBSA for the pilot project and the other by the CCLS on the 1994/95 scheme. The purpose of the former evaluation was to monitor progress and 'evaluate critical elements in the Training and Placement Scheme (TPS) and to report on these elements in such a way as to assist the development of the scheme; to reach more conclusive judgements on the objectives of the scheme and its elements insofar as the data available allows and to determine what the indicators of success should be; to present evidence on the replicability of the scheme' (DBSA 1994). The findings of the evaluation were positive with trainees agreeing that the scheme proved to be a valuable learning experience. Responses from the former DCC mentors were less positive than UDW mentors on the mentoring aspect of the programme. UDW mentors felt that they had learnt a lot from their involvement in the scheme, especially about the workings of the DCC, of which they had not had much knowledge.

The only negative responses concerned the coordination of the institutions involved in the scheme, with trainees 'strongly disagreeing that they were happy with the way the scheme was coordinated'. This probably was the case because the three different organisations (UDW, DCC and CCLS) were not involved in the initiation of the programme, the former DCC taking greater ownership of the programme only after the pilot year. Also, restructuring at the DCC in 1992/93 afforded much 'corporate style' autonomy to the different service units. This made coordinated action more difficult, but the problem is gradually being overcome.

The second evaluation conducted (on the 1994/95 scheme) proved informative and enlightening. The focus group was the interns themselves and the aim was to establish the quality of their experience on the scheme. A sample of 22 interns was taken, nine of them from the KZNPA and the rest, trainees from the DCC.

Trainees were asked questions relating to the following areas (see Appendix 1 for questionnaire):

- internship experience (overall work experience);
- mentorship experience;
- the course in development management;
- visiting lecturers;
- assignments; and
- syndicate sessions.

2 THE WORK EXPERIENCE

2.1 The internship experience/overall work experience

Eighty-seven percent of the trainees found that they generally benefited from the TDS. One participant 'found the programme to be very helpful'. Another said that the 'scheme has made it possible for me to gain a work ethic and professionalism' and another agreed that the 'scheme makes one feel that one belongs to the workforce'. These are just some of the many positive responses elicited from participants on their experience as interns.

Trainees were generally enthusiastic about their work experience with most being ardent about their internship role. They found the work experience rewarding and, in most cases, challenging and agreed that it contributed to their development.

There were mixed feelings concerning the level of work assigned to trainees in their various placements. Some found the level of work was not sufficient and too low. They felt that more duties could have been allotted to them, while others found the level of work to be appropriate, stating that it did enhance their working knowledge. Most agreed that the work experience exposed them to understanding how decisions were made; it improved their communication and planning skills, enlightened them on project management and helped improve their people handling skills. 'I enjoyed project management, that is, being involved in all stages of a project. It enabled me to improve a good deal' said one trainee on the subject of skills acquisition.

There was unanimity among trainees that the work experience was helpful and developmental, enabling them to become more efficient in the working environment. It also contributed to their work discipline and taught them how to tolerate other peoples' opinions. On the subject of gaining work experience, a participant said 'the scheme exposed students to the realities of working life and allowed for the total development of the trainee'.

2.2 The mentorship experience

The mentorship component was the centrepiece of the scheme. Its failure would have exposed the interns to all the insecurities experienced by public sector employees in this period of transition and structural change. On the mentorship experience, participants were excited about having a mentor as it was a relatively new concept to them (there was no culture of mentoring in the council or the province prior to the TDS). Only a few trainees felt that they could have easily coped without a mentor in the workplace.

When asked if their mentors helped them deal with conflict in the workplace, trainees were not unanimous in their responses (see figure 3). There was a slender majority who felt their mentors did not help them deal with conflict in the workplace and that they had to learn how to deal with it themselves. Others were more positive and felt that their mentors did help alleviate workplace problems. One participant described her internal mentor in the following way: 'My mentor was a good listener, was very open to discussion and always willing to offer a helping hand.'

There were wide differences of opinion among trainees on whether or not mentors helped them to be 'upfront' with any problems they experienced. The question was placed in the questionnaire to gauge the extent to which confidence had been gained during the internship. Most of the trainees found that they could be candid about their problems because the advice they received from their mentors bolstered their confidence to deal with conflict.

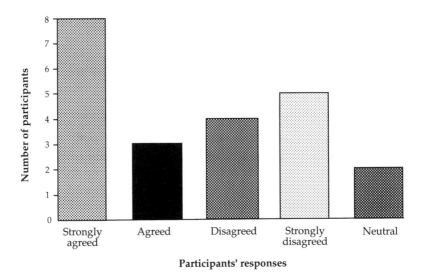

Figure 3: Dealing with conflict in the workplace

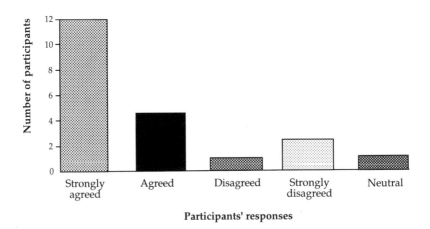

Figure 4: Improved confidence

One trainee described her mentor somewhat euphorically: 'My mentor boosted my self-confidence by making it known to me that nothing was unattainable when you put your mind to it' (figure 4).

Others were less inclined to this position and stated that they were assertive because they took the initiative (figure 5). Most agreed that their mentors helped them improve their confidence, develop good relations with their workmates, enabled them to set goals, to plan ahead and work more effectively; enlightened them on how to work as a team and to trust their own decisions.

Optimistic remarks such as 'relationship with internal mentor was healthy, positive and helpful' or 'my mentor was assertive and demanded high standards',

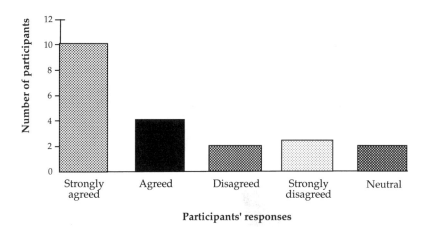

Figure 5: Being assertive

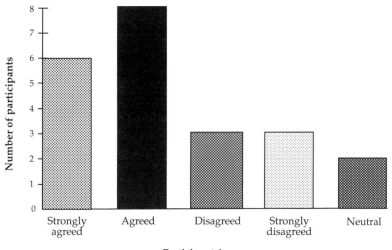

Figure 6: Dealing with stress

were just some of the positive responses that characterised the relationship of trainees with their workplace mentors.

The question concerning dealing with stress (figure 6) elicited responses that were equally weighted. About half the participants interviewed found that talking to their mentors helped them deal with stress. The other half were negative about this aspect and did not see how their mentors helped them in this matter.

Most students agreed that mentors helped them organise their time and manage projects (figure 7). The following statement highlights this: 'mentor informed me on the corporate culture, coached me on specific skills such as leadership, communication and time management' (figure 8).

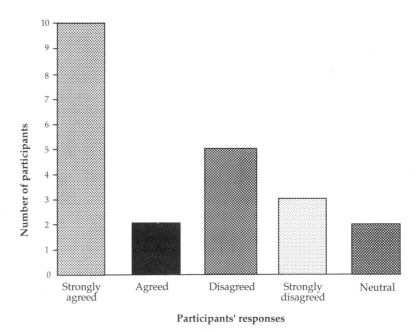

Figure 7: Time management

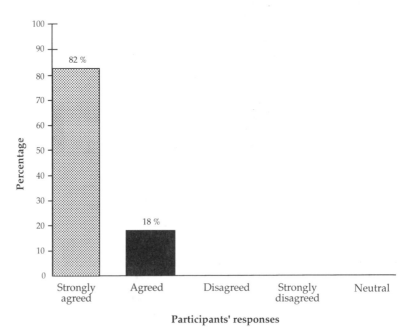

Figure 8: Improved communication skills

There was a mixed response as to whether mentors enabled trainees to cope with the power relations in the workplace and 'submit to authority'. Half agreed that they could submit to authority after the coaching received from their mentors ('mentor demonstrated warmth and empathy at all times'). The other half were disappointed by the apathy displayed by their mentors. The following statements made by interns emphasise this apathy: 'internal mentor did not fully understand the role of a mentor' and 'my mentor was not committed to the scheme and in creating opportunities for me'.

3 EXTERNAL MENTOR EXPERIENCE

The 'external' mentor to some extent mediated the trainee's relationship with his internal mentor, was responsible for overseeing the participants' progress, the level of the work experience and generally ensured that the objectives of the scheme were being achieved.

About half the trainees interviewed found that external mentoring differed from internal mentoring (figure 9). Students were enthusiastic about their external mentor experiences and positive responses were received ('... found UDW mentor to be a facilitator who readily provided direction and advice'). According to one participant the 'external mentor acted as both facilitator and intervener and always worked in my interest'.

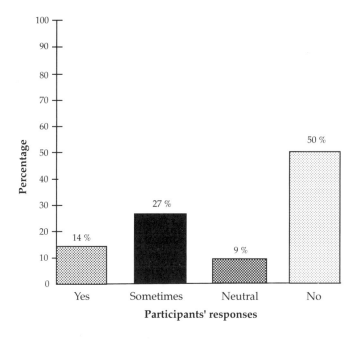

Figure 9: External mentors were exactly the same as internal mentors

Trainees agreed unanimously that the external mentor contributed to their confidence in that they helped them to deal with problems at their workplace. They were strongly opposed to the idea that the external mentor was unhelpful.

There was an overwhelming majority agreeing that the external mentor intervened to their benefit, saw them regularly and 'followed up' their queries. An equally strong majority agreed that the external mentor was objective in his advice and proved to be both a friend and adviser ('external mentor acted as friend and confidant'). Generally most of the trainees disagreed that the external mentor was too personal.

3.1 The course

Several questions were asked of the modules covered during the course. These modules included:

☐ Reorientation of professional management: this component of the course aims to develop political sensitivity and gender awareness, improve skills in communication, internal accountability, approaches to problem solving, and strategic planning;

☐ Change management: this module attempts to review the distribution of function between services and centre; the interrelationship of tasks, rules and structures; the location of decision making; decentralisation; organisational changes and management responses; local government financing and reviewing resource planning systems;

☐ Human resource planning: this section of the teaching programme covers planning development in human resources; applying affirmative action strategies; identifying training needs; developing leadership skills; encouraging teamwork; communication and decentralised decision making;

☐ Issues in urban administration and development: this module explores key concepts in urban politics, transport, housing; urban development programmes and community-initiated projects;

☐ Development administration: the course material in this module is aimed at developing a value-critical approach; covers issues in development and urban transformation; public management; and

☐ Legal framework of local and provincial government: this element of the course programme looks at legal issues relevant to the ethos, content and structures of the new dispensation in provincial and local government.

On the subject of which modules were relevant/useful to the trainees at their place of work, the following responses were evoked. The modules dealing with human resource management and organisation proved to find the most favour, the participants agreeing that the modules were useful, relevant and sufficient.

On the other hand, the module on the orientation to local government financing and law, elicited mixed responses. There was a slender majority that felt the module was helpful. Others did not think it was of any relevance to their field of work. There was a general tendency for trainees to approve the 'practical' course modules relevant to their field of work and reject the theoretical components as 'irrelevant'.

A large majority found the public administration module helped them gain a clearer focus on their role and the scope of their work in the local authority. Unusually, this component of the course, which dealt with the ethics of the public service (for the most part considered to be 'abstract' in the participants' thinking), was recognised as important and appropriate.

Urban administration and the orientation and democratic management of local government modules proved to be popular, with most saying they were 'interesting and useful'. The module on orientation and democratic management of local government enabled some trainees to gain a better understanding of local government and what it entails.

The following charts indicate the popularity of the human resource management (figure 10) and organisation (figure 11) modules:

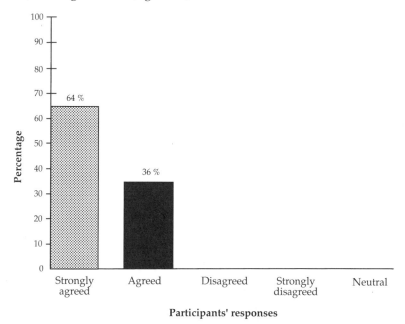

Figure 10: Human resource management well presented and interesting

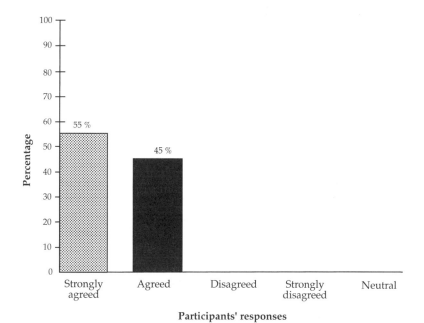

Figure 11: Organisation module well presented and interesting

Despite its importance, few participants were interested in 'finance', finding the module 'just average and of no particular relevance'. On balance, most agreed that the human resource management and organisation modules were the best presented and most enjoyable modules.

Trainees were quite positive in their responses concerning the usefulness of the course packs. The majority strongly agreed that the course material helped them organise their time, understand how local authorities functioned, improved their leadership qualities and interpersonal skills, enabled them to understand what management is about and also helped them gain insights into the problems of human resource development. Trainees were of the opinion that the human resource management and law modules should be given more time and were 'special' to them.

On leadership qualities the following graph (figure 12) illustrates their views on the question 'Did the workplace help you to improve your leadership qualities?'

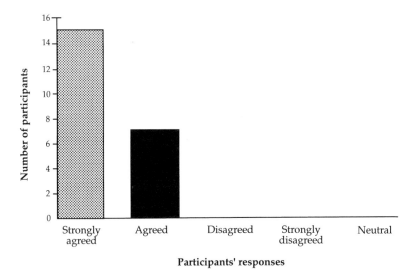

Figure 12: Improving leadership qualities

3.2 Visiting lecturers

This was an important, even crucial, component of the course as it provided opportunities for participants to learn from the wider experience of practitioners, civic leaders, specialists and external academics. The programme proved beneficial to trainees. Those interviewed strongly disagreed that the visiting lecturers programme 'interrupted the flow of the modules and should be discontinued'. Trainees found this part of the programme to be 'fruitful, informative and stimulating'.

A large majority were of the opinion that the visiting lecturers programme provided an opportunity for deeper treatment of themes which gave them more meaningful insights into their subject of study. Many felt that the visiting lecturers programme should be expanded. They felt that more visiting practitioners should be included in the visiting lecturers programme, ie employees from the council or the province. Most interviewees also agreed that the topics presented by the visiting lecturers should be more varied. Trainees suggested a range of subjects they could lecture on, including:

- project management;
- public relations;
- strike management;
- conflict management, labour law;
- law (in particular, procedures on sentencing and dismissal);
- decision making by senior management;
- law and the workplace; and
- government budgeting.

Trainees did not see the need for more opportunity to discuss their problems with TDS staff. On the subject of assignments and exams, responses were mixed. A slight minority felt that there should be more assignments and exams.

The following graph (figure 13) illustrates trainees' responses on whether or not they should be given more assignments and exams:

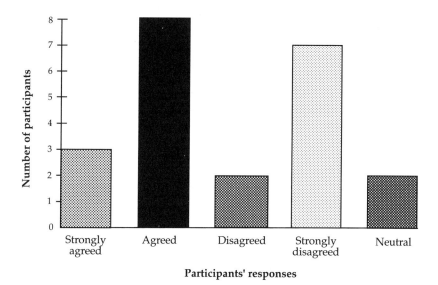

Figure 13: There should be more assignments/examinations

3.3 Syndicate groups

Trainees found the syndicate group sessions to be a better learning forum than the plenary sessions, with a strong majority agreeing their participation in syndicate group sessions was useful and helped them 'analyse problems, present an argument clearly, improve their interaction with others, provide them with the opportunity to discuss problems more frankly and in detail, make them more assertive and enhance their communication skills'. One participant said 'I found syndicate groups to be a good confidence-building technique'.

Trainees were fiercely opposed to the ideas that syndicate groups were time-wasting, that they interrupted information flow and that they should be 'scrapped'. Most interviewees disagreed that syndicate sessions 'were dominated by one or two individuals' and felt that they had all made substantial and serious contributions to syndicate group discussions. The trainees also agreed that the time allocated to syndicate sessions was 'just right'. They unanimously agreed that report-backs to plenary assisted them in their presentation skills, although many trainees felt that report-backs were not given sufficient time to do justice to the group discussions.

4 CONCLUSION

The trainees' general comments summed up their main feelings about the TDS. In listing other questions they would have liked to have been asked, their responses suggested a range of questions that possibly would not have reflected such positive responses, eg:

☐ Has your personal interest and qualification been matched?
☐ Did your mentor try to impose his opinion on you?
☐ Did you feel 'condemned' to the status of trainee?
☐ What opportunities does the course offer to trainees?
☐ Can you manage better now after having done the course?
☐ Who should choose internal mentors?
☐ Was the course relevant to your work situation?
☐ Do you view your mentor as having a positive attitude?
☐ What influence do UDW mentors have on the TDS?
☐ How should they select their syndicate groups?

The answers to the questions the trainees would have liked to have been asked would provoke stimulating debate on the experience of internship, mentoring and 'fast-track' learning. The overall impression gained by the TDS organisers was that the trainees found the scheme to be a useful learning experience, equipping them with skills to meet the challenges and demands of a working environment. It provided them with opportunities to develop managerial skills, helped them map a career path for themselves, widened their horizons and provided them with meaningful insights into local government and public administration. There may be some hyperbole in their comments but there is no doubt that the experience was generally positive.

Questionnaire

Training and Development Scheme (TDS): Evaluation 1994/95

NPA	DCC

A   Personal Details
(Please complete/leave blank/circle wherever appropriate)

1 Surname: . . . .
2 First names: . . . .
3 Degree/diploma . . . .
4 Institution from which you obtained your degree/diploma: . . . .
5 Service unit/department: . . . .

B   Overall work experience
Rate your score from 1 – 5 (5 is the highest)

6	Did you feel you benefitted from the TDS?	0	1	2	3	4	5

7	The work experience was:	Rating					
	Rewarding	0	1	2	3	4	5
	Challenging	0	1	2	3	4	5
	Boring	0	1	2	3	4	5
	Level of work was too low	0	1	2	3	4	5
	Level of work was appropriate	0	1	2	3	4	5

8	The work experience exposed me to:	Rating					
	Understanding how decisions are made	0	1	2	3	4	5
	Improving communication skills	0	1	2	3	4	5
	Planning	0	1	2	3	4	5
	Project management	0	1	2	3	4	5
	Improving my leadership skills	0	1	2	3	4	5
	People handling skills	0	1	2	3	4	5
	Improving my work discipline	0	1	2	3	4	5
	Tolerating other people's opinions	0	1	2	3	4	5

9	The work experience was:	Rating					
	Positive	0	1	2	3	4	5
	Unhelpful	0	1	2	3	4	5
	A good learning experience	0	1	2	3	4	5
	Frustrating	0	1	2	3	4	5

C The mentorship experience

		Rating					
10	I would have coped as well without a mentor	0	1	2	3	4	5
	My mentor helped me to:						
	Deal with conflict	0	1	2	3	4	5
	Be upfront with my problems	0	1	2	3	4	5
	Be assertive	0	1	2	3	4	5
	Improve confidence	0	1	2	3	4	5
	Develop good relationships with my workmates	0	1	2	3	4	5
	Enabled me to set goals	0	1	2	3	4	5
	Plan ahead	0	1	2	3	4	5
	Work more effectively	0	1	2	3	4	5
	Work as a team	0	1	2	3	4	5
	Trust my decisions	0	1	2	3	4	5
	Accept criticism	0	1	2	3	4	5
	Deal with stress	0	1	2	3	4	5
	Organise my time	0	1	2	3	4	5
	Manage projects	0	1	2	3	4	5
	Stand up for my rights	0	1	2	3	4	5
	Submit to authority	0	1	2	3	4	5
	Express my feelings when pleased	0	1	2	3	4	5
	Express my feelings when sad or disappointed	0	1	2	3	4	5

D The external (UDW) mentor experience
(tick where appropriate):

11	The role of my external mentor was exactly the same as that of my internal mentor	Yes	No	Sometimes			
	My external mentor enabled me to confront problems in the workplace that my internal mentor could not	Yes	No	Sometimes			
	My external mentor:	Rating					
	Was helpful	0	1	2	3	4	5
	Unhelpful	0	1	2	3	4	5
	Intervened to my benefit	0	1	2	3	4	5
	Saw me regularly	0	1	2	3	4	5

Followed up my queries	O	1	2	3	4	5
Met me with my internal mentor	O	1	2	3	4	5
Was objective in his/her advice to me	O	1	2	3	4	5
Was a friend and adviser	O	1	2	3	4	5
Was too personal	O	1	2	3	4	5

12 The course: the following modules were relevant and useful in the workplace:

Module	Rating					
Organisation	O	1	2	3	4	5
Human resource management	O	1	2	3	4	5
Law	O	1	2	3	4	5
Public administration	O	1	2	3	4	5
Orientation and management of local government	O	1	2	3	4	5
Urban administration development	O	1	2	3	4	5
Finance	O	1	2	3	4	5

The following modules were interesting and well-presented:

Module	Rating					
Organisation	O	1	2	3	4	5
Human resource management	O	1	2	3	4	5
Law	O	1	2	3	4	5
Public administration	O	1	2	3	4	5
Orientation and management of local government	O	1	2	3	4	5
Urban administration development	O	1	2	3	4	5
Finance	O	1	2	3	4	5

The following course pack remains a good source of reference which I refer to:

Module	Rating					
Organisation	O	1	2	3	4	5
Human resource management	O	1	2	3	4	5
Law	O	1	2	3	4	5
Public administration	O	1	2	3	4	5
Orientation and management of local government	O	1	2	3	4	5
Urban administration development	O	1	2	3	4	5
Finance	O	1	2	3	4	5

The course material helped me to:	Rating					
Think strategically	O	1	2	3	4	5
Organise and manage projects	O	1	2	3	4	5
Organise my time	O	1	2	3	4	5
Understand how local authorities function	O	1	2	3	4	5
Become more development-minded	O	1	2	3	4	5

Improve my leadership qualities	0	1	2	3	4	5
Improve my interpersonal relations	0	1	2	3	4	5
People handling skills	0	1	2	3	4	5
Understand what management is about	0	1	2	3	4	5
Understand human resource development	0	1	2	3	4	5
Understand organisational systems	0	1	2	3	4	5
Understand financial planning	0	1	2	3	4	5
Learn the legal framework of local government	0	1	2	3	4	5
Appreciate the basics of labour law	0	1	2	3	4	5

The following were special and should be given more time:						
Module	Rating					
Organisation	0	1	2	3	4	5
Human resource management	0	1	2	3	4	5
Law	0	1	2	3	4	5
Public administration	0	1	2	3	4	5
Orientation and management of local government	0	1	2	3	4	5
Urban administration development	0	1	2	3	4	5
Finance	0	1	2	3	4	5

13	The visiting lecturers:	Rating					
	Interrupted the flow of the module and should not be continued	0	1	2	3	4	5
	Provided an opportunity for deeper treatment of themes	0	1	2	3	4	5
	(Tick whichever is appropriate)	Yes		No		Don't know	
	Were too few						
	Programmes should be increased						
	Should be more varied in their chosen topics						

If yes, please list such topics: . . . .
. . . .
. . . .
. . . .
. . . .
. . . .
. . . .

There should be more visiting practitioners (employees of council/province or others)	Yes	No	Balance is just right
Most of the lectures should be taken by invited, outside lecturers and practitioners	Yes	No	Balance is just right

14	TDS organisation	Rating					
	CCLS communication with trainees is adequate	0	1	2	3	4	5
	There is sufficient access to staff	0	1	2	3	4	5
	There is sufficient feedback on assignments	0	1	2	3	4	5
	More time is required with TDS staff	0	1	2	3	4	5
	There would be more assignments	0	1	2	3	4	5
	The syndicate groups operate regularly	0	1	2	3	4	5

15	The syndicate group helps develop my ability to:	Rating					
	Analyse	0	1	2	3	4	5
	Present an argument clearly	0	1	2	3	4	5
	Interact with others	0	1	2	3	4	5
	Discuss problems more frankly	0	1	2	3	4	5
	Discuss problems in more detail	0	1	2	3	4	5

The syndicate system is:	Rating					
Time-wasting	0	1	2	3	4	5
Interrupts information flow	0	1	2	3	4	5
Dominated by one or two individuals	0	1	2	3	4	5
Not taken sufficiently seriously by trainees	0	1	2	3	4	5
Not sufficiently practised by lecturers	0	1	2	3	4	5
Too short and needs more time for discussion	0	1	2	3	4	5
Plenary report-backs assist my presentation skills	0	1	2	3	4	5
Report-backs do not have sufficient time	0	1	2	3	4	5
Should be scrapped	Yes		No		Don't know	

16 Own opinion: what other questions would you have liked to have been asked? . . . .

. . . .
. . . .
. . . .
. . . .
. . . .
. . . .
. . . .

What are your general comments on the TDS? . . . .

. . . .
. . . .
. . . .
. . . .
. . . .
. . . .
. . . .
. . . .
. . . .

5 REFERENCES

Centre for Community and Labour Studies. 1993. *Training and Placement Scheme — Evaluation Report.* Durban: Centre for Community and Labour Studies, School of Public Policy and Development Management.

Centre for Community and Labour Studies. 1994/95. *Training and Development Scheme — Evaluation Report, 1994/95.* Durban: Centre for Community and Labour Studies, School of Public Policy and Development Management.

Hemson C, K Naidu & D Tapson. 1994. *Training to Placement to Training and Development.* Affirmative action case study, Development Bank of Southern Africa.

— CHAPTER 9 —

Women in Local Government Management and Development

P Maharaj & P S Reddy

1 INTRODUCTION

The Reconstruction and Development Programme (RDP) outlined by the African National Congress (ANC) recognises that local government plays a pivotal role in the promotion of community welfare. It is the level of representative democracy closest to the people and it is this tier of government which is involved in the allocation of resources directly affecting communities (RDP 1994:129). To achieve this effectively and efficiently, local government must be restructured on a democratic, non-racial and non-sexist basis. This view is reinforced in the RDP which states that a 'women's portfolio should be established with powers to scrutinise local authority programmes and budgets for gender sensitivity' (RDP 1994:130). In view of the foregoing, the aim of this chapter is to:

☐ Provide a brief overview of women in employment and in local government;
☐ Highlight the role of women in local government; and
☐ Identify strategies local authorities can embark on to ensure adequate representation of women in local government management and development.

2 WOMEN IN THE SOUTH AFRICAN LABOUR MARKET

Women constitute one-third of South Africa's labour force. Fifty-two percent of economically active women are employed, in contrast to 84% of men (Barrett 1993:9). Women generally remain less likely than men to be employed. Although women constitute half the population, they constituted only two-fifths of the paid workforce in 1991. Within the formal economy, occupational segregation between women and men is also clearly evident: women workers continue to be concentrated within particular sectors and occupations (Maconachie 1993:43). In analysing the 1991 census figures, Maconachie (1993:43) drew the following conclusions:

☐ Although women made up 40% of the workforce, they account for as many as two-thirds of all service workers, more than half of all clerical and sales workers, and half of all professional, semi-professional and technical workers.
☐ Within each broad occupational category, women usually do certain kinds of jobs: 75% of women in service occupations are listed as domestic workers, and

nearly all domestic workers are women; 75% of women in clerical and sales occupations are listed as clerical workers and two-thirds of clerical workers are women.

☐ Nearly 75% of women in professional and technical occupations are listed specifically as teachers or fall under registered nursing occupations. While two-thirds of all teachers are women nearly all those in registered nursing occupations are women.

☐ Women workers are under-represented in categories including artisan, apprentice and related occupations. White women are over-represented in managerial, executive and administrative occupations (77,6% of women workers are white), in clerical and sales occupations (57,8% of women workers are white), and in professional and technical occupations (45,4% of women workers are white).

Women's subordination in South Africa remains interwoven with significant race and class differences. White women generally still have access to higher status and better-paid jobs. White women, in particular, are concentrated in white-collar occupations (as clerical, sales or technical workers, or as professional or semi-professional workers), whereas women classified Asian, coloured and African tend to be over-represented in lower status jobs (Maconachie 1993:46).

In local government, the top jobs are held by white men. Statistics show that 86,1% of town clerks/treasurers are male and only 13,9% are female (ANC Women's League 1993:31). Given these alarming statistics and the need to effect changes in the local government labour force so that it reflects gender equity, it becomes imperative to examine the role of women in local government.

3 LOCAL GOVERNMENT AND WOMEN

The local government sector is of major importance to the South African economy for two important reasons. First, it provides a wide range of public services, including transport, water and waste reticulation, electricity and community services; secondly, it is a provider of jobs. Local government is the level of government charged with responding to local needs. For this to happen effectively, it is imperative that all are involved in the decision-making process. Therefore, there is a strong case to examine the role of women in local government (Gwagwa 1991:73).

Local government can play a pivotal role in satisfying women's practical gender needs and transforming gender relations which will lead to the empowerment of women. According to Gwagwa (1991:73) low-income women in the Third World have three roles, namely reproductive, productive and community management roles.

3.1 Reproductive role

In their reproductive role, women are important consumers of local government services such as health, housing, infrastructure, childcare and transport. Women are therefore directly affected by the organisation of local government. Robinson (1995:15) highlights this by stating that 'exactly how, where, and under what conditions these services are delivered are important questions for most women, and the gender-specific nature of these facilities needs to be taken into account by planners and service providers'.

3.2 Productive role

Women, in a productive role, contribute significantly to the South African economy. However, this role is given very little attention and women are regarded as secondary earners. Local government institutions need to recognise this, for they are employers, creators of potential employment, and examples of well-represented labour forces comprising both men and women. In South Africa, it is evident that women are under-represented in senior management and policy-making structures. A study of the gender profile of the Durban City Council (DCC) undertaken by the Centre for Community and Labour Studies (CCLS) indicates that women employees are concentrated at the clerical level. Women labourers and clerical staff also dominate in the divisions of culture, recreation and health. Women comprise 20–40% of middle management in some sections, but senior management is dominated by white men (Robinson 1995:16). It may be concluded that decision making in local authorities is controlled by men.

3.3 Community management role

South African women have constantly fought consumption related issues, confronting the state through protest and struggle. Women have been actively involved in rent boycotts and the struggle to upgrade informal settlements. The main reason for this is their engendered position as wives and mothers, which puts them in an ideal position to participate in democratic and participatory local government structures. It is therefore important that women's political participation be enhanced. This can be achieved only if the political and institutional structures set up allow for and encourage this process.

It is important, however, to examine the various barriers that women experience in the workplace before elucidating strategies for their advancement.

4 BARRIERS TO THE ADVANCEMENT OF WOMEN IN THE WORKPLACE

Within an organisation, one's access to power and one's ability to succeed depend, in part, on the structural constraints and possibilities in the organisational structure and climate (Anderson 1993:128–129). In this section, factors affecting women's work in the organisation are examined. The barriers to the advancement of women fall into three categories:

☐ Barriers external to the organisation;
☐ Barriers in the organisational culture; and
☐ Barriers in the organisational structure.

4.1 Barriers outside the organisation

Women face various barriers external to the organisation. These barriers include sex segregation, socialisation experiences, and balancing work and family issues.

4.1.1 Sex segregation

An organisation with a completely integrated workforce in terms of sex would have an equal percentage of male and female personnel in each of the occupations in which people work. For example, if 6% of males were accountants, 6% of females would be accountants, and the same would apply for all occupations. Sex segregation exists where females and males are not similarly distributed across occupations (Powell 1988:72).

In South Africa, senior managerial positions remain male-intensive. Given the statistics quoted earlier, this holds true for local government. Women and men also differ in earnings. This is due to the low wages earned in female-intensive occupations. In addition, a sex difference in wage exists within almost every occupation, with men tending to either hold the higher-paying jobs or to earn more than women for the same job (Powell 1988:79). In addition to wage disparity, women also experience less career mobility than men. Women receive less on-the-job training so they have fewer resources than men to advance their status and wages. In female-intensive occupations, workers achieve their maximum status in a relatively short time. As a result, women tend to gain less occupational status over the course of their careers than do men (Powell 1988:79).

According to Anderson (1993:115) most women work in gender-segregated jobs. This means that women work in jobs where most of the other workers are women, and women constitute a minority of workers in jobs that have been traditionally identified as men's work. Women also work in fewer different occupations than do men and, within occupational categories, women tend to be concentrated in sexually stereotyped jobs. For example, women outnumber men among semi-professionals (ANC Women's League 1993:21). However, more detailed studies reveal that these women are employed either as nurses or primary and secondary school teachers. So, although a greater proportion of women hold semi-professional jobs, men are still positioned at a higher level in the better-paid professions (Anderson 1993:115).

4.1.2 Socialisation experiences

The way women think about their circumstances and act upon them is influenced by social ideology, social norms, and social organisation. According to Gilbert (in Rickel 1984:5) it is well documented that sex-role socialisation influences the personality development of men and women, as well as the observed sex-related differences in various achievement areas. Several variables are closely related to achievement and the professional development of women. These include intellectual competence versus femininity, expectancy of success, and self-confidence (Rickel 1984:6).

4.1.2.1 Intellectual competence vs femininity

Women's achievement behaviour is inhibited and circumscribed by the effects of sex-role socialisation. A key question in the socialisation of women is whether to socialise females to be competent or to be feminine. This implies that the goals of femininity and competence are not necessarily the same (Rickel 1984:6). A woman, for example, need not be intellectually competent to be considered feminine in the stereotypic sense of the word. However, if she is considered intellectually competent, her femininity will be doubted, and if she is considered feminine, her intellectual competence will be doubted. Moreover, many women internalise the belief that competence and achievement are incompatible with their femininity or with their desirability. Achievement-oriented women often feel they must choose between a career and a family (Rickel 1984:6).

Thus many women, although no less achievement-oriented than their male peers, are more sensitive to the negative consequences of educational and professional success. The rewards of such success for them are still far less certain than for their male peers, and the possible costs — in the form of affiliative loss — far more certain. As a result, many women may satisfy achievement needs and reduce some of the conflict with cultural sex-role demands, by choosing a 'feminine' occupation and/or by remaining in a low-status position in their occupation.

4.1.2.2 Expectance of success

A related factor is the expectance of success, the expectations of what one can attempt and successfully accomplish. Across various areas of achievement, females tend to hold lower expectations of what they can accomplish. Two aspects of this expectancy are prevalent. Women either believe they cannot be as successful or as competent as men in certain areas or, alternatively, they feel that they are performing less well than their male peers, even when they are, in fact performing as well, if not better (Rickel 1984:6).

4.1.2.3 Self-confidence

Another important area to consider is women's self-confidence in achievement setting. Women vary their opinions of their own abilities and confidence in response to specific achievement situations. Rather than viewing themselves as having a lower degree of self-confidence than males, women are discriminative in making self-evaluations of confidence and competence, and these self-evaluations are largely situationally determined. Important characteristics of the situation are gender related and include sex-appropriateness of the task, sex composition of the group, and the nature of the achievement domain (Rickel 1984:7).

4.2 Barriers in the organisational culture

In organisations, women confront male-oriented organisational cultures in which they are relegated to lower-level jobs. In addition, strained relations between races and sexes are reflected in sexual harassment and exclusion from informal systems of support.

4.2.1 Sexual harassment

Recent statistics indicate that sexual harassment is prevalent in many South African commercial and industrial organisations (*Focus* 1991). On 18 August 1990 (*Daily News*) it was reported that a staggering 76% of South African women experience sexual harassment of some form in the workplace, yet as many as 80% of these incidents are not reported.

Sexual harassment may be defined as unwelcome sexual advances, requests for sexual favours, and other verbal or physical conduct of a sexual nature when (Karsten 1994:58):

☐ submission to such conduct is explicitly or implicitly a term or condition of an individual's employment;

☐ a person's submission to or rejection of such conduct is used as the basis for employment decisions affecting that individual; or

☐ the conduct unreasonably interferes with a person's work performance or creates an intimidating, hostile or offensive work environment.

According to Stringer, Remick, Salisbury & Ginorio (1990:43), the literature on sexual harassment generally characterises it as an abuse either of role power or sexual power. For example, role power is abused where an employer demands sexual activity as a condition of hiring an applicant (Sing & Maharaj 1993:62). Two major motivators for harassment are to obtain sexual activity and/or to abuse or increase one's power.

Local authorities must recognise that sexual harassment in the workplace is not acceptable, regardless of the power issues or the motivation. The following observations were made in an Industrial Court judgement (Sing & Maharaj 1993:65):

☐ sexual harassment is a serious disciplinary offence;

☐ employers have a duty to protect employees from sexual harassment; and

☐ if allegations are made, steps must be taken to ascertain the facts and the actions or steps dictated by the circumstances must be taken.

Broad legislation, however, is inadequate to address this issue. Sexual harassment costs individuals and organisations a great deal in both economic and non-economic terms. Employees subjected to it may feel angry, humiliated or embarrassed. Frequently, their self-esteem drops. They may fear that others will not believe they have been harassed. Sexual harassment also hurts the entire organisation. It causes morale to drop and contributes to absenteeism and staff turnover. This has an effect on productivity. Opportunity-cost also is associated with sexual harassment. It drains time and energy that could have been used to pursue other goals (Karsten 1994:65).

It is therefore very important for local authorities to formulate and implement policies prohibiting sexual harassment, written in easily understandable language, published and distributed to all employees. Managers must be fully conversant with the policy and must discuss it with employees. If the policy is published in a manual relegated to a shelf, no one will be aware of its existence (Karsten 1994:66).

A policy is insufficient in itself to protect organisations from liability for sexual harassment. Organisations must conduct training, covering the nature of the of-fence, suggestions for dealing with it as an individual, internal channels for report-ing harassment, investigation procedures, and links between harassment, discipline and grievance procedures.

4.2.2 Access to role models and mentors

Same-sex role models are important to women's professional development. Women look for models who successfully combine professional and personal roles, and who integrate professional and feminine qualities. They also seek out role models who are likely to affirm them as professionals and encourage and support their professional goals. Such affirmation is more likely to come from females than from males, and is perhaps most likely to come from females who are selected on the basis of their lifestyles, attitudes to work and parental roles (Rickel 1984:10). Moreover, female role models, so selected, would be more able than others in the work environment to show sensitivity to female-related issues such as claims of discriminatory practices against women and sexual harassment.

The difficulties women have in locating and establishing relationships with role models are compounded when it comes to mentors (Rickel 1984:10). The mentor process is largely unavailable to women. In view of the key role mentors have in the professional development of men, this lack of access for women places them at a distinct disadvantage. Mentors act as teachers to enhance skills and intellectual development. As sponsors, they use their influence to promote an individual's entry and advancement. Mentors are essential because they generate power. Men-tors can speak up for their mentees and they can short-circuit established policies and procedures.

Three reasons are often cited to explain why mentoring is a predominantly male phenomenon (Rickel 1984:10). Males are in higher positions, male protégés are more assertive in initiating mentoring relationships, and relationships are unlikely to become sexual. Essentially these three 'reasons' are rationales for maintaining the status quo. Males in power select other males, rather than females, as protégés because women are too unassertive, too sexy, or both — a clear example of an expedient interpretation of a social problem. The focus (or blame) is on charac-teristics that reside within the individual (here, women as a group), and relevant situational or structural factors external to the individual are ignored.

4.3 Barriers in the organisational structure

The structure of organisations mirrors social norms and cultural stereotypes as well as power and privilege in the broader society. These forces, in turn, influence which jobs and opportunities are available to certain workers. For example, the low-paying jobs with the largest number of women in them are not connected to any career ladder or job pipeline. The most pervasive structural barriers to women are sex discrimination in educational and occupational settings and attitudes about women's abilities and roles.

4.3.1 Sex discrimination in educational and occupational settings

Male dominated occupations are not typically open to women. Those few women who are admitted receive fewer promotions than men with similar credentials and are directed into career paths that are lower in status, power and pay. Women are encouraged, if not forced, to become 'homogenised' into a narrow range of fields which offer little chance for advancement or prestige. Women at all educational levels continue to earn considerably less than men and are greatly under-represented in nearly all professions. Thus women's acceptance and promotion in careers, unlike that of men, may be based on factors related more to their gender than to their ability.

In 1975 Broverman et al (in Tanton 1994:34) noted that men held stereotypical perceptions of women as dependent, passive, non-competitive, illogical, less competent and less objective than they are. They also felt it desirable for women to be less ambitious. Other studies have found that males tend to underestimate the importance of motivators for females. These included desire for responsibility, advancement, challenging work and a voice in decision making. It seems that when one thinks manager, one thinks male (Tanton 1994:34). These stereotypical perceptions have contributed to women confronting a 'glass ceiling' when they aspire to managerial positions. The term 'glass ceiling' has been coined to portray the artificial barriers preventing women attaining senior managerial positions in private industry (*Women in Public Service* 1991/92:1). An analysis of state and local government employment in the USA indicates that women in the public sector also confront a glass ceiling (*Women in Public Service* 1991/92:1). A glass ceiling in local government limits the participation of women at the higher levels of the policy-making process. In addition, most women in government, especially black women, face barriers restricting their opportunities beyond the lowest-level jobs.

The glass ceiling is not the only obstacle to employment equity for women. Studies reveal the existence of a 'sticky floor'. This traps women in low-paying, low-mobility jobs at the bottom of the labour market. The term 'sticky floor' was used by Catherine White Berheide, Associate Professor of Sociology at Skidmore College, USA. While the glass ceiling keeps a select group of women from government's top jobs, more women employed by state institutions work on the 'sticky floor' of low-paying, low-mobility jobs. These historically undervalued jobs, essential for effective and efficient government services, offer little prestige and limited opportunity for promotion.

Local governments should recognise the particular and important contributions that women may bring to modern institutions. The importance of this is aptly stated by Metcalfe:

> 'The old bureaucratic monoliths with military type, rigid hierarchies, multilayered and which place people in tight boxes in specific functions that prevent cross-specialism and cross-functional boundaries, are dying or dead. To succeed in times of unparalleled change organisations need to be slimmer and flatter, decentralised, creative fluid shapes ever adapting to new challenges and demands. To benefit from experience the organisations must create a culture which supports risk-taking and encourages reflection, analysis and learning

from mistakes. A learning organisation is one that continuously trans-
forms itself in a process reciprocally linked to the development of its
members' (in Tanton 1994:38).

She goes on to add that these organisations need leaders different from those who
controlled the structures of the past. This is especially significant since research
shows that women lead in ways different to those of men (Metcalfe in Tanton
1994:40). Women use transformational leadership, which requires motivating
others by changing their self-interest into an interest in achieving the goals of the
organisation. Women are also likely to use power based on charisma, track record
and contacts (personal power) as opposed to power based on organisational
position, title and the ability to reward and punish, or structural power (Metcalfe
in Tanton 1994:40).

Another important factor reflecting sex discrimination in the workplace are the
criteria and methods of selection and promotion in organisations. The most popular
selection technique used in local government recruitment is the selection interview.
The selection interview is highly susceptible to the influence of stereotyping and
prejudice on the part of the assessor (Metcalfe in Tanton 1994:28).

For women interviewed by men there is substantial opportunity for discrimination, particularly when women apply for non-traditional jobs (management, engineering). Assessors have notions of the 'ideal' candidate who often bears a striking
resemblance to themselves.

One would expect that assessors know the skills and traits required for the job.
They then use the selection interview as a means of 'objectively' collecting relevant
data in order to inform the final decision. However, research suggests that when it
comes to interviews of women applying for traditionally male jobs, dress, physical
attractiveness and even the wearing of lipstick significantly affect the assessor's
decision (Metcalfe in Tanton 1994:28).

Local government institutions should become more aware of the poor reputation
that the selection interview has and should adopt a more systematic and rigorous
approach to selection and assessment. The criteria, techniques or instruments used
and the assessors need to be reviewed .

4.3.2 Attitudes to women's abilities and roles

One of the greatest structural barriers to women's achievement involves attitudes
to women's abilities and women's roles. Related to these attitudes is the manner in
which individuals are evaluated on the basis of gender. According to Gilbert (in
Rickel 1984:11) men are rated higher than 'equivalent' women in performing certain
tasks, speaking effectiveness, job qualifications, and other areas. Similarly, women
receive lower recognition and economic rewards for their work than men, and
lower prestige, knowledge, and expertise are attributed to them as well. Widely
accepted stereotypes depict men, but not women, as having the requisite skills and
characteristics for managerial and leadership positions. These stereotypes persist
even though sex differences are not found in leadership ability and job performance
(Rickel 1984:11).

Personal belief systems about roles as mothers also have a profound effect on
women's achievement. In dual-working families the female continues to assume

most of the home and parental role responsibilities. Thus, the demands of parenting continue to have a far greater impact on the achievements and career paths of women than of men. These sets of demands limit both women's opportunities to participate in public life and the time and energy they have to devote to it (Stivers 1993:5).

Local authorities must recognise the various structural and attitudinal barriers confronting women in society in general and, more particularly, in the workplace. There is therefore a need to lobby for changes through strategic means.

5 STRATEGIES FOR THE ADVANCEMENT OF WOMEN IN LOCAL GOVERNMENT MANAGEMENT AND DEVELOPMENT

In order to improve the position of women in local government employment, the development of legislative and institutional strategies in South Africa becomes imperative.

5.1 Legislative and institutional measures in South Africa

The right to equality is entrenched in the interim constitution. Section 8(1) of the interim constitution provides that (Basson 1995:22)

> '... every person shall have the right to equality before the law and to equal protection of the law.'

Gender equality is ensured in section 8(2) which states that

> '... no person shall be unfairly discriminated against directly or in-
> directly and without derogating from the generality of this provision,
> on one or more of the following grounds in particular: race, gender,
> sex, ethnic or social origin, colour, sexual orientation, age, disability,
> religion, conscience, belief, culture or language.'

Many women recognise these rights as means of achieving non-sexism and sub-stantive equality between the sexes. However, the question is whether these hopes are justified and whether the entrenchment of a right to equality will translate into real and substantive equality for all women in South Africa (Van der Walt 1995:83). South Africa's interim constitution also makes provision for a commission on gender equality. Section 119(1) states that (Basson 1995:182):

> 'there shall be a Commission on Gender Equality, which shall consist
> of a chairperson and such number of members as may be determined
> by an Act of Parliament.'

The object of the Commission on Gender Equality (CGE) is to promote gender equality and to advise and make recommendations to parliament or any other legislature with regard to any laws or proposed legislation which affect gender equality and the status of women (Basson 1995:183).

The Constitutional Assembly Workshop on National Machinery for the Advancement of Women held at the World Trade Centre, Kempton Park in June 1995, produced the following ideas on the functioning of the CGE (Neophytou 1995:63):

☐ the CGE should be part of a broader package of national machinery;

☐ there should be separate structures to deal with women's issues/concerns as the concerns of women may not be effectively addressed in the 'general structure' of women and men;

☐ the CGE should receive a level of budgetary prioritisation and there should be equitable allocation of resources; and

☐ one of the functions of the CGE should be to act in a proactive and interventionist manner in terms of policy development affecting women. Further, it should have a strong monitoring function and a strong training and capacity-building function.

While all political parties agreed that the commission should be concerned with full political, social and economic equality for women, there is as yet no draft text on its powers and functions (Sithole 1995:3).

Legislation itself is not adequate to address issues relating to gender equity. Gwagwa (1991:77) stresses the need for both a political and administrative structure to address gender inequality and to ensure opportunities for women at all levels, including local government. The political structures of local government, namely the local government councils, should have women councillors. Women in different areas need to mobilise to ensure that at least some level of representation is secured through party lists or ward-based candidates (Robinson 1995:17). However, having women on local government councils is not a guarantee that women's rights and issues will be highlighted. An effective strategy is to set up the CGE similar to that in existence in Port Elizabeth. A gender commission has been set up as part of the Port Elizabeth transitional local council. The object of such a commission is to consider ways in which council policies can be made more gender sensitive. Furthermore, an affirmative action committee has been put in place to deal with the question of women in the council's employment structure (Robinson 1995:13).

At the administrative level, a committee of women administrators should be set up. The function of this committee would be to ensure that policies aimed at providing opportunities and ensuring equality are implemented. It is important that there be a good working relationship between the women councillors and the committee of women administrators (Gwagwa 1991:78).

5.2 A review of the international experience

In deliberating on how local government can set up structures to ensure that policies reflect the needs of women, South African local authorities also need to undertake research and consider lessons from the UK and the USA. A number of local authorities in the UK and USA have established political and administrative structures designed to further the formulation and implementation of policies which result in equal opportunities for women in their employment (Stone 1988:17).

By way of example, attention is drawn to the USA where there are commissions on the status of women.

5.2.1 Political structures

Most commissions on the status of women are units of government. They are created and mandated to work on behalf of women, either by executive order or by legislation in the form of statutes or municipal laws. Since they are sanctioned by government, they enjoy the same rights as other government agencies, and therefore acquire the prestige and aura associated with officialdom, position and power.

5.2.1.1 Commissions on the status of women in the USA

Local commissions perform several basic functions which include, *inter alia*, education, lobbying, administrative oversight and a few commissions receive and resolve complaints alleging sex discrimination. The commissions devote the greatest portion of their time to educational activities — sponsoring conferences, holding hearings and workshops, publishing newsletters, and distributing materials on women's concerns. Educational activities serve two purposes: they raise communities' awareness of women's issues, and they gain visibility for the commissions. Educational activities have the advantage of being relatively uncontroversial and they therefore attract little political opposition (Boneparth 1982:39).

Local commissions also devote substantial amounts of time to lobbying. State commissions monitor the state legislative process, occasionally initiate policy proposals, direct grass-roots lobbying campaigns, and lobby office-holders directly. Local commissions occasionally lobby at the state level as well. Lobbying occurs more informally at the local level as commissions work with local officials for changes in government operations (Boneparth 1982:40). One specialised form of lobbying performed by both state and local commissions is for the appointment of more women to public office, both elected and appointed. Several commissions maintain talent banks of women willing to serve in order to expedite the appointment process.

In performing the oversight function, commissions on the status of women monitor state and local government operations as they affect women. They engage in a variety of activities including the investigation of personnel procedures and law enforcement practices, and the review of government publications for sexism (Boneparth 1982:41). While several commissions have made progress in revising job tests or eliminating veteran's preference points, only limited progress has been made in hiring or promoting women to high-level positions in local government.

However, women's commissions have the potential to perform several critical roles in relation to the advancement of women. First, because women's commissions are governmental bodies, they speak with greater authority than private interest groups, both to office-holders and the public. While they are not able to use the normal political rewards and punishments to pressure office-holders because they are governmental bodies, they have the tool of publicity, positive or negative, to persuade politicians, bureaucrats, and private interests such as employers, to attend to women's concerns (Boneparth 1982:44).

Commissions on the status of women also provide a link between women's interest groups and political actors. They provide access for interest groups to public officials. Equally important, they may be used as a vehicle for public officials seeking to reach out to the grass roots, although, in fact, commissions have not made much use of their ability to facilitate communication in this direction.

Lastly, commissions on the status of women are a means of institutionalising women's concerns in the policy-making process. While individual interest groups attempt to influence policy in their particular areas, women's commissions, by virtue of their location in government, are privy to the broad range of governmental activity, most of which has an impact on the status of women but which is rarely scrutinised from that perspective.

5.2.2 Institutional arrangements: an international perspective

Political mechanisms are by no means sufficient to ensure the management and development of women in local government. In addition, various institutional structures are required.

5.2.2.1 Institutional structures in the USA

Westchester was the first county in New York State to establish an Office for Women in August 1980. Since its inception, the Westchester County Office for Women has served as a model for similar agencies in three other counties and two cities in New York (*Westchester County Office for Women — A Decade of Service 1980–1990* undated:8).

The Office for Women has three divisions, namely, Public Policy and Advocacy, Public Education and Research, and a Direct Service Division. Through the Public Policy and Advocacy Division, the Office for Women seeks to:

- ☐ influence public policy and its implementation on all levels of government; and
- ☐ advocate for needed changes in all sectors of society.

The Public Education and Research Division seeks to empower women through the dissemination of accurate and comprehensive information. This is done through:

- ☐ responses to specific enquiries from the community;
- ☐ printed materials;
- ☐ educational programmes, such as workshops and conferences;
- ☐ specialised training; and
- ☐ research reports.

Women seek help from the Office for Women regarding personal, family and work related problems. Over the years the major problems presented have included (*Westchester County Office for Women — A Decade of Service 1980–1990* undated:8):

- ☐ homelessness or imminent homelessness due to various problems;
- ☐ rape and sexual assault of adult women and children;

- □ all forms of family violence — spouse, elder, parent and child abuse, including incest;
- □ sexual harassment and other forms of sex discrimination;
- □ workplace problems, including all forms of discrimination, benefits, pay equity and questionable grounds for termination;
- □ alcohol and substance abuse;
- □ separation and divorce; and
- □ child support enforcement.

5.2.2.2 Institutional structures in the UK

In the Birmingham City Council in England, a women's unit was created in 1984, reflecting the city council's commitment to tackling the many forms of discrimination which women face. The aims of the women's unit are (*Birmingham City Council Women's Unit Annual Report, 1992/93*:10):

- □ to initiate and develop corporate policies promoting women's equality;
- □ to highlight the disadvantages that women in Birmingham face;
- □ to ensure that all forms of discrimination which women face are addressed;
- □ to facilitate the delivery of quality services to women;
- □ to promote women's access to services, opportunities and resources;
- □ to consult with women to enable them to identify issues of concern;
- □ to produce and disseminate information on issues affecting women's lives; and
- □ to assist the council in complying with its legal obligations — for example, the 1976 Sex Discrimination Act.

a)   Locus of the women's unit within the council structure

The women's unit is structured so that it falls under the Community Affairs Committee of the City Council. The organisational structure can be depicted as follows (*Birmingham City Council Women's Unit Annual Report, 1992/93*:10):

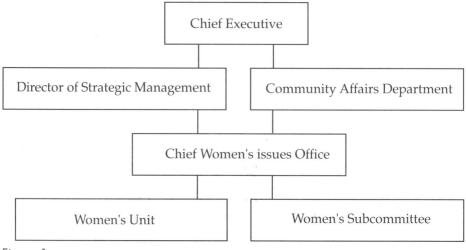

Figure 1

The Women's Unit, a constituent part of the Strategic Management Department, ensures that the interests of women are properly served by the city council and that no discrimination is suffered (*Birmingham City Council Budget Report 1994/95*:24).

5.3 Reassessment and restructuring of local authorities

In addition to the creation of effective political and institutional arrangements, local authorities can embark on various strategies to improve the position of women. Marks (1995:20) is of the view that to change gender power relations in local government, the following issues pertaining to reassessment and restructuring need to be examined:

☐ the structure, policies and representation of women in local government will have to be addressed;

☐ the attitudes of male councillors who determine how policy, powers and functions of local government are carried out, need to change;

☐ the dual role some female councillors play, as councillors and mothers, needs to be recognised and a gender-sensitive work environment with childcare facilities needs to be put in place;

☐ female councillors need to look at ways of forming support networks enabling them to influence gender-sensitive policies and practices of local government;

☐ female councillors in rural areas in particular, need to be more visible to other women within their constituency, so that women can play a positive community management role; and

☐ a forum needs to be created where women can discuss and develop strategies of intervention on issues affecting them.

6 CONCLUSION

The success of initiatives regarding improving opportunities for women depends on a strong management commitment to the belief that women can and should participate in the management of local government institutions. While legislation entrenching equality for women and the provision of a Commission on Gender Equality are essential to the eradication of sexism, they are by no means adequate. Women face numerous barriers in the workplace which cannot be removed by legislation alone. These obstacles may be attributed to barriers external to the organisation, barriers in the organisational culture and barriers in the organisational structure itself. Local authorities serious about improving the status of women should consider establishing political and management structures for the advancement of women. The new, democratic, non-racial local authorities have the opportunity of impacting on such a process.

7 REFERENCES

African National Congress. 1994. *The Reconstruction and Development Programme: A Policy Framework.* Johannesburg: Umanyano Publications.

African National Congress Women's League. 1993. *Status of South African Women*. Pinetown: Pinetown Printers.

Anderson ML. 1993. *Thinking about Women*. 3rd ed. USA: Macmillan.

Barrett J. 1993. Women and the economy. *Agenda* (18).

Basson D. 1995. *South Africa's Interim Constitution*. Kenwyn: Juta & Co Ltd.

Birmingham City Council. 1992/93. *Women's Unit Annual Report*. Birmingham: Birmingham City Council.

Boneparth E (ed). 1982. *Women Power and Policy*. USA: Pergamon Press.

Centre for Women in Government. Women face barriers in top management. *Women in Public Service 1991/92*. Bulletin of Centre for Women in Government. State University of New York.

Daily News. 18 August 1990.

Focus. 17 March 1991. The Women's Bureau of South Africa.

Gwagwa NN. 1991. Women in local government: towards a future South Africa. *Environment and Urbanisation*. Vol 3 no 1.

Karsten MF. 1994. *Management and Gender*. USA: Quorum Books.

Maconachie M. 1993. Patterns of women's employment in the 1991 census. *Agenda* (18).

Marks R. 1995. The contested terrain of local government. *Agenda* (26).

Neophytou V. 1995. Developing the Commission for Gender Equality. *Agenda* (26).

Powell GN. 1988. *Women & Men in Management*. USA: Sage Publications.

Rickel AU, M Gerrard & I Iscoe. 1984. *Social and Psychological Problems of Women*. USA: Hemisphere Publishing Corporation.

Robinson J. 1995. Act of omission: gender and local government in the transition. *Agenda* (26).

Sing D & P Maharaj. 1993. Sexual harassment in working life: theoretical perspectives and management solutions. *Politieia*. Vol 12 no 1.

Sithole E (ed). 1995. Ensuring equality for women. *Constitutional talk* (13). Cape Town: The Constituent Assembly.

Stivers C. 1993. *Gender Images in Public Administration*. USA: Sage Publications.

Stone I. 1988. *Equal Opportunities in Local Authorities: Developing Effective Strategies for the Implementation of Policies for Women*. London: HMSO.

Stringer DM, H Remick, J Salisbury & AB Ginorio. 1990. The power and reasons behind sexual harassment: an employer's guide to solutions. *Public Personnel Management*. Vol 19 no 1.

Tanton M (ed). 1994. *Women in Management*. London: Routledge.

Westchester County Office for Women. Undated. *Westchester County Office for Women: A Decade of Service 1980–1990*. New York: Westchester County.

— PART 4 —

Finance and Development

— CHAPTER 10 —

Local Government and Development Planning in South Africa

M Wallis

1 INTRODUCTION

This chapter focuses on the planning functions of local authorities with particular reference to how such functions relate to local development. While planning can, in a certain sense, be traced as far back as Plato, it has certain features characteristic of modern times. From the 1920s planning by the state became an important element of the Soviet Union's development and India embarked on planning after independence in 1947 (Thornhill 1995:93; Nove 1969; Hanson 1966). For present purposes:

☐ it is forward looking;

☐ it usually involves forecasting conditions;

☐ it means proposing actions for which it requires reviews of possible alternatives;

☐ it aims to serve the developmental needs of some but not necessarily all members of a geographic entity (cities, provinces, nations and so forth). The people thus served are commonly called beneficiaries;

☐ it normally involves many actors and stakeholders, some in government but many outside it (for example, private companies and households); and

☐ it is, at least in part, an activity carried out by trained specialists called planners.

Much of this is obvious. After all, everyone uses 'planning' in some sense; a motorist plans a route to reach a destination, and a student plans an assignment. What is critical, however, is that in the public sector planning is seen as a professional activity related to the welfare and development of people, and in local government it is specifically concerned with geographic entities or localities defined by law (through, for example, recent processes of demarcation as in South Africa). It is important to realise that it is an interdisciplinary field, with economics as the core discipline for most planners in most countries (Edmunds & Paul 1985:19; Waterston 1979:516). In South Africa the pattern is different. The planning profession here is rooted in an approach that is not seen elsewhere as development planning at all. In South Africa planning has not had a particularly strong economic content. The lack of technically competent economic development planners is one of the country's most serious obstacles to realising the Reconstruction and Development Programme.

2 HISTORICAL BACKGROUND

There are two broad influences of note. The first concerns the Anglo-Saxon influenced 'town and country' planning approach. Traditions and methods of planning stemming from the UK were implanted. These focused on the spatial or physical location of activities, facilities, etc, meaning that planners in local authorities often worked with maps to decide where to allow schools to be built, where to establish industry, and so on. This was often called land-use planning. Often this form of planning involved control rather than development. For example, it has meant restrictions on where income generating activities can be carried out; some suburbs being 'off limits' to factory development or the building of flats. In the 1960s there was a movement in the UK to change this approach (Johnson & Cochrane 1981:15) but it did not influence this country until much later. Even then, it was largely the province of NGOs and university planning departments rather than local authorities; it therefore had limited impact.

The second influence was, of course, the apartheid city that obliged planners — some enthusiastically, others less so — to separate the races, particularly as far as places of residence were concerned. Cities were therefore planned so that areas were set aside for housing black labour. Usually road construction was planned to limit access and egress to white areas for residents of townships such as Soweto and Guguletu. Legislation on 'group areas' provided the legal framework within which apartheid planning took place.

It can be argued that this planning was essentially a negative force, serving white privilege as opposed to facilitating or promoting the interests of historically disadvantaged communities. Until quite recently, planners were either unwilling or unable to do very much to address the questions associated with urban poverty. It has been estimated that about a third of African households in urban areas are living in poverty, defined as the 'minimum living level'; the income required for basic food, clothing, fuel, lighting, washing, cleansing, rent, transport, medical expenses, education and household equipment for an average family of 5,45 people (Tomlinson 1994:16,17). On a comparative note, the observation has been made that 'indicators of poverty, inequality and economic and social deprivation are reminiscent of the Dickensian conditions facing British cities and public authorities over 140 years ago' and show the magnitude of the task that will face the new metropolitan and local government administrations (Benington 1992:2).

3 THE BENEFITS OF LOCAL GOVERNMENT PLANNING

Potential benefits accruing to local governments involved in development planning include:

☐ sustainability of development initiatives if local people, through councils and councillors, come to feel a sense of owning projects and programmes; better-quality information being obtainable and exchanged to the benefit of project planning. The staff and councillors of local authorities are more in touch with local realities such as aspirations and constraints than can be expected of central or other levels of government;

☐ easier consultation with local people so that joint planning between formal institutions of government and communities can be simplified; and

☐ speedier decision making on issues affecting localities, and avoiding the 'red tape' of which central governments often stand accused.

Allen (1990), Cheema & Rondinelli (1983:14–16) have detailed analyses of these and other points. This kind of advocacy has been questioned by those who see widespread failure to achieve development through decentralisation and argue that countries like Malaysia have achieved much without strong local authorities (Ingham & Kalam 1992). No convincing evidence exists to correlate decentralisation with development. All that can be said is that the potential benefits of decentralisation can only be realised if various conditions are met. For example:

☐ there needs to be a policy of devolution in which the planning responsibilities of local authorities are firmly identified. These may form part of the national constitution, form part of the legislation concerning local government generally, or be contained in specific planning legislation (it can also be a permutation of these three types);

☐ an adequate resource base from which local authorities can operate (this includes finance, people, land and physical assets);

☐ an atmosphere must prevail in which it is possible for communities to participate freely and willingly in the planning process, a genuine partnership with local government included;

☐ there must be support from higher levels of government, rather than unnecessary obstruction of local initiatives. This would include, for example, central government grants for development projects; and

☐ there must be an adequate understanding of what planning is about by all stakeholders and, most important, an understanding of what roles various organisations and individuals must play. This includes a solid commitment to the planning process.

Related to much that has already been said, it is important that local government enjoys widespread support as an institution and is not seen (as in the recent past) as a privileged island for an elite to maintain what it sees as an appropriate way of life. Significant legitimacy problems can arise if this support is not forthcoming.

To summarise, the mere creation of local government does not make it developmental. While it may be a necessary condition for local development, it is not sufficient. A host of other conditions need to be met if planning is to be effective.

4   LOCAL GOVERNMENT AND THE RECONSTRUCTION AND DEVELOPMENT PROGRAMME (RDP)

The RDP has several important implications for performing planning functions in local government. It is a useful point of departure to refer to the basic principles of the programme, which are directed at the entire public sector including local government, in the white paper on the Reconstruction and Development Programme (1994:6–7):

☐ A sustainable and integrated approach, as opposed to one that is piecemeal and lacks coordination. Affordability is an important component because, if it is not considered, sustainability will not be achieved. Services will collapse if they are not paid for;

☐ The second principle is that the RDP must be 'people-driven'. This really involves two points. One is that the programme should be about people's immediate needs, such as housing and sanitation; the other, in counterpoint, is that there is reliance on their energies. The notion of a 'passive citizenry' is disowned;

☐ The third principle of the programme is the need for peace and security. Important roles are thus accorded to the security forces and the judiciary. Specific emphasis is placed on the taking of hostages, vandalism, drug trafficking, gun-running and the abuse of women and children. The importance of peace and security for the encouragement of investment is stressed;

☐ Fourthly, the point is made that a process of 'nation building' is essential to success. Unifying factors are strongly suggested here, reference being made to South Africa being a single country with a single economy; and to a constitutional framework 'that establishes provincial and local powers' (Republic of South Africa 1994:7). The latter point is of particular significance for local government;

☐ The fifth principle is the notion of linking reconstruction and development. What this means is that attacking the inequalities of the past — providing infrastructure, etc — is integrated with an emphasis on increases in output throughout the economy; and

☐ Finally, the idea is put forward that all five points depend on the creation of a democratic society, meaning active processes in which much more is involved than the holding of periodic elections. Participation in decision making by the people affected by those decisions is stressed. In addition, review and restructuring of government is essential.

All these points relate to local government. The first requires local authorities to *pursue integrated and sustainable development activities*, and the second requires that it relate its work to *the needs of the people and draws on their energies*. The third is also relevant as local authorities are involved in the maintenance of peace and security and depend in many ways on a stable context to undertake development.

The fourth principle is also relevant as it focuses on the *framework of constitutionalism within which local government powers are spelt out*. The fifth is vital to our concerns as many local government functions are involved in *the provision of infrastructure*, water and electricity. Finally, democratisation is clearly not going to be completed until local government is a part of it; provincial and central levels are too remote from communities.

The RDP white paper has more to say about local government than the original (or 'base') document issued just before the April 1994 elections. The base document confined itself to stating a few important principles, but did not contain much detail and does not discuss local government in a developmental context. This is under-standable as its authors did not have the benefit of being experienced in govern-ment at any level (African National Congress 1994:129–131). The white paper is an improvement on the base document as it is more specific, although it leaves key questions unanswered — for example, the procedures by which RDP funding is to be allocated to local authorities.

More recently, a report by RDP minister Mr Jay Naidoo has reinforced the importance of local government as a route to more effective local economic devel-opment strategies and projects; it also anticipates a second white paper in Septem-ber 1995 (Republic of South Africa 1995a:3). It also links the RDP to the Masakhane campaign, defined as a 'vehicle for implementation of a people-driven RDP at the local level' with emphasis on: accelerated service delivery; local economic devel-opment compacts; community responsibility to pay for services; maintenance of investments by communities and local authorities; and community policing It also calls for a 'bold vision of developmental local government', drawing on traditions of community organisation and activism (Republic of South Africa 1995b:13).

It is recognised by government that 'local authorities are key institutions for delivering basic services, extending local control, *managing local economic develop-ment*, and redistributing public resources' (Republic of South Africa 1994:22). This implies going beyond what most councils have been doing and, although several have attempted to do so, their undemocratic nature has hampered them. On this point see, for example, the case study of Durban's 'Operation Jumpstart' (Robinson & Boldogh 1994). What is, however, stated to be more clearly a new development is the idea that 'emerging democratic local authorities must work with community-based organisations and NGOs to establish minimum conditions of good govern-ance and to implement effective development projects' (Republic of South Africa 1994:22).

This notion would, in essence, bring local authorities closer to more progressive ones in Europe and North America (Benington 1992; Tomlinson 1994). The priorities are twofold and need to be approached in tandem. The first is the improved delivery of services; restoring and upgrading them in the many areas where they have collapsed, and extending them to new localities. The other is the development of institutional capacity in ways that can create better conditions for carrying out the RDP. This is a tall order, involving many variables. Some of these are spelt out in the white paper: moving towards democracy; amalgamation where appropriate; a developmental orientation; proactive in seeking the trust of the public; sensitive to affordability, financing and efficiency; shifting resources to more developmental activities; and engaging in debate with community groups. The document does not say this, but what is implied is a strengthening of *strategic planning* where it already exists and its introduction where it does not. A useful account of what this entails is found in John Benington's report (Benington 1992). (See also the chapter on strategic planning and management by PS Reddy in this volume.)

An important point about institutional capacity is that local government is a key RDP agency in considerable disarray in many places countrywide, partly because of non-payment for services, a problem that is unlikely to disappear in the short to medium term. Such capacity problems are clearly critical and require urgent attention, not just from local government but also from central and provincial authorities (Cameron & Stone 1995). A complicating factor here has been the delay in converting local authorities from apartheid to democracy.

The danger, of course, is that local government will be left behind and marginalised, thus becoming incapable of providing the support for the RDP envisaged in the white paper. This means planning will be an exercise of limited value in that it will probably not make a significant impact on the communities supposed to derive benefit from it.

4.1 Capacity building for RDP implementation: what are the key issues?

The 1995 RDP report to parliament refers to capacity constraints in using RDP funds. In this context, a 'key challenge' is developing capacity in provinces and local authorities. Particular concern is expressed about the quality of project preparation. To address this, 'project preparation facilities' are being established 'to develop capacity at local level to prepare project plans' and thus 'help to ensure that local needs are the starting point for budgeting' (Republic of South Africa 1995a:18–19). It is also vital to stress that capacity is needed for implementation as, even when funds are available, implementation may not occur owing to several constraints, eg managerial skills.

There is a tendency to see capacity building purely in terms of training. While this is an important factor, the idea is actually a broad one involving several dimensions. To assess the issues better, it is necessary to review in more detail what the RDP expects of local government. This demands a review of the project approach central to RDP implementation and the specific types of project for which it is anticipated councils will be responsible. These can be categorised in various ways but, using the RDP's own framework, referring to two broad types seems appropriate: presidential or 'lead' projects on the one hand, and projects initiated by the local authorities themselves, but aimed at RDP objectives, on the other. The first of these serves a catalytic function, enabling the programme to start and ensuring that certain identified needs are met as soon as possible. They are catalysts in the sense that they are supposed to generate other projects and activities of a similar type.

4.2 The project approach

The white paper implies that projects will be the devices through which various agencies will be expected to implement the RDP. Baum & Tolbert, writing from a World Bank viewpoint, define a project as 'a discrete package of investments, policies, and institutional and other actions designed to achieve a specific development objective (or set of objectives) within a designated period' (Baum & Tolbert 1985:333). There is, however, no agreed definition.

Some common features of the project approach include: an emphasis on development finance or investment (grants or loans or a mixture of the two); an activity or set of activities aimed at specific objectives; a time-frame in which objectives are to be achieved; a specified organisational framework; a notion of who is to benefit (the 'beneficiaries'); a coherent plan in which the various project activities are linked to a network or chain; and a breakdown of activities in terms of inputs and outputs.

In addition, most projects can be said to follow a 'project cycle' with the following sequence: identification (a preliminary assessment of need and a thumbnail sketch of what might be involved in terms of cost, timing, etc); preparation (in which detailed project design is done after identification has been accepted by the authorities concerned); negotiation and appraisal (primarily a matter of potential funders being convinced of the desirability of funding the project); implementation (when the main activities are carried out, for example, construction, training, marketing, credit provision. This also involves monitoring what is being achieved); and, finally, evaluation of the project once accomplished.

The cycle is then linked back into the identification stage because the evaluation results should benefit the identification of further projects. Many projects also involve efforts to improve the capacities of organisations through restructuring and training. This account of the project approach, derived largely from the World Bank work referred to above, is essentially what is intended in South Africa, if not in detail, then at least in broad outline.

4.3 Presidential projects

Government stated that it would be following a project approach when the President addressed parliament in May 1994. He stated that certain projects were being identified 'which would launch the delivery of the RDP in the first 100 days' (Republic of South Africa 1994:17). It is not clear how much detailed consultation with communities took place before this announcement and the subsequent identification of specific projects although, before the elections, the RDP as a whole had been presented to a series of workshops attended mostly by ANC activists. Given the circumstances facing the government at that stage, it is perhaps unfair to call the process 'top–down'; nevertheless, it is hard to see how there could have been community involvement of any weight, given the rapidity with which the announcement was made.

The white paper is clear in stating that most of the consultation was with national departments and provincial administrations. Community bodies may have had some indirect involvement, through their influence at provincial level for instance, but their position may be characterised as essentially marginal. The presidential projects were identified in line with eleven criteria:

□ high impact on the communities they serve;
□ empowerment of these communities;
□ economic and political viability and sustainability;
□ job creation;
□ provision of basic needs;
□ training and capacity development;
□ affirmative action with respect to gender and race;
□ visibility;
□ transparency;

☐ potential to lever funds from old to new priorities by requiring departments to provide matching funds from their budgets and to carry all recurrent costs (other than in exceptional cases no recurrent costs would be funded); and

☐ some existing capacity to start implementation' (Republic of South Africa 1994:18–19).

Almost in line with the project cycle, 'business plans' were to be prepared for projects; these corresponding with the preparatory stage of the cycle. These plans use a standard format that should ease their preparation.

Annexure One of the document sets out in more detail the content of these projects concerning sectors, objectives, costs, etc. Projects are listed under various headings such as clinic-building, small scale farming development and national literacy. A substantial number involve local government, either directly or indirectly. On the rural side, a couple of examples can be given, involving 'local government to be' rather than extant. Under the rubric 'Rural Water Provision' the task of meeting the needs of communities in deprived rural areas was to be carried out through twelve projects in eight provinces (the Western Cape excluded). The object is not only to provide water; it is also to 'develop local water boards as institutions for local government' (Republic of South Africa 1994:55). 'Land Reform Pilots' are to take place in one district per province. The primary aim is to 'develop and support integrated, sustainable rural development and rural local government models through land restitution, redistribution, tenure reform and settlement support to kickstart a wider land reform process' (Republic of South Africa 1994:55).

Not surprisingly, urban projects figure prominently; three types suggest strong local government involvement. One of the smaller ones is 'Urban Infrastructure Investment Planning' which entails the creation of teams 'to facilitate the development of local infrastructure investment plans'. This is important to the theme of this chapter as the pivotal feature of this project is to develop capacity for local planning, an activity in which local government is inevitably involved though the white paper does not specifically say so (Republic of South Africa 1994:56).

Although important in developing planning capacity, a necessary condition for successful projects of greater significance if measured in terms of funding, are two other projects in which local government will play a greater role: 'extension of municipal services' and 'urban renewal'. While urban infrastructure planning is only allocated R2,9 million for 1994–1996, the extension of municipal services is given R850 million and urban renewal not much less at R791,1 million over the same period. These obviously represent developmental activities that are likely to preoccupy planners in local authorities (assuming the delay in starting RDP projects does not lead to reduction in the sums available). Therefore, setting out some details concerning these components of the programme is necessary.

Extension of municipal services is a wide-ranging set of projects in two senses; it covers most municipal services and can benefit any area of the country providing certain conditions are met. There are three related aims. The first is to improve the provision of municipal services; the second is to bring about the democratisation of local government, and the third is to provide a basis for 'the sustained payment of rent and services by local communities' (Republic of South Africa 1994:59). Particular emphasis is placed on the restoration of collapsed infrastructure and the extension of services to new areas. There is also a concern with ensuring that measures are taken to create the required institutional and financial capacity. The conditions to be met are:

☐ Funds to be made available only when a Transitional Council has been established under the Local Government Transition Act.
☐ Evidence of how the provision of services and infrastructure will be financed and sustained must be provided.
☐ There must be a system of planning and budgeting, managed in an integrated way.
☐ The prime beneficiaries should be the poorest members of the community.

From an organisational point of view there might be a strong element of the top-down approach. Leading roles are played by the Department of Constitutional Development and the Department of Environmental Affairs, but local government is recognised as having an important place in the scheme of things.

Urban renewal projects are more focused, particularly in terms of locality. The aim is to bring development to areas affected by violence and other forms of crisis. As for what is to be done there is overlap with the other major initiatives outlined above, but specific localities have been selected. Thus it is envisaged that projects of this type will be planned and carried out in certain areas. They are:

☐ Katorus in the East Rand (Katlehong, Thokoza, Vosloorus);
☐ Kwazulu Natal: the only province to be included as a whole, presumably because of its high level of violence;
☐ Duncan Village, East London;
☐ Ibhayi, Port Elizabeth;
☐ Botshabelo and Thabong in the Free State; and
☐ Cape Flats in the Western Cape

The preliminary identification is to be developed into detailed projects. Clearly the needs differ from one area to another, making it essential to vary the content of the projects concerned. However, the more rural provinces are excluded from this list.

While saying there is some meat in the white paper for local government is correct, sounding some notes of caution is also necessary. First, the sums made available are not enough to meet all needs; local authorities must find funds elsewhere (from within their own budgets or from other, outside sources). Secondly, the selection of areas for urban renewal is problematic as areas that can claim similar devastation are excluded, and this may be resented. Thirdly, it was almost inevitable that the RDP should come across in these projects as a top-down initiative, and understandable, given the circumstances of its preparation (urgency and the illegitimacy of local government being of particular importance). In the longer term, this could cause problems because local authorities are unlikely to see themselves as mere implementing agencies with only marginal roles as policy makers and initiators of new development. Fourth, the question of finding funds is a concern. Although procedures are being worked out, it is far from clear how the system is supposed to work, and frustration is evidently growing as a result.

The RDP has been reviewed in detail because it is a framework local authorities must come to terms with as they strive to become more developmental. This central fact should not, however, be allowed to obscure several other points. One is that the principle of autonomy is not necessarily undermined by the RDP. In as much as it is an agenda determined from above it does not negate the possibility of councils developing their own priorities in their own ways. Much will therefore depend on the context in which they are operating. Secondly, it is possible to take this a step further since it is now common for ministers to make the point that the RDP cannot work if it is entirely dependent on central government directives and decisions. Although this point is more commonly made about community development activities rather than local government, the implication is clear: if central government direction is both undesirable and unattainable, then local authorities, once legitimated by elections, are logical alternative institutions to initiate and manage projects.

Thirdly, local authorities have a political complexity and unpredictability that might mean their programmes will not always reflect the RDP approach and philosophy. Councillors are important actors in the determination of development priorities. Thus, after elections are held, a local authority may find itself with a body of councillors who belong to a social class that does not see its interests being served by the RDP. Where this is the case, and where disadvantaged communities do not comprise a significant portion of the voting population, perhaps because of demographic factors, the protection afforded the former wards in the Local Government Transition Act, low voters' registration or low turnouts at the polls, it is possible that RDP objectives will not be seriously entertained by councillors. For example, for a combination of these reasons, predominantly white middle class suburbs can vote into office councillors for whom the priorities are to keep the rates down while maintaining the privileged life styles of their voters. Within this scenario — which is possible in many parts of the country — lip service may be paid to the RDP while little is done for disadvantaged communities such as informal settlements within these localities.

It may then become essential for such communities to have ways of securing funds without using council channels. In practice this may prove difficult unless steps are taken to ensure that RDP funds can be reached.

Fourthly, many developments are going on around the country that predate the RDP (as Tomlinson's book shows). Reference is made to Operation Jumpstart in Durban that arose in 1990 from a concern in business and local government circles that there was a crisis in the region (Robinson & Boldogh 1994:191). The development activities of the metropolitan chamber in Gauteng (Hunter 1994) and Cape Town's 'Vision 2000' programme (Cape Town City Council 1993), which aims to create jobs, affordable housing and transportation within the wider Cape Town region are two further programmes. The point here is that these initiatives need not be displaced by the RDP (although some may be). They may continue despite the RDP, especially if they have the funds to see them through to completion. This is, of course, more likely to be the case where local authorities have financial resources in reserve because of their prior operations and the effectiveness of their financial management. The latter is an important variable often overlooked. This is not to say that these initiatives are to be seen as separate from the RDP; on the contrary, they might fit well into the broader strategies of the programme even if they do not have formal status within it. They may also be usefully redesigned or carried out in different ways, considering the RDP.

Sources of policy other than the RDP documents themselves but parallel to them also need to be considered. For example, a white paper on the development and promotion of small business published by the Department of Trade and Industry has a short but important section on local authorities (Republic of South Africa 1995b:46). Several points are made which relate to our concerns. It is noted, for example, that 'All over the world there is increasing realisation that the most effective level for the promotion of SMMEs (small, medium and micro enterprises) is the village, town, city or metropolitan area. Local authorities have direct 'contact' with each enterprise, down to those involved in survival activities, and their administrative infrastructure could be useful for the implementation of support programmes'(Republic of South Africa 1995b:46).

The paper goes on to note the lack of support for these businesses in the past, especially those in the informal sector, but recognises a recent trend that is more conducive (informal markets, hives and incubators, flexible zoning, and business infrastructure facilities, for example). All these phenomena are necessary for job creation and 'rates generating business activities'. Calling for 'effective orchestration' (coordination) of the various bodies concerned, the white paper highlights the need to strengthen local economic development, and support small enterprises through bodies such as local authorities — which are urged to play more proactive facilitating and coordinating roles. To this example can be added the under-studied question of privatisation by local authorities. This has potential to create business opportunities. For example, the Durban City Council recently privatised disconnection and reconnection of electricity supply (personal communication from a contractor, 1995).

What this boils down to is that the RDP documentation is not 'the only show in town'. It may in fact be seen as a rather broad framework that some local authorities may choose to opt out of. Few will probably do this. However, questioning the apparently reasonable assumption that is sometimes made that government will want to spell out (or even dictate) in detailed fashion to local government what it should do regarding development, is prudent. If this becomes reality, it would imply a significant reduction in local autonomy, and if that occurred it would clearly have major implications for the achievement and maintenance of democracy in the country. RDP planning will be a major factor for local authorities to be aware of and become involved in but that does not, however, exclude their using other approaches and initiatives.

5 THE LOCAL GOVERNMENT TRANSITION ACT

Examining the legislation that coexists with the RDP to establish the precise nature of the framework within which local government development planning is to operate is necessary. The Local Government Transition Act, passed towards the end of 1993, arose from the deliberations of the Local Government Negotiating Forum (LGNF) which began its deliberations early in the same year. With the constitution (chapter 10), this Act provides the legal framework for local government in the new South Africa (Republic of South Africa 1993a; Republic of South

Africa 1993b). These documents are more comprehensively reviewed elsewhere in this volume. What is important from a development planning point of view is highlighted in this chapter.

The listing of functions of councils is not explicit regarding planning, but is implied in several ways. For example, schedule 2 of the Act refers to the powers and duties of transitional metropolitan councils, *inter alia*, as follows:

☐ Many functions and services that clearly imply planning, especially if the introduction of new services and facilities, improvement or expansion is involved (for instance, airports, refuse dumps, produce markets).

☐ '... the promotion of economic development and job creation', which clearly provides scope for a wide range of development activities for which planning will be essential.

☐ 'Metropolitan coordination, land usage and transport planning', which also suggests the need for planning capacity within the new local authorities.

Thus there might be no serious legal restriction on local government's developmental role, but there are nevertheless constraints to which we now turn.

6 CAPACITY AND CONSTRAINTS: CLOSING THE GAP

For reasons embedded in South Africa's history enormous pressures are being placed on those charged with the tasks of designing and implementing development. Given the track record of past efforts at development, whether at central, 'homeland', provincial or local level, the existing institutional framework could only provide an inadequate platform for progress. To take but one example, the activities of the Department of Development Aid during apartheid's terminal years suggests that a combination of incompetence and corruption has characterised much development planning and management in this country (Sing & Wallis 1995). With this factor, it is essential to take into account the high priority attached to affirmative action, a strategy that inevitably will mean that members of historically disadvantaged communities will occupy key positions with which they are not immediately able to cope, mainly because of their lack of experience. This therefore means that, for some time, a considerable gap will exist between what needs to be done — RDP goals essentially — and existing institutional capacity.

As far as local government's developmental role is concerned, there are several constraints to be discussed here that require the attention of the authorities at various levels. While noting that many of the problems are part of a wider national picture, there are others specific to our concerns.

6.1 Shortages of appropriate planning officials

The issues here are complex and vary from one part of the country to the other. It can perhaps be argued that some bigger councils were well endowed in relation to what was expected of them in the *ancien regime. However, in the new era the inadequacies are alarming almost everywhere*. There is evidence that problems are worse in some areas than others. The big cities have relatively sophisticated and large-scale planning capacities but even these are unlikely to be able to cope with the following changes: the emergence of metropolitan local government that, in itself, changes planning demands dramatically (Durban incorporating townships such as Umlazi, Clermont, etc, Johannesburg incorporating Soweto); the need for forms of planning appropriate to the RDP as opposed to the town planning of the past; and the need to take into account community needs and their organisational frameworks (civic associations, etc). The Centre for Community and Labour Studies (CCLS) has compiled a data base on local authorities in the greater Durban area, most of which is now within the metropolitan council area; it reveals woeful capacity problems in most of the outlying districts, especially those within the former Kwazulu, such as Umlazi (CCLS 1994).

Yet the picture is even worse when one turns to rural areas. Take the Northern Province as an example. It has been argued on the basis of fairly detailed research that capacity is severely limited, the only exceptions being the former white areas (McIntosh & Vaughan 1994:ch 1). The new transitional councils in rural areas of former homelands such as Lebowa are, in some instances, entirely without staff and are obliged to depend on provincial officials over whom they have no direct authority and who are limited in capacity (personal communication; member of Ngwaritsi Transitional Local Council and Northern Province planning officials: field visit, 1995). Under these conditions it is no surprise that talk of urban bias in planning is often to be heard. It clearly has solid factual foundations.

What is increasingly recognised is the need for a new emphasis on project planning and management. The RDP white paper has a little to say about this, reference being made to 'business plans' for projects; this has since been elaborated into quite detailed procedures orchestrated at provincial level. Also important is the involvement of the donor community. The World Bank, for example, is expected to become heavily involved, the government having agonised for some time over the desirability of making major repayments (*Sunday Times* 23 April 1995). An important consideration is that such sources of funds can normally only be made available following an exercise much more elaborate than RDP procedures. The same applies to the German 'zopp' (goal-oriented project planning). This particularly difficult exercise could result in delays in donor fund usage and reinforce criticism that government is not acting decisively.

6.2 The status of local government

The transition to democracy at local level has lagged approximately eighteen months behind the central and provincial levels. This may even be an underestimate of what is clearly a major problem surrounded by tension and uncertainty. Given the central role of local authorities in so much of the RDP, this is a constraint of extraordinary importance. Local authorities under these conditions will be understandably tentative in making critical decisions, preferring to wait until democratic processes have been completed; and there is still a legitimacy problem to be solved. As a result there are, even now, areas where local economic issues are being tackled by forums established for that purpose, essentially bypassing local government per se.

This issue — the continued failure to form democratic local authorities – is probably the greatest obstacle to progress in this area. From a planning point of view this is important as it is the body of politically recruited councillors who have to give the go-ahead once projects have been identified. If they are reluctant to take that on, then delay is the result. Paralysis can mean living conditions deteriorate further, and the backlog of what needs to be done grows. It can also mean that data may be out of date by the time the project comes on-stream, creating further difficulty.

6.3 Political, social and economic change

To put matters simply, South Africa is *changing* even if it is not doing so in any clear-cut direction. From a planning point of view, dealing with change is a big challenge. A few examples may suffice. Areas such as Cato Manor in Durban have been targets of planning initiatives for years, but the emerging informal settlements in the area constantly render proposals for land-use unworkable since areas identified for shops or schools may be occupied or 'invaded' by informal settlers who build shacks there. This uncontrolled, unplanned pattern of change results from many factors: escape from violence, the ending of influx control and the encouragement of politicians and civic associations are some relevant factors. Thus, in many parts of the country, planners are challenged by the fact that the areas for which they are drafting plans are changing too rapidly for them to keep pace; under these conditions it is understandable that a kind of fatalism sets in.

Another example concerns the much emphasised notion that communities have to be fully involved in the planning process. This is complex for several reasons, but what is perhaps most important, is the likelihood that the leaders being consulted at one stage may move on (to political office for example) and be replaced by others. This is particularly frustrating in circumstances where the winning over of local leaders has been a painfully slow process. If 'social compacts' are reached under these conditions, sustaining them for long may not be easy. Another factor is that many communities contain deeply entrenched divisions that can undermine projects. These cannot be eliminated by planning alone. There are political, moral and cultural concerns here which need to be addressed. Reconciliation is needed for many reasons, one of which is that it is a prerequisite for development in many areas of South Africa.

7 CONCLUSIONS

Planning, in common with many South African activities, has a legacy that retards development. With local authority planning the issue is not simply apartheid. We need to consider the tradition derived from the British model that has linked planning with control rather than with development. Concerns with transformation need to recognise this legacy and remedy it. Despite delays in the creation of democratic local government, in the RDP there is a strong emphasis on planning and implementation by local authorities. For example, roughly half the presidential projects, either directly or indirectly, require action from councils. The project approach is needed to achieve RDP goals but the traditions of planning are not appropriate to its full adoption. A similar point can be made in relation to community involvement to which much importance is attached. The pace and uncertainty of political, economic and social change create further difficulty as recent experience in cities such as Durban and Pietermaritzburg show us. Ending on a pessimistic note would be wrong and, happily, we do not have to do so. The political, social and economic climates are clearly more encouraging than before 1994, and there are many planners anxious to go on with the required work. That they have a hard road to travel is unquestionable, but to prophesy failure cannot be justified.

8 REFERENCES

African National Congress. 1994. *The Reconstruction and Development Programme: A Policy Framework.* Johannesburg: Umanyano Publications.

Allen H. 1990. *Cultivating the Grassroots.* The Hague: International Union of Local Authorities.

Baum WC & SM Tolbert. 1985. *Investing in Development.* Washington DC: The World Bank.

Benington J 1992. *Preparing for Power: Local Government and Local Administration in a New South Africa.* UK: University of Warwick.

Cameron RG & AB Stone. 1995. *Serving the Public.* Pretoria: J L van Schaik.

Cape Town City Council. 1993. *Annual Report of City Planner.* Cape Town City Council.

Centre for Community and Labour Studies. 1994. *Towards Restructuring Local Government: Part 2.* Durban: CCLS.

Cheema GS & DA Rondinelli. 1981. *Decentralisation and Development.* Beverley Hills: Sage.

Edmunds, W Starl & S Paul. 1985. *Training Guide for the Implementation of Development Projects.* Brussels: International Institute of Administrative Sciences.

Hanson AH. 1966. *The Process of Planning Oxford.* Oxford University Press.

Hunter R. 1994. Local economic development strategies in the PWV. In Tomlinson R *Urban Development Planning.* Johannesburg: Witwatersrand University Press.

Ingham B & AKM Kalam. 1992. Decentralisation and development: theory and evidence from Bangladesh. In *Public Administration and Development.* Vol 12, London.

Johnson N & A Cochrane. 1981. *Economic Policy-Making by Local Authorities in Britain and Western Germany.* London: George Allen and Unwin.

McIntosh A & A Vaughan. 1994. *Towards a System of Rural Local Government in Northern Transvaal.* Halfway House: Development Bank of Southern Africa.

Nove A. 1969. Soviet political organisation and development. In Leys C (ed) *Politics and Change in Developing Countries.* Cambridge: Cambridge University Press.

Republic of South Africa. 1993a. Local Government Transition Act 209 of 1993.

Republic of South Africa. 1993b. Constitution of the Republic of South Africa Act 200 of 1993 (as amended by Act 2 and 3 of 1994).

Republic of South Africa. 1994. *White Paper on Reconstruction and Development.* Pretoria: Government Printer.

Republic of South Africa. 1995a. *Taking the RDP Forward*. Pretoria: Office of the State President.

Republic of South Africa. 1995b. *White Paper on National Strategy for the Development and Promotion of Small Business in South Africa*. Cape Town: Department of Trade and Industry (WPA 1995).

Robinson J & C Boldogh. 1994. Operation Jumpstart: an urban growth initiative in the Durban functional region. In Tomlinson R *Urban Development Planning*. Johannesburg: Witwatersrand University Press.

Sing D & M Wallis. 1995. Corruption and nepotism. In Cloete F & J Mokgoro (eds) *Policies for Public Service Transformation*. Kenwyn: Juta & Co Ltd.

Thornhill C. 1995. Public sector planning. In Thornhill C & SX Hanekom (eds) *The Public Sector Manager*. Durban: Butterworths.

Tomlinson R with D Dewar, R Hunter, J Robinson & C Boldogh. 1994. *Urban Development Planning*. Johannesburg: Witwatersrand University Press.

Waterston A. 1979. *Development Planning: The Lessons of Experience*. Baltimore: Johns Hopkins.

CHAPTER 11

Local Government Financing in South Africa

S Moodley & D Sing

1 INTRODUCTION

The theory and practice of local government financing in South Africa are expected to undergo major changes before an acceptable paradigm of sustainable local government financing is formulated. Therefore, at this stage of local government transition there can be no 'absolute' measures for financing. It is expected that several approaches, systems and processes from a pot-pourri of financing options, will be tried and tested over the next few years. In the long term, both experiential learning and changing local government dynamics should determine how local authorities will be financed.

This chapter provides an overview of local government financing. It focuses on transitional arrangements, administrative and management issues, factors which impact on financing, and current and new sources of financing.

2 TRANSFORMING LOCAL GOVERNMENT IN SOUTH AFRICA

Since the Government of National Unity (GNU) took office in April 1994, historic changes have taken place in South African politics and governance.

2.1 Legislative measures

The Constitution of the Republic of South Africa Act 200 of 1993 provides, in a preamble, fifteen chapters and seven schedules, fundamental provisions for common citizenship in a sovereign and democratic constitutional state, where all people can enjoy and exercise their fundamental rights and freedoms. Nowhere is this provision more relevant and apparent than at the local government level. This is the level at which citizens experience the tangible provisions of local government services.

Chapter 10 of the Constitution Act sets out broad policy guidelines for the establishment, structures and functions of local government in South Africa. Sections 174(1) and (2) provide for the establishment of different categories of metropolitan, urban and rural local government with powers and functions peculiar to their environment. Regarding this, the Local Government Transition Act 209 of 1993 provides for transitional arrangements in three specific phases viz: pre-interim phase, interim phase and the final phase. The pre-interim phase covered the period up to the local government elections held for transitional structures in November 1995/early 1996. The interim phase commenced with local and metropolitan elections and the final phase starts with implementation of a local government model according to the final constitution of South Africa.

Under section 175(3) of the Constitution Act, local government is expected to provide a wide range of services within its area of jurisdiction, including water, sanitation, transportation, electricity, primary health services, education, housing and security. Note that the above provision includes a qualification: 'provided that such services and amenities can be rendered in a sustainable manner and are financially and physically practicable'. Services can only be provided to the extent that funds are available for delivery. An important consideration is that services must be both sustainable and affordable to local citizens.

The constitutional architects were evidently aware of the enormity of the task facing local authorities in meeting service provisions and expect reality and practicality to prevail when determining and implementing local government policies.

2.2 Financial provisions

Section 178(2) and (3) of the Constitution Act covers the important areas of financing of local government activities. Local governments are empowered to levy and recover on a uniform basis a series of levies, fees, taxes, tariffs and rates. Moreover, local government shall be entitled to an equitable allocation of funds from the provincial government. The recommendations of the Financial and Fiscal Commission must be considered in respect of finances.

When the Local Government Transition Act was promulgated on 2 February 1994, a multilateral Agreement on Local Government Finances was signed at the World Trade Centre in Kempton Park. This agreement on finances committed the stakeholders to a statement of intent regarding future financing and service delivery by local authorities. Briefly, the agreement provided that TLCs should promote services in historically disadvantaged areas with the intention of improving, upgrading and extending such services in a visible and sustainable manner (Cloete 1994:61). An important principle for service delivery was cost recovery. Tariffs should be structured to address poverty and unemployment. TLCs must use available resources in an equitable, efficient and effective manner. Moreover, municipal finances must be based on the principle of one municipality, one tax base.

The outstanding institutional debts of black local authorities that cannot be paid (approximated at R360 million), will be taken over by the state. Individual service charge arrears, approximated at R2 billion, must be considered by local negotiating forums and dealt with as seen fit. All debts to be written off by the local authority must be approved by the provincial government. Moreover, accurate and updated records and accounting procedures must be maintained to ensure control and accountability.

In the following section, local government financing is discussed with particular reference to conceptualising, administering and managing the financing function, followed by factors impacting on financing and lastly, viewing current and future sources of financing.

3 CONCEPTUALISATION, ADMINISTRATION AND MANAGEMENT OF LOCAL GOVERNMENT FINANCING

No institution can expect to perform any activity or reach a desired goal without finance. Finance is a golden thread running through all activities undertaken in the public and private sectors. The government of any country is there essentially to serve the community. Governments strive towards predetermined goals that are collectively directed to improving the quality of life of the community. The nature and extent of government involvement are determined by the prevailing political ideology and community perception as articulated by their elected representatives (Gildenhuys 1993:3). Therefore, one cannot ignore the fact that both politics and ideology play a determining role in formulating the financial policies of a government.

In South Africa the social welfare ideology is considered both pertinent and relevant to conditions in this country. Given the policies of apartheid, this ideology is highly suited to meet the needs of the communities by (Gildenhuys 1993:10):

- □ providing assistance, not only financially but also in many other ways, to the poor and the less privileged to enhance their quality of life; and
- □ identifying and eradicating the causes of poverty and destitution that affect most South Africans.

These considerations are, in a measure, being addressed by the GNU in its policy on reconstruction and development. In addressing local government financing, the following questions are considered relevant to the discussion (Gildenhuys 1993:3):

- □ What are the financing functions by which the goals and objectives of local government can be realised?
- □ How and from which sources of income should local services be financed?

3.1 Conceptualisation

The financing function only assumes significance if it is contextualised. The financing function or activity in the public sector is referred to by different names. Public finance, government finance, state finance, public sector economics, public economics, public financial administration and public financial management, are terms often used interchangeably to describe the financial activity of governments and other public authorities (Rosen 1988:5; Aronson 1985:7; Stiglitz 1988:8–9)

An understanding of the financing function may be twofold. At the first level, which is at the macro or national level, the impact of economics is pertinent to the raising, collecting, and redistributing of resources, the setting up of national priorities, the evaluation, monitoring and control of different public programmes, building infrastructure (facilities) and carrying out different methods of public service delivery.

At the second level, that is, at the micro or local level, managers need to understand financial management to decide whether resources are being used optimally to achieve predetermined goals. In the same vein, Gardner (1978:4) submits that the three general economic responsibilities of government are to ensure:

☐ a high level of economic resource (full employment) and stable price levels;
☐ the society's resources are used efficiently, effectively and economically, ie the value for money principle, for the satisfaction of the wants of the people; and
☐ that the distribution of income among individuals who comprise society is satisfactory or acceptable.

These responsibilities are labelled stabilisation, allocation and distribution functions respectively. In this regard, Croeser (1992:16) argues that central government must accept basic responsibility for economic stabilisation while the allocation function should, as much as possible, be vested with provincial and local tiers of authority. Moreover, the distribution function through vertical and horizontal tiers is essential to ensure equity in the development and growth in all regions (Croeser 1992:16).

Public finance, therefore, could be defined as

'... the study of the financial activities of government and public authorities. It describes and analyses the expenditures of governments and the techniques used by governments to finance these expenditures' (Aronson 1985:7).

In a similar vein, Rosen (1988:8) submits that

'Public finance, also known as public sector economics or public economics, focuses on taxing and spending activities of government and their influence on the allocation of resources and distribution of income'.

It is therefore argued that in South Africa, at the national level, the GNU determines financial policies directed to specific goals to meet the welfare of citizens. Within a unitary state such as South Africa, regional and local government policies must be directed to meet national goals and priorities. Within this context, local government financing could be construed to include a series of processes involved in the collecting, budgeting, appropriating and expending of public moneys; auditing income, expenditure receipts and disbursements; accounting for assets and liabilities and for the financial transactions of the government; reporting on incomes and expenditures; receipts and disbursements, and the condition of funds and appropriations (Bhambhri 1992/93:536–537).

The efficient and effective administration and management of local government finances will be critical to the nature and scope of local service provision.

3.2 Administration and management of local government financing

The administration and management capacity of local government is important to its goal achievement. Under section 178(1) of the Constitution Act, a local government must be managed on sound principles of public administration, good governance and public accountability, to render efficient services to the local community and to ensure effective administration of its affairs.

Local authorities in the new South Africa will come under increasing financial pressures as they can expect growing demands for urban services because of urbanisation and rapid population growth. This, coupled to the existing deficiencies caused by the years of apartheid, can only exacerbate the situation. Therefore, their capacity to provide local government services and also undertake infrastructural development will be severely constrained by the shortage of money (McMaster 1991:1).

3.2.1 Strategic vision and mission statement

In any situation there is a need for purposeful, goal-oriented action. This applies no less to financing local government. There is a need for foresight and planning in financing, ensuring a balance between justifiable expectations and available financial resources for delivering local government services. A strategic vision for local government generally and for financing specifically, is an essential guideline for monitoring and evaluating goal achievements. To this end, local government must provide essential services on a sustainable basis at affordable prices. Within the context of local government financing, Evans (1991:300) contends that

> 'The short answer to requirements for financially viable local authorities is to say that local authorities must be accorded or must be able to generate or receive sufficient or adequate funding to pay for the functions and services allocated by the constitution and the servicing and development expected by the local population in the urban content. A statement such as this is so broadly descriptive as to be of little quantitative assistance'.

One could counter this argument by stating that such a vision is nevertheless essential, especially in a fledgling democracy such as South Africa, where local governments have the stupendous task of meeting gross imbalances that defy easy quantification — at the least, only estimates are being made for achieving the goals of the RDP, ranging between ten and twenty-five years.

In determining a strategic mission statement for local government financing, which is the realisation of efficient, viable or adequate financing on a rational basis, consideration of the following issues is necessary (Evans 1991:302):

☐ the nature and scope of functions and services to be performed by local governments;

☐ the jurisdictional area, metropolitan or other related resources, distribution or reticulation of functions and services and other needs of the local community;

☐ functions and services provisions based on equal funding or weighting criteria or whether there are different degrees of need and requirement that must be met, and the duration/timescale for these;

☐ the current and potential sources of funding and other available resources of local communities; and

☐ the level of infrastructural base and development of the local government communities, eg black and white local authorities have widespread differences in this regard.

Rademan (1987:10) submits that the following characteristics could form the basis of a mission statement for local government financing:

☐ it would be broadly formulated allowing for flexibility and changes and for financial objectives to be logically deduced from it;

☐ it would be open to pioneering ventures;

☐ it must be worthwhile and contribute to the improvement of the quality of life of the local citizenry; and

☐ the duration/time-span would not be specifically stated for its achievement, as this would be influenced by different variables in each area of local government jurisdiction, for example, economic status of local authority and levels of prosperity of its residents.

The first financial mission of any local authority would be one based on financial self-sufficiency or adequacy. The extent to which each local authority strives to attain this goal will be determined by its peculiar environment and variables such as economic, social and physical constraints. Therefore, there can be no uniform timescale for achieving financial self-sufficiency or viability by any local authority.

Rawlinson & Tanner (1993:3) submit that to achieve effective financial management the following are essential ingredients of the process:

☐ need for clear objectives at all levels;

☐ clearly defined levels of authority and responsibility;

☐ the means and availability of accurate, current and understandable management information;

☐ logical and uncomplicated control and reporting methods and procedures;

☐ ensuring relevant training and advice; and

☐ implementing effective performance monitoring systems.

These fundamental guidelines would ensure that the functions constituting local government financial management are undertaken both efficiently and effectively.

3.2.2 Functions constituting local government financial management

Several important activities constitute local government financial management. Rawlinson & Tanner (1993:1–2) submit that the following are specific functions of local government financial management:

☐ the exchequer function that entails payroll, creditors, income, pension, VAT administration and insurance;

☐ coordination, control and accountability aspects that include financial and strategic planning, budgeting control, final accounts, cash flow and debt management;

☐ audit function both internal and external; and

☐ information and advice aspects including financial advice, management advice and information, financial trading and performance review.

The Local Government Transition Act 209 of 1993 provides for the orderly development of local government from the apartheid to the post-apartheid era. It only provides for broad policy guidelines during the transition phase. Local government transitional models, either transitional councils or local government coordinating committees, must clearly address policies and procedural details of administration and management by way of enacting local legislation, rules and regulations.

However, these prescriptions may be meaningless without strong local government leadership from councillors, chief executive officers and chief finance officers.

3.2.3 Roles of councillors and top officials in local government financing

The roles of councillors and top officials are expected to be very important to the administration and management of the new local government structures. They are expected to provide dynamic leadership to achieve the goals of local government transformation.

3.2.3.1 Councillors

The Constitution Act, section 179, provides for democratic local government elections every three to five years. The electoral system for local government provides for proportional and ward representation. Section 245 of the Act further provides that 40% of councillors shall be elected by proportional representation and the remaining 60% shall be elected on a single member, ward basis. Thirty percent shall represent traditional white, coloured and Indian areas and the other half (30%) current black local authorities, both these groups falling under the jurisdiction of the local government authority. This approach is a compromise addressing itself to local government unity in a manner protecting the status quo and interests of minority groups in the elections (Cloete 1994:46).

Councillors are either elected or nominated to the local government council by the electorate. Widespread public participation in local government elections is essential, so that the local community is truly represented by a council vested with powers to deliberate and decide in the government and administration of civic matters.

This is reinforced by Craythorne (1990:27) who submits that two of the more important functions of councillors are their representative and decision-making capacities. In representing their constituency, councillors must serve the public interest by ensuring that all decisions are fairly and judiciously considered and applied for the benefit of the local authority as a whole. Councillors, in serving the public interest, must not seek to enrich themselves.

Evidently, councillors play decisive roles in financial management. The Constitution provides, in section 176(a), that the budget of the local government shall be decided by a two-thirds majority of all its members. Moreover, in terms of section 177, it provides for the establishment of an executive committee of a council to exercise such powers and functions that a council may determine. Matters shall be resolved within the committee either through consensus decision making or by a two-thirds majority.

3.2.3.2 The chief executive officer (CEO)

The chief executive officer plays a dynamic role within the local government authority. The importance of his position is highlighted by the fact that it is often entrenched by statutory provisions that prescribe both the role and responsibility of the chief executive officer. The following are the pertinent executive functions, having financial implications, undertaken by the chief executive officer (Cloete 1981:9 adapted):

- ☐ in executing the financial decisions and directions of the finance committee and council, he provides advice and guidance to his subordinate officials, including the chief finance officer, materials manager, town engineer, town planner and the medical officer of health, emphasising the necessary steps that have to be taken to give effect to the financial decisions and directions;
- ☐ in rendering accounts both to the finance committee and council of the outcome of the specific financial decisions and directives implemented, and recommending corrective and remedial measures where necessary;
- ☐ in actively participating in governmental relations, communications are made vertically with provincial and central authorities, and horizontally with other local authorities regarding the execution of local government financial administrative functions of the council, the finance committee and other officials; and
- ☐ in communicating with interest groups and citizens about the financial implications of goods and services rendered by the local authority, provides feedback to the finance committee and council about the merits and demerits of the financial policies of the council.

The chief executive officer is supported in his role by the chief finance officer who is responsible for financial administration and management of the local authority.

3.2.3.3 The chief finance officer (CFO)

The chief finance officer is directly responsible for financial management in the local authority. He has a traditional and proven record to maintain within the local authority. He has to ensure the professional integrity of his occupation within the local government financial sphere. In recent times, local government financial management has become so complicated and intensive that specialists such as financial and management accountants, programmers, budget analysts and financial economists have been employed to help the chief finance officer (Gildenhuys 1989:190).

The prime function of the chief finance officer is to develop and set up an integrated financial system, thereby providing a coordinated policy and procedure for financial management. (Gildenhuys 1989:190).

Modern local government financing demands that the chief finance officer is proactively involved in coordinating the policy of the council and supervising the financial activities of various other functional departments so that account can be rendered on various facets of financial management. Marshall (1974:284–288) lists further important functions of the chief finance officer:

i. In a general sense, the chief finance officer functions both as an accountant and financial adviser to the council. He is responsible for, *inter alia*:
    (a) financial administration and management of the local authority;
    (b) administration and management of his department;
    (c) training and development of finance department personnel; and
    (d) reporting annually to the council on the financial structures of the local authority with recommendations for future development.

ii. To provide, develop and operate a centralised accounting system for the local authority ensuring the:
    (a) supervision of all financial records;
    (b) preparation of accounting manuals;
    (c) preparation and submission to committees, council, and auditors, the accounts relating to all council's activities;
    (d) prompt supply of financial data to departments, committees and council when needed; and
    (e) control of all the local authority's assets.

iii. To develop and maintain a central audit system by:
    (a) auditing the financial records of all departments;
    (b) reporting to committees and council on the work of the internal audit and the state of financial records in each department; and
    (c) promptly reporting irregularities discovered during the process of an audit to committees and council.

iv. To ensure payments by making arrangements for the:
    (a) verification of all accounts for payments;
    (b) payments of allowances, salaries, wages and pensions; and
    (c) preparing, signing and despatching of all cheques and similar documents.

v. To make all arrangements for income of the council by:
    (a) collecting and recovering all the money due to the council;
    (b) handling, custody, security and banking of cash; and
    (c) maintaining proper custody of stocks of all receipts, tickets and similar documents.

vi. To participate in the planning and supervision of the council's annual budget in conjunction with the chief executive officer and heads of departments by:
    (a) coordinating and controlling the annual estimates and participating in evaluation and appraisal exercises;
    (b) submitting estimates to operating committees;

(c) forwarding summaries and reports to finance committee or management committee; and

(d) reporting over-expenditure or unauthorised expenditure of the budget to finance committee and council.

vii. To administer all funds of the council subject to the chief executive officer, finance committee and council by:

(a) ensuring available money is suitably invested; and

(b) advising finance committee and council on raising of capital funds.

The important role the chief finance officer plays in local government financial administration and management cannot be underplayed. He is the hub of the administrative wheel and provides the chief executive officer with substantial support in the day-to-day administration and planning of the local authority's activities.

3.2.3.4 Heads of departments

Finance is required to attain the objective of every local government department. Gildenhuys (1993:174) stresses the following with respect to the role of heads of departments in financial management:

'The head of department must accept that he is responsible and accountable for the financial administration of his department. He is his department's accounting officer and must account for the financial activities of his department to his chief officer.'

In this regard, the head of department therefore ensures the purposeful and effective execution of the departmental budget for which he is responsible. Consequently, it is essential that, with the chief finance officer of his department, he decides budgeting measures that ensure adequate control over the expenditure of funds (Gildenhuys 1993:175). In this context, the heads of departments and other senior officers entrusted with financial duties perform the following functions (Van Straaten 1985:434):

☐ compiling of financial reports and the preparation of the draft departmental budget;

☐ determining the goods and services required for the following financial year and its financial implications;

☐ identifying new requirements and obtaining the permission of the committees of the council, and if these are accepted, providing accordingly in the draft budget;

☐ ensuring that the financial rules and prescriptions of the treasury are strictly followed;

☐ ensuring that all departmental transactions with financial implications are thoroughly checked; and

☐ providing information to the chief executive officer, chief finance officer, committees and council about present or new services for which provisions in the budget must be made.

It is evident from the foregoing that the administration and management of local government are critical to its success.

4 FACTORS IMPACTING ON LOCAL GOVERNMENT FINANCING

The development of an acceptable model for local government financing depends on several factors. The most central challenge facing the GNU is how best to improve the quality of life of South Africans, given the effects of apartheid. In the main, these factors arise out of, and affect the political, economic and social environments, and include issues such as governmental relations, decentralisation, autonomy, management and administrative capacity and the role of the Financial and Fiscal Commission (FFC).

4.1 Political environment

The current problems experienced by most South Africans originated in the political milieu. Apartheid, entrenched in a range of legislative measures, perpetuated racial discrimination and created widespread inequities in, *inter alia*, employment, housing, health and education. Moreover, apartheid marginalised blacks, ie most South Africans, excluding them from meaningful political decision-making institutions. The policy of separate development, underpinned by the Group Areas Act, divided South Africans according to race. From 1948, the National Party government systematically used legislation to inhibit black advancement and approved large budgetary allocations to promote the development of whites through better education, housing and health facilities (Nkuhlu 1993:11).

The policies of central government impacted on regional and local governments. Administration boards and black local authorities were responsible for providing local government services to black residents. The black townships, situated some distance from city centres, were initially designed as dormitory towns to provide cheap labour for white commercial, industrial and domestic needs (World Bank Report 12596 SA:1). As a consequence, black local authorities suffered serious inequities in the provision of services. Moreover, they lacked a strong fiscal base and, in comparison with white local authorities, had a low level of infrastructural development (World Bank Report 12596 SA:1). At the local level, the merging of cities and townships to create unified local authority structures, posed an important challenge. The local government demarcation boards, created under section 11 of the Local Government Transition Act 1993, had to identify optimal areas of jurisdiction to ensure the greatest financial viability for new local authorities (Cloete 1994:60). It is expected that the new local government structures will work for the good of their communities by:

☐ allowing for widespread public participation;
☐ operating with responsibility, transparency and accountability;

☐   promoting and improving the quality of life of their citizens; and

☐   collectively contributing to the national objective of community welfare.

4.2 Economic environment

Political objectives cannot be achieved without the necessary economic development to provide the fiscal base to meet such expectations. The greatest challenge
facing new local authorities in South Africa is how best to carry out redistribution
and poverty alleviating policies and raise the standard of living of most South
Africans. History has recorded that attempts by blacks to compete in the economic
sphere were thwarted by the National Party government. Legislative measures
which afforded racial privilege included section 77 of the Industrial Conciliation
Act and section 12 of the Mines and Works Act that set the basis for the policy of
job reservation: systematic measures favouring whites over blacks (Thompson
1993:22). The impact of these economic inequalities is evident in a recent World
Bank report (1994:1):

> 'However 51 percent of annual income goes to the richest 10 percent
> of households. Under 4 percent goes to the poorest 40 percent. Poverty
> afflicts fewer than 2 percent of whites, but more than half the African
> population. In rural areas and former homelands two-thirds of all
> Africans are poor.'

The Report goes further to emphasise that

> 'The cumulative effect of such inequity carries through life. Per capita,
> whites earn 9.5 times the income of blacks and live, on average, 11.5
> years longer.'

To curb this trend, an approach that addresses sustainable poverty reduction
through equitable growth and redistribution is essential (World Bank 1994:1–2). In
this respect, the World Bank Report recommends a strategy for redistributive
growth that entails the accomplishment of three mutually reinforcing goals (World
Bank 1994:3):

☐   ensure an equitable pattern of growth, specifically more labour demanding
pattern;

☐   try to achieve a more equitable distribution of assets, services and access to
markets; and

☐   maintain macro-economic stability.

In addition, activist measures envisaged in the RDP to broaden economic participation must be encouraged. In this regard, the following have been identified as
primary investment areas (World Bank 1994:3):

☐   Investing in people: by improving the quality of life and providing greater
opportunities for self-development by ensuring access to services such as

education, health and employment. These would contribute significantly to the rate of growth.

☐ Investing in cities: cities are part of the urban sector and, as such, are the hubs of economic growth and development. Well-functioning and productive cities will be critical in renewing urban growth and promoting equity and contributing to national growth.

☐ Investing in private enterprise: broadening this base to include smaller agricultural and industrial enterprises is necessary. The development of black entrepreneurship, in this field, is seen as a positive endeavour. The measures will ensure equity and accelerate a shift towards a more labour demanding and efficient pattern of growth.

Restructured local authorities, as core institutions, have the potential to provide a strong foundation for future economic growth and development. They are expected to change the face of South African society and provide acceptable standards of living for all.

4.3 Social environment

In South Africa, apartheid severely damaged the nature and fabric of the social environment. The policies of separation created racial division, psychological complexities, mutual distrust, anxieties and cultural intolerance. This situation must be decisively addressed by local government. Of particular importance to the social environment is the social system that has distinctive characteristics and interrelates with stable patterns of the social order (Anderson & Carter 1978:10).

A social system could be a family, interest group organisation, neighbourhood, society or cultural group, with the individual being the primary unit of all social systems (Anderson & Carter 1978:10). The object of local government is to ensure that the social environment is always worthy of the human being. The integration of society is essential to foster South African nationalism and mutual respect among race groups. There is urgent need to understand the diverse cultures, traditions and customs of South Africa's heterogenous society. The local authority must act as facilitator and coordinator in bringing about greater interaction between communities. It should direct its expenditure to this end by providing (Rademan 1987:16):

☐ energy: this relates to resources such as finance, personnel moral support, recognition and information; and

☐ organisational arrangements: necessary for bringing organisations and groups together, giving role perceptions and definitions, and providing basic elements of communication and feedback.

Moreover, this environment lends itself to encourage community participation and self-help in civic matters. It serves as an important locus for nation building. The local authority must coordinate and, if necessary, direct such activities so that a stable, tolerant and well-balanced society evolves.

4.4 Governmental relations, decentralisation and autonomy

These three concepts are closely related and will have considerable impact on local government financing options in South Africa. Governmental relations are dependant on the nature of the constitutional system. South Africa has a three-tier unitary system of government. The system is characterised by a centralised authority and territorial integration, with the central government vested with constitutional authority (Gildenhuys 1993:181). The establishment of various governmental authorities at different tiers within a unitary state is aimed at dividing labour, allocating and executing functions with the greatest efficiency and effectiveness (Gildenhuys 1993:183).

The nature and scope of governmental relations in South Africa are not specifically stated, but implied, in many provisions of the interim constitution. Sections 126(3) and (4) stipulate that an Act of parliament shall prevail over a provincial law only to the extent it impacts on national interests and provided it is applied uniformly in all parts of the Republic. In terms of section 175(4), a local government may legislate only if such laws are consistent with Acts passed by parliament or the laws of a province.

Evidently, provincial and local government legislation is subject to laws passed by parliament. Therefore, parliament is the supreme body applying the doctrine of residual authority (Gildenhuys 1993:182). Within this context, central government dictates the financial relations between provincial and local authorities based on the amount allocated to these subordinate tiers of government. Although the National Party government, before the transitional era, had committed itself to decentralisation, and more especially to the devolution of power to local authorities, in practice this did not materialise.

Christianson (1993:13) submits that local government in South Africa is extremely weak, has been given minimal political authority from the centre, no constitutional status and extremely restricted powers and functions. Support for 'strong' local government is evidently an international trend because plural policies and market-based economics have generated a move away from highly centralised governments (Christianson 1993:4).

Moreover, there is a growing consensus over the importance of decentralisation among development policy networks. Croeser (1992:14) strongly supports this perception defining devolution as

> 'creating or strengthening financially or legally — of sub-national units of government, the autonomy of which are substantially outside the direct control of the central government. Under devolution, local units of government are autonomous and independent and their legal status makes them separate or distinct from central government. Central authorities exercise only indirect supervisory control over such units.'

Croeser (1992:14) further argues that devolution has many advantages for South African local authorities and includes, *inter alia*, the following:

☐   decisions on public services are brought closer to affected communities and can therefore improve the effectiveness of government delivering those services demanded by specific communities;

☐   community involvement in public service delivery could be encouraged and should contribute to a greater willingness by the community to contribute financially and otherwise to local projects since it is an integral part of the decision-making process; and

☐   owing to the scarcity of resources, efficiency and effectiveness of public services could be enhanced through devolution, involvement, reporting and proper accountability.

Within the context of a development focus to local government objectives, redistribution can still be maintained in a decentralised structure (Croeser 1992:14). Rhyneveld (1992:28), on the other hand, contends that redistribution should be coordinated on a national basis because the geographic distribution of resources and needs in South Africa are so out of balance that centralised control is essential.

Many see the dominance of a development vision as one that, of necessity, must be centrally driven. Given the enormity of deficiencies and inequities perpetrated during the apartheid era, central decision making is seen as the key to rapid socio-economic development, a coordinated planning of services, controls of scarce resources, ensuring provincial/local equality, resolving implementation problems and centrally providing funds (Mawhood 1983:6; Smith 1985:194 in Christianson 1993:4). Moreover, an added motive to centralisation in South Africa, racked by racial intolerance and misunderstanding, is the desire to encourage nation building. It is possible that, between these two extremes, there is a balanced and acceptable option. Croeser (1992:14) cautions that a pragmatic approach for South Africa is one including both elements of devolution and centralisation.

Autonomy, an important aspect of local government relations, implies the degree to which authorities can decide and determine their own priorities within the expenditure, taxation and borrowing powers assigned to them by the constitution (Croeser 1992:15). In theory, maximum fiscal autonomy implies that each level of government could probably draw on enough of its own revenue sources to finance all services without financial assistance from another level of government (Croeser 1992:5). In practice, however, Croeser (1992:15) argues this would not be possible because of vertical and horizontal inequities in intergovernmental fiscal relations and the overriding need for policy and service coordination between the different tiers of government. To increase the autonomy of South African local government, devolving more taxes to this tier of authority is necessary. However, because of vertical and horizontal disparities, and also the need for coordination, fiscal transfers will remain an important part of the financing of lower levels of government (Croeser 1992:15).

Cloete (1994:64) aptly concludes that the main issue in future will probably be the degree of autonomy local government obtains from central government. He further argues that intergovernmental conflict of this nature is part of a normal, worldwide trend.

4.5 Administrative and management capacity

This raises an important concern as to the calibre and ability of councillors and officials in local authorities. Concerning black local authorities, Christianson (1993:12) argues that their poor financial position, coupled to a boycott tradition that has created strong, sometimes violent, pressures against the system, has resulted in a situation in which black local authorities lack both resources and personnel to effectively and efficiently administer and manage their areas of jurisdiction. Although there have been secondments from provinces, there have always been massive personnel inadequacies in black local government (Christianson 1993:12).

With the metropolitan system being a prominent feature of the new local government restructuring, it is expected that white officials would play a leading role in its administration and management. A legitimate concern in this regard is that one assumes that previous white local authority officials could probably administer townships effectively whose problems, needs and political dynamics are very different to those of white local authority areas (Christianson 1993:13).

In the present situation there is a lack of trained black personnel who could be employed in new local government structures. It is important that urgent attention be given to the training and development of a well-qualified corps of local government personnel in, *inter alia*, financial and human resources management. Such personnel must be trained in the theory and practice of local government administration and management. An action-oriented learning approach that stimulates creative and critical thinking should be encouraged. This should be the priority of universities, management training institutes, schools of local government, technikons and the Local Government Training Board. A comprehensive and coordinated action plan must be determined by these teaching and training institutions in consultation with other stakeholders such as the local authorities, civic, and political bodies and other interested parties such as the Institute for Municipal Treasurers and Accountants (IMTA). The impact of this endeavour on the efficiency and efficacy on the future administration and management of local government cannot be overemphasised.

4.6 The role of the Financial and Fiscal Commission (FFC)

This commission was established in terms of chapter 12, section 198 of the Constitution Act. It is an advisory body charged with rendering advice and making recommendations on the following:

- [ ] financial and fiscal policies;
- [ ] equitable financial and fiscal allocation to national, provincial and local governments;
- [ ] potential sources of revenue which provincial governments intend to levy;
- [ ] norms for the raising of loans by local and provincial governments; and
- [ ] the criteria for allocating financial and fiscal resources.

The main objective of the FFC is ensuring fairness and efficiency in fiscal relations between governments. Morobe (1995:14), chairperson of the FFC, submits that among other things, the FFC will look at matters of process, particularly in terms of how role players participate/interact within the evolving system. Evidently, the FFC will play a leading role in reviewing the sources of local government financing in South Africa, to develop a financing system appropriate to the needs of South African local authorities.

5   CURRENT AND FUTURE SOURCES OF LOCAL GOVERNMENT FINANCING

In most developing countries, local government must strive to meet the costs of developing and sustaining urban facilities and services. This task is made difficult by an increasing population and rising inflation that place enormous demands on local resources. Revenue must cover both capital investment and recurrent expenditures, and also service debts. There is therefore a continuous need to ensure that revenue growth is in line with expansion of services and rising costs (McMaster 1991:223).

In South Africa, the determination of an economic local government tax base that in the long term would ensure financial self-sufficiency of local authorities, is a worthy ideal for which to strive. However, this is easier said than done. The policy of separate development has created myriad problems, the most pressing being the need to address the imbalances of the past and to restructure local government to play a meaningful role in sustainable development. The debate on current and future sources of financing for local government is taking place against a backdrop of the important processes outlined below (Rhyneveld 1995:1):

☐   the demarcation process resulted in white and black local authorities amalgamating to ensure uniform and acceptable standards of local government services in their areas;

☐   constitutional change has focused on decentralisation, resulting in provincial governments with elaborate powers and functions being established, and independent institutions such as the FFC to provide inputs and advice on financial and related matters;

☐   the GNU has focused on the RDP and spending is being directed more specifically towards providing basic local government services such as electricity, water, sanitation and refusal removal. This implies that most government spending will be at the local level;

☐   the worldwide trend in exploring new and dynamic ways of rendering local government services, such as the entrepreneurial spirit advocated by Americans Osborn & Gaebler, is now impacting on South Africa; and

☐   financing options at this stage of the transition are fluid and opportunities abound for innovative and creative strategies in this respect.

The assignment of revenue in South Africa is currently as follows:

☐   central government receives the bulk of its revenue from value-added tax (VAT), personal income tax (PIT) and corporate income tax (CIT). Additional sources include customs duty, excise taxes and the fuel levy.

□ provincial governments' sources of revenue include betting and totalisation taxes, taxes on vehicles, and user charges for various services, including health.
□ local government revenue sources comprise RSC and JSB levies (payroll and turnover taxes); property taxes, consumer tariffs, user charges, fees and rents.

With the present restructuring and reallocation of functions to different tiers of authority, and the focus on the decentralisation and devolution of power, it is expected that revenue assignments will be reviewed.

To ensure maximum use of current (as well as determining and raising new) sources of revenue, it is important to bear in mind the basic principles of a good tax system, as espoused by Adam Smith. These are equality, certainty, convenience and economy (Stapelberg & Steyn 1988:332–333). Moreover, within the South African context, one must consider the question of affordability, given that many South African citizens are poor and cannot afford to pay on the quid pro quo principle.

5.1 Current sources of financing

Current sources of local government revenue are inadequate to meet the extensive service provisions set out in the RDP. This will become apparent in the following discussion on financing instruments used by white and black local authorities.

5.1.1 Property tax

Property tax, or assessment rates, is an important source of revenue for South African local authorities. The tax is on land and/or buildings and is imposed on all types of property including commercial, industrial, institutional and residential. The basis for taxing real property is its capital value, determined by a valuation process. Gildenhuys (1993:290) submits that the valuation procedure must establish a basis for fair distribution of the tax burden and be the heart of the real property tax system. The tariff in any one locality, therefore, is normally a uniform percentage, although it may differentiate between different property types, for example, the rates may be higher in industrial or commercial than residential properties. Property valuation is based as follows (McMaster 1991:26):

□ Annual rental values, that is, the potential income to the owner from letting a property (whether it is actually rented or not);
□ Capital improved site values, that is, the potential market sale price of the land or the land plus its improvements (meaning the buildings, infrastructure, and amenities developed on the land); and
□ Unimproved site values, that is, the potential market sale price of the land as if it were vacant, disregarding any actual development on it.

In South Africa, the property tax is a valuable source of revenue, primarily used by white local authorities to provide for most of their general services. The well-developed and clearly demarcated residential and industrial areas in white local authority areas lend themselves to this form of taxation. Industrial and commercial properties are situated mainly in white local authority areas and are charged higher assessment rates than residential properties. Stewart (1991:18) states that in 1988/89

property taxes generated by commerce and industry provided white local auth- *(contra-diction!)*
orities with an income of R870 million and constituted 53% of all property taxes
collected from non-governmental agencies. Therefore, this tax is obviously an
important source of revenue for white local authorities.

In contrast, apartheid policies have concentrated lower income households into *administrative crisis for local gov't finance*
black townships with little or no industrial and commercial sectors to support
growth and development (World Bank Report 12596 SA:6). Moreover, these regulations have deprived the black community of land ownership and housing and
have thus seriously affected the growth of the property tax system (World Bank
Report 12596 SA:6). Consequently, a lack of land ownership rights has prevented
the black community from using land and housing as a form of collateral to generate
a growing economy and a taxable income base (World Bank Report 12596 SA:6).

Clearly, property tax cannot be stopped as a financing source for local govern- *connect to Project Liquidity*
ment, especially as they are easily assignable to local authorities, have been used
for some time and mechanisms for its valuation, collection and monitoring have
been in place in many local authorities throughout the country. As a local tax, it
serves the cause of autonomy for local government and also enhances accountability. With the process of restructuring and unifying black and white local
authorities, extending this form of taxation even further is possible. There is a need
to find an uncomplicated model for valuation and assessment of property using
modern information technology. Moreover, the system should be sufficiently
flexible to allow for review and rebate, and for waivers under special circumstances.

Masakhane is thus central to process of legitimation

5.1.2 Service charges

In this category, the public usually pays for such services by the way of user charges,
consumer tariffs, nominal levies and sundry revenues. These three types of taxes
are closely related, but distinguishable from each other (Gildenhuys 1993:362–387):

☐ User charges: These amounts are charged for using public services. The service
   is not exhausted but available to other users for a prescribed charge. User
   charges cover services of a quasi collective nature and include fire protection,
   health, environmental, educational and preventive health services.
☐ Consumer tariffs: This tax differs from user charges to the extent that consumer
   tariffs are paid for public goods that must be replenished as consumption
   continues. The primary objective of consumer tariffs is that they should yield
   adequate revenue to cover the costs of supplying such services to consumers.
   Consumer tariffs are charged for water, sewerage and electricity. Often these
   services are referred to as public utilities or public trading services.
☐ Nominal levies: often nominal levies do not recover the cost of services, but are
   necessary as they serve to relieve the tax burden by recovering part of the cost
   from the consumer. Nominal levies are charged for services rendered sporadi-
   cally, on special request, or for a privilege or a right granted to an individual
   or a business enterprise. At the local government level, this group of levies
   includes trading licences, dog licences, building plan fees and searching fees.
☐ Sundry revenues: This group is difficult to classify as it possesses characteristics
   of one or more of the previously mentioned revenue sources. In the main, these
   revenues are determined randomly, without any rational basis. Examples of

sundry revenues include, *inter alia*, public library membership fees, rent for the lease of sporting facilities, and registration fees. Other sources of sundry revenue are fines and forfeitures. Traffic fines often yield considerable revenue for local government and are sometimes used to cover the full cost of the traffic control function.

In this group of taxes the discussion will focus primarily on consumer tariffs as they are considered the most substantial sources of revenue. Consumer tariffs for services such as electricity and water represent an important source of revenue for white local authorities. Many of these local authorities have obtained exclusive rights to distribute electricity and water through their own distribution networks (World Bank Report 12596 SA:8). It is estimated there are approximately seven hundred distribution utilities at the local government level in South Africa. These distribution utilities make large volume purchases of water and electricity that they then supply, at a profit, to users in the local government boundaries (World Bank Report 12596 SA:8).

Consumers of electricity pay the full tariff, covering capital, operating and maintenance costs. The high level of taxation of the utilities, especially electricity and water, has generated a surplus in the trading account of major white local authorities. These surplus revenues are often used to cross-subsidise other revenues and are also used to provide a rebate on property tax. In large white local authorities, property tax is set residually only after the local authorities have determined the level of surplus to be derived from their utility services (World Bank Report 12596 SA:9).

The case of black local authorities is markedly different. Few black townships had electricity until the late 1980s, and water provision was not measured. Therefore, consumer tariffs were not a viable source of income. Most businesses were zoned into white local authorities forcing blacks to work and consume goods and services in these areas. By zoning businesses within white local authorities' jurisdiction, blacks were forced to work and consume goods and services in white local authority areas, thus indirectly financing part of the cross-subsidisation made to white residents (World Bank Report 12596 SA:10). This has been a serious source of tension in the politics of local government.

The consumer tariffs evidently provide substantial revenue for local authorities and they would expect them to continue. Within the process of amalgamation, service provisions would be extended, and the tariff tax base widened. Consumer tariffs encourage efficient and prudent use, since consumers would be expected to pay according to consumption. There is also an appreciation of the relationship between cost and standards of services delivered. Rhyneveld (1995:9) contends that a progressive consumption tariff, with prices rising per unit as consumption increases, is a financing option being considered. In the main, the advantages are that there will be a redistributive cross-subsidisation within the service of small consumers by large-volume users. Moreover, poor consumers can reduce their service charges by reducing consumption to basic need levels (Rhyneveld 1995:9). Caution should be exercised in structuring consumer tariffs to ensure that the burden of cross-subsidisation is appropriately spread over many consumers to avoid high prices being borne by a few volume consumers (Rhyneveld 1995:9).

5.1.3 Loans

Although loans are not really a source of revenue they, nevertheless, are the means to obtain funds for major capital programmes. Loans could be raised externally from capital markets and the central government, or internally from trust funds or from capital development or revolving funds. Loans raised with the central government are lent at subsidised rates of interest and are often called 'soft loans'. The government obtains its funds from taxes but has access to international financial markets as well. Since borrowing implies repayment of capital plus interest, loans from central government are made for priority projects justified by local authorities. In South Africa, loans could be obtained for local government capital projects from the Development Bank of South Africa (DBSA), South African Housing Trust (SAHT) and the Independent Development Trust (IDT).

Local government must borrow circumspectly. Greater autonomy to local tiers may provide easy access to the loan markets as a mark of their independence. The principle is to ensure that such actions are done within a regulatory framework and without compromising macro-economic policies of the state. Moreover, such policy guidelines will ensure that capital loan financiers or local governments do not implicitly assume that central or regional authorities will ultimately 'bank guarantee' all local government borrowing (World Bank Report 12596 SA:3).

5.1.4 Regional Services Councils' (RSCs) and Joint Services Boards' (JSBs) levies

The RSCs and JSBs were established from 1987 to finance infrastructural development in areas of need and provide certain collective functions on a subregional basis (Rhyneveld 1995:3). These bodies had representatives from both black and white local authorities according to the value of services consumed. To finance their services, the RSCs and JSBs raised revenue through two levies, viz the regional levy based on a percentage of the wage bill; and a regional establishment levy, based on a percentage of turnover.

From 1993/4 these organisations received one cent for every litre of fuel and diesel sold in their areas, to be used primarily for financing commuter subsidies.

The purpose of RSC and JSB levies was to finance the establishment, improvement and maintenance of infrastructural services and facilities. However, in some areas, these levies have been used to meet financial crises being experienced by black local authorities. For example, in 1993/4, the Central Witwatersrand RSC allocated R144,2 million to finance the current deficit of black local authorities in its area. Other RSCs have also followed this trend.

Although RSCs and JSBs are important sources of revenue for local authorities, there are problems with administration and there is scope for evasion. These problems are expected to increase if levies are raised. Nevertheless, these levies, in some form or other, will continue to be a source of financing for local government in the future.

5.1.5 Subsidies, grants-in-aid and revenue sharing

Intergovernmental relations are significant to local government financing. South African local authorities favour devolution of power so they can enjoy a greater degree of autonomy and independence. Subsidies, grants-in-aid and revenue sharing are provided by other tiers of government and serve as important sources of intergovernmental financing.

5.1.5.1 Subsidies

In most countries, subsidies from higher to lower tiers of authorities are necessary for advancing national, regional and local quality of life objectives. Subsidies may originate either from central government or through the provincial authorities. Subsidies are payments made to local authorities to cover services rendered by the local authorities on behalf of both central and provincial government. There is no reason to suggest that this method of financing will not continue. In fact, given the amalgamation process and the number of deficiencies in the provision of basic services, there is strong justification for subsidy payments. However, local authorities must ensure maximum use of such subsidies and not increase the tax pressure on central and provincial tiers of authority by becoming reliant on subsidies as a source of financing.

5.1.5.2 Grants-in-aid

Grants-in-aid are a form of assistance given to local authorities experiencing problems in meeting their obligations. Grants-in-aid can be grouped as follows:

☐ categorical grants — where money is provided for a specific programme, activity or facility, eg water provisioning;
☐ block grants — where money is provided for a number of projects, activities, etc with spending conditions stated in broad terms only; or
☐ formula grants — where the amount is calculated according to a predetermined formula without any spending conditions being prescribed.

Grants-in-aid, as a source of finance, are expected to continue on a selective, priority basis.

5.1.5.3 Revenue sharing

Gildenhuys (1993:197) explains that

> 'Revenue sharing means that a specific government level or a specific government institution has the authority to exploit a specific tax or revenue source and then distribute the yield according to a predetermined formula against various governmental levels vertically or horizontally amongst governments at the same level'.

Revenue sharing could take two forms, vertical or horizontal. Vertical revenue sharing is between different tiers of authority within a state. Grants-in-aid and subsidies are examples of vertical revenue sharing sources. Croeser (1992:21) argues that revenue sharing should not be seen as a grant by central government but as revenue to which lower tiers of government are entitled and which is allocated at the central level on their behalf.

Horizontal revenue sharing means sharing of revenue between government on the same tier of authority (Gildenhuys 1993:197). Croeser (1992:21) contends that horizontal redistribution of revenue by revenue sharing should be undertaken on the basis of the fiscal capacity of different authorities, based on a formula that considers, *inter alia*, factors such as population density, per capita income, own revenue capacity and cost disparities. In this regard, obtaining reliable data to decide realistic formulas is essential.

Within the restructured local government environment, it is expected that both vertical and horizontal revenue sharing will be maintained to ensure continuity of services and uniform development.

5.1.6 Savings and maximum revenue collections

In the Report of the Committee of Inquiry into the Finances of Local Authorities in South Africa (the Browne Committee) it was suggested that savings on expenditure could be an important source of revenue to local authorities. However, this can only be maintained with a high degree of cost-efficiency and effectiveness. Local authorities in South Africa do not have a positive record in this respect and need to address the matter decisively.

Maximum collection of all moneys due to a local authority is quite clearly an equally important source of revenue. The culture of non-payment by black communities was a response to apartheid at the local level, to the unfair distribution of resources and to the fragmentation of towns and cities (Kroukamp 1995:190). Rapiti (1995:14) argues that if non-payment persists it could lead to anarchy and a breakdown of local government. Although the Masakhane Campaign is underway to promote payment for services, much more has to be done to reverse the culture of non-payment. According to Ndlovu (1995:6) if the policy on non-payment is to be effectively countered, the following are essential:

□   adequate legislative support measures;
□   capacity and commitment of the administrator to carry out council policy decisions;
□   unwavering support of the administration by policy makers at local and national levels; and
□   a culture of civil responsibility needs to be engendered.

Moreover, consideration should be given to a nationwide publicity campaign emphasising the need for, *inter alia* (Kroukamp 1995:197–199):

□   dialogue and communication;
□   public education; and
□   determining a local government flat-rate for services rendered in the short term.

If local government is to be viable and provide for sustainable development, payment for services is imperative.

5.2 New sources of financing

There is considerable scope for reviewing current sources of finance at the different levels of government and to reallocate them on sound principles of taxation. In the evidence submitted to the Committee of Inquiry into Finances of Local Government in South Africa (1980:65) reference was made to the following additional sources of revenue for local government:

☐ A review of motor vehicle licence income: this should be devolved to local authorities, since 90% of all motor vehicles were owned by persons living in the urban sector.

☐ A local fuel tax: on visitors to urban areas and on large commercial vehicles as a contribution towards defraying expenses on traffic control and road construction.

Currently, a levy of 1 cent per litre on diesel and fuel has been allocated to RSCs and JSBs. There is clearly scope for this tax to be increased for local government development. Fuel tax is a buoyant source, with a wide incidence and impact, allowing for the enhancement of accountability (Rhyneveld 1995:11).

☐ Service levies based on direct quid pro quo — those who derive benefit from a service rendered should pay the price of the service. This may be difficult, especially in respect of citizens who might require services but are unable to afford them.

☐ Tourist tax has the potential to bring additional income from hotels, boarding houses, holiday flats and camping grounds. However, local government investment and support for tourism are essential to make it a success. Widespread publicity and marketing must be undertaken to attract tourists.

Rhyneveld (1995:11) recommends fixed property transfer taxes and a piggyback personal income tax. The fixed property transfer tax is considered a suitable source of additional revenue. Within a local authority mechanisms are already in place for registering transfers and administering it would therefore be easy. The piggyback personal income tax, according to Rhyneveld (1995:11), is the most significant source of potential revenue for local government, except that less than 20% of the country's voting population pays income tax.

This list of proposed additional revenue sources is not exhaustive. McMaster (1987:28–29) provides a series of local government sources of financing from an international perspective. These are, *inter alia*, assignment of national income tax based on a percentage of tax collected within the local authority; a tax on professions such as, teaching, engineering, doctoring, and lecturing. One could include in this category a tax on the strongly debateable vice, prostitution. Another tax could be levied on the movement of goods between different local authorities. It is collected at tax stations on the borders of local authorities.

Many taxes can be imposed at local government level in South Africa. They must, however, be suited to the local government environment peculiar to South Africa. Therefore, any future sources of financing must be thoroughly researched before being implemented.

6 CONCLUSION

This chapter provided an overview of local government financing pertinent to the South African environment. It focused on important issues in local government financing. The financing of local government will, ultimately, be determined by events currently unfolding including, *inter alia*, the demarcation of areas, the nature and scope of local government functions, the degree of decentralisation and autonomy, and the viability of new local government structures. Moreover, there is a need for macro economic and fiscal coordination to ensure the stable growth and development of South African local authorities.

7 REFERENCES

Anderson RE & I Carter. 1978. *Human Behaviour in the Social Science Environment.* Chicago: Aldine.

Aronson JR. 1985. *Public Finance.* New York: McGraw-Hill Inc.

Bhambhri CP. 1992–93. *Public Administration (Theory and Practice).* Meerut City: Jai Prakash Nath & Company.

Christianson D. 1993. *Strong Local Government in South Africa: Exploring the Options.* Johannesburg: The Urban Foundation.

Cloete F. 1994. Local government restructuring. *Politikon.* Vol 21 no 1 June.

Cloete JJN. 1981. *Administration of Health Services.* Pretoria: JL van Schaik.

Croeser G. 1992. *Financing of Local Government.* Paper presented at the Conference on Critical Aspects of Local Government in a Post-apartheid South Africa, University of Durban-Westville, 16–17 September.

Evans S. 1992. Requirements for financially viable local authorities. *SAIPA Journal of Public Administration.* Vol 27 no 4 December.

Gardner WD. 1978. *Government Finance: National, State and Local.* Englewood Cliffs, New Jersey: Prentice Hall Inc.

Gildenhuys JSH. 1989. *Owerheidsfinansies.* Kenwyn: Juta & Co Ltd.

Gildenhuys JSH. 1993. *Public Financial Management.* Pretoria: JL van Schaik.

Kroukamp H. 1995. *The Culture of Non-payment of Services as a Constraint in Financial Policy Management for Local Authorities in South Africa.*

Marshall AH. 1974. *Financial Management in Local Government.* London: George Allen & Unwin.

McMaster J. 1991. *Urban Financial Management: A Training Manual.* Washington DC: The World Bank.

Ndlovu MN. 1995. *The Experience of Bulawayo in Local Government Finance and Service Delivery.* Paper presented at an IDASA Conference, Port Elizabeth, 23–24 February.

Nkuhlu W. 1993. Affirmative action for South Africa in transition: from theory to practice. In Adams C (ed) *Affirmative Action in a Democratic South Africa.* Kenwyn: Juta & Co Ltd.

Rademan DJ. 1987. *Financing of Municipal and Urban Councils in Bophuthatswana.* Mmabatho.

Rapiti L. 1995. Start paying rent. *The Sowetan.* 8 March.

Republic of South Africa. 1980. Report of the Committee of Inquiry into Financing of Local Authorities in South Africa.

Rosen HS. 1988. *Public Finance*. Illinois: Irwin.

Stapelberg NH & FG Steyn. 1988. *Economics: An Introductory Study*. NHS Publishers.

Stewart J. 1991. The business of sharing. *Finance Weekly*. 27 September, 121, 18.

Stiglitz JE. 1988. *Economics of the Public Sector*. New York: WW Norton & Company.

Thompson C. 1993. Legislating affirmative action: employment equity and lessons from developed and developing countries. In Adams C (ed) *Affirmative Action in a Democratic South Africa*. Kenwyn: Juta & Co Ltd.

Van Rhyneveld P. 1992. *Decentralisation and the Financing of Local Government*. Paper presented at the Conference on Critical Aspects of Local Government Administration in a Post-apartheid South Africa, University of Durban-Westville, 16–17 September.

Van Rhyneveld P. 1995. *Current and Future Sources of Finance for Local Government*. Paper presented at Inlogov Conference on Financing Democratic Local Government, 10–11 March.

Van Straaten FP. 1985. Munisipale begrotings. In Kotze HJN et al *Teorie en Praktyk van Munisipale Regering en Administrasie*. Bloemfontein: PJ de Villiers Akademiese Boekhandel.

World Bank. 1994. *Financing the Metropolitan Areas of South Africa*. Report no 12596 SA.

World Bank 1994. *Reducing Poverty in South Africa: Options for Equitable and Sustainable Growth*.

— CHAPTER 12 —

Local Economic Development: Reflections on the International Experience and Some Lessons for the Reconstruction of South Africa's Cities

F Khan

1 INTRODUCTION

All over the world, cities are the centres of innovation, growth, dynamism and, ultimately, the linchpins for pervasive modernisation and development. Cities, argues Harris (1990a), are the engines of growth and development producing a unique bundle of goods and services. The specific composition of the bundle in these spatial configurations varies, but in sum they constitute the main and dynamic part of the national economy. The economic success of countries and regions is thus inextricably bound to the productivity and competitiveness of their cities and towns (Cohen 1990; Heymans 1995).

Despite this broad consensus, controversy rages as to how improvements in city efficiency and productivity can be reconciled with the broad aims of social justice, sustainability and participation (Cheema 1993). Seductive orthodoxy posits that the path to prosperity lies in 'simplification, deregulation and privatisation' (Gilbert 1992:447). Localities and cities, according to this view, are locked in an interminable 'bidding war', tirelessly attempting to attract hypermobile capital by providing as many preconditions as possible for unbridled profit maximisation (Beauregard 1989). Underpinned by a development agenda that privileges urban efficiency, cost recovery and privatisation, the focus in this approach is on ensuring that cities are efficient sites of production. Thus government should assume the role of *facilitator/ enabler*, striving to enhance city efficiency through managerial innovation; public–private partnerships; deregulation; decentralisation; intergovernmental reorganisation; and fiscal rationalisation (see World Bank 1991).

Enlightened policy makers challenge this orthodox conception, arguing instead for city governments to 'bet on the basics' (Markusen & Carlson 1989), targeting existing heavy industry for economic development efforts.

'This brand of development agenda rejects the sunrise industry route because it is not believed that heartland economies will be successful candidates for such activities or that the sunrise jobs created will be sufficient in number and of an appropriate kind to solve the unemployment problem. In addition, it rejects the notion that the culprits are uncompetitive cost structures. It points instead to localities' unique industrial histories, structure, product and process designs, and fates under alternative macroeconomic policy regimes. In such plans, greater emphasis is given to retention and expansion strategies, including governmental aid for technology improvement, marketing, management and ownership changeovers, and region-wide organising around national economic policy' (Markusen & Carlson 1989:50).

Betting on the basics requires new socio-institutional modes of regulation, including an active and innovative role for the public sector (Clavel & Kleniewski 1990; Porter 1990; Wade 1990; Murray 1992; Best 1993; Geddes 1994). This entails the construction of new state–market relations centred around *interventionist corporatism* wherein local governments and political parties assume the role of social leader and reformer by organising collaboration, orchestrating consensus, limiting uncertainty, avoiding dislocative losses for important agents and defining directions of expansion (Zeitlin 1989; Grahl & Teague 1989; Scott 1992; Vonk 1989; Totterdill 1989; Logan & Swanstrom 1990).

Whether the development agenda is approached from the efficiency or equity perspective, or both, it is apparent that progress towards either/both objective/s must necessarily include increased understanding and support for the role of policy and action at the city level (Marshall 1989). In this context, policy makers in South Africa have a window of opportunity for policy influence, before spatial and economic patterns become fixed as established forms of uneven development. On the eve of local government elections in South Africa, a unique opportunity exists to investigate and embark on new creative ways of operating and thinking about local economic development (LED). The challenge is to develop understandings and methods for planning and management that neither blindly follow the market nor naively seek to structure it (Healey 1992). Regional and local authorities must be ready not simply to cope with, but to respond with vigour and imagination to decisions made by firms with markets or headquarters outside the boundaries of the nation as well as the region (Rodwin 1991).

Engineering 'appropriate' LED policies and strategies has only recently captured the attention of the major stakeholders. The South African National Civic Organisation (SANCO) and the Reconstruction and Development Programme Office (1995) have released weighty and thoughtful documents in this regard. The common thread running through both documents is the rather 'unsophisticated' view that LED is a practical and material extension of the RDP. While the scope of the SANCO and RDP (1995) documents vary quite dramatically, both lack a clear perspective of how LED initiatives will be affected by and effect changes in our conservative macro-economic policy regime. It is no small wonder, therefore, that both documents pay considerable attention to 'inoffensive' small business support and incremental redistribution of tax revenues through improved public services for the poor; ie the economic low road. These themes will be discussed in the final section.

Against the backdrop of a novel combination of monetary orthodoxy, fiscal restraint and supposedly 'progressive social policy' (Craine 1995:23),[1] a crucial question for national policy makers and LED experts is whether South Africa can generate the economic growth and employment opportunities for the vast majority in an age of fundamental changes in the material logic of production; ie the appearance of new core technologies, the widespread diffusion of advanced technological capabilities, dramatic convulsions in long-standing patterns of international competition, global economic restructuring, and the complexity and pace of technological change (Gordon 1994). Addressing the Seventh National Conference of the Institute of Personnel Management, the former deputy finance minister, Alec Erwin, stated that the challenge for South Africa was not just to be export competitive, but to hold back the de-industrialisation tide.[2]

The need to address the imperatives of employment creation has been central to several programmes and proposals for rethinking national economic development planning in the new post-apartheid South Africa (see Rogerson 1995). Underscoring much of this thinking is a recognition of the declining absorptive capacity of the formal economy, the persistent upward trajectory of national unemployment and urban distress. The broad geography of economic development suggests that cities have performed very poorly. Although the metropolitan areas generate 80% of the GDP and accommodate more than 60% of the population (Turok 1994:244), recent research shows that in almost every sector the performance of the cities was worse that of the country. This decline cannot be attributed solely to the country's economic malaise.

> 'Manufacturing employment in the Central Witwatersrand decreased at a remarkable rate of 4.47 per cent per annum (compound) between 1980 and 1991. The annual rates of decline in the PWV as whole, Durban, and Cape Town were less, at 2.88 per cent, 2.03 per cent and 1.59 per cent respectively. By 1991 manufacturing employment in the Central Witwatersrand was no more than 60.5 per cent of its 1980 level; in the PWV, 72.5 per cent; in Durban, 79.8 per cent; and in Cape Town 83 per cent. The decline of manufacturing in the cities is all the more striking when contrasted with the country as a whole where employment in manufacturing rose slightly from 1.46 million to 1.49 million, over the period' (Tomlinson 1993:336).

As South Africa's largest employer, resuscitating this declining manufacturing sector is viewed by many as the only serious route to a high-productivity, high-wage economy with low levels of income inequality. Studies of the East Asian industrialisation miracle demonstrate this quite clearly (see Henderson 1993).

Yet, there are significant problems in this regard. South African industry is characterised by its high capital intensity, low productivity, high concentrations of ownership and control, inability to establish a secure foothold in export markets, continued dependence on capital and technology imports, and its failure to generate a significant volume of employment opportunities. South Africa ranks poorly in industrial competitiveness. According to the findings of the Global Futures

Project[3] conducted under the auspices of the Boston University Manufacturing Roundtable, local industries fail to implement new techniques and suffer from a lack of discipline top-to-bottom, often starting an approach and backing off after difficulties arise at the lower corporate echelons. Distribution and delivery problems are endemic and management culture is autocratic. The Monitor Report,[4] inspired by the works of Michael Porter, rates South African industry as 'weak' and 'poor' on most of the determinants of modern competitiveness; ie clustering, strategic capability, strong and integrated skill bases, inter-firm rivalry and cooperation, and capable bureaucracies.

All, however, is not bleak. The negotiated settlement is daily proving that the 'democratic impulse towards socio-economic transformation has hardly been fully tamed' (Saul 1994:32) and, as such, the room for progressive manoeuvres may have widened as other avenues close. South Africa has considerable infrastructural and manufacturing capacity; a well-developed financial sector; forums for structured, continuous engagement of labour in corporate decision making and economic policy formulation. The multilayered, institutionalised negotiation process between classes created through NEDLAC, workplace forums and the industry wide councils in the new Labour Relations Bill represents for Webster (1995) a 'creative challenge to the global agenda of neo-liberalism'[5] (see Hyslop 1994; Nattrass & Seekings[6] 1995 for an alternative perspective). The question then becomes one of how to develop, upgrade and reconfigure national, regional and local advantages and strengths in order to improve our global competitiveness in a way that is economically viable, politically feasible and socially responsible.

The objective in this chapter is to present some preliminary findings on LED, and to highlight the shortcomings of the present debate. The paper is divided into three sections. The first section traces some international developments with particular reference to the strategic and structural reorientation of the capitalist state in the era of global restructuring. The next part briefly examines the applicability of the mainstream approach to the development dilemmas of South African cities. The final section raises normative issues about LED and suggests new ways of thinking and operating based on a different set of case studies.

2 GLOBAL ECONOMIC RESTRUCTURING AND THE STRATEGIC REORIENTATION OF THE CAPITALIST STATE

During the past two to three decades, several fundamental and irreversible changes, usually captured under the rubric *global economic restructuring*, have transformed the world economy.

> '"Restructuring" refers to the transformation of the economic bases of cities in the advanced capitalist world from manufacturing to services; the rapid growth of the producer services sector within cities at the top of the global hierarchy; the simultaneous concentration of economic control within multinational firms and financial institutions, the decentralisation of their manufacturing and routine office functions; the development of manufacturing in the Third World; and

the rise of new economic powers in the Pacific Rim' (Fainstein 1990a:120).

Economic change has in turn produced important political, spatial and institutional changes in all countries (Boviard 1992, 1993, 1994). Dominant trends in the urban economies of industrialised countries during the 1980s include: rapid decline of manufacturing employment relative to service employment; suburbanisation and ruralisation of employment (especially in the manufacturing sector); long-term persistence of derelict or under-used sites in inner city areas, at the same time as major growth and development in other parts of the city; employment casualisation and informalisation; the increasing role of SMMEs in employment creation; prolonged disparities in unemployment rates between cities and regions within countries; and a stubborn persistence of low wages and high unemployment in specific social groups and even in particular families in local areas.

2.1 Restructuring, national responses and the hollowed-out Schumpetarian workfare state

The competitive pressures associated with restructuring have redefined the policy agenda in a thoroughly revolutionary manner. In the words of Judd & Parkinson (1990:19), 'adjustment rather than resistance to global change became the *leitmotif* of national policies on both sides of the Atlantic'.

Competitive restructuring has prompted a strategic and structural reorientation of the capitalist state *from Keynesian welfarism to Schumpetarian workfarism* (Jessop 1994). The new state is dedicated to the promotion of product, process, organisational and market innovation aimed at strengthening the structural competitiveness of the national economy. Domestic full employment is deprioritised and redistributive welfare rights take second place to growth (Cochrane 1994; Peck 1995; Peck & Tickell 1995).

The productivist reordering of social policy is accompanied by changes in the institutional, territorial and political fabric of the capitalist state. The shift towards internationalised (and regionalised) flexible production systems has decisively weakened the capacity of the late capitalist state to project itself even within its own borders. In turn, this loss of autonomy creates both the need for supra-national coordination and the space for sub-national resurgence. Thus we find that the powers of the nation–state are being limited through a complex displacement of powers — upward, downward and outward. The strategic reorientation of the capitalist state is thereby complemented by its structural hollowing out.

The subordination of the public sector to the needs and demands of international competition through wholesale and indiscriminate deregulation, commercialisation, liberalisation, decontrol, privatisation, etc is promoting an ad hoc, uncoordinated, conflictual, market-guided transition to a flexible post-Fordist economy (Jessop 1994; Harvey 1989; Cochrane 1994; Mayer 1994). In the wake of these changes there have been many losers and winners, and enormous economic, social and human costs: blighted communities and regions, erosion of skills, increasing income inequality and human misery. The public policies guided by this market ideology devastated the poor and minorities of inner cities. They exacerbated the exodus of jobs and industries from the central city, accelerated disinvestment from inner city neighbourhoods, widened an already polarised income spread, and failed dismally to lift the underclass from their legacy of poverty and despair. Fear, hostility and concern have been aroused in numerous quarters and many people are convinced that a better way to handle the incidence of costs and benefits of restructuring must be found.

2.2 Changes in the territorial organisation of the state

From the mid-1970s, changes in the relations between territorial levels of the state and in local policies have been significant in all the Western countries. In some respects (eg sources of funding) they show a trend towards decentralisation that runs counter to the centralisation trend of the Golden Age, but in other respects (eg policy control) they show a trend towards centralisation. Second, these changes are closely related to the economic restructuring dynamic.

In lower to middle income countries, the World Bank (1991) places great emphasis on decentralisation. The Bank argues the case for decentralisation on economic grounds and envisages a broad shift in central functions away from direct infrastructure provision and service delivery towards the creation of an enabling regulatory and financial environment. Gilbert (1992) questions the seemingly obvious validity of the prescription.

> 'Is it totally coincidental that this enabling strategy has been adopted enthusiastically precisely at a time when government is least able to help the poor?' (Gilbert 1992:444).

Hoisting the decentralisation banner is now fashionable for creatures of different political hues and persuasions. Parties to the right of the political spectrum, the World Bank for example, anchor their call for increased decentralisation and autonomy in the belief that it will automatically lead to the maximisation of local choice and accountability (defined in narrow fiscal terms). They welcome variation between local authorities in service provision and standards in accord with public choice theory as espoused by conservative administrations. Those on the left are acutely aware of the importance of local choice, accountability and customer and service-delivery orientations. However, their call for decentralisation is grounded in broader social democratic objectives with its emphasis on redistribution and the social rights of citizenship (King 1989).

While decentralisation admittedly opens the space for greater participation and increased governmental responsiveness, Preteceille dissects the underlying logic for decentralisation in the age of restructuring:

> 'A decentralisation policy makes it possible to get rid of that [Fordist] norm of consumption in a flexible way, fractioning it into local social policies by moving state responsibilities for welfare and consumption from central to local levels. Such a shift to fragmented localities helps to dissolve the global social compromise as well as established class identities, which are an absolute to the restructuring of wage relations. It accelerates locally the dismantling of recognised social rights to public provision of collective consumption, by setting up a quasicom-

modity link between taxes and public provision. And finally, by fostering competition between local authorities in the race for investment in new technology firms, it helps impose "flexibility" on local economies, on local labour markets, and mobilises local resources in favour of that flexibility' (Preteceille 1990:51).

Preteceille does, however, caution us against deducing the meaning of institutional changes and subsequent urban policies from the dynamic of economic restructuring only. One should rather consider this dynamic as shaped and channelled through political relations of power (see Hambleton 1989). Changes in state structures and urban policies are closely related to hegemony and accumulation crises. Centralisation of control was a response to local opposition to neo-liberalism in Denmark and the UK. Decentralisation in Canada, the USA and France was used to promote neo-liberalism by appealing to local support (Preteceille & Pickvance 1991).

2.3 LED initiatives

In the course of intensified inter-local competition, cities have gone over to concentrated promotion of their economies and growth which, with the founding of various quasi governmental public development sponsors and mixed public–private partnerships, is based on new political–institutional regulatory forms, far removed from public control and the public sphere (Kratke & Schmoll 1991).

Pivotal to the new forms of social and institutional regulation are changes in the nature and substance of state intervention. Informed by a broad development paradigm whose foundations rest on 'bidding down' and 'bailing out', mainstream local government policies for regeneration are passive and broad, rather than active, targeted and carefully administered as is the case in progressive policy. The focus of intervention is on the supply side, particularly in relation to the labour and property markets, from urban development corporations to deregulated enterprise zones. The institutional framework for local policy has sidelined elected local government in favour of executive agencies controlled by central government. Entrepreneurship has replaced employment as the primary policy goal. Local level planning has become more market and private sector-led. Neo-liberalism has also created strong pressures for the reorientation of local public expenditure and services towards the needs and priorities of unfettered capital accumulation.

The shift to entrepreneurialism and supply-side oriented interventions is a direct response to global economic restructuring associated with increased inter-urban competition and profitability crises (Leitner 1990). Inter-urban competition for investment means that cities with a competitive advantage cannot count on retaining that advantage for an extended period, because the spatial reorganisation of production is now occurring at a more rapid pace. This heightened pace is linked to the accelerated turnover time of capital and the increased freedom of corporations to relocate production across space. One result is that the character and health of the local economy are constantly being redefined, forcing cities to compete more intensely with one another. Not surprisingly, there seems to be a consensus emerging throughout the world that positive benefits are to be had by cities adopting an entrepreneurial stance to economic development. In many instances, the entrepreneurial role conceals the 'marriage of convenience' (Clavel & Kleniewski 1990:229) between political officials being pressured to create jobs, and corporations interested in maintaining the upward redistribution of income.

2.3.1 The new urban entrepreneurialism

2.3.1.1 Public–private partnerships

As the centrepiece of the new urban entrepreneurialism, the notion of public–private partnerships features prominently and has become a leading 'buzzword' in economic development circles. Public–private partnerships refer to a set of institutional relationships between government and various actors in the private sector and civil society in which boosterism is integrated with the use of local government powers to attract external sources of funding, new direct investments, or new employment sources.

For economic development practitioners, public–private partnerships are indispensable tools for urban revitalisation. Public support for private development is assumed to generate public benefits and is viewed as a fundamental, accepted function of local government, in the same category as 'public safety and sanitation' (Levine 1989:13). Yet, this literature contains little empirical research on the actual impact of public–private partnerships on individual cities.

Urban political economists adopt a more critical perspective, arguing that the creation of formal public–private partnerships have often amounted to corporations doing the planning while city governments facilitate corporate plans using municipal powers (see Feagin, Gilderbloom & Rodriguez 1989). Municipal democracy and social control over development is diminished as business control over public resource allocation is increased, and as economic development policy is removed from the channels of municipal governance and lodged in public–private development institutions. Moreover, political economists assert that because public–private partnerships reflect the agenda of urban business elites, they tend to have minimal impact on the central economic problems of urban areas; ie inner city poverty, neighbourhood decay, the shrinking number of quality employment opportunities available to city residents, etc.

In the USA, public–private partnerships are premised on the assumption that business and community interests are largely compatible and that the mobilisation of public support for business adventures should be viewed as consistent with the public interest (Logan & Molotch 1987). Yet research on urban redevelopment clearly indicates that the traditional public–private approach has

> '... succeeded in creating a "profit machine" for developers and investors. Downtowns have been revitalised and transformed into centres of corporate services and tourism, but the great majority using these facilities are not city residents. Neighbourhood distress and shrinking economic opportunities remain serious problems for large numbers of urban dwellers. Urban democracy has been compromised by a partnership approach that views city government as a hindrance to "fast track" redevelopment deal-making, rather than as a genuine

redevelopment partner representing the public interest' (Levine 1989:28).

The interests of the local community and those of the business coalitions do not coincide. Private sector elites usually resist policies that would reduce their wealth, power and prestige. In the case of Houston,

> '... business interests have opposed partnerships for such government activity as public housing, cooperative housing, rental aid programs, new infrastructure for moderate income neighbourhoods, many types of general public services, and social welfare programs' (Feagin, Gilderbloom & Rodriguez 1989:256).

In Britain, public–private partnerships have in many instances supplanted strategy, representing a reversion to a simple form of project-based interventions divorced from the wider urban context (see Totterdill 1989:515–516; Fainstein 1994; Peck & Tickell 1995). Lawless's (1990) review of the Sheffield public–private partnership initiative highlights the virtual impossibility of longer term land-use planning; and the relegation of distributional issues to a secondary status. The partnership ignores questions of collective consumption and the serious problems associated with unemployment.

In the Third World, critics have charged that public–private partnerships hide their dependent corporatist orientation, artificially separating it from the wider dynamic of deregulation, privatisation and the harsh realities of structural adjustment (Mitchell-Weaver & Manning 1991). But the picture in developing countries is less uniform than often assumed (see Fergusen 1992; Harris 1993).

2.3.1.2 Urban Development Corporations (UDCs)

The activity of public–private partnerships is essentially entrepreneurial in nature and in many instances the public sector takes the risk and the private sector appropriates the benefits. The institutional forms that it often assumes are urban development corporations (UDCs). UDCs, promoted by the UK Conservative government in the 1970s, are quasi-government bodies established and funded by the central government. They are charged with expanding the range of job opportunities, facilitating local skills acquisition, improving housing provision, enhancing the quality of the physical environment, and promoting investment opportunity areas.

UDCs are single-purpose agencies functioning outside local political interference and attuned to market opportunities by virtue of their 'superior' managerialist/technocratic attributes. They are based on market investment criteria and wealth creation as opposed to public planning, community control and social welfare. While local authority actors do sit on UDC boards, they are there in a personal capacity and not as representatives of the local community. UDCs are favoured by private developers because they offer structural independence from central government, privacy in negotiations, rapid coordination of public and private resources, and easy access to public officials by private developers.

The success of UDCs in meeting the broad aims of urban revitalisation and employment generation are mixed. While they might seem effective in stimulating, initiating and expediting development, they are criticised for being unrepresentative, unaccountable and non-transparent, sometimes operating as a 'shadow government' (Judd & Parkinson 1990:330) that makes the most important decisions affecting urban citizens.

Others have voiced concern over the narrow sectoral focus of UDC projects centred around financial services and the construction of upper income residential areas. Case studies examining the London Docklands Development Corporation's (LDDC) record on housing, employment and democracy, demonstrates that property-led urban regeneration has led to the creation of 'islands of prosperity being developed in a sea of disadvantage and deprivation' (Nicholson 1989:54). The LDDC actively discriminates against industrial capital through its land policies, leading to a mismatch between jobs occurring and their availability to local residents. The astronomical increase in land prices has in large measure contributed to homelessness (Lawless 1990).

UDCs are rapidly coming to be regarded as the panacea for the ills of urban administration in major Third World cities. In common with UDCs in Britain, Third World UDCs are made up of appointed rather than elected officials, and they replace, to some degree, local government. The general assumption is that administrative efficiency replaces 'political chicanery and incompetence' —

> 'The real world of urban society, however, is not always so straightforward. Shown out the front door, politics and politicians have a tendency to slip in the back door' (McAuslan 1985:111).

Development planning experts charge that UDCs cannot serve as a substitute for responsive elected local government, properly funded, adequately staffed, and supported by central or state governments. Increased administrative efficiency does not simply flow from new institutional forms of administration but entails broader reforms in law, internal functioning and policy. The direction of development in municipal administration should be upwards as well as downwards and not by displacement through UDCs (see Moore 1990).

2.3.1.3 Image making and place marketing

Entrepreneurialism focuses more closely on the speculative construction of spaces than on the enhancement of place. Much energy and planning in many Western cities have gone into image making and place marketing. Heritage cities, cultural cities, new civic centres, etc are efforts used by city governments to promote a particular centre as an appealing destination, and to improve the possibilities of attracting commercial, retail and government investment (Robinson 1993). Often this leads to gentrification, increased income inequality and accelerated social dualisation (see Fainstein 1990a; Hula 1990).

2.3.1.4 Privatisation

Entrepreneurialism focuses on deregulation and privatisation. In the USA and Britain, privatisation assumes several forms: the elimination of public functions or transferral to the private sector; shifts in the production and delivery of goods from the public to the private sector while maintaining public financing; the sale of assets (public land, infrastructure and enterprises); and the deregulation of services. Often, privatisation and deregulation have produced increased market competition, efficiency and innovation against the backdrop of skyrocketing consumer costs and increased burdens on the national fiscus. The arguments for privatisation of public services and facilities often ignores the enormous public subsidies required for capital costs (Banerjee 1993).

In Britain, Thatcher's privatisation drive did occasionally improve productivity and efficiency, but the costs were high. One hundred and fifty thousand jobs were slashed. Gas and water prices spiralled, with the latter increasing by 67% during 1985 to 1990. In the same period, salaries of the chairmen of the ten water companies rose between 108% and 571%. Disaffected Tory voters have begun to question the value of privatisation because they believe 'the rich are getting richer on the backs of the poor'.[7]

In the Third World, privatisation seems to be emerging as a nostrum for two reasons: first, there is simply no money to fund government activity and, secondly, pressure from the IMF and World Bank who hold back emergency loans if governments are not prepared to accept some measure of privatisation.

Privatisation in the Third World has been slowed by the difficulties encountered in selling off unprofitable, debt encumbered state enterprises. The politically sensitive nature of privatisation has translated into little public agency divesture. But in practice, privatisation of a different kind is taking place very rapidly. Lacking public provision of services (even when fees are charged), small entrepreneurs have taken over the supply of water, housing, building lots, transport, marketing facilities, etc. Many of these small entrepreneurs are poor, and most of their clients are poor. The services are often inferior to those available in the regulated sector, but they are offered where they are needed, and at a cost that is at least affordable to people who otherwise would have no services at all (Stren 1991:21).

For progressive policy makers concerned with empowerment and equity, the critical issue in the privatisation and deregulation debate is how they can be linked to local strategies for job creation, small business development and economic growth. Privatisation and deregulation should aim to enhance the liquidity of local capital markets; broaden participation in local capital markets through mass share-ownership schemes; improve the administrative environment by separating the commercial and regulatory functions of government-owned enterprises; form strategic public–private joint ventures; further black economic empowerment; and redistribute wealth. Privatisation needs to be viewed in a holistic manner and not simply confined to public debt retirement as this would merely entrench, rather than challenge, inefficient power imbalances.[8]

3 APPLICABILITY OF THE MAINSTREAM APPROACH TO THE DEVELOPMENT DILEMMAS OF SOUTH AFRICAN CITIES

In the South Africa of the 1990s, a key issue facing the cities is overcoming the fragmentation of space, with its implications for decreasing segregation and enhancing urban efficiency (Mabin 1994). Attempting to overcome apartheid in a postmodern world in which some of the key forces affecting cities globally are those of fragmentation, segregation and surveillance, it is doubtful whether a market-led planning style can achieve the objectives of progressive urbanism; ie diversity, complexity, freedom and equity. The socially divisive and clandestine nature of market-guided planning (Brindley, Rydin & Stoker 1989:180–183) could potentially frustrate the creation of a democratic post-apartheid urban order by exacerbating disparities between localities. According to Tomlinson (1992), adherence to market principles and market-guided planning will tend to reinforce the form of the apartheid city. Preliminary findings show that the costs in terms of unemployment, income distribution, displacement and fiscal crises will weigh down quite heavily on our fledging democracy.[9]

Yet the Urban Foundation (1994), while attempting to strike a balance between strategies for the attraction of industry, and those to promote indigenous economic growth from within the urban centre, comes down heavily in favour of competition and entrepreneurship. In an interview, the ex-Executive Director of the Urban Foundation (UF), Anne Bernstein, warned that if controls are placed on the ability of South African cities and towns to compete, it will reduce their economic potential in the global economy.[10]

Housing research group PLANACT has criticised the UF's position paper on the need for South African cities to compete for development funds.[11] Leilia McKenna of PLANACT argues that the UF's approach would reproduce the lopsided and uneven allocation of national resources. The system of funding allocation for local government was already based primarily on the existing resource base, capacity and institutional ability of local authorities, and was therefore not a new approach. The criteria used by the UF — population size, incomes, facilities — were those used traditionally in the grading of local authorities and in defining decision-making powers in regional services councils:

> One of the major criticisms of the local authority system is that this grading system has resulted in an unbalanced allocation of resources to those local authorities who are in a position of strength, leaving others with a continuing problem of lack of basic services' (McKenna 1994).[12]

There is a great deal of evidence, international and local, to indicate that inter-urban competition places onerous burdens on poor cities who are forced to pay more than well-endowed centres (Rubin & Rubin 1987; Rubin 1988). Inter-urban competition seems to operate not as a 'beneficial hidden hand', but as an external coercive law forcing the lowest common denominator of social responsibility and welfare provision. Competition helps discipline geographical variation in accumulation and class struggle within the bounds of the endless lurching between the stabilising stagnation of monopoly control and the disruptive dynamism of competitive growth (Harvey 1989a). Inter-urban competition also has dangerous macroeconomic consequences including regressive impacts on income distribution, volatility within the urban network and landscape ephemerality. Concentration on spectacle and image rather than on the substance of economic and social problems can also prove deleterious in the long run, even though political benefits can all too easily be had (Harvey 1989:12–16).

Tomlinson (1994) notes two reasons why American-style local development planning might be inappropriate for South Africa. First, South Africa looks forward to functionally defined urban areas/cities where resources will be spread more equitably (Smith 1992) than in the USA (see Soja 1971). Secondly, traditional competition between cities and states has not featured prominently in South Africa.

The fundamental problem with the urban entrepreneurship hypothesis is that they represent blanket prescriptions for different diseases, and are unconcerned with struggles to create liveable cities and workable environments. To the extent that there is policy reliance purely on market mechanisms and entrepreneurship 'then there is the danger of risk-reducing strategies that discourage spending on research and development and worker training but encourage, instead, cheap labour policies including [capital relocation and flight]' (Cox 1993:20–21).

The lesson from this short discussion is that models cannot be uncritically imported. The specific outcomes of and responses to the restructuring process are contingent on the interaction of world economic forces and particular local factors (Fainstein & Fainstein 1989; Fainstein 1994). Approaches to urban governance and revitalisation are the product of interaction of various social forces that exploit the strategic selectivity and structurally uneven terrain of the capitalist state (Jessop 1990). South African policy makers will have to engineer their own model, grounded in the material and political exigencies of reconstruction and development, and sensitive to the needs/aspirations of the urban poor.

So what are the alternatives? Cooke (1989) has emphasised the possibility of proactive intervention by localities; Totterdill (1989) has outlined wider lessons for progressive economic policy; and Harloe et al (1989) have highlighted the range of local economic policies that could be followed. The next section tries to unpack alternative strategies for urban governance and development that might prove useful as we chart our way through the treacherous seas of post-apartheid urban reconstruction.

4 NORMATIVE ISSUES AND NEW WAYS OF THINKING AND OPERATING

How stakeholders view economic restructuring may be as important as the facets of economic restructuring themselves. Between the stimulus of economic restructuring and the response of urban policy lies the 'image' that politically relevant actors have of economic change and what problems need to be addressed by public policies. But what needs to be realised is that

> '... explanations in society are not simply scientific responses to a problem. They are weapons in a fight, the basis for praise or blame. It is for this reason that social science can contribute least where the social and political significance of the problem is the greatest. The study of economics has its "black holes", but they are not the blindness of economists so much as the blindness of the social order. For blindness serves its functions too, protecting and defending the status quo' (Harris 1983 in Cole 1994:35).

The apathy confronted in unpacking ideologies and their substructures of economic theory reproduces the prejudices of the age and classes from which these
ideologies derive (Harris 1986). The resulting blindness to alternative development
strategies narrows the political agenda favourable to conservative political interests. As DH Lawrence notes in *Lady Chatterley's Lover:* 'What the eye doesn't see
and the mind doesn't know, doesn't exist' for in this world of interconnected
moments and fleeting experiences, 'sufficient unto the moment is the appearance
of reality'.

In mainstream urban policy, the dominant image and rhetoric of economic
change as presented by the business coalition have legitimated conservative
policies in the present period.

> 'The dominant metaphor is the image of mobile capital spanning the
> globe in search of the lowest-cost production sites. The implications
> are far-reaching: economic development is a matter of attracting more
> of this thing called capital, which is increasingly demanding of its
> potential suitors' (Logan & Swanstrom 1990:19).

An alternative image of economic development would recognise that the most
valuable forms of capital investment are embedded in particular social and geographical contexts (see Smith 1984). While the physical barriers to capital mobility
have increasingly been overcome by technology, many sectors of capital remain
dependent on what could be called a 'spatially organised ecological system' (Duncan, Goodwin & Halford 1988:113; also see Duncan & Goodwin 1988; Hudson 1988)
of production technologies, inter-industry linkages, physical and social infrastructure, and consumption patterns. The industries embedded in this ecology are more
attractive than hypermobile capital, because they will not suddenly relocate when
asked to contribute to the common wellbeing of citizens. Experiments in alternative
LED are based on an image of economic development that does not revolve solely
around attracting mobile capital but focuses instead on nurturing community
relations between labour and capital, between networks of small businesses, between the political system and firms.

Entrapping spatially dependent/embedded firms forces policy makers to develop new ways of doing things based on notions of *strong competition*; ie continuous and ceaseless reconfiguration, differentiation and improvement of products
through a dynamic redeployment of specialised production skills and equipment
(Storper 1993). The geography of strong competition is one of localised complexes
of social relations tying firms to one another, one fixed investment to another,
employees and employers, and firms to the state, in a manner that enhances the
competitive edge of all firms participating in it (Cox & Mair 1988). This approach
embraces traditional ideas of agglomeration, the formation of knowledges, of
relations and communities of trust that facilitate cooperation between constituent
firms, and of coalitions for political and distributive purposes. Forging the relations
of trust and cooperation is only possible through the creation of an institutional
matrix that leads the market in strategically delineated directions alongside complex interpellation projects that secure the conditions for continued and sustained
valorisation (see Best 1993; Wade 1990).

Drawing their inspiration from this alternative conception of economic develop-ment; ie embeddedness, a number of UK, Labour-led local authorities tried, in the 1980s, to develop their own local strategies in response to recession and deindus-trialisation. One of the major characteristics of this approach was the overwhelming reaction against competitive industrial promotion that were regarded as costly and often ineffective advertising campaigns. Strategic emphasis was placed, instead, on restructuring and reorientating indigenous industry directed at building on the skills, knowledge and expertise of the workforce, the local community and the business sector (see Mawson & Miller 1986).

Interventionist local authorities in the UK started from the assumption that the economic domain was not simply about job creation and investment, but also involved questions concerning the quality of work, industrial democracy, access to opportunities, the distribution of incomes, and, ultimately, living standards. For the Greater London Council (GLC) economic planners, restructuring was to be achieved in ways consistent with the interests of workers and communities (Rustin 1986; Palmer 1986). By combining collective consumption, community participa-tion and economic revitalisation through a bottom-up rather than a trickle-down approach, the GLC planners pioneered a unique local development paradigm premised on *radical* supply-side strategies.

In Chicago, Giloth & Mier (1989) provide examples of initiatives by local com-munity groups aided by a progressive mayor and local state resourcing of com-munity inputs. A task force consisting of a network of neighbourhood organisations and specialised organisations provided technical advice and assist-ance to community created business incubators and worker-owned factories. The focus in this experiment was on preserving industrial productive capacity, oppos-ing initiatives that encouraged relocation. Competition between localities was seen as divisive and expensive, all grants were performance linked and were at times contested in courts. Gentrification for residential and commercial use was vigor-ously resisted on the premise that it enticed industries to relocate.

Molotch & Vicari's (1988) study of growth machines in Japan and Italy shows that alternative growth machines based on *public–public partnerships* do exist. Whereas private sector dominated growth coalitions feature prominently in the USA, yielding dramatic unevenness within and across urban areas and local governments that often serve as mere 'adjuncts of the real estate business' (207), this is not true of Japan and Italy. National government, organically linked to conglomerate firms, plays a significant role in Japanese development producing high levels of GNP, but poor environments.

In Italy, the national party system features prominently in setting the conditions of local development. The power of space entrepreneurs is seriously curtailed and business has woken up to the futility of attempts aimed at manipulating locational decisions. Land use is nationally regulated, governed by strict city zoning laws. Government specifies percentages for public services, commercial functions and residential use. The municipality carefully defines the portions of land and the built cubic volumes to be devoted to each function. Municipalities, in general,

> '... [expect] to gain all public facilities from developers, including roads, buildings, parks, libraries and cultural centres — and to make a substantial profit in addition. This system of developer "exactions"

... is far more widespread in Italy, than the USA, and much less likely to result in net public losses so common in US cities under similar "partnership" arrangements...This arrangement in which public authorities define in advance the configuration of a given parcel of land and then demand amenities as a condition for the right to develop, means that profitability of private investment necessarily depends on negotiation and partnership with government — referred to in more general terms as "concertation". Private developers thus see collaboration with local government as the only viable means of doing business. They speak ...of their need for a "fair gain" but have no conception of being able to profit by alerting spatial relations. Nor do they presume that projects they build will be provided necessary infrastructure; some past projects remain half-empty because government never provided transportation access. Prudent entrepreneurs wait for government to act on these matters; their passivity is evidence that they themselves have little capacity to influence such outcomes. They will use their special influence and connections (which are not extensive) not to alter spatial relations, but to cut themselves into the development deals that public policies eventually make possible' (Vicari & Molotch 1990:615).

Rennes, regional capital of Brittany, is another example of a public–public partnership driven by aggressive public sector elites committed to the dynamic regeneration of the city. During the 1980s, it was agreed by the major stakeholders that Rennes's regeneration would occur through scientific and technical research and training. The urban elite consisting of academics, intellectuals from the voluntary sector and new social movements, young entrepreneurs, and the local authority decided to build on the cultural dynamism of the city and to link new technologies, education and training. The cultural dynamic combined with the development of a science park was used for a massive marketing campaign to promote the city as a modern place of sophistication and intelligence. Simultaneously, a variety of traditional economic policies were pursued which included the provision of financial assistance, land, premises and advice to business; renovation of the historic city centre; modernisation of housing stock; place marketing; and special provisions for poor people.

In the 1980s, Rennes became one of the four most dynamic French cities, with Montpellier, Grenoble, and Toulouse. The new urban elites and the regional civil servants were the driving force behind the city's economic development initiative. The private sector played a limited role (Le Gales 1990).

In contrast to other regeneration efforts, the 'partnership' developed between the public and non-profit (universities) sector in Pittsburgh used public resources to help key non-profit institutions enhance their role as exporters of services and importers of new advanced technology firms.

'At the very least, city officials have moved beyond an exclusive focus on supporting and bargaining with the private sector. As public–private partnerships become ever more fashionable elsewhere, Pittsburgh has already recognised that certain non-profit organisations are economic engines, and thus should receive public sector attention. The non-profit sector, in brief, can be as strategic to economic development policy as is the private sector' (Sbragia 1990:64).

The strategy adopted does not focus on the speculative construction of space, but views real estate development as facilitating strategic economic activity rather than being an end in itself, and relies on non-profit and variants of public monies rather than simply on private firms and private investment. City rejuvenation is viewed in a holistic manner. The strategy is characterised by a consensual style of policy making.

Summarily, the public sector strategies of Rennes, Pittsburgh, Chicago, London and Italy were proactive in nature; supportive of a diverse range of growth sectors; involving many institutional, political and community leaders, and relying on relatively inclusive growth coalitions. The institutional fabric, the traditions of leadership and the political coalitions that sustained them, have been carefully engineered allowing rapid strategic reorientation. The public sector leadership coalitions defended, adapted and revolutionised inherited spatial fixes in line with the demands of changed national and international forces. In short, they *bet on the basics* in which local governments and political parties assumed the role of social leadership. Local government was central in organising collaboration, orchestrating consensus, limiting uncertainty, defining directions of expansion and avoiding dislocative losses for important agents.

These experiments in alternative LED strategies offer valuable lessons and point to the multitude of policies that we can creatively appropriate to suit the developmental needs of our cities. Nevertheless, as Fainstein notes:

> 'Which strategy is followed within a city and the city's commitment to targeting low income groups are consequences of political struggle and are largely independent of external forces... although...whether the growth strategy works is less open' (Fainstein 1990b:37).

5 CONCLUSION: REFOCUSING THE SOUTH AFRICAN LOCAL ECONOMIC DEBATE

The contemporary process of organisational, sectoral and spatial restructuring is probably the most fundamental economic and social change that has occurred since the industrial revolution (Cheshire 1991). It should come as no surprise that, as in the past, phases of the industrial revolution, we are now witnessing

> '... the battle of ideologies around the inexorably growing economy, some blindly opposing, some seeking to retard its more ruthless thrust into the social fabric, some single-mindedly or simple-mindedly hailing its every advance. We witness the rearguard action of the champions of the old order, the impotent discomfiture of the upholders of [tradition — LR], the easy triumph of the orthodox economists who neatly explain it all. But the advancing front leaves ruin in its train, and the hastily built defences crumble before it. We see how with a

new liberation went a new servitude, and we [must — LR] measure and [confront — FK] the challenge that now faces our age' (MacIver 1957 in Rodwin 1991:4).

The revival of metropolitan areas in the 1980s has commonly followed the strategy of 'rupture-filiation' (Gordon 1994:32); ie building on traditional territorial strengths while substantially changing them simultaneously. This approach stands in stark contrast to the capital mobility model which is oriented more often than not to speculative profiteering and unfettered accumulation. 'Betting on the basics' or 'rupture-filiation' rejects the whole notion that the economic domain is simply about job creation and investment. The strategy focuses attention on quality of work, industrial democracy, access to opportunities, income distribution and living standards. This approach forces South African policy makers to reassess many of their core assumptions concerning growth, development, empowerment and urban planning.

The SANCO, RDP (1995) and Urban Foundation documents correctly acknow-ledge that the urban sphere must be viewed as a 'functional unit' encompassing employment, housing, services, living conditions, etc. Unfortunately, they fail to translate this holism into concrete policy recommendations, mooring their boats to the conservative private–public partnership jetty. Their glorification of conserva-tive partnership arrangements is politically expedient. The public sector strategies of Rennes, Chicago, Pittsburgh, Italy and London compel local policy makers to break from their orthodox and politically expedient mindsets. The search for a socially just economic dispensation demands that we actively confront exploita-tion, marginalisation and powerlessness (see Harvey 1992) by widening the par-ameters of the economic discourse to encompass alternative institutional and political arrangements in the form of public–public and public non-profit partner-ships. This is critical if we are to creatively challenge the global agenda of neo-lib-eralism.

Another disturbing trend in the local debate is the narrow and parochial focus on the 'locality'. Stakeholders seem to share the naive belief that the local economy can be 'hived off' from developments in the national political economy. There is no mention in the SANCO and RDP (1995) documents of how the national economic policy will constrain growth, proscribing alternative investment and development strategies. For example, the present administration's emphasis on monetary and fiscal conservatism, financial sustainability, deficit reduction and competitive econ-omic restructuring,[13] while palatable to the IMF,[14] suggests that government has surrendered its crucial leadership role in industrial restructuring to the private sector (see Heilbronner & Bernstein 1989). For the first few years, therefore, gov-ernment will have to rely on voluntary initiatives by the private sector to promote RDP objectives such as outsourcing to small firms, removal of anti-competitive practices, redirection of production from luxury to mass markets, balanced regional development, affirmative action, etc. Private industry did little of this in the past since it was not commercially attractive and would undermine profitability and growth. The SANCO and RDP (1995) documents do not explain why companies will suddenly change their focus and support community-driven projects.

At a macro-economic level, the space for alternative local investment and devel-opment strategies is severely circumscribed. Government has continued the restrictive policy of previous administrations, prioritising the control of inflation and maintaining high interest rates (Turok 1995). The pursuit of monetary orthodoxy and fiscal conservatism

> '... has gone hand in hand with excessive caution in advancing real policies for generating employment and getting the economy along a path of sustainable growth' (Pillay & Millward 1995:28–29).[15]

Coupled to this has been a shift in government rhetoric from 'sustainable development' to the 'prioritisation of economic growth'. President Mandela's neo-liberal obsession with growth found its organisational expression in the appointment of a Special Cabinet Committee charged with the task of investigating ways to boost growth. This high-profile *Council of Wise Men* could effectively bypass NEDLAC in future, privileging 'short-term growth spurts' at the expense of long-term socio-economic upliftment (Sam Shilowa, General Secretary of COSATU, August 1995).[16] This broad macro-economic policy orientation could drastically reduce the investment capital required for interventionist type LED initiatives.

Against this backdrop of conservative economics and social policy, the RDP (1995), Urban Foundation and SANCO documents argue quite vociferously for the installation of developmental local government. But is this possible? The deplorable white bias in the forthcoming local elections (whites get three votes for every black vote, and on top of that will enjoy virtual veto power over budgeting (Bond 1995)) and market financing for infrastructural development (80% of the funds needed for infrastructure development must be raised by local authorities through the market)[17] raises crucial questions as to whether socially responsive programmes can be embarked upon at the local level. This is worsened by the fact that local authorities have no tradition of flexibility or external consultation in state planning.

The constraints on progressive urban economic policy suggest that alternative development and investment strategies must be championed at all levels. Case studies show that the need for region-wide organising around economic, institutional and infrastructural policy is critical.

What about the role of the state? The SANCO and RDP (1995) documents on LED stress the need for local authorities to become more developmentally focused. Encouraging as this might be, the alternative case studies suggest that the achievement of stable economic growth requires a more productive, interventionist role for the public sector as strategist, coordinator, animator, and promoter of new initiatives (see Murray 1992). The state needs to push, challenge, lead, follow and signal (Porter 1990) through the creation of advanced factors, encouragement of domestic 'co-opetition' (competition + cooperation), the shaping of national priorities and influencing demand sophistication.

> 'The growth of the new post-Fordist economic practices, structures and industrial sectors, and the restructuring of old sectors, requires new institutional modes of regulation, including an active and innovative economic role for the public sector, both to achieve environmentally sustainable growth and to combat the strong tendencies towards a polarised society and labour market, which in turn limit consumption. If we wish to influence the outcome of the struggle over the shape

of the post-Fordist state, we should be developing the case for a more active, innovative, productive and sustainable private sector, as part of broader strategic alternatives to neo-liberalism' (Geddes 1994:174).

State policies regarding rupture-filiation need to be *'interstitial'* in character, coordinating a new framework of state–market interactions (Gordon 1994:33) as in the GLC, Rennes, Pittsburgh, Chicago and Italian experiences.

'In this context, the state should play a key role in defining an appropriate incentive structure, in facilitating the growth of national, sectoral, regional and firm-level capabilities, and in promoting the development of an effective institutional infrastructure' (Kaplinsky, Joffe, Lewis & Kaplan 1993:124).

At an administrative–organisational level, a productive role for the state implies an outcome-oriented approach with emphasis on education and training, devolution of management responsibility, meaningful decentralisation of power to ensure maximum involvement by communities in the governing process, and service delivery that is flexible and efficient (De Bruyn, Patel & Tshiki 1995). Local authorities, civics and NGOs could benefit immeasurably by forcing this policy recommendation onto the national and regional agenda. In so doing, they will transform themselves from passive recipients of national industrial restructuring to active, transformatory agents.

Progressive policy orientations demand different forms of governance centred around interventionist local corporatism, in which local governments and political parties assume the role of social leadership through the organisation of collaboration, and orchestration of consensus among diverse and potentially conflicting social interests (Zeitlin 1989). The corporatism called for is a critical type and radically different from the ones presently in vogue (see Brindley, Rydin & Stoker 1989:166–7).

'The critical factor here is the framework within which the "local negotiation" of this corporatism takes place, specifically the extent to which a strategic analysis determines its operation and agenda. It is thus important to distinguish between "dependent" and "interventionist" corporatism. In the former, the state, whether central or local government, is relegated to the role of servicing capital...On the other hand, an interventionist corporatism would take the form of a structured discourse in which the local authority negotiates (and reformulates) its social and economic objectives through a series of alliances with different sections of labour and capital' (Totterdill 1989:517–518).

An interventionist corporatism, as demonstrated by the case studies, is by its very nature pragmatic, focusing on strategic analysis as the principal means of identifying routes by which workforce and community gains can be secured. An interventionist corporatism would create structures offering a potential forum in which the private strategies of investment, management practices and employment could be examined and interrogated within the public sphere. The creation of 'economic advisory or intelligence units' (Harris 1993:194), linking the local administration, business associations, educational and infrastructure agencies, communities and NGOs could potentially facilitate participative, accountable and integrated development action. This is an advance over the SANCO proposal that envisages the creation of an 'economic development unit' within the local government administration. While many local authorities have gone this route (Durban, Port Elizabeth, Cape Town, etc), what needs to be recognised is that administrative tinkering is not a substitute for meaningful institutional change; ie crafting a progressive dialectic between local state institutions and the wider civil society by changing the political–administrative interface. Economic development units do not ensure that private economic and investment decisions are brought into the public realm. Although economic development units are critical in effecting organisational reorientation, they need to be firmly situated within the broader governance dynamic.

A key task for such a forum would include detailed sectoral and labour market analysis to guide coherent action. The analysis should encompass a thorough examination of the pace of sectoral change, geographical spread, size of plants, ownership patterns, class structure, sectoral specialisation and the existing socio-cultural infrastructure (Markusen 1989). Newly elected regional and local authorities in South Africa may be tempted to neglect this strategic consideration in the interests of political expediency and immediate delivery of urban infrastructure. Progressive forces need to guard against the quick-fix solution.

Economic development strategies forged at state and local levels should be directed not only towards the maintenance of basic public services, but towards a decent quality of life as demonstrated by the case studies. The goals of growth and redistribution should be viewed as mutually reinforcing and integrated. Priority should be given to public sector programmes for such basic needs as health, education, housing and electrification (Fine 1994). The envisaged public works programmes should be linked to basic needs, the development of new tourist sites and infrastructural support for tourist activity. Tourist development could be linked to expanding the clothing and textile industry in 'new and creative ways ... which would then be targeted to the tourist market' (Padayachee 1994:25). Manufacturing development in certain product lines could be tailored to meet the basic needs of a growing market for consumer durables, especially as the effects of electrification become more apparent. Joint ventures between global firms and local companies of all sizes should be promoted to produce globally competitive products incorporating local skills, resources and talents, in ways that develop indigenous technological capacity and promote more sustainable long-term development.

Local industrial policy should focus on retention and expansion strategies; government aid for ownership changeovers, technology upgrading and management improvement; strengthening firms of different sizes, abilities and functions in relation to a system of firms embedded in a production process. Policy should strive towards fostering intricate formal and informal relations between firms; identifying product niches for local industry; promoting product development, training; and marketing local inputs (Khan 1993; Fainstein 1994). Progressive manufacturing policy should focus on using existing infrastructure and skilled labour, but reorganising them with new interests, new markets, and new products. Through the self-conscious linking of economic goals to wider political, social and urban dynamics, local authorities can produce sophisticated responses to industrial restructuring and change.

Progressive policy in the service sector should primarily be oriented to the needs of labour and community groups. Local governments should attempt to harness, shape and encourage the private sector in pursuit of social goals defined by the community as a whole. They may nurture alternative forms of production and investment, such as public companies, cooperatives, and worker-managed enterprises, as well as maintaining the traditionally liberal emphasis on redistributive public services, eg GLC. For progressive policy to be viable, officials must decide which industries have potential for growth and transformation; ie targeting.

Another avenue for progressive local policy is through *linkage programmes*, eg Chicago. These programmes permit developers to build high-profit projects only if they build low-profit projects (low income housing, daycare centres, etc) or contribute to their funding. Linkage policies have been used in the USA to mitigate the social costs of commercial development. It must, however, be cautioned that linkage programmes are only a 'partial solution to internalising the social costs of development'.

> 'It cannot be viewed as a panacea to all development ills but, nevertheless, it provides a useful mechanism, particularly in economically booming areas, for local authorities to pursue social objectives at a time of central government restraint on local spending' (Dawson & Walker 1990:168).

Other ways of harnessing service sector growth for progressive purposes include enforced hiring practices, mandatory affirmative action schemes, land trusts to curb speculation, revolving loan funds for small and worker-owned businesses, etc. Participating companies are given preferential treatment when requesting city loans, access to city-owned property, and other economic assistance.

In conclusion, socially and economically sustainable LED initiatives revolve around local government harnessing, shaping and encouraging the growth of a productive private sector. An approach is required in which the state drives the investment process in partnership with communities and, that this investment is complemented by the private sector (Adelzadeh & Padayachee 1994). This role involves traditional functions of local government, such as infrastructure provision and land-use planning, but may also extend into more novel activities such as the laying out and operation of science parks, the underwriting of venture capital activities, the organisation of worker training programmes, and the formation of public–private and public–public development corporations (Scott 1992). However, what is important is the fact that the local state, as leader (Vonk 1989; Luke et al 1988) and redistributor (Kohli 1993), enhances and entrenches territorial embeddedness concentrating on ameliorating and improving economic conditions rather than speculatively constructing space.

7 REFERENCES

Adelzadeh A & V Padayachee. 1994. The RDP white paper: reconstruction of a development vision. *Transformation — Critical Perspectives on Southern Africa* no 25 1–18.

African National Congress. 1994. *The Reconstruction and Development Programme.* Base Document, Johannesburg.

Africa Today: The International Magazine.

Banerjee T. 1993. Market planning, market planners, and planned markets. *JAPA* Summer 353–360.

Beauregard RA. 1989. Space, time and economic restructuring. In Beauregard RA (ed) *Economic Restructuring and Political Response.* Newbury Park: Sage 209–240.

Best M. 1993. *The New Competition: Institutions of Industrial Restructuring.* Cambridge: Polity.

Bond P. 1995. Fly-fishing in Southern Africa. *Southern African Review of Books.* No 37 May/June 11–12.

Boviard T. 1992. Local economic development and the city. *Urban Studies.* Vol 29 nos 3/4 343–368.

Boviard T. 1993. Analysing urban economic development. *Urban Studies.* Vol 30 nos 4/5 631–658.

Boviard T. 1994. Managing urban economic development: learning to change or the marketing of failure. *Urban Studies.* Vol 31 nos 4/5 573–603.

Brindley T, Y Rydin & G Stoker. 1989. *Remaking Planning: The Politics of Urban Change in the Thatcher Years.* London: Unwin Hyman.

Business Day. Johannesburg (daily newspaper).

Cheema GS. 1993. The new agendas. In Harris N (ed) *Cities in the 1990s: The Challenge for Developing Countries.* New Delhi: Research Press 24–42.

Cheshire P. 1991. Problems of regional transformation and deindustrialisation in the European Community. In Rodwin L & H Sazanami (eds) *Industrial Change and Regional Economic Transformation: The Experience of Western Europe.* London: Harper Collins 237–267.

Clavel P & N Kleniewski. 1990. Space for progressive local policy: examples from the United States and the United Kingdom. In Logan JR & T Swanstrom (eds) *Beyond the City Limits: Urban Policy and Economic Restructuring in Comparative Perspectives.* Philadelphia: Temple University Press 199–236.

Cochrane A. 1994. Restructuring the local welfare state. In Burrows R & B Loader (eds) *Towards a Post-Fordist Welfare State.* London: Routledge 117–135.

Cohen MA. 1990. Macroeconomic adjustment and the city. *Cities* February 49–59.

Cole K. 1994. The intellectual parameters of the real world: experience, reality and ideology. In *Economic Analysis — Implications for the Teaching of Economics.* School of Development Studies, University of East Anglia, Discussion Paper no 234.

Cooke P. 1989. Locality, economic restructuring and world development. In Cooke P (ed) *Localities: The Changing Face of Urban Britain.* London: Unwin Hyman 1–44.

Cox KR & A Mair. 1988. Locality and community in the politics of local economic development. *Annals of the Association of American Geographers*. Vol 78 no 2 307–325.

Cox R. 1993. *Taking Localities Seriously*. Paper presented at the Urban Policy Workshop at the Institute for Social and Economic Research, University of Durban-Westville, August.

Dawson J & C Walker. 1990. Mitigating the social costs of private development: the experience of linkage programmes in the United States. *Town Planning Review*. Vol 61 no 2 157–170

De Bruyn J, I Patel & N Tshiki. 1995. A productive public service: what's needed? *South African Labour Bulletin*. Vol 19 no 1 74–80.

Duncan S & M Goodwin. 1988. *The Local State and Uneven Development*. Oxford: Polity Press.

Duncan S, M Goodwin & S Halford. 1988. Policy variation in local states: uneven development and local social relations. *International Journal of Urban and Regional Research*. Vol 12 no 1 107–128.

Fainstein S. 1994. *The City Builders: Property, Politics, and Planning in London and New York*. Oxford: Basil Blackwell.

Fainstein S. 1990a. Economics, politics, and development policy: the convergence of New York and London. In Logan JR & T Swanstrom (eds) *Beyond the City Limits: Urban Policy and Economic Restructuring in Comparative Perspectives*. Philadelphia: Temple University Press 119–149.

Fainstein S. 1990b. The changing world economy and urban restructuring. In Judd D & M Parkinson (eds) *Leadership and Urban Regeneration: Cities in North America and Europe*. Newbury Park: Sage 31–50.

Fainstein S & N Fainstein. 1989. Technology, the new international division of labour and location: continuities and disjunctures. In Beauregard RA (ed) *Economic Restructuring and Political Response*. Newbury Park: Sage 17–40.

Feagin JR, JI Gilderbloom & N Rodriguez. 1989. The Houston experience: public–private partnerships. In Squires GD (ed) *Unequal Partnerships: The Political Economy of Urban Redevelopment in Postwar America*. New Brunswick: Rutgers 240–259.

Fergusen BW. 1992. Inducing local growth — two intermediate-sized cities in the state of Parana, Brazil. *Third World Planning Review*. Vol 14 no 3 245–265.

Finance Week. Johannesburg (weekly magazine).

Fine B. 1994. *Flexible Production and Flexible Theory: The Case of South Africa*. Centre for Economic Policy for Southern Africa: SOAS (unpublished).

Geddes M. 1994. Public services and local economic regeneration in a post-Fordist economy. In Burrows R & B Loader (eds) *Towards a Post-Fordist Welfare State*. London: Routledge 154–176.

Gilbert A. 1992. Third World cities: housing, infrastructure and servicing. *Urban Studies*. Vol 29 no 3/4 435–460.

Giloth RP & R Mier. 1989. Spatial change and social justice: alternative economic development in Chicago. In Beauregard RA (ed) *Economic Restructuring and Political Response*. Newbury Park: Sage 181–208.

Gordon R. 1994. *Industrial Districts and the Globalisation of Innovation: Regions and Networks in the New Economic Space Centre for the Study of Global Transformations*. University of California. Working Paper 94–7.

Grahl J & P Teague. 1989. 1992: The neo-liberal agenda. *New Left Review.* No 174 March–April 33–50.

Hambleton R. 1989. Urban government under Thatcher and Reagan. *Urban Affairs Quarterly.* Vol 24 no 3 359–388.

Harloe M, C Pickvance & J Urry. 1989. *Place, Policy and Politics: Do Localities Matter?* London: Unwin Hyman.

Harris N. 1986. *The End of the Third World.* London: Penguin.

Harris N. 1990a. *Urbanisation, Economic Development and Policy in Developing Countries.* Development Planning Unit: University College, London.

Harris N. 1993. Productivity and poverty in cities of the developing countries. In Harris N (ed) *Cities in the 1990s: The Challenge for Developing Countries.* New Delhi: Research Press 173–198.

Harris N. 1990. *The End of the Third World.* London: Penguin.

Harvey D. 1992. Social justice, postmodernism and the city. *International Journal of Urban and Regional Research.* Vol 16 no 4 588–601.

Harvey D. 1989. From managerialism to entrepreneurship: the transformation in urban governance in late capitalism. *Geografiska Annaler* 71B 1 3–17.

Harvey D. 1989a. *The Urban Experience.* Oxford: Basil Blackwell. Chapter 5.

Healey P. 1992. The reorganisation of state and market in planning. *Urban Studies.* Vol 29 no 3/4 411–434.

Heilbronner R & P Bernstein. 1989. *The Debt and the Deficit.* New York: WW Norton & Company.

Henderson J. 1993. Against the economic orthodoxy: on the making of the East Asian miracle. *Economy and Society.* Vol 22 no 2 200–217.

Heymans C. 1995. Cities: engines of prosperity or sites of decay? *Indicator South Africa: Quarterly Report.* Vol 12 no 3 47–53.

Hudson R. 1988. Uneven development in capitalist societies: changing spatial divisions of labour, forms of spatial organisation of production and service provision, and their impacts on localities. *Transactions.* Institute of British Geographers. Vol 13 no 4 484–496.

Hula RC. 1990. The two Baltimores. In Judd D & M Parkinson (eds) *Leadership and Urban Regeneration: Cities in North America and Europe.* Newbury Park: Sage 191–215.

Hyslop J. 1994. South Africa in the era of globalisation. In Webster E et al (eds) *Work and Industrialisation in South Africa.* Johannesburg: Ravan Press 337–348.

Jessop B. 1990. *State Theory: Putting the Capitalist State in its Place.* Pennsylvania: University Press.

Jessop B. 1994. The transition to post-Fordism and the Schumpetarian workfare state. In Burrows R & B Loader (eds) *Towards a Post-Fordist Welfare State.* London: Routledge 13–37.

Joffe A, R Kaplinsky, D Lewis & D Kaplan. 1993. Meeting the global challenge: a framework for industrial revival in South Africa. In Baker PH, A Boraine & W Krafchik (eds) *South Africa in the World Economy in the 1990s.* Claremont: David Philip 91–126.

Judd D & M Parkinson. 1990. Urban leadership and regeneration. In Judd D & M Parkinson (eds) *Leadership and Urban Regeneration: Cities in North America and Europe.* Newbury Park: Sage 13–30.

Khan F. 1993. Product-based technology learning; small to medium sized manufacturers and industrial districts: challenges confronting SMMEs in penetrating the export markets (unpublished).

King DS. 1989. The new right, the new left and local government. In Stewart J & G Stoker (eds) *The Future of Local Government*. London: Macmillan 185–211.

Kohli A. 1993. Democracy amid economic orthodoxy. *Third World Quarterly — Journal of Emerging Areas*. Vol 14 no 4 686.

Kratke S & F Schmoll. 1991. The local state and social restructuring. *International Journal of Urban and Regional Research*. Vol 15 no 4 542–552.

Logan JR & H Molotch. 1987. *Urban Fortunes: The Political Economy of Place*. California: University of California Press.

Leitner H. 1990. Cities in pursuit of economic growth — the local state as entrepreneur. *Political Geography Quarterly*. Vol 12 no 2 146–170.

Lawless P. 1988. Urban development corporations and their alternatives. *Cities*. Vol 5 no 3 277–289.

Le Gales P. 1990. Economic regeneration in Rennes: Local social dynamics and state support. In Judd D & M Parkinson (eds) *Leadership and Urban Regeneration: Cities in North America and Europe*. Newbury Park: Sage 69–85.

Levine MV. 1989. The politics of partnerships: unequal development since 1945. In Squires GD (ed) *Unequal Partnerships: The Political Economy of Urban Redevelopment in Postwar America*. New Brunswick: Rutgers 12–34.

Logan JR & T Swanstrom. 1990. Urban restructuring: a critical view. In Logan JR & T Swanstrom (eds) *Beyond the City Limits: Urban Policy and Economic Restructuring in Comparative Perspectives*. Philadelphia: Temple University Press 3–25.

Luke JS, C Ventriss, BJ Reed & CM Reed. 1988. *Managing Economic Development: A Guide to State and Local Leadership Strategies*. San Francisco: Jossey Bass.

Mabin A. 1994. *'Forget democracy, build houses': negotiating the shape of the city tomorrow*. Paper presented at University of the Witwatersrand history workshop — Democracy: Popular Precedents, Practice and Culture 13–15 July.

Mail & Guardian International (weekly newspaper).

Markusen AR. 1989. Industrial restructuring and regional politics. In Beauregard RA (ed) *Economic Restructuring and Political Response*. Newbury Park: Sage 115–148.

Markusen AR & V Carlson. 1989. Deindustrialisation in the American Midwest. In Rodwin L & H Sazanami (eds) *Deindustrialisation and Regional Economic Transformation: The Experience of the United States*. Boston: Unwin Hyman 25–59.

Marshall JN. 1989. New industrial horizons and local responses. *Local Government Studies*. November/December 17–22.

Mawson J & D Miller. 1986. Interventionist approaches in local employment and economic development: the experience of Labour local authorities. In Hausner VA (ed) *Critical Issues in Urban Economic Development*. Vol 1 Oxford: Clarendon Press 145–199.

Mayer M. 1987. Restructuring and popular opposition in West German cities. In Smith MP & JR Feagin (eds) *The Capitalist City: Global Restructuring and Community Politics*. Oxford: Basil Blackwell 343–364.

Mayer M. 1994. Postfordist city politics. In Amin A (ed) *Postfordism: A Reader.* Oxford: Basil Blackwell 316–338.

McAuslan P. 1985. *Urban Land and Shelter for the Poor.* Washington DC: Earthscan.

Mercury Kwazulu Natal (daily newspaper).

Mitchell-Weaver C & B Manning. 1991–1992. Public–private partnerships in Third World development: a conceptual overview. *Studies in Comparative International Development.* Vol 26 no 4 45–67.

Molotch H. 1976. The city as growth machine: towards a political economy of place. *American Journal of Sociology.* Vol 82 no 2 309–332.

Molotch H & S Vicari. 1988. Three ways to build: the development process in the United States, Japan and Italy. *Urban Affairs Quarterly.* Vol 24 no 2 188–214.

Moore C. 1990. Displacement, partnership and privatisation: local government and urban economic regeneration in the 1980s. In King DS & J Pierre (eds) *Challenges to Local Government.* Newbury Park: Sage 55–78.

Murray R. 1992. *Local Economic Development Planning: A Response to Questions in Relation to Economic Development Policy in Durban.* Sussex: Institute of Development Studies.

Nicholson G. 1989. A model of how not to regenerate an urban area. *Town and Country Planning* February 52–55.

Padayachee V. 1994. *Economic Development in Metropolitan Durban: Reflections on an Integrated, Multi-Layered Strategy in the Context of Global and National Restructuring.* Institute for Economic and Social Research, University of Durban-Westville (unpublished).

Palmer J. 1986. Municipal enterprise and popular planning. *New Left Review* 159 Sept/Oct 117–125.

Peck J. 1995. Moving and shaking: business elites, state localism and urban privatism. *Progress in Human Geography.* Vol 19 no 1 16–46.

Peck J & A Tickell. 1995. Business goes local: dissecting the business agenda in Manchester. *International Journal of Urban and Regional Research.* Vol 19 no 1 55–78.

Porter ME. 1990. *The Competitive Advantage of Nations.* London: Macmillan.

Preteceille E. 1990. Political paradoxes of urban restructuring: globalisation of the economy and localisation of politics? In Logan JR & T Swanstrom (eds) *Beyond the City Limits: Urban Policy and Economic Restructuring in Comparative Perspectives.* Philadelphia: Temple University Press 27–59.

Preteceille E & C Pickvance (eds). 1991. *State Restructuring and Local Power: A Comparative Perspective.* London: Pinter.

Reconstruction and Development Programme Office. 1995. *Local Economic Development: Discussion Document* (unpublished).

Redeye. 1995. Bosses on the move and other stories... . *South African Labour Bulletin.* Vol 19 no 4 4–5.

Republic of South Africa. 1994. *White Paper on Reconstruction and Development.* Cape Town: Government Printer.

Robinson J. 1993. *Local Economic Development Planning* (unpublished).

Rodwin L. 1989. Deindustrialisation and regional economic transformation. In Rodwin L & H Sazanami (eds) *Deindustrialisation and Regional Economic Transformation: The Experience of the United States.* Boston: Unwin Hyman 3–28.

Rodwin L. 1991. European industrial change and regional economic transformation: an overview of recent experience. In Rodwin L & H Sazanami (eds) *Industrial Change and Regional Economic Transformation: The experience of Western Europe*. London: Harper Collins 3–38.

Rogerson C. 1995. The employment challenge in a democratic South Africa. In Lemon A (ed) *The Geography of Change in South Africa*. England: John Wiley and Sons Ltd 169–196.

Rubin IS & HJ Rubin. 1987. Economic development incentives: the poor (cities) pay more. *Urban Affairs Quarterly* September 37–62.

Rubin H. 1988. Shoot anything that flies; claim anything that falls: conversations with economic development practitioners. *Economic Development Quarterly* 2 236–251.

Rustin M. 1986. Lessons of the London industrial strategy. *New Left Review* 155 Jan/Feb 75–87.

Saff G. 1995. The changing face of the South African city: from urban apartheid to the deracialisation of space. *International Journal of Urban and Regional Research*. Vol 18 no 3 377–391.

Saul J. 1994. *Liberation without Democracy? Rethinking the Experiences of the Southern African Liberation Movements*. Paper presented at the University of the Witwatersrand history workshop — Democracy: Popular Precedents, Practice and Culture 13–15 July.

Sbragia AM. 1989. Pittsburgh's 'Third Way': the non-profit sector as a key to urban regeneration. In Judd D & M Parkinson (eds) *Leadership and Urban Regeneration: Cities in North America and Europe*. Newbury Park: Sage 51–68.

Scott AJ. 1992. The Roepke lecture in economic geography: the collective order of flexible production agglomerations: lessons for local economic development policy and strategic choice. *Economic Geography*. Vol 68 no 3 219–233.

Smith N. 1984. *Uneven Development*. Oxford: Basil Blackwell.

Smith D. 1992. Redistribution after apartheid: who gets what where in the new South Africa? *Area*. Vol 24 no 4 350–358.

Soja E. 1971. *The Political Organisation of Space Commission on College Geography*. Washington DC: Association of American Geographers, Resource Paper no 8.

South African National Civic Organisation. 1995. *Strategies and Policies for Local Economic Development in the New South Africa*. Johannesburg: SANCO/FES.

Squires GD. 1989. Public–private partnerships: who gets what and why. In Squires GD (ed) *Unequal Partnerships: The Political Economy of Urban Redevelopment in Postwar America*. New Brunswick: Rutgers.

Storper M. 1993. The limits to globalisation: technology districts and international trade. *Economic Geography*. Vol 68 no 1 60–93.

Stren R. 1991. Old wine in new bottles? An overview of Africa's urban problems and the 'urban management' approach to dealing with them. *Environment and Urbanisation*. Vol 3 no 1 9–22.

Sunday Times National (weekly newspaper).

Tomlinson R. 1992. Competing urban agendas in South Africa. *Urban Forum*. Vol 3 no 1 97–110.

Tomlinson R. 1993. Urban economic development in South Africa. *Development Southern Africa*. Vol 10 no 3 335–359.

Tomlinson R. 1993a. From regional planning to local development planning. *Development Southern Africa*. Vol 10 no 2 167–175.

Tomlinson R. 1994. *Urban Development Planning: Lessons for the Economic Reconstruction of South Africa's Cities*. Johannesburg: Witwatersrand University Press.

Totterdill P. 1989. Local economic strategies as industrial policy: a critical review of British developments in the 1980s. *Economy and Society*. Vol 18 no 4 478–526.

Turok I. 1994. Urban planning in the transition from apartheid. Part 1: The legacy of social control. *Town Planning Review*. Vol 65 no 3 243–260.

Turok I. 1995. Restructuring or reconciliation? South Africa's Reconstruction and Development Programme. *International Journal of Urban and Regional Research*. Vol 19 no 2 305–318.

Urban Foundation. 1994. Local economic development: new strategies and practical policies. *UF Research*. No 10 November.

Vicari S & H Molotch. 1990. Building Milan: alternative machines of growth. *International Journal of Urban and Regional Research*. Vol 14 no 4 602–624.

Vonk FPM. 1989. Managing the metropolis. In Knight RV & S Sappert (eds) *Cities in a Global Society*. London: Sage 181–194.

Wade R. 1990. *Governing the Market: Economic Theory and the Role of Government in East Asian Industrialisation*. Princeton: Princeton University Press.

Watts K. 1993. National urban development policies and strategies: a review of country experience. In Harris N (ed) *Cities in the 1990s: The Challenge for Developing Countries*. New Delhi: Research Press 123–172.

World Bank. 1991. *Urban Policy and Economic Development: An Agenda for the 1990s*. Washington DC: World Bank Policy Paper.

Zeitlin J. 1989. Local industrial strategies: introduction. *Economy and Society*. Vol 18 no 4 367–373.

ACKNOWLEDGEMENTS

Sathi Moodley, Brij Maharaj, Vishnu Padayachee, Jennifer Robinson and Linda Bailey are thanked for their advice and editorial comments. The generosity and support of June Hilder, William, Alice, Little One, Rosey, Nicholas and Fennela is acknowledged, while the usual disclaimers apply.

NOTES

1. Craine, David. 1995. Mandela's second miracle. In *Africa Today. The International Magazine* May, 1, 1, 23–26.
2. Gebhardt, Claire. 1995. State-of-the-art technology crucial for SA. In *Mercury Business Report* 1 June.
3. SA industry near-worst for efficiency worldwide. In *Mercury Business Report* 3 February 1995.
4. Cited in John Smith. 1995. Creating competitive industry should be government's priority. In *Mercury Business Report* 6 April.
5. Webster E. 1995. Speak out, social democrats. In *The Weekly Mail & Guardian* 18–24 August.

6. Nattrass N & J Seekings. 1995. And the jobless? In *The Weekly Mail & Guardian* 8–14 September.
7. Elsor, Linda. 1995. Profiteering CEs give privatisation a bad name in the UK. In *Business Day* 8 February.
8. Moseneke T & R Roberts. 1995. Privatisation more than a fiscal device for government. In *Business Day* 27 March.
9. Perhaps the debate as to whether or not a market-led planning style is appropriate has already been settled. Geographers and political economists argue that the post-apartheid dispensation is prompting a new class stratification gradually beginning to overlay old racial strata, 'never completely eliminating the old divisions but blurring them and adding a new dimension' (Bond 1995: 12). Access to urban space and amenities is now based on wealth rather than racial criteria. For some, this is fast 'becoming *the* defining characteristic of South Africa's cities' (Saf 1995:377).
10. Cited in *Finance Week* 10–16 November 1994:7.
11. *Business Day* 28 December 1994.
12. Ibid.
13. Minister of Trade and Industry Trevor Manuel is so keen to open our economy to international competition that he plans to reduce tariffs in the motor, textile and clothing industries faster than even the timetable provided in GATT. This has raised the ire of both business and unions. Anglo American's Leslie Boyd sums up the concern of many cynics: 'We don't need ministers to be holier than GATT' (cited in *Redeye* 1995:5). The holier-than-thou attitude is compounded by the recent preferential trade deal struck with Zimbabwe (*Business Day* 30 August 1995). The clothing and textile industries warn of hundreds of thousands of job losses and scaling down of their proposed R3,5 billion capital investment in training and technology. These measures could plunge some cities into severe crisis.
14. Cameron, Bruce. 1995. IMF pleased with SA's progress. In *Mercury Business Report* 24 August.
15. Pillay, Vella and Charles Millward. 1995. Opportunity lost. In *Finance Week* 6–12 July.
16. Cited in COSATU criticises liberalism. In *Mercury Business Report* 4 August 1995.
17. Payne, Beatrix. 1995. Urban development bond unlikely. In *Business Day* 24 May.

CHAPTER 13

Rural Local Government in South Africa — The Context, the Theory and the Process

A McIntosh

1 INTRODUCTION

This chapter analyses current developments in the establishment of a local government system in South Africa's rural areas and their implications for the future. The chapter describes pre-existing systems for administering the rural areas during the apartheid period and difficulties arising from them, outlines proposals that have emerged to address these difficulties and assesses the local government transition process in rural areas. This provides a basis for projecting two possible scenarios for rural local government in the future.

2 THE ADMINISTRATION OF RURAL AREAS DURING THE APARTHEID PERIOD

During the apartheid period local government services in the rural areas were not provided by local government bodies but by homeland, provincial and national line departments and parastatal agencies. As autonomous, representative structures with capacity to provide services, local government existed only in South Africa's towns and cities. Even these, as other chapters make clear, only existed in any real sense within white group areas, the largely discredited Indian and coloured management committees or local affairs councils and the black local authorities relying on government line ministries to provide services and finance. The history of these arrangements, the opposition they caused, and the distortions and inefficiencies of South Africa's racially-based cities have been well documented. Indeed, until the establishment of RSCs in the late 1980s (to be discussed below), local government did not exist in any form within the rural areas.

Within the white commercial farming areas, responsibility for providing various services was vested in central line ministries or departments of the provincial administration (education, transport, agriculture, welfare, etc). Since, under the tricameral system, these responsibilities were also racially defined, different central ministries were responsible for providing the same services to different race groups, whether falling within the House of Assembly (whites), the House of Delegates (Indians) or the House of Representatives (coloureds). Since Africans resident on white farmlands were deemed to be citizens of the various homelands, less emphasis was placed on their requirements. Nominal attention was paid to certain services (eg farm schools and clinics) by the various departments responsible for Africans in 'white' South Africa (including the Department of Development Aid, formerly known as Bantu and Native Affairs). As far as the so-called 'black spot' areas — areas in which Africans had purchased land and had managed to evade removal to the homelands — were concerned, a policy of deliberate neglect by the relevant ministries resulted in many of these areas receiving no infrastructure or services until the latter part of the apartheid period.

In practice, the bulk of those living in white farming areas, namely farm workers, obtained most 'local government' services from their employers. Although some farm workers resided in neighbouring homelands, many remained resident on farms, relying on the farmer for housing, water, transport and even recreation.

Administration of the homelands was highly centralised within the regional or central administrations created for the various national states and self-governing territories. In this sense, the system was similar to the administration of the colonial period. This was because service delivery had previously been centralised within the Department of Native Affairs. There was one significant difference, however. The Department of Native Affairs made extensive use of commissioners and magistrates to administer local affairs. As the government's supreme representative in a locality it was the task of this officer to assure implementation of government policy according to local conditions. The magistrate/commissioner thus had an important coordinating role at a local level and had authority over the various divisions of the department providing local services. Since commissioners and magistrates did not have extensive policing or military forces at their disposal, they also tended to consult traditional leaders to ensure that government policy was implemented in a way that did not generate opposition. In this sense, traditional leaders became intermediaries between government and communities through the offices of magistrates and commissioners.

Apartheid reforms saw the powers and functions of the commissioners and magistrates being undermined in favour of the new 'national' governments. This took the form of establishing regional authorities (amalgams of tribal authorities) and subsequently territorial authorities in which service provision was centralised within various functional departments falling under the various legislative assemblies and cabinets. Whereas decision making regarding service provision had been through the magistrate (with traditional leaders as intermediaries), decision making regarding service provision was now centralised within line departments without local level coordinating mechanisms (see McIntosh 1992).

Decisions regarding the provision of services were usually made by senior officials within the homeland centre, who had little knowledge of local conditions or priorities. The field officers who interacted with the public were usually junior, without departmental support, and their accountability was upwards to their line department rather than to their community. The homeland line ministries themselves were also usually very insular. Since local government or coordinating mechanisms did not exist at a local level, cooperation between departments at the point of implementation could usually not take place. It would consequently be very difficult to mount health education programmes in conjunction with spring protection programmes, for example, as both these functions fell under different departments. Not only was coordination usually weak in the locality. It was also weak at central levels, the imperatives of the line departments usually taking precedence over joint planning structures that were put in place at a 'national' level (see McIntosh 1994 for a case study dealing with these issues).

Finally, it has been argued that traditional authorities were undermined during the apartheid period. Since local services were often provided independently of tribal authorities by officers of the line ministries, traditional leaders were bypassed in respect of decision making on service delivery and development. Concerns of amakhosi were meant to be channelled through regional authorities, to the chief minister's office and, in turn, to the various line departments. This was a cumbersome, lengthy process that did not work effectively (see McIntosh 1990). This meant that the de facto powers and functions of traditional leaders were fairly limited to judicial functions under customary law, to dispute resolution, and most important, to land allocation.

Even in respect of these functions, traditional authorities were severely neglected by responsible government departments and obtained little funding to perform their duties. Indeed, greater emphasis was placed on the traditional leaders as individuals. They were often drawn into the party political arena as members of legislative assemblies, functions that often undermined their roles as traditional authorities.

The common shortcomings of local administration across the different contexts described above might be summarised in terms of the highly centralised, non-responsive and unrepresentative character of local administration and service delivery; and the fragmentation of administration. This apparently took place along ethnic lines, taking intergovernmental and intra-governmental forms.

3 TOWARDS A THEORY OF RURAL LOCAL GOVERNMENT

Many challenges emerge from the situation outlined above. One challenge is the establishment of a viable local government system in areas where there are such limited revenue-raising capacities. They fall outside the metropolitan centres and secondary cities, where the majority rely on urban remittances or welfare disbursements and where there are distinct limits to what the commercial agricultural and the trading sectors within the market towns could contribute to local government.

Another is how to build on the very limited existing capacity of local institutions, given the absence of any local government — outside market towns — within the commercial farming areas and the limited role and inadequacy of tribal authorities within the homelands. Can new local government systems, built on such a weak base, overcome the problems associated with existing systems of fragmented, centralised and uncoordinated delivery? Can they be expected to deliver responsively? Would they be able to ensure that services from higher authorities or outside organisations are provided in a way that is consistent with local political and developmental priorities?

A third challenge is how to establish and sustain local structures of representation and accountability. To what extent does the institution of chieftainship retain popular legitimacy? Should it be accommodated within future local government arrangements? Could rural (or district) councils be expected to be truly representative and accountable where institutions of civil society are so weakly developed and where local elites tend to monopolise local affairs and development resources to the exclusion of marginal groups such as farm workers, landless people and women? How might the specific needs of such marginal groups be accommodated at a local level? Will the franchise suffice?

This section outlines several principles to address these challenges. They were developed by rural NGOs and popularised during the transition period. It is against these suggestions that the final section outlining the progress of the local government transition process in rural areas will be evaluated.

3.1 Institutional support for rural local government

There is a need for central (and provincial) support for rural local government. The weak economic and political position of rural people and their institutions highlight the difficulties of sustaining a viable local government system and the importance of outside support. Unless rural constituencies become more assertive within national politics and, unless vested interests in sustaining an independent local government system can be created and sustained at provincial and national levels, there is a danger that rural local government will simply become an agent of central or regional government. It has been suggested that institutional support for rural local government should ideally come from the centre, since the centre is likely to be less threatened by local government than the regions. Caught between local and central government, regionally-based political parties often try to agglomerate power to themselves at the expense of local government where central government can resist such incursions. However, it is not clear whether it will be possible to sustain the argument for central rather than regional support for rural local government.

The one suggestion then is that if central (and provincial) support for a viable rural local government system is to be sustained, a strong ministry of local government is required. This is not only necessary to ensure the defence of the interests of local government within the centre (and/or provinces) where such a ministry has an interest in defending localities from the tendency of other provincial and central ministries to agglomerate powers and functions of localities to themselves. Ensuring the defence of localities' interests at a local level is also necessary. Newly established structures of local government with relatively weak constituencies can hardly be expected to carry the necessary political authority to pursue their local political and developmental priorities. Therefore, it has also been suggested that field representatives of a ministry of local government (ie district commissioners) fulfil certain functions of rural local government structures in the short term. For example, in themselves, district councils may not carry the central or provincial political authority to ensure the delivery of services according to local priorities, or to challenge them when they overstep their jurisdiction. Where service delivery organisations have to contend with district councils and powerful district commissioners attached to such councils, their scope for unilateral action is diminished.

However, support from district commissioners is necessary to lend district councils the political authority they are unable to muster. District councils will also need to rely on the professional support of such officers where, usually, these are being built upon weak or non-existent institutional bases.

3.2 Financial support for district councils

Central (and/or provincial) support for district councils should take the form of block grants in recognition, on the one hand, of their limited revenue-raising capacities and, on the other, of the contribution of rural people to urban economies — whether through migrant/commuter labour or purchasing. It is suggested that such grants be calculated according to a national formula based on populations in rural council areas. Apart from providing a basis for dispersing resources equitably, these criteria would be aimed at maximising decision-making autonomy. Although other criteria would, no doubt, need to be attached to funding district councils — to ensure that statutory duties are performed, and that national performance standards are stuck to — it would be important for at least part of these funds to be made available as discretionary grants. Without such discretionary funding, district councils could find that their role is limited to performing duties specified by higher authorities. Under these conditions district councils could face difficulties addressing local priorities and acquiring political legitimacy at a local level.

3.3 Local government staffing

Another element of outside support relates to the staffing of district councils. The one possibility is for central or provincial government tiers to second staff to district councils. The problem with this is that although staff are formally accountable to the council, in practice they will follow the lead of their mother departments. Also, regional or central government departments typically do not value the contribution of staff seconded to local authorities. A result is that the least able staff are the ones who are seconded and ambitious individuals seek promotion to regional or central tiers. A second possibility is for different councils to hire their own staff according to service conditions. Although this gives greater autonomy to local councils, the general tendency is for better qualified and more capable local government professionals to find work in more attractive and lucrative city environments. The third option is to establish a national local government service commission, independent and parallel to the national government service commission, to decide conditions of service in local government and make appointments. Although this could undermine local government autonomy, it could establish clear career and promotion structures in local government and ensure that the more capable local government officers are not enticed by opportunities in central or provincial government agencies.

3.4 The boundaries of district councils

A viable rural local government system cannot be founded on support from higher tiers of government alone. It is imperative that district council boundaries are delimited according to criteria maximising their revenue-raising potential and facilitating scale economies in service delivery. There are two ways in which these principles may be fostered, both of which could undermine prospects of local representation. The first is to, where possible, incorporate rural hinterlands of the major metropolitan centres and secondary cities into single local government bodies, thereby maximising possibilities for redistribution. Although this may be justified for commuter settlements on the outskirts of — or even distant from — the cities, there is a valid fear of rural constituencies being overwhelmed by powerful urban constituencies with different interests. The second is for district councils to incorporate areas serviced by the major rural service centres (or market towns) in a way that incorporates trading centres, commercial farmlands, tribal landholdings and, where possible, other rural settlements. The theory is that district councils delimited in this way could probably provide some of their own revenue, support a cadre of local government professionals and carry some political weight.

However, size is a problem posed by district councils demarcated to generate revenue and achieve scale economies in service delivery. Given the existing spatial distribution of wealth in South Africa, boundary demarcations that meet the above criteria could encompass massive areas, similar in size to the present RSCs and JSBs. In this context, if district councils do not incorporate those urban settlements (or towns) outside the metropolitan centres and secondary cities the possibility of their generating a reasonable proportion of their own revenue is small. This diminishes the likelihood of their sustaining political autonomy, and they will become dependent on central or provincial government grants.

3.5 Representation and composition of district councils

The reason large district council demarcations are problematic relates to representation. Will such large local authorities be able to represent their constituents adequately? Large, directly elected local authorities imply distance between councillors, officials and the many location-bound constituents in different types of rural settlement (such as farm dwellers, relict women in tribal lands, etc), suggesting the prospect of distant, unresponsive, bureaucratic and expensive councils. This underlies the suggestion that district councils should be composite, incorporating elected primary local councils. Not only would local councils provide selected services but they would also provide local representation on district councils. Consequently it is argued that local councils should be indirectly elected onto district councils. However, indirect representation on district councils should be complemented by direct election to ensure the political accountability of district councils and to encourage district councillors to acquire supra-local perspectives.

Of course, whether district councils of whatever complexion become meaningful channels of representation is not only a question of their size, composition or voting criteria. It also depends on the process embarked on in establishing a new rural local government system. In this context, it is important to recognise that many existing representative local bodies (whether development committees, civics or tribal authorities) already have legitimacy and some capacity to deliver services and to raise funds.

Consequently, a failure of new local government arrangements to incorporate existing, legitimate institutions risks alienating the public and undermining existing mechanisms of mutual support. This raises the question of whether criteria underlying incorporation should consider traditional practices like chiefly inheritance. Making such concessions may be important, although they need not undermine the requirements of democracy and accountability. Ex officio representation of traditional leaders on local or district councils in recognition of chiefly inheritance need not affect the capacity of these bodies to represent local people where the other office-bearers are elected, for example, and have voting powers to over-rule chiefly preferences.

The difficulty posed by the need to incorporate existing, representative local institutions into a new local government system is that many existing local bodies lack legitimacy and represent few sectors of the population (such as tribal authorities in the Ciskei) (see Manona 1991). An interim process enabling legitimate local institutions to be included — and illegitimate local bodies to be excluded — from a new local government system is imperative.

4 THE LOCAL GOVERNMENT TRANSITION PROCESS: PROGRESS AND SHORTCOMINGS

This section reflects on the process of local government transition in South Africa's rural areas and evaluates likely prospects for a strong, developmentally oriented local government system. It argues that this preferred course is by no means assured, and that some problems associated with the local government transition process in the period leading up to the first democratic local government elections suggest a possibility of weak representative structures at a local level becoming reliant on provincial or central patronage.

4.1 The transition process

The rural local government issue was first raised by the National Land Committee (NLC) in collaboration with SANCO and the ANC before the elections at the time the Local Government Transition Act was being negotiated in the national Local Government Negotiating Forum (LGNF). Although a technical committee established by the forum produced a set of broadly acceptable principles according to which the matter might have been pursued, these principles did not find their way into the Local Government Transition Act.

Briefly, the Act makes provision for local or metropolitan negotiating forums comprising statutory and non-statutory members (that is, representatives of organisations having participated in local government and/or local government elections and organisations that have not). Transitional local councils (TLCs) (made up of representatives chosen from lists drawn up by statutory and non-statutory sides within the forums) then replace existing local authorities until local government elections are held. Under the Act, decisions regarding these processes are made by the provincial premier acting in concurrence with multi-party provincial committees on local government in each province. Provision is also made for demarcation boards making recommendations if there are disputes around the demarcation of forum and council areas.

While the Act, in theory, applied to the whole country, the process it set out for local government transition, for establishing forums and TLCs in the pre-interim period, could not be applied in rural areas where there are no pre-existing local authorities.

When this anomaly was pointed out to the Transitional Executive Council's (TEC) sub-council on provincial government, local government and traditional authorities, a similar subcommittee was established, developing a set of more detailed principles and recommendations (see Working Group 1994). By this time, however, the TEC had run its course and these recommendations were simply handed over to the new government.

Since the 1994 national elections, the Ministry of Constitutional Development and Provincial Affairs has established a national task team on rural local government whose job it has been to liaise with the provinces and to ensure that the provinces meet the requirements of the interim constitution for elected local government countrywide. Since, by this time, local government had become a provincial competence under the interim constitution, no national vision or framework for local government had been articulated for rural areas. This, at a time shortly before local government elections were meant to take place throughout the country.

Before reflecting on how the provinces have responded to the rural local government issue, suggesting a few reasons why too little was done too late is necessary. First, urban concerns and issues (especially the service and rates boycotts) have overshadowed those of the rural areas, a bias reflecting where political party support has been most organised.

Secondly, insufficient attention has been given to local government as a national priority. This is suggested by an anticipated national ministry of local government failing to materialise. This, in spite of recognising that support and funding will be needed by the provinces and local governments if local government is to be effective, especially within the rural areas. That local government became a provincial competence at the time some provinces lacked the capacity to deal with the issue has exacerbated the situation.

A final possible reason for the neglect of rural local government at a national level relates to the nature of our transition. National and provincial elections occurring before local government elections have created a situation in which sets of interests that may prevent effective local government have been entrenched at these levels (whether in bureaucracies or political parties). Some bigger municipalities can and will protect their interests from provincial and national government by virtue of their size and political influence. Some metros, for example, have larger budgets than their provincial governments. For the smaller towns and the yet to be established rural local government bodies, obtaining the necessary support and autonomy will be more difficult. The provincial quest for power could be at the expense of local government.

The provinces are responsible for developing rural local government systems, but have no clear, national direction or a legal framework equivalent to the Local Government Transition Act. The North West, Northern and Eastern Cape provinces are, in any event, facing enormous administrative difficulties amalgamating their existing regional administrations. It is perhaps not surprising, given the capacity problems existing in these provinces, that progress should have been slow in dealing with the rural local government issue. This is reflected in delays encountered in finalising provincial approaches to rural local government.

The national task team established by the Ministry of Constitutional Development and Planning spent some time attempting to find consensus on a common framework for rural local government in the various provinces. Eventually some points of departure, in line with the arguments developed in section two, were suggested. Those generally accepted by the provinces included:

☐ the suggestion that a two-tier system of local government would be appropriate where it is unlikely that a single tier system will be viable;

☐ the principle that all citizens could elect some form of local government;

☐ the suggestion that the pre-interim phase (for establishing forums, TLCs, etc) may or may not be applied in rural areas, depending on circumstances; and

☐ the principle that the entire country would be serviced by some form of local government.

Generally, the provinces appointed their own task teams to develop suggestions for provincial models and pre-interim arrangements for rural local government as well as appropriate legislative mechanisms for introducing the new system.

Most of the provinces originally opted for what has become known as the two-tier district council model described in the previous section. They argued that primary local government bodies would then be directly elected. Some argued for district councils to be elected indirectly by the primary local government bodies while others argued for an element of direct representation in district councils. More recently, however, it became clear to most provinces that they did not have the capacity to establish new primary local government structures within rural areas in time for elections. The result is that most provinces went into elections without primary structures in rural areas. Thus, the general trend is for direct election from rural areas to district councils based on proportional representation, with only council representatives on the TLCs being indirectly elected onto district councils.

The system will be built on the administrative infrastructure existing in the old RSCs and JSBs. These were established in the late 1980s as a mechanism to finance bulk services at a supra-local level and to extend the political and constitutional principles of the 1983 tricameral constitution (particularly the principles of own and general affairs) to the third tier (Humphries 1991:60). They also became regarded as one of the main constitutional strategies to deal with the economic and political problems of black local authorities. These problems included a lack of own revenue and legitimacy. RSCs/JSBs allocate resources/services (raised through a variety of local taxes) according to a voting system between members of the council (that is local authorities or other RSC/JSB members) determined by the financial contribution to services by member local authorities (or equivalents).

RSCs/JSBs have been built on ethnically-based local authorities. They also exclude large sections of the population (such as farm workers), and are not devolved local authorities in their own right. Rather, they are agencies servicing a variety of existing local bodies. However, they have been delimited according to criteria that include the ability to raise local revenue and to achieve scale economies in service delivery. They also provide the only existing local (supra-local) institutional framework on which a new rural local government system might be built.

The modified district council model (without primary structures in rural areas) might be the general trend in spite of difficulties associated with it. These include district councils remaining remote from many communities, councillors not being elected on a ward basis, and district councils having to accommodate many councillors, making councils' meetings difficult and expensive to organise. The general weaknesses of the transition process discussed have previously had several consequences.

4.2 Delays in finalising rural local government models

First, there have been considerable delays in finalising provincial models for rural local government. Although a similar framework is emerging regarding rural local government in South Africa, most provinces had only recently finalised their approach. In other cases, an approach to the rural local government question remains elusive. Difficulties around voter registration have undoubtedly arisen from a lack of knowledge of local government among rural constituencies. Nor has there been clarity about which local government bodies they will be voting for. Other difficulties arising out of delays in formulating and implementing policies on rural local government will become apparent in the run-up to elections. They include the local government demarcation process and the process of ward demarcation, affected by the slow registration process.

4.3 Lack of pre-interim arrangements

Secondly, while pre-interim arrangements have been set in motion in most towns and cities, this has not happened in the rural areas. Pre-interim structures, it will be recalled, are designed to fulfil a similar role to the TEC: to provide legitimate multi-party bodies mechanisms to take decisions before elections and to oversee election preparation. The procedure outlined in the Local Government Transition Act allowed forums to decide boundaries and to appoint statutory and non statutory representatives to the TLCs taking over existing local government administrations.

In rural areas, where there are no existing local government administrations, such pre-interim processes have not taken place. Under these conditions, many provincial governments have tasked the RSCs with voter registration and other aspects of election preparation. This is controversial in some provinces since, in their structure and composition, RSCs remain untransformed, apartheid institutions. The provinces have usually had little choice in this since they are obliged to use whatever capacity exists to meet existing deadlines around voter registration.

There is recognition nationally and provincially that the procedures laid down for the pre-interim phase are not appropriate for the rural areas. They would, in any event, be impossible to apply given the tight schedules drawn to meet election deadlines. This was one of the reasons for amendments being made to the Local Government Transition Act that, among other things, enable pre-interim structures to be established according to procedures other than those outlined in the Act. These include allowances for representatives for pre-interim structures being elected at public meetings. For many provinces, however, it was even questionable whether such 'fast-track' pre-interim solutions could be carried out.

4.4 Poor management of conflict between stakeholders

Thirdly, the absence of a pre-interim process for rural areas and the failure to consult timeously in developing and implementing rural local government systems, has led to conflict among rural stakeholders. Traditional leaders lack clarity on their future role. In this regard, chapter 11 of the interim constitution recognises traditional authorities and makes provision for advisory roles at provincial and national levels. However, it does not specify what roles such authorities should play at a local level except by reference to other applicable laws. Since the various self-governing territories and independent states that promulgated much of this legislation have now been dissolved, much of the legislation that has typically underlaid traditional authorities will probably be repealed. It is unclear with what the new provinces will replace this legislation.

It is perhaps understandable that the national negotiation process preceding the framing of the interim constitution should have fudged this issue, particularly in the light of the national elections that followed. As one of the most organised rural constituencies, the need to address the interests of the traditional leaders had to be set against (the largely urban-based) objections of the women's lobbies to discriminatory aspects of customary law and to competing claims of what local democracy should consist of.

Arising out of the constitution's failure to address the roles of traditional authorities at a local level, is the question of how they should relate to elected local government entities. Under chapter 10 of the interim constitution these 'shall be established for residents of areas demarcated by law of a competent authority'. It further specifies a service delivery role for elected local government in providing access to water, sanitation, transportation facilities, electricity, etc. Service delivery and development have rarely been the prerogatives of traditional authorities in practice, but of the various line departments of the homeland governments. The role of traditional authorities has usually been limited to cultural, ceremonial or religious functions; dispute resolution and judicial functions concerning customary law; and, importantly, land allocation. However, existing legislation (promulgated by the former homeland governments) governing the operation of traditional authorities, provides wide-ranging powers to traditional authorities, including those of a service delivery nature.

Difficulties arising include a perception by civics that the national election presages the imminent dissolution of chieftaincy and a perception by traditional leaders in other places that their role will not change (see McIntosh & Vaughan 1994 and 1994a for the case of the Northern Province and Mpumalanga). Generally, however, there is great uncertainty among traditional leaders stemming from the dissolution of their former patrons — the former homeland governments — and a lack of clarity about whether, and to what extent, the new provincial governments will become suitable substitutes. Such insecurity could well discourage traditional leaders from willingly giving up existing *de jure* powers, even those that have not been exercised.

The failure to establish houses of traditional leaders or to deal with some other insecurities felt by traditional leaders has engendered a reluctance to encourage the voters' registration process in certain provinces or to accept a minority role in elected local government structures. To argue that traditional authorities should participate in decision making regarding service delivery matters is not to suggest that they should be responsible for providing such services. In instances where traditional authorities have been viewed by communities as responsible for providing services, their legitimacy and authority have been undermined by non-delivery. Ex officio representation of traditional leaders in local government thus implies participation in decision making regarding local government services, but not responsibility for providing such services. A potential difficulty arises when many councillors, who are traditional leaders, hold the perception that service provision is a responsibility of traditional leaders rather than elected local government.

What needs to be emphasised is that such insecurities and the potential for conflict could have been better managed in many provinces. Mpumalanga provides an example. The early establishment of a task team to negotiate the composition of the provincial house of traditional leaders, provided a structure that could be used to negotiate a workable relationship between envisaged rural local government structures and traditional authorities. This involved establishing councils of traditional leaders from each proposed rural council area that would elect representatives to serve ex officio on that elected local council.

Indeed, it is suggested that the threat traditional leaders pose to establishing a strong local government system derives more from their current insecurities than a principled objection to an elected rural local government system. It could be argued that, ultimately, an elected local government system would serve their interests. For, quite apart from the problems created by the politicisation of the chieftaincy during the apartheid period, traditional leaders have been compromised by their inability to orchestrate the delivery of development resources in their localities, due to centralised and poorly coordinated service delivery. Elected structures responsible for accessing or delivering such resources would distance traditional leaders from these immediate pressures. Simultaneously, a devolved and rationalised local government system would ease locally accountable and responsive service delivery. Under these conditions, traditional leaders, in their ex officio capacities on elected local councils could, conceivably, have much greater influence over local affairs, in spite of their *de jure* powers being more limited. More intensive education and negotiation processes emphasising these points might have done much to limit the threat posed by traditional leaders to the local government transition process.

It is necessary to concede, however, that such difficulties have been magnified in Kwazulu Natal by the Inkatha Freedom Party's (IFP) linkage of participation in local government elections to the international mediation around the future of the Zulu kingdom, the resulting withdrawal of many Zulu traditional leaders from local government transition processes, and to the controversy around the provincial house of traditional leaders. This has resulted in limiting the role of the King within that house and in making the IFP leader the chair of the house (see McIntosh, Vaughan & Xaba 1995).

However, not only traditional leaders have laid claim to ex officio representation. The white farming community has also done so based on their likely tax contribution to rural local government revenue. These lobbying efforts have been followed by rural NGOs laying claim to special representation for rural women (because of their relatively powerless position in society) and for farm workers on similar grounds.

Attempts have been made by the national government to satisfy these competing claims by allowing the provinces provide special representation for these interest groups, but limiting the proportion of unelected representatives (to 20% of any single council). However, this raised the ire of certain traditional leaders for reducing their representation in rural local government bodies and for placing them on a similar footing to other 'interest groups'.

Quite how representatives of these 'interest groups' are going to be selected is unclear, since many of these groups are not organised. However, the knee-jerk reaction of government to such pressures highlights shortcomings in processes that should have been managing these competing interests.

4.5 Fragmentation of line functions in relation to rural local government

Fourthly, the inadequate process of local government transition has discouraged provincial and national line ministries from gearing their activities towards an anticipated rural local government system. Rather than channelling their activities into local government, or at least a local coordinating administration upon which local councils could be built, the trend is towards establishing parallel statutory or semi-statutory bodies that relate directly to the relevant line ministries. These include water committees in the case of Water Affairs, Community Land Trusts in the case of Land Affairs, and proposed structures for rural housing, including trusts, section 21 companies and utility companies. In addition, the RDP office has been pushing hard for RDP committees at a local level '... which have access to funding to manage and set up development projects' (see Westaway 1995).

The *raison d'être* of some ministries for establishing what could become parallel and competing structures of local government is that these are interim mechanisms for service provision, which should be integrated into the local government system. Whether they will be remains to be seen. Many provincial officials and politicians have not experienced or developed local government perspectives. Since power is already entrenched at the provincial and national levels, they might be reluctant to devolve powers to local government or to undertake their activities through, or with, newly established local government bodies. The temptation to dispense patronage through their own sectoral-based user committees might be overwhelming under these circumstances.

5 CONCLUSION: LOCAL DEVELOPMENT OR CENTRAL CONTROL?

The shortcomings of the local government transition process in the run-up to the first democratic elections in South Africa highlights the aptness of suggesting a possible alternative for local government in South Africa's rural areas. A common compromise throughout Africa is where a local structure of representation is recognised, but not given the finance, authority or staff to be effective. Under these conditions, departmental staff who are seconded to the local government structure tend to follow the orientation of their mother department and, in any event, try to avoid such secondments as local government is regarded as a backwater. To the extent that the representative body, under such conditions, remains weak and dependent on a higher authority, it is questionable whether such arrangements can be distinguished substantially from the regionally centralised arrangements that existed in the homelands during the apartheid period. The fragmentation and competition existing between various government agencies will persist, and the difficulties centralised ministries have supervising field-based officers in local conditions will continue.

South Africa has a choice to make. In not providing the requisite commitment to a strong local government system, it can choose to follow a centrist route. However, the alternative is not only imperative for local democracy but also a precondition for rural development. Furthermore, it is not too late to pursue such opportunities, given that South Africa will be bound by the interim constitution until 1999. Sufficient commitment by national government and the provinces to put systems of administration and processes for establishing a strong primary level of local government in place, is urgently required.

6 REFERENCES

McIntosh AC. 1990. Chieftainship and the future of rural local government: a preliminary investigation. *Transformation*. Vol 13 27–45.

McIntosh AC. 1994. Reforming local administration in South Africa's rural areas: lessons from the upper Tugela catchment experience. *Development Southern Africa*. Vol 11 no 3.

McIntosh AC. 1992. *Options for Rural Local Government and Administration with Particular Reference to Kwazulu*. Unpublished PhD thesis, Development Administration Group, University of Birmingham.

McIntosh AC & A Vaughan. 1994. Towards a rural local government system in the Northern Transvaal. In Inlogov *Rural Local Government in South Africa*. Cape Town: Page Arts.

McIntosh AC & A Vaughan. 1994. Establishing a rural local government system in the Eastern Transvaal: options and possibilities. Consultant report for the Development Bank of Southern Africa.

McIntosh AC, A Vaughan & X Thokozani. 1995. *The Rural Local Government Question in Kwazulu Natal: Stakeholders' Perspectives*. Durban: Regional Consultative Forum.

Westaway A. 1995. *The Development Framework and Local Government: Whatever Happened to the RDP?* Paper presented at the Rural Local Government Summit, hosted by the National Land Committee, Midrand.

Wittenburg M & AC McIntosh. 1993. Regionalism: a hall of mirrors. *Indicator SA* Autumn.

Working Group on Non-metropolitan Government. 1994. Report to the sub-council on regional and local government and traditional authorities. In *Rural Local Government in South Africa*. Cape Town: Inlogov.

— CHAPTER 14 —

NGOs, Civil Society and Development — The South African Experience

B Maharaj & S Jaggernath

1 INTRODUCTION

The essential function of government is to uphold the rights of its citizens. The government's role is enhanced by formal and non-formal institutions of society. These are made up of state-created structures and of non-governmental organisations (NGOs) including civic groups, other community-based organisations and private interest groups with social responsibility programmes. Organisations falling outside governmental structures may be called organs of civil society. The relationship between government and civil society is strongest at the local government level. This is because organisations at the local level articulate an immediacy of community needs.

Until April 1994 blacks in South Africa were denied political power and participation in government at all levels. Their political exclusion influenced the rise of social movements that 'mobilised civil society around a wide range of politicised causes such as housing, basic services, transport, development and culture' (Copans, Darbon & Faure 1992:29). Civic organisations have played an important role in articulating the needs of those who were disenfranchised, and in many respects were at the forefront of the struggle for a democratic society in South Africa (Botha 1992).

Parallelling the civic organisations, many other types of service organisations, all falling within the framework of NGOs, were established to alleviate problems experienced by the victims of apartheid. Since democratic elections were held in South Africa, the future of NGOs has been hotly debated. The aim of this paper is threefold, namely, to provide a brief theoretical perspective on NGOs, to examine their role in the South African context, and finally, to suggest future directions for them in South Africa.

2 THEORETICAL PERSPECTIVES

2.1 Emergence of NGOs

The term NGO embraces a variety of organisational forms and activities, ranging from small, informal local initiatives to more formalised structures, their composition and goals varying from, for example, a radical rural peasant organisation to a conservative cultural women's movement. NGOs are voluntary, non-profit organisations that function independently of the state apparatus. A working definition that perhaps proximates all the features ascribed to NGOs is offered by Bernstein (1994:27):

> 'In the broadest sense, NGOs are non-profit groups outside of government, organised by communities or individuals to respond to basic needs that are not being met by either the government or the market. Some produce goods; others deliver services; and some of the largest do a combination of both. The groups are either formed at the neighbourhood level, by and for the community, or at a regional level where they have intermediary functions.'

Since the 1980s, there has been a rapid growth of NGOs 'both in numbers and in the volume of resources they mobilise' (World Bank 1991:136). According to the World Bank (1991:136), about $5,5 billion from industrial to developing countries filtered through NGOs in 1977, nearly $1 billion more than that handled by the International Development Association, underscoring the impact NGOs have made in influencing world affairs. At the very least the unprecedented growth of NGOs in all parts of the world, both developed and undeveloped, is interpreted as an indisputable statement that the welfare of communities rests as much on organs of civil society as it does on government. It has also become increasingly apparent that the significance of NGOs lies in their capacity to work with communities at grass-roots level in carrying out development projects. These organisations are increasingly being viewed as 'possible alternatives to government in addressing the needs of populations otherwise unreached by official development programmes' (Brown & Korten 1989:1). According to Garilao (1987:114), in many cases NGOs have developed out of:

- □ social tensions and conflict;
- □ the necessity to react more competently to difficult circumstances, especially when conventional structures are unable to respond effectively;
- □ differences between government and community in the design and execution of development projects; or
- □ the inability of the government or the private sector, because of a lack of determination, resources or capacity to respond to urgent social problems.

NGOs have emerged as an influential force in the development process that has alleviated the costs of 'institutional weaknesses, which often include administrative shortcomings and an inability to carry out efficiently, essential development tasks, such as providing social services or protecting the environment' (World Bank

1991:135–36). There are various reasons for the rapid development of NGOs, including:

☐ increasing interest among international donors and national governments in augmenting the developmental capacities of institutions functioning outside the formal public sector;

☐ NGOs being more capable than government agencies in reaching the poor;

☐ governments being forced to seek more cost-effective alternatives to orthodox state development programmes because of a rapid decrease in development resources;

☐ NGOs displaying an ability to mobilise large sums of money for development projects; and

☐ recognition that some NGOs have shown an ability to advocate and start projects on a national level and influence central government policies and institutions (Brown & Korten 1989:1).

The development of most NGOs can be traced to a very basic human tendency to right a wrong, either through compassion or protest. However, the attention of most NGOs was in the past focused on immediate concerns or protest actions. More recently, there has been some consideration of 'questions of development theory and strategy and their implications for policy and programme action' (Korten & Quizon 1991:6).

Another factor that influenced the development of NGOs was disillusionment with the role of the state and market in contributing to development and progressive social change. Many examples of state incompetence, corruption and repression revealed that social development could not be achieved through public sector policies. Equally disappointingly, the profit-oriented marketplace has not shown much willingness to annihilate poverty or to empower the disadvantaged (Farrington & Babbington 1993:2).

This rethinking has led to the identification of a 'third sector' to relieve poverty, reinforce civil society and encourage participation in grass-roots development in ways that go 'beyond the capability — or willingness — of the state and the market' (Farrington & Babbington 1993:2). NGOs and other voluntary, self-help organisations form this 'third sector'. Some analysts have argued that NGOs are more concerned in ameliorating poverty, some that they are more interested in empowering the poor and contributing to a stronger civil society, and others have maintained that NGOs focus on environmental issues (Farrington & Babbington 1993:2).

2.2 Stages in the development of NGOs

NGOs have evolved over time, and analysing stages in their development is useful. Most indigenous NGOs began operations at the local level, focusing on micro projects in the village. As their skills and experience increased, they began to work with 'village clusters', subsequently functioning in larger areas, and addressing more complex problems. As their grass-roots support increased 'NGOs began to affect other institutions and to confront directly other social forces and groups' (Garilao 1987:115). According to Garilao (1987:115) NGOs go through three stages in their organisational evolution — formation and development; consolidation; and institutionalisation.

2.3 Formation and development

In this stage, a small group recognises common problems and decides to organise itself collectively towards responding to them. The NGO's emphasis on organising people is related to a philosophy that identifies the 'centrality of people in development policies and action programmes, and the importance of self-organisation' (Cernea 1989:119). Many NGOs have developed as a reaction to the philanthropic and benevolent yearnings of individuals to 'contribute toward making a better world. They have relied on high moral purpose, goodwill, hard work and common sense to make them successful' (Korten 1987:155). The epitome of the NGO approach is not to encourage 'development financially, but to mobilise people into organised structures of voluntary group action for self-reliance and self-development' (Cernea 1989:119). This has been emphasised by Cernea (1989:119) as follows:

> 'The first and foremost NGO emphasis is on organising people for reaching their common objectives. In this way, NGOs are putting people first in their work, both as methodology and as a goal — particularly the poor groups — and are themselves an embodiment of this principle ... The organisational capacity that comes to life through and becomes engaged in development action represents its fundamental strategic resource and crucial contribution.'

Generally the intervention in this stage is at the micro level. Members define their expectations and elect their leaders. The rules and regulations for the functioning of the organisation, however, have yet to be clarified. The aim is to address immediate, or short-term, problems.

2.4 Consolidation

In this stage the NGO 'consolidates its gains'(Garilao 1987:115). A strong, respected leadership emerges, and the NGO's expertise is developed and used in support of its aims and objectives. In fact the ability to conduct its activities efficiently 'gives the NGO a distinctive competitive edge in carrying out its programmes vis-à-vis other groups' (Garilao 1987:115). Many NGOs do not develop beyond this stage, some may ultimately become dormant because of the inability of leaders to sustain the interest of members in pursuing the aims of the organisation, and others are sometimes unable to adapt to the changing environment in which they function. Some NGOs fail to develop internally because of concerns that 'in responding to calls for professionalisation, they would become more like the conventional bureaucracies of government that they commonly believe to be ineffective' (Korten 1987:155).

2.5 Institutionalisation

Some NGOs become institutionalised through fulfilling all the requirements for long-term existence. Besides performing their functions efficiently, they also have 'a certain strategic impact in (their) geographic localities. In fact, the programme becomes the model after which other NGOs, and even government, pattern their programme' (Garilao 1987:115). NGOs acquire a secure resource foundation from internal and external sources. They also develop regional, national and international alliances and linkages, a significant indicator of the institutionalisation stage. This stage is often characterised by a geographic expansion in the area of coverage of the activities of the NGO. For example, the 'combined efforts of NGOs in Brazil, the United States, Europe and other Third World countries succeeded in persuading the World Bank to stop funding a road-building and resettlement scheme that was destroying a large portion of the Amazon' (Clark 1991:6). However, ultimately, it is not the size but the 'quality of the organisation that matters' (Garilao 1987:115). In this third stage the NGO is highly organised and influential. People are empowered to use their own local productive resources and services to advance equity and relieve poverty, and also influence government policies to achieve these objectives, and establish new institutional frameworks to sustain community-centred grass-roots development (Cernea 1989:119).

3 NGOs AND DEMOCRACY

NGOs have often been viewed as vital for democracy because of their strong support at grass roots and their capacity for development and empowerment of the poor. As Farrington & Lewis (1993:6) point out, the focus is not on western democracy, 'but rather on the institution of "checks and balances" to prevent the abuse of power, channels for the articulation of views that oppose dominant interests, and the increasing capacity to represent the interests of the poor'. NGOs are an important constituent part of civil society that is a crucial element in the conceptualisation of democratic society. Both the state and civil society may be perceived as integrally part of the processes of government, the one representing the 'politics of domination' and the latter the 'politics of consent' (Walters 1993:15).

In several countries the growth of NGOs has parallelled the transition to democracy, resulting in NGOs being an important component in the increased attention to the notion of civil society (Bernstein 1994:58). The strengthening of a vibrant civil society may be seen as a critical component towards preventing government 'statism' which is characterised by centralisation of power and linked public participation (Dangor 1994:16). International experience suggests that a democratic government would need NGOs to exist and expand. This is because NGOs could probably design policies for, and advocate the interests of, those whose needs are overlooked through the state's failure to ensure equal quality of services for everyone (Bernstein 1994:61–62).

Since the state does not have the capacity to respond to expanding demands in a developing country experiencing rapid urbanisation, it would be difficult for it to act both as the provider and guarantor of services and simultaneously ensure quality. The endemic nature of poverty cannot be tackled by government departments that seldom have the resources, versatility, information or creativity needed to design programmes that can reach diverse, individual and community needs. Further, NGOs serve as a safety mechanism against too powerful a state, and can function as a 'school for democracy' (Bernstein 1994:61–62).

NGOs can help shape civil society in two distinct ways: through their own position and through their work with communities. At the micro level this takes place at three levels, namely:

☐ material base — achieving sustained improvements in the physical wellbeing of individuals, households and communities;

☐ organisational base — strengthening local organisations, building and increasing people's representative organisations; and

☐ ideological expression — promoting empowerment through psycho-social strengthening and mobilisation (Fowler 1994:29).

According to Fowler (1994:32) three key issues underpinning NGOs as effective civic actors are:

☐ identity — the more clearly defined the constituency, the more firmly the NGO will be located in civil society and the greater its legitimacy as a civic actor;

☐ relationships — NGOs must ensure that they do not accept resources that weaken their civic position by, eg simply taking over government functions or shifting towards operating as a parastatal; and

☐ development programmes — NGOs must engage in micro interventions, macro action, organisational reframing, and fostering of civic awareness.

According to Walters (1993:6) the period 1989–1991 marked the shift within NGOs internationally from protest to proactive politics. This occurred within the context of the emergence of the 'global imperial state' through the ascendancy of the 'free market' ideology, the 'discrediting of socialism' and the 'interventionist policies' of agencies such as the World Bank and the International Monetary Fund. The dismantling of state supported social welfare systems through donor insistence on the removal of mechanisms built to 'decolonise the economy' has led to underdeveloped countries being 'integrated into global capitalism' (Walters 1993:6).

4 NGO STRENGTHS

Against the background of the increasing democratisation of the developing world since the late 1980s, there has been a great expectation, especially from funding agencies and development policy makers, that NGOs would contribute to a stronger civil society, and promote 'people-oriented' development. Development agencies have therefore been encouraging the formation and growth of NGOs, and have often given more funds to these organisations than to governments (Walters 1993:7). Overall, NGOs have a special capacity to:

☐ fend for the poor and other groups not served by public or private sectors. This commitment is related to their dedication to helping the poor and other disadvantaged groups;

☐ ease the mobilisation of local resources and the establishment of private organisations to promote participatory development. NGOs are very versatile and can easily identify and adapt to local needs and circumstances;

☐ provide basic services at low cost. This is related to the NGOs' capacity to galvanise local resources and voluntary labour; and

☐ find creative solutions to unique problems and to promote successful innovation in the public sector. This capacity is related to 'their small size, administrative flexibility, and relative freedom from political constraints' (Brown & Korten 1989:16).

According to Carroll & Reilly (cited in *Urban Edge* October 1989:6), successful NGOs focus on one rather than many tasks; prudently choose staff who sympathise and identify with the poor; develop an administrative structure that is modest, more user-friendly, and has more flexibility than the public or private sectors; adopt an 'incrementalist' and creative approach to development; notice, and respond sensitively to the needs of clients who also participate in the design and execution of projects; establish linkages to influential forces in the political, public and private sectors; and sensitively merge social issues with technical expertise.

5 NGO WEAKNESSES

Brown & Korten (1989:16–17) identify several reasons for criticism of some NGOs, namely:

☐ they are not able to undertake complex projects. This is related to their limited budgets and small size, especially in terms of staff, pay scales and capacity to attract qualified professionals;

☐ they are unable to implement successful projects on a regional or national basis. This is because of their limited size and resources, restricted 'administrative systems, intensive focus on a few communities, and inattention to developing real efficiency and expertise in a well-defined technology';

☐ they are unable to establish community organisations that can function independently. This is linked to the small scale and short-term operations of NGOs, as well as their limited funding. Also, NGOs do not give sufficient attention to sustainability in project planning;

☐ they often work in isolation, focusing on the micro level, and ignoring the wider context in which they function, as well as the strategic linkages that could be forged with other major actors. Such deficiencies may arise from a combination of 'commitment to locality-specific interventions and a sense of moral superiority that leads to undervaluing the ability and intentions of other organisations'; and

☐ they have weak administrative, managerial and organisational skills. There are several interrelated reasons for these weaknesses: limited skills, scarce resources and the inflexibility associated with administrative bureaucracies.

6 RELATIONSHIP BETWEEN NGOs AND GOVERNMENT

The relationship between NGOs and government is important because of the 'strategic development and impact of NGOs' on public activities (Cernea 1989:136). The socio-political environment is significant because NGOs do not operate in a political vacuum, however hard they may try to distance themselves from politics or from the political regime under whose authority they operate. They are part and parcel of the political system and consequently the socio-political environment within which they function. This environment can help or constrain the activities of NGOs through policy or legislative outputs (Cloete 1991:4).

To realise greater significance and be influential in reproducing their activities on a massive scale, there is a need for NGOs to influence government at local, regional and national levels. Relations between government and NGOs have often been ambiguous and contradictory. For example, governments may value the resources mobilised by NGOs, but oppose the political empowerment associated with popular movements (Bratton 1989:569). This dilemma is apparent in societies where the state predominates, and where NGOs did not play an important role in development (Williams 1990:31). Several factors have been identified for tensions between NGOs and government, *inter alia*, 'differences in values and ideology; differences in development priorities; and differences in development approaches' (Garilao 1987:117).

NGOs were initially aloof from the state, and there was often a great deal of antagonism between them. NGOs are generally 'committed to social change, that is, to increasing not just the living standards but also the power of the people' (Clark 1991:152). According to Landhim (1987:37) NGOs are always oriented to the strengthening of civil society, particularly within regimes that have strong authoritarian traditions, that deny the majority access to minimal material living conditions, participation and cultural expression.

A reason for NGO/government conflict is that they are sometimes forced to compete with each other economically and politically. Many NGOs have displayed an amazing capacity to collect large sums of money independently of the government. This generates suspicion that some governments would like to tax these resources and/or control the NGOs. Some governments feel threatened by the capacity of NGOs to organise and mobilise the poor around important social issues neglected by the state. However, there are strong grounds to support collaboration between NGOs and governments. For example, 'getting experienced NGOs into national and local policy making, programme design and project formulation may contribute to development that is more sensitive and responsive to the needs of the poor' (Williams 1990:32).

The increasing trend towards democracy in most parts of the world, however, has forced NGOs to review their interaction with the state, and they have begun debating certain critical issues that could define a new relationship paradigm with government. Landhim (1987:32) states that the essential question being debated is whether NGOs should cooperate with state projects, whether they should seek state funding, and whether they should occupy positions within state structures. If there is consensus to work with the state, then the remaining question would be at what level and under what conditions?

A basic requirement for NGOs would be to develop more favourable policy and administrative structures. Decentralised development, especially in regional and local planning, would provide opportunities both to governments and NGOs to work together and devise 'appropriate administration' strategies to manage development projects at the local level (Cernea 1989:136).

Although it may appear paradoxical, the progress of NGOs depends to some extent on government support. However, governments are often disinclined to cooperate with, and are sometimes openly antagonistic to, such organisations. NGOs in turn often put restrictions on the extent to which they are prepared to cooperate with governments because of the limited benefits, and a concern that they may be coopted. Perhaps it is time for NGOs to rethink this approach, and to consider strategies that use 'government policies, mechanisms and resources to be more responsive to the development needs and initiatives of the people they represent' (Cernea 1989:136).

The existence of diametrically differing relationships — open collaboration on the one hand and animosity or distrust on the other — could be viewed from two perspectives. The first is that the NGOs accept, support and sometimes complement the government's development agenda, and stems from the realisation that the state's resources are limited. The second is the view that 'government cannot do anything right', and is not likely to respond to the needs of the people, and leads to NGOs rejecting government initiatives (Garilao 1987:116–117). There is a need for careful management of NGO/government relations, and three areas of concern have been identified:

□ NGOs must prove that their activities directly benefit the poor, and their expertise and services are required by the community;

□ Once an NGO proves its ability to deliver low cost, efficient services, it must transfer this capacity to other institutions, especially government; and

□ Once it has proved its organisational and administrative capacity, and its ability to deliver efficiently, an NGO can move into the policy advocacy arena. In addressing these concerns NGOs have the challenging task of preparing themselves for the role of policy advocacy above that of programme implementation. This is critical to their long-term survival and status as viable and effective institutions of civil society (Garilao 1987:117).

7 NGOs AND FUNDING

The issue of funding is of crucial significance to NGOs, especially in a period of global economic crisis and restructuring, and 'the accompanying search for alternative approaches to development' (Antrobus 1987:95). The process by which NGOs obtain funding is complex, and has to take cognisance of the following issues:

□ the question of sources (against the background of the political realities and ideological conflicts of the day);

□ institutional procedures, priorities and practices of donor agencies;

□ the constraints of the short-term nature of most funding; and

☐ problems of vulnerability and dependency for NGOs whose main sources of finance are from external quarters (Antrobus 1987:95).

Some factors that influence the ability of NGOs to attract funds include level of success; ability to deliver; credibility with donors; extent to which their aims and objectives are compatible with those of donors; their awareness of and access to foreign funds; efficiency of their administrative and management systems; and the level of support they receive from their governments (Antrobus 1987:98).

Many NGOs function on a 'project to project' basis. This is mainly due to a shortage of local resources that constrains their long-term plans. Therefore, a stable resource base that can sustain programmes is a necessity for any development-oriented NGO. If an NGO is to survive in the current environment of scarce resources, it would have to show a capacity to be competitive as an organisation, a characteristic that is not common to NGOs. NGOs would therefore have to develop strategic visions that define their future and allow them to harness resources towards implementing these goals in the form of relevant and viable programmes (Garilao 1987:117). In enhancing their capacity to secure funds an NGO would need to consider the following:

☐ As an institution, what does it have to offer a society that traditional institutions cannot or do not offer? NGOs must have a competitive edge vis-à-vis these other structures.

☐ What strategic linkages should it activate to leverage for greater resources? This may be achieved through networking, alliance building or tie-ups with other organisations and agencies in the private and public sectors.

☐ What resources can it generate? How should it choose its resource partners? How should such funds be used? (Garilao 1987:17)

8 THE SOUTH AFRICAN EXPERIENCE

There are very few countries that have sought a negotiated transition from authoritarian rule in the way South Africa has 'and which encapsulate both First and Third Worlds cheek by jowl. In this context unique organisations are likely to emerge' (Cross 1994:11). In South Africa a major emphasis of NGOs has been on politicisation and conscientisation towards realising structural transformation. This approach contrasts from the rest of Africa where NGOs functioned within a convention negotiated with the government, focused on basic community needs and operated with more subtle political agendas.

In the past South Africa had neither a coherent, formal public policy, nor any legislation that lucidly enunciated government policy towards NGOs. However, often there were conflicts between the state and NGOs because of the apartheid government's support for a top-down, growth-centred model of development as opposed to people-oriented development (Lee 1991:10–11).

The objectives, constitution and modus operandi of NGOs were influenced by political considerations. The NGOs were critical of the apartheid status quo, and were often assessed for their 'socio-political positioning' than their development capacity. The notion of an NGO performing social welfare functions in a politically neutral manner was rejected. Unless an NGO could show that it was actively committed in the struggle for a new, just, non-racial democracy, and enjoyed community participation, its right to exist through funding or popular mandate was challenged. Hence, most productive NGOs functioned from an anti-apartheid base (Allwood 1992:29). NGOs did not form a uniform community, and reflected rich diversity. Some are mass-based constituencies, others are restricted to a limited membership, and comprise unions, lobby groups, self-help organisations; service agencies and charitable associations.

Estimates of the number of NGOs in South Africa range from 20 000 (Lee 1994:35) to 54 000 (*Daily News* 26 May 1994). They were funded by the international community and by the private sector. These organisations generated funds of about R6 billion annually, and they ranged in size from national bodies to local churches:

> 'The NGOs that emerged varied in size and mission from Operation Hunger, sending food shipments to the destitute, to the Get Ahead Foundation, creating jobs and micro businesses for the unemployed, all the way to hundreds of small church groups that stirred impoverished communities into action to launch do-it-yourself projects of their own' (*Daily News* 26 May 1994).

8.1 Characteristics of NGOs in South Africa

While South African NGOs share many characteristics of organisations in other parts of the world, they have certain unique attributes that arose largely from their functioning within the apartheid milieu. Often, for reasons that are understandable, these have hindered the effective functioning of NGOs and have made the task of transforming their purpose and mode of existence even more challenging. Among these are the following:

☐ Many NGOs originated from an anti-apartheid constituency, and therefore viewed the state as an enemy or hostile entity. Therefore, there was a great deal of opposition between NGOs and the state.

☐ Many NGOs developed around charismatic individuals who emerged during the era of mass struggle, who assumed leadership positions, and who now find themselves engaged in development work. In the process an element of possessiveness about their NGOs has taken root. An innate propensity towards rivalries and 'turf wars' between NGOs has also developed. This has become more problematic and intensified as some NGOs constitute a vehicle for the ambitions of particular individuals.

☐ Some NGOs could more appropriately be described as 'tribunate' ('claiming to speak in the name of the people') organisations rather than as purely voluntary. They are structures that have a particular political intent with an implicit agenda to capture and manage the process of community mobilisation at an intermediate level. This is the aftermath of decades of political struggle. Such organisations tend to impede the goal of promoting social and economic advancement, as their dominant purpose is to control the development process in order to benefit from the patronage, status and prestige derived from the delivery of basic social services. Arguably, in the South African NGO context, 'populism, development and democracy' have often been viewed as 'strange bedfellows' (Cross 1994:8–9).

Despite the areas mentioned by Cross, there is ample justification to claim that, largely, NGOs in South Africa have kept the tradition of democratic governance by civil society institutions alive and acted as a bulwark against political and civil oppression. In effect, for the vast majority they came to represent an alternative to traditional government. One strength of NGOs in South Africa

'is the robust tradition of the radical critique of the state. Simply having a transition to a democratic government is unlikely to mean that this tradition of a critique of the state by civic organisations will cease. Far from it. There is a healthy growth in frank criticism of the state and the NGOs continue to represent interests in this fashion' (Cross 1994:10).

However, Fitzgerald (1991:3) states that despite the spread of political organisation and mobilisation in the 1980s, South African society has very little experience of effective community self-organisation around development goals. This arose because of the plethora of racist apartheid controls that prevented this kind of community self-empowerment.

8.2 NGOs, local government and development

NGOs have found themselves in the historical predicament of not being able to be exclusively developmental in their approach. However, the emergence of political democracy based on the popular will has opened new vistas of opportunity for NGOs to make a meaningful contribution to the development of South African society, particularly at a local government level.

It is at the local government level that citizens actually 'experience' democracy as they try to influence local processes. Local government is perceived as playing a key role in building democracy, bringing government closer to the people and actively involving them in decision making and the planning processes that affect them. In South Africa the deracialisation of local government represents a major challenge. Transformation at the local level has been impeded by the high level of fragmentation and duplication of administrative and institutional structures. Also, the socio-spatial distortions of the apartheid era must be addressed through a more equitable distribution of resources, and the redrawing of geographical boundaries. It is in this regard that local governments have a key role to play in the new South Africa as they will be involved in providing services, and influencing and implementing the RDP which will make a major impact on the wellbeing of communities.

A partnership that is constructive and dynamic can be ensured through NGOs being enabled to participate in policy formulation and planning at local government level. Community involvement tends to secure greater sustainability in development. Local government structures offer greater potential for community participation and development because of their closeness to communities and their more area-specific orientations (Heymans 1992:1).

The emergence of effective civil society is essential for negotiating development. Negotiated development planning could inject public participation and account- ability into development. This would enable communities to identify their needs and develop strategies and action plans. In this way parameters for development in particular spatial and functional areas could be established. NGOs lend them- selves to effective development programmes because they can maintain a grass- roots developmental approach that effectively empowers communities through the process; coordinate the different initiatives of the democratic movement to present a coherent response to the state and other initiatives; and launch, manage and control development programmes in a variety of sectors so that they combine into a coherent national strategy (Heymans 1992:11).

The present government's RDP recognises local government as 'the level of representative democracy closest to the people' (ANC 1994:129). The policy provi- sions call for a developmental culture among local government administrations to be encouraged, and for local authorities 'to be structured in a way that ensures maximum participation of civil society and communities in decision making and developmental initiatives of local authorities' (ANC 1994:130–131). Regarding the role of civil society, the RDP states:

> 'Many social movements (and community-based organisations) will be faced with the challenge of transforming their activities from a largely oppositional mode into a more developmental one. To play their full role these formations will require capacity-building assis- tance. This should be developed with democratic government facilita- tion and funded through a variety of sources. A set of rigorous criteria must be established to ensure that beneficiaries deserve the assistance and use it for the designated purposes. Every effort must be made to extend organisations into marginalised communities and sectors like rural black women' (ANC 1994:131).

However, if the government wishes to uphold its promise that the RDP will be people-driven and sustainable it would have to strengthen the policy and legal environment in which organs of civil society participate and actively build partner- ships with NGOs in the planning and implementation of development initiatives (Bernstein 1994:61–62).

The lack of sustainable and effective institutions to engage in negotiations around development has been identified as a major problem in South Africa. The admin- istrative and functional capacities of institutions and organisations need to be enhanced (Heymans 1992:11). In this regard NGOs have an important role to play. Any competent NGO should be able to explain how it is realising micro and macro level development action in its work. At the micro level the challenge is to help people improve their material wellbeing in sustainable ways. At the macro level, lobbying, advocacy, public education, etc, which have a bearing on equity, poverty and sustainability, can be effected in three distinct areas, namely, trying to bring change to the international economic order, advocating changes in public policies and behaviour at the national level, and attempting to reform the nature of the country's political economy (Fowler 1994: 26–27).

Throughout the various discourses on NGOs and local government the emphasis has fallen heavily on urban areas. This reflects the general tendency for civic movements and NGOs to have organised themselves most effectively in the urban areas since political activity itself has been heightened in such areas. The consequence has been a severe neglect of the problems and needs of rural areas. Although poverty is essentially rural and the vast bulk of the poor live in rural areas, effectively mobilised civic organisations that are not controlled by traditional authorities, charismatic individuals or non-representatives, are rare (Cross 1994:10–11). The RDP, noting the problems in rural areas, states that elected local government, with responsibility for the delivery of services, should be extended into rural areas, including traditional local authorities. Rural district councils that incorporate a few primary local councils must have a key role in rural local government (ANC 1994:129).

The poverty and demobilisation of the rural poor make it difficult to produce democratic civic structures. When small-scale local village and street-based organisations such as friendly societies, burial associations, mutual credit groups and stokvels, reach a certain level of scale and bureaucracy, they drift away from the interests of the poor (Cross 1994: 10–11). The challenge therefore remains on how to sustain rural community participation in development projects.

8.3 The future of NGOs in South Africa

The challenge facing NGOs is aptly summarised by Abugre (1994:133):

> 'The challenges facing South African NGOs are immense, the biggest being the challenge of building a new society out of the smouldering lava of apartheid. The scale of confidence rejuvenation, trust building and reconciliation that is required is almost without precedent in Africa. Given the unique role of NGOs in the struggle, the expectation of their role is equally high.'

NGOs in the civic sphere have played a political, economic, social and psychological role in development, ie of organising and mobilising people in campaigns against apartheid, coupling political action with a focus on resource distribution, bringing together diverse groups around common social objectives, and building self-esteem and self-reliance within individuals and communities (Meintjies 1994:13).

Apartheid was the *raison d'être* for the existence of many NGOs. After the democratic elections in April 1994 and the installation of a government of national unity, many NGOs became redundant. For example, in 1994 a Nelspruit-based NGO employed four thousand people on community projects. In 1995 it employed seventeen people, who were also likely to be retrenched (*Sunday Times* 5 May 1995). In February 1995 the Urban Foundation closed its doors. International funders were changing their priorities and redirecting their funds to the democratic government. This is a disturbing trend:

> 'The closure of NGOs which provide invaluable services to people who, in spite of the elections, are still poor, still jobless, still ill-

informed and often still homeless, seems a very worrying portent. One fears a future South Africa where an overburdened and inexperienced state bureaucracy will battle alone and ineffectually to provide the consolations promised by the RDP. International experience has shown that NGOs can provide a vital auxiliary service within newly democratised societies' (*Mail & Guardian* 18–24 November 1994).

There has also been closer scrutiny of NGO activities, and calls for greater accountability. Some NGOs have been criticised for being inefficient and corrupt. NGOs also have other limitations:

'Among these are poor implementation skills, lack of trust, an absence of dispute resolution mechanisms, resource constraints, fluidity of membership ... difficulty transforming protest organisations into development promotion, and a failure to formulate strategies and skills for negotiating with external interests' (Abugre 1994:133).

In spite of this,

'NGOs have contributed more to developing leadership for the new order than any other sector; have tackled the daunting tasks that everybody else ignored; were responsible for considerable inflows of foreign exchange throughout the sanctions era; and have implemented inventive and worthwhile ideas in development and education. In short, they have changed the way we think about civil society' (*Mail & Guardian* 24 February — 2 March 1995).

NGOs have an important role to play in the implementation of the RDP. The government does not have the experience or structures to reach the poor. In this regard the government will have to turn to NGOs who have the expertise and linkages to reach out to the poor. NGOs could then receive government support without losing their autonomy or being coopted. The government was also concerned about the implications of the collapse of NGOs. In August 1995 it urged international and local donors to continue to support NGOs. However, there is a need for stronger government support. If government wishes to give meaning to its promise that the RDP will be people-driven and sustainable, then it should 'strengthen the policy and legal environment in which organs of civil society, especially NGOs ... operate in, and also actively build partnerships with NGOs in the planning and implementation of development initiatives' (Dangor 1994:16).

NGOs would need to be provided training and assistance in development theory and planning to cope with a wave of new projects that require technical proficiency, management competence, and strategic perspectives. Some NGOs may not survive this process of transformation, while 'others may effectively negotiate the learning curves and develop to enlarge their role in the development process' (Meintjies 1994:16).

NGOs in South Africa need to explore new ways of relating to the government, communities and funding agencies. For example, many NGOs are trying to shift their emphasis from protest and activism to one concerned more directly with the developmental process. Both NGOs and the government would need a paradigm shift towards working symbiotically. Their functioning must be commensurate with the community interests they set out to serve, the one recognising its interdependence with the other, not only for the sake of credibility but for the wider purpose of ensuring the progress of civil society. Fitzgerald (1991:4) argues that while the new state should make a shift from 'a culture of opposition' to 'a culture of responsible governance', wider civil society must move from 'a culture of resistance' to 'a culture of development'. NGOs would have to 'contemplate the rather more difficult future role of maintaining their independence from a government they support, as vigorously as they did from a government they opposed' (Lee 1994:35). In South Africa, civic organisations in particular have considerable experience in functioning within a democratic framework. It is here that they can make a significant contribution to the transformation process.

9 CONCLUSION

The past two decades have been characterised by a rapid growth in NGOs, especially in developing countries. While they do not fulfil the role of formal governance, NGOs have played an important role in articulating and responding to the development needs of poor communities. NGOs support a strong civil society, functioning at the grass roots, and beyond the state authorities. However, NGOs have been criticised for functioning at the micro level, and their projects often lack sustainability. This was primarily related to their limited funding. The administrative and managerial skills of NGOs also need to be upgraded.

In South Africa, NGOs have played a significant role in championing the cause of the disenfranchised and opposing the apartheid state. The emergence of a political democracy, based on the popular will, has opened new vistas of opportunity for NGOs to make a meaningful contribution to the development of South African society. There is a need for NGOs to redefine their goals and agendas. NGOs would now have to focus on a development mode in contrast to their previous protest orientation. Their recognition by a democratic government as having a legitimate role to play in transforming South African society means that NGOs hold the unique position of being central to fostering a meaningful relationship between people and government.

However, a disturbing trend has been the decline in the number of NGOs since the democratic elections of April 1994. This was because international funders who had previously supported NGOs were now redirecting their funds to the GNU. NGOs have the experience and should be given the resources to contribute creatively to the process of reconstruction and development in South Africa.

10 REFERENCES

Abugre C. 1994. NGOs, institutional development and sustainable development in post-apartheid South Africa. In Cole K (ed) *Sustainable Development for a Democratic South Africa*. London: Earthscan Publications 121–134.

Allwood J. 1992. *The Developmental Role of NGOs: The South African Paradigm*. University of Stellenbosch.

African National Congress. 1994. *The Reconstruction and Development Programme: A Policy Framework.* Johannesburg: Umanyano Publications.

Antrobus P. 1987. Funding for NGOs: issues and options. *World Development* 15 (Supplement) 95–102.

Bernstein A. 1994. NGOs and a democratic South Africa. *Development and Democracy* 7 55–66.

Botha T. 1992. Civic organisations as autonomous organs of grassroots participation. *Theoria* 79 57–74.

Bratton M. 1989. The politics of government–NGO relations in Africa. *World Development* 17 569–587.

Brown LD & DC Korten. 1989. *Understanding Voluntary Organisations — Guidelines for Donors.* Washington DC: World Bank.

Cernea MM. 1989. Non-governmental organisations and local development. *Regional Development Dialogue* 10 117–142.

Cloete F. 1991. *The Socio-political Environment of NGOs in a New South Africa.* Paper presented at the NGOs in Development Conference, University of Stellenbosch 24–25 October.

Clark J. 1991. *Democratising Development — The Role of Voluntary Organisations.* West Hartford: Kumarian Press.

Copans J, D Darbon & V Faure. 1992. Civil society arises the phoenix. *Indicator SA.* Vol 9 no 4 29–32.

Cross S. 1994. South African NGOs in world perspective. *Development and Democracy* 7 7–11.

Dangor Z. 1994. NGOs and government RDP partnership. *Matlhasedi* Nov/Dec 15–18.

Farrington J & A Bebbington. 1993. *Reluctant Partners? NGOs, the State and Sustainable Agricultural Development.* London: Routledge.

Farrington J & DJ Lewis. 1993. *NGOs and the State in Asia.* London: Routledge.

Fitzgerald P. 1991. *Networks and Structures for Development in a Democratic South Africa.* Paper presented at the NGOs in Development Conference, University of Stellenbosch 24–25 October.

Fowler A. 1994. Development, democratisation and NGOs: lessons from experience. *Development and Democracy* 7 25–33.

Garilao ED. 1987. Indigenous NGOs as strategic institutions: managing the relationship with government and resource agencies. *World Development* 15 (Supplement) 113–120.

Heymans C. 1992. *Setting Agendas where the Issues are: The Developmental Limits and Possibilities of Local-level Urban Planning and Management Processes.* Paper presented at the Logopop conference, Bellville 23–25 October 1992.

Korten DC. 1987. Third generation NGO strategies: a key to people centred development. *World Development* 15 (Supplement) 145–159.

Korten DC & AB Quizon. 1991. *Toward Common Ground among Governments, NGOs and International Assistance Agencies.* Paper presented at the Regional Dialogue on GO–NGO Relations in Asia, Thailand.

Landhim L. 1987. Non-governmental Organisations in Latin America. *World Development* 15 (Supplement) 29–38.

Lee R. 1991. *No Perfect Path: Cooperation for Development.* Paper presented at the NGOs in Development Conference, University of Stellenbosch 24–25 October.

Lee R. 1994. From projects to advocacy: NGOs in search of greater impact. *Development and Democracy* 7 34–43.

Meintjies F. 1994. Community-based organisations and development. *Development and Democracy* 7 13–16.

NGOs gain clout, recognition. *Urban Edge*. Vol 13 no 8 1–6.

Walters S. 1993. *Continuity and Change in Community Organisations*. Cape Town: Cace Publications.

Williams A. 1990. A growing role for NGOs in development. *Finance and Development* December 31–33.

World Bank. 1991. *Annual Report* Washington DC.

CHAPTER 15

Urban Environmental Planning and Management — The Challenge of Sustainable Development

D Roberts

'Who would be foolish enough to eat today the seed corn for next year's crop? Only the person who will otherwise starve tomorrow!'
Manfred Max Neef (quoted in Local Government Management Board *1993)*

1 INTRODUCTION

The pace and scale of global urbanisation in the latter half of the twentieth century have signalled the beginning of a new and challenging era for local authorities around the world. Statistics suggest that by the end of the century most of the world's population will live in urban areas and, if the current trends continue, that urban populations will be twice the size of rural populations by the year 2030! Nowhere is this rapid urbanisation more pronounced than in the developing world. According to the United Nations Centre for Human Settlements (UNCHS), the global population is expected to grow by 3,7 billion people during the period 1990 to 2030 (UNCHS 1994a:v). Ninety percent of this increase will take place in developing countries and 90% of this growth will be urban. In the ten years from 1990 to 2000 alone, it is expected that cities in the developing world will increase their population by nearly 50%, adding an extra 737 million people to the world's population (UNCHS 1994b:2).

The effects of urbanisation are particularly pronounced in Africa: the continent with the highest rate of urbanisation in the world. Urban populations in Africa are presently increasing at a rate of 5,1% per annum, and are set to double every 14 years (Huntley, Siegfried & Sunter 1989:50). Similar trends are evident in South Africa where the urban population is expected to grow from 16,2 million in 1985 to 35,7 million in the year 2000 (Huntley et al 1989:51). Already most South Africans live in urban areas (approximately 57% in 1985) (Urban Foundation 1990:7) and it is anticipated that this proportion will increase rapidly to an estimated 79% by the end of the century (Huntley et al 1989:51). Urbanisation will be particularly striking among the black population, which is expected to increase from 53% urban in 1985 to 69% in 2010. In absolute terms, this means that the black population of urban areas in South Africa will increase by around 20 million between 1985 and 2010 (Urban Foundation 1990:22).

2 CITIES AND THE GLOBAL ENVIRONMENTAL AGENDA

As global population growth becomes increasingly synonymous with urban growth, so the focus of the global environmental agenda has shifted increasingly from rural to urban-based issues. The rationale is clear: urban areas are the areas where most of the world's population will eventually live and work, where most economic activity will occur, where most pollution will be generated and where most natural resources will be consumed. Furthermore, the environmental consequences of this growth will not be limited to towns and cities, but will impact well beyond urban boundaries at local, regional and often global levels, creating escalating problems of air and water pollution, land and natural resource degradation, traffic congestion and noise pollution. According to Rees (1992:125) these negative externalities can be called an urban area's 'ecological footprint'. The 'ecological footprint' of a town or city is the total area of land required to sustain that urban region (ie to provide resources and a sink for waste products) and is typically larger than that contained within the municipal limits or associated built-up area. The 'ecological footprint' for a city such as London is estimated to be at least 124,5 times larger than the city and is global in impact! Outspan oranges in British supermarkets and shiploads of toxic waste from Finland destined for Durban harbour are all consequences of living in the shadow of a rapidly urbanising world.

It is against this backdrop of escalating global urbanisation and environmental degradation that this chapter reviews current thoughts and debates in the field of urban environmental planning and management. The intention is not to offer a retrospective view, but to encourage a proactive look at the future and to emphasise the need for a new approach to planning and managing the environment in South Africa's towns and cities.

3 THE 'BROWN AGENDA' — A LINK BETWEEN POVERTY AND ENVIRONMENTAL DEGRADATION

The greatest challenge facing local authorities in South Africa during its period of reconstruction and development is the need to safeguard the health, productivity and quality of life of all urban dwellers by managing the interaction between urban populations and the built and natural environments that surround them in a sustainable and integrated manner. This can only be achieved if the indisputable link between environmental quality and human quality of life is acknowledged and actively addressed in the planning and management of our urban areas.

It is known that the poor suffer more from environmental degradation than any other income group. In urban areas they are the sector of society most threatened by environmental hazards and health risks caused by air and ground pollution, inadequate housing, poor sanitation, polluted water and lack of other basic services. The scale of this problem at a global level is immense. In the developing world alone the poor comprise 25–50% of the population of most cities (UNCHS 1994b:4). Current figures indicate that at least 600 million people in cities, towns and villages around the world currently live in 'health and life threatening' situations (UNCHS 1994a:v). At least 250 million urban residents have no easy access to safe, piped water and 400 million lack sanitation (UNCHS 1994a:v). In some countries, as little as 2% of sewage is treated and from 30–50% of urban solid waste is left uncollected (UNCHS 1994a:2). About 1,3 billion people, again mostly in developing countries, live in urban areas that do not meet World Health Organisation (WHO) standards for sulphur dioxide (UNCHS 1994a:2).

Many urban poor also live in the most ecologically vulnerable areas, ie on marginal lands such as steep slopes and floodplains characterised by a high susceptibility to environmental degradation. The net result is a 'downward, mutually reinforcing, spiral of poverty and environmental degradation which is endangering current and future generations in the urban areas of the developing world' (UNCHS 1994a:v). In South Africa an ill-conceived and too narrowly focused process of reconstruction and development (eg one focused exclusively on economic growth and housing) could exacerbate rather than improve the environmental conditions to which the urban poor are exposed. There is no value in giving poor people a home and employment if the house is on a floodplain and their job takes them to factories where their health (and even their lives) might be at risk!

The Urban Management Programme (UMP) — a partnership programme between the United Nations Development Programme (UNDP), the United Nations Centre for Human Settlements (UNCHS) and the World Bank — has identified the most important environmental problems facing cities in the developing world as (Bartone, Bernstein, Leitmann & Eigen 1994:11):

□   access to basic environmental infrastructures and services;
□   pollution from urban wastes and emissions;
□   resource losses such as groundwater depletion and land degradation; and
□   natural and human-made environmental hazards.

Collectively called the 'brown agenda', it is acknowledged that by effectively addressing these key issues in cities in the developing world it will be possible to improve the quality of life of all urban residents significantly, especially that of the poorest sectors of society. It would be ill-conceived, however, to see the 'brown agenda' as something separate or distinct from the concerns of the 'green agenda' eg the degradation of environmentally fragile lands, the conservation of indigenous landscapes and communities, the occupation or areas prone to floods or landslides, deficient public transport, overcrowding and noise pollution, etc (Bartone et al 1994:11). In fact, rather than excluding a concern for 'green' or 'social' issues, the 'brown agenda' recognises that solving the 'brown' issues has crucial implications for the resolution of many natural resource or 'green' issues that extend beyond urban boundaries. For example, a reduction in urban air pollution in cities will reduce carbon dioxide emissions and thus slow global warming. Both the 'green' and 'brown' agenda must therefore be included in any future process of urban planning and management developed for South African urban areas.

4 SUSTAINABLE DEVELOPMENT — THE WAY FORWARD?

How are South African local authorities to move toward a more holistic planning and management approach that addresses the 'green' and 'brown' agendas equally? The first step in this process is the acceptance of sustainable development as a key planning and management objective. This will in turn require a *participative planning* process by which all sectors of the urban community become partners in developing and implementing a vision for their city or town. But what is sustainable development? Even a cursory scan of the current literature suggests that there is extensive debate regarding the definition and meaning of the term.

The Brundtland Commission defined sustainable development as:

> 'Development that meets the needs of the present without com-promising the ability of future generations to meet their own needs' (World Commission on Environment and Development 1987:8).

In *Caring for the Earth* the World Conservation Union, United Nations Environmental Programme and the World Wide Fund for Nature define it as:

> 'Improving the quality of life while living in the carrying capacity of supporting ecosystems' (IUCN/UNEP/WWF 1991:10).

ICLEI (the International Council for Local Environmental Initiatives) has developed a definition for use by local authorities that emphasises their role as environmental service providers:

> 'Development that delivers basic environmental, economic and social services to all without threatening the viability of the natural, built and social systems upon which these services depend' (ICLEI 1995:12).

Despite the semantics, the essence of sustainable development is the need to develop a planning and management approach in our urban areas by which economic expansion can continue without destroying the natural resource base on which it depends, or negatively affecting the human communities that it is intended to serve. It brings together two strands of thought concerning the management of urban areas. First, the need to concentrate on development goals, ie economic, social, cultural, health and political needs within the urban area, and secondly, the need to focus on controlling or limiting the harmful impacts of human activities on the urban environment, ie ensuring there is no depletion or degradation of environmental capital so that the ecological base for human activities can be sustained indefinitely (Mitlin & Satterthwaite 1994:2). The two, interrelated as environmental problems (caused through the depletion or degradation of environmental capital), can and do undermine the process of development. Based on this understanding, four key objectives have emerged as significant in the move to achieve sustainable development in urban areas, namely: futurity, a healthy environment, quality of life, and equity.

4.1 Futurity

Futurity (Local Government Management Board 1993:7) is essentially a concern for the wellbeing of future generations, ie the principle that the people currently living should not deprive their successors of the chance to enjoy opportunities, choices, amenities and resources as good as those presently available. It highlights the fact that current consumption should not be financed by incurring debts that others must repay in the future, particularly that natural resources should not be used in ways that create ecological debts by over-exploiting the carrying and productive capacity of the earth (UNCHS 1994a:1). The message is clear, a concern for futurity requires that investments must be made in the health, housing, basic services and environmental infrastructure of today's urban areas so as not to create a social and environmental debt for future generations.

4.2 Healthy environment

The health and integrity of the natural environment are critical to human wellbeing (Local Government Management Board 1993:8), and therefore any concern for futurity (ie the responsibility to future generations) must include a duty to safeguard critical aspects of the environment. This approach implies more than just giving the environment more weight in decision making. It means accepting that there are absolute limits to how far the environment can sustain human activities before natural systems begin to deteriorate, sometimes irreversibly. The costs of certain activities, through their impact on environmental integrity and the subsequent effect on future generations, must therefore be regarded as unacceptable. For example, no development or economic gain could compensate humanity for the loss of the climate regulating, waste recycling and life support 'services' that the atmosphere provides for human and other life. Quite simply, sustainable development means accepting that people must live within their environmental means ie within the earth's carrying capacity. Determining where these environmental limits lie, however, is not easy for even where (as is in the case of the greenhouse gases) there is reasonable evidence that an important 'absolute' limit is being exceeded, scientific knowledge may currently not be advanced enough to decide where the limit actually is.

In view of this difficulty, the precautionary principle has been identified as an important principle of policy development and choice in urban planning and management (Local Government Management Board 1993:22). The precautionary principle suggests that where there is uncertainty about environmental impacts it is far more dangerous to make optimistic assumptions than pessimistic ones. This is because damage to the life-support functions that the natural environment provides can have very serious effects on the quality of life of present and future generations, and may be difficult or even impossible to repair. Natural systems also often have long time-lags in their ability to recover from disturbance. The consequences of present human impacts may therefore not become clear until long after the damage is done. For example, CFC molecules can take decades to move from the surface of the planet where they are released to the upper atmosphere, damaging the ozone layer. For these reasons, policy design must have a strong bias towards the avoidance of potential environmental risks that, in turn, will ultimately preclude certain activities and projects in urban areas where the possible environmental effects are either very serious, uncertain or unknown.

4.3 Quality of life

The concept 'quality of life' (Local Government Management Board 1993:10) recognises that there is more to life than can be measured by economic indicators or the growth of income. It acknowledges that many other elements are crucial for human wellbeing, for example: physical health, the quality of family, community, social and cultural life, physical security, social continuity, opportunities for education, personal development, employment, and the quality of the natural environment, etc. Non-income measures of wellbeing and development are hard to define and difficult to measure. Nevertheless, the development of such measures is an essential component of any sustainable development programme and is required to facilitate discussions regarding what kind of development is best for future generations, and how human welfare and environmental sustainability can best be reconciled.

4.4 Equity

The notion of equity (Local Government Management Board 1993:11) is critical to the concept of sustainability. Equity implies that any concern for future generations (ie futurity) must be accompanied by a concern for fairness to present generations (ie people currently living). This is critical because under present global conditions it is the poor, disadvantaged and vulnerable groups (especially women) who are worst affected by environmental problems and least able to solve them. Wealthy people, for example, can afford to ignore or escape the environmental consequences of their actions, thereby often exacerbating the plight of the poor. Policy responses to environmental issues will also affect people differently according to their relative wealth or poverty. For example, increasing the price of domestic energy may not make the better-off save energy because the extra cost is insignificant to them. But it may make people already suffering from fuel poverty live in colder and more polluted environments. Alleviating poverty is therefore a prerequisite to enabling people to live more sustainability. In effect, reducing environmental impacts will only be possible if the poor and disadvantaged groups (such as women) are given greater access to global resources and decision making. A regard for equity therefore requires that social and gender issues inform sustainable development planning for our urban areas.

In summary, sustainable development is a process by which economic, social, environmental, fiscal, trade, energy, agricultural, and industrial and technological policies bring about development that is economically, socially and environmentally sustainable (UNCHS 1994a:1). It implies a new notion of development — one that promotes fairness and opportunity for all the world's people, not just the privileged. It requires that current and future development proceeds without further destroying the world's natural resources and without further compromising the carrying capacity of the globe. Most important, it recognises that in some situations the carrying capacity of the environment must be treated as an absolute limit to human activities rather than just traded off against development benefits.

5 LOCAL AGENDA 21: MEETING THE CHALLENGE OF SUSTAINABLE DEVELOPMENT

The endorsement of Agenda 21, the United Nations' global action plan for the implementation of socially, economically and environmentally sustainable development, at the United Nations Conference on Environment and Development (the Earth Summit) in Rio de Janeiro in 1992 has made sustainable development a crucial pillar of international strategic policy. One hundred and twenty heads of state attended the Earth Summit, evidence of the increasing political significance being given to environment and development issues and the urgency facing governments around the world in the race to achieve a sustainable future for all (Global Forum '94 1994:5).

From an urban planning and management perspective, Agenda 21 is a highly significant document emphasising the importance of dealing directly with urban environmental problems and issues. It acknowledges that while cities are key contributors to the global environmental crisis, they are also a necessary and vital part of the solution. Agenda 21 contains two chapters of particular relevance to any discussion of environmental planning and management in urban areas, ie chapters 7 and 28.

Chapter 7 ('Promoting Sustainable Human Settlement Development') outlines the human settlement objective as follows:

> 'The overall human settlement objective is to improve the social, economic, and environmental quality of human settlements and the living and working environments of all people, in particular the urban and rural poor. Such improvement should be based on technical cooperation activities, partnerships among the public, private and community sectors and participation in the decision-making process by community groups and special interest groups such as women, indigenous people, the elderly and disabled' (Johnston 1993:182).

Chapter 7 also outlines programme areas for action that include: human settlement planning, management and capacity building, the provision of environmental infrastructure, basic services and housing, land-use planning and management, more efficient uses of energy and energy-efficient transport systems, and sustainable construction activities. The need for an enabling approach and cooperation with a wide range of public, private and community partners in the pursuit of sustainable development is also highlighted in the chapter.

Chapter 28 supports and builds on these principles and concepts by underscoring the unique role of local authorities in achieving global sustainability:

> 'Because so many of the problems and solutions being addressed by Agenda 21 have their roots in local activities, the participation and cooperation of local authorities will be a determining factor in fulfilling its objectives. Local authorities construct, operate and maintain economic, social and environmental infrastructures, oversee planning processes, establish local environmental policies and regulations, and assist in implementing national and sub-national environmental

policies. As the level of governance closest to the people, they play a vital role in educating, mobilising and responding to the public to promote sustainable development' (Johnston 1993:423).

Because most global resource and waste issues arise from local or regional activities, chapter 28 emphasises local government as the logical level for action around most sustainability issues. For example, the global freshwater resource is made up of many separate watersheds and aquifers whose condition is determined by *local* extractions, discharges, nutrient runoffs, leachates, etc. Similarly, traffic causes both local environmental concerns such as noise, odour, congestion and global ones such as acid rain and global warming. Therefore the same traffic control actions which local residents may demand for quality of life reasons will also have a global impact by reducing global warming (Local Government Management Board 1993:41).

Recognising the pivotal role to be played by local government in the drive to achieve global sustainable development, the following directive was issued to local authorities around the world at the Earth Summit in 1992. This mandate is contained in chapter 28 of Agenda 21:

> 'By 1996, most local authorities in each country should have undertaken a consultative process with their populations and achieved a consensus on a "local Agenda 21" for the community' (Johnston 1993:423).

The mandate requires that local authorities should interact with civic, community, non-governmental, business and industrial organisations in the preparation and implementation of sustainable development strategies for their cities through a process of thorough consultation and consensus building. The International Council for Local Environmental Initiatives (ICLEI) reports that some 1200 local authorities from more than 30 countries around the world are actively engaged in Local Agenda 21 activities. In some countries, such as Australia, the Netherlands, the United Kingdom and Finland, national Local Agenda 21 programmes have been established to support and coordinate such local initiatives. In South Africa, Durban, Cape Town and Johannesburg have all recently initiated Local Agenda 21 programmes.

6 HABITAT II AND THE GLOBAL PLAN OF ACTION

The second United Nations Conference on Human Settlements (Habitat II or the City Summit) will be convened in Istanbul in 1996 and will mark an important milestone in the journey towards greater urban sustainability. Habitat II will focus the world's attention on one of the greatest challenges the human race will face in the twenty-first century, ie the need to make 'the world's cities, towns and villages healthy, safe, equitable and sustainable' (UNCHS undated). The vehicle for realising this objective will be through the adoption (and subsequent implementation) of a Global Plan of Action (GPA). The GPA is proposed to be the 'instrument by which governments and key groups commit themselves to a long-term strategy to create sustainable and equitable human settlements and by which the international community commits itself to programmes in support of governments and key groups' (Habitat II Secretariat 1995:2).

It is significant that the draft GPA (prepared for discussion at the second preparatory committee meeting for Habitat II held in Nairobi in April 1995) highlights environmental quality and sustainability as essential elements in achieving an improved quality of life in human settlements around the world. The principles of civic engagement, sustainability, equity and partnerships, which feature strongly in the draft GPA, all underscore the need for a strategy of enablement, whereby women and men work with governments at all levels, with the private sector and with other NGOs to decide the collective future they want, to decide priorities for action, to identify and allocate resources fairly and to build partnerships to achieve common goals (Habitat II Secretariat 1995:9). Particular emphasis is placed in the draft GPA on addressing the special needs of vulnerable groups (such as women and children) in the drive to achieve greater sustainability in human settlements. The revised draft GPA (prepared by the informal drafting group of the preparatory committee for Habitat II convened at the second preparatory committee meeting in 1995) also re-emphasises the need for local governments to 'formulate and adopt Local Agenda 21 in partnership with local NGOs, CBOs, industry, trade and commerce' (Informal Drafting Group of the Preparatory Committee for Habitat II 1995) as a necessary step in achieving sustainable urban development.

7 THE RECONSTRUCTION AND DEVELOPMENT PROGRAMME (RDP) — A SOUTH AFRICAN FRAMEWORK FOR SUSTAINABLE DEVELOPMENT

In South Africa, both Local Agenda 21 and the GPA find a compatible and mutually supportive framework for action in the RDP. Although the RDP is primarily concerned with meeting the basic needs of the country's population and addressing the inequity of the past, there is little argument that the provision and maintenance of a high quality environment are two of the most basic of all human needs. Both the RDP base document and (to a lesser extent) the RDP White Paper therefore identify environmental quality and the right of people to participate in the management of their living and working environments as essential and critical steps in meeting the basic needs of all South African citizens (African National Congress 1994; Government of National Unity 1994). Such an approach is particularly critical in urban areas, where the environmental implications of upgrading the living standards of the poor through mass improvements to housing, electrification, water supply and sanitation, education and employment are potentially enormous. A successful housing programme, for example, will lead to an increased consumption of energy, water and raw materials; a large-scale expansion of transport networks and vehicles; and increased pollution and waste management requirements (Walmsley & Walmsley 1995:106). Unless this large-scale development and redevelopment of our urban areas occurs within the carrying capacity of the natural environment, any improvement to the quality of life of the urban poor achieved could be as short-lived as the political agendas that initiated it in the first place.

8 THE WAY FORWARD

How do local authorities in South Africa begin implementing environmental planning and management programmes that are responsive to the challenges of sustainable development, reconstruction and development, and participative planning? First, it is important to remember that neither sustainable development nor community participation will happen as byproducts of other planning or policy goals:

☐ Both must be consciously and actively planned for and managed by local government.
☐ Both must become central to the political agenda and accepted as a major part of the responsibility of local government (of whatever political persuasion!).

Secondly, although there is no blueprint for environmental planning and management in urban areas, it is possible to identify certain elements belonging to international programmes that have universal applicability and could be of use to South African local authorities in developing city-specific strategies. The programmes reviewed here include:

☐ the UNDP/UNCHS/World Bank's Urban Management Programme (UMP) and UNCHS/UNEP's Sustainable Cities Programme (SCP) (figure 1);
☐ ICLEI's Strategic Services Planning Framework (SSPF) (figure 2); and
☐ the United Kingdom's Local Government Management Board's 'Framework for Local Sustainability'.

All these international programmes highlight the need to (UNCHS 1994b:7):

☐ work out procedures and mechanisms for building consensus and developing cooperation between stakeholders;
☐ identify and understand local environmental issues;
☐ establish priorities among such issues;
☐ develop up-to-date strategies and action plans that command widespread support to address these issues;
☐ set up strategies and convert action plans into projects and programmes; and
☐ monitor and follow up the actions taken.

These key elements are reviewed in more detail below.

8.1 Participative planning

Environmental problems affect all people, groups and organisations in an urban area. They affect them in their homes, their neighbourhoods and their workplaces, in all aspects of their lives (UNCHS 1994b:9). To be effective and to make optimum use of resources, environmental management and planning must therefore involve all actors in a process of participatory decision making and concerted action. This participation should encompass all aspects of the planning and management process: ie strategy formulation, planning, implementation and evaluation, in order

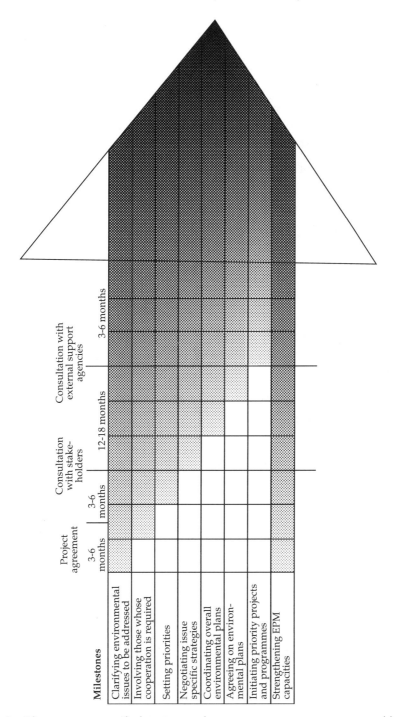

Figure 1: The environmental planning and management process proposed by the Urban Management Programme and the Sustainable Cities Programme (Source: Bartone et al 1994)

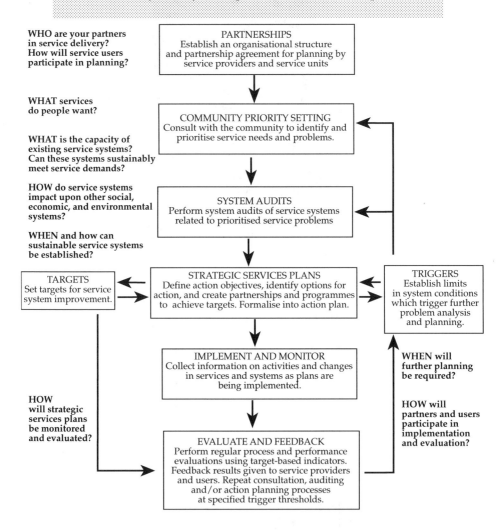

.I.C.L.E.I
**The International Council for
Local Environmental Initiatives**

STRATEGIC SERVICES PLANNING
A Framework for Local Agenda 21
Sustainable development is development that delivers basic
environmental, economic and social services to all without threatening
the viability of the systems upon which these services depend.

**WHO are your partners
in service delivery?
How will service users
participate in planning?**

PARTNERSHIPS
Establish an organisational structure
and partnership agreement for planning by
service providers and service units

**WHAT services
do people want?**

COMMUNITY PRIORITY SETTING
Consult with the community to identify and
prioritise service needs and problems.

**WHAT is the capacity of
existing service systems?
Can these systems sustainably
meet service demands?**

**HOW do service systems
impact upon other social,
economic, and environmental
systems?**

SYSTEM AUDITS
Perform system audits of service systems
related to prioritised service problems

**WHEN and how can
sustainable service systems
be established?**

TARGETS
Set targets for service
system improvement.

STRATEGIC SERVICES PLANS
Define action objectives, identify options for
action, and create partnerships and programmes
to achieve targets. Formalise into action plan.

TRIGGERS
Establish limits
in system conditions
which trigger further
problem analysis
and planning.

IMPLEMENT AND MONITOR
Collect information on activities and changes
in services and systems as plans are
being implemented.

**WHEN will
further planning
be required?**

**HOW
will strategic
services plans
be monitored
and evaluated?**

**HOW will
partners and users
participate in
implementation
and evaluation?**

EVALUATE AND FEEDBACK
Perform regular process and performance
evaluations using target-based indicators.
Feedback results given to service providers
and users. Repeat consultation, auditing
and/or action planning processes
at specified trigger thresholds.

Figure 2: ICLEI's strategic services planning (Source: ICLEI 1995)

to give all actors a sense of common purpose and ownership in addressing the environmental problems that confront them, and also to ensure a participative approach to implementation that mobilises the skills and commitment of the total urban community (Local Government Management Board 1993:18; UNCHS 1994a:22).

An inclusive approach to planning and management is critical for local authorities concerned with improving the living and working environments of the urban poor. To involve the poor and their organisations — NGOs, community and women's groups, political associations — effectively, together with business (which must play a central role in local, industrial and commercial development), requires not just public education and awareness-raising, but also sharing responsibility and power over such matters as land-use decisions, budget allocations and service delivery priorities (UNCHS 1994a:4). Experience has shown that generating such widespread participation is not easy and that a full-scale participatory process usually emerges slowly in most situations (UNCHS 1994a:22). Nevertheless, strong and consistent efforts must be made to shift the planning process towards this goal of establishing effective planning partnerships if sustainable development is to remain a realistic goal at the local authority level. It is for this reason that the draft GPA stresses the need for a strategy of enablement which establishes:

'(a) the conditions for women and men to exercise their individual rights and responsibilities and to engage their abilities effectively in activities that will more equitably improve and sustain their living environments; (b) the conditions for all organisations and institutions to interact and network, building partnerships for sustainable development; and (c) the conditions for self-improvement for government' (Habitat II Secretariat 1995:9).

Current models for partnership that have been suggested and/or are being used in facilitating broad enablement in urban planning and management in urban areas around the world include (Local Government Management Board 1993:18):

☐ Environmental forums and other consultation and liaison mechanisms with residents and community organisations, businesses and others, eg the Canadian Roundtables;

☐ Liaison, coordination and joint environmental planning between agencies, such as health authorities and river authorities;

☐ Participative and enabling environmental programmes, eg recycling and habitat management;

☐ Grants and support to voluntary organisations and activities; and

☐ Leadership and mobilisation of community environmental views and action.

According to the general partnership model suggested by ICLEI (figure 3) the creation of effective partnerships (using any or all of these mechanisms) will depend on the success achieved in the following areas.

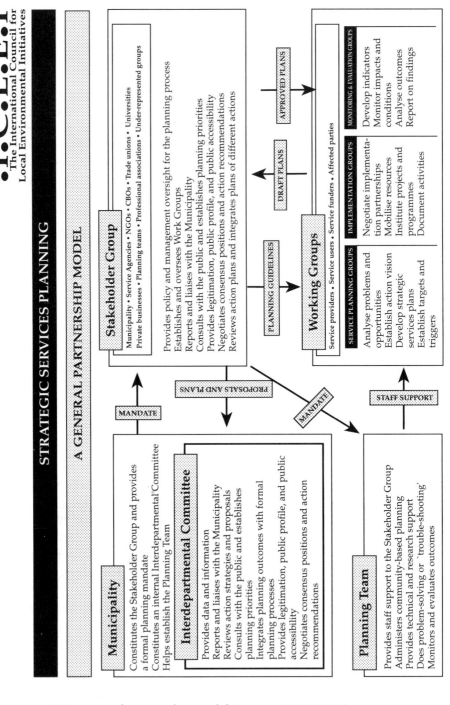

Figure 3: ICLEI's general partnership model (Source: ICLEI 1995)

8.1.1 Defining the types of partnerships needed for each aspect of the planning effort

According to ICLEI (1995:20), partnership-based planning requires the establishment of different kinds of partnerships for different tasks and responsibilities in the planning and management process. For example, the overall strategic planning process will need to be governed by a specific partnership group (called the 'stakeholder' or 'coordinating group') which includes representatives from key public, private and civic institutions, interest groups and different disciplines. This proposal is compatible with the steering committee proposed by the UMP (Bartone et al 1994:75) which provides guidance on major project policies and issues, attains the consent of those with legal responsibilities, and assures full coordination of effort throughout the planning process.

Once specific issues of concern have been identified by the stakeholder group or steering committee, 'specialist working groups' or 'forums' can be created for those priority issues or problems requiring strategic planning and immediate action. These forums are referred to as 'issue-specific working groups' in the context of the UMP and SCP (Bartone et al 1994:75; UNCHS 1994b:50). The SCP proposes that each working group should have a convener or moderator, ie a widely respected expert in the field, as well as a coordinator. The members of the working groups should consist of the stakeholders relevant to that particular environmental issue, ie: representatives from the public, private and community sectors, those with technical knowledge and those who have decision-making powers. Although a variety of criteria may be used to determine the appropriate membership, the general aim is always to ensure a broad base of participation. In other words, the membership should be cross-sectoral, inter-institutional, and multidisciplinary; it should combine experts and non-experts; and most important, it must comprise people who have the time and energy to commit to the work (UNCHS 1994b:51). To achieve the required outputs, the working groups must meet regularly and frequently.

The ICLEI partnership model suggests that each specialist working group reports back to the stakeholder group or steering committee, which then facilitates the integration of the efforts of the various working groups and helps to develop a coherent overall environmental strategy from the work done on individual issues.

8.1.2 Identifying appropriate partners in the community

Participative planning requires that all those who have a 'stake' in the process be involved. Key stakeholders in the field of environmental planning and management usually include (UNCHS 1994b:47):

☐ those whose interests are affected by environmental management strategies and action plans, to reconcile competing interests;
☐ those who possess the relevant information and expertise needed for addressing a wide spectrum of environmental issues; and
☐ those who control relevant implementation instruments, to use the full range of possible interventions.

Moreover, these various 'stakeholders' include persons and organisations from three sectors:

- ☐ the public sector (especially at the local level);
- ☐ the private sector (especially the business community); and
- ☐ the popular sector (especially communities and NGOs).

Identifying appropriate partners in the planning process is critical for local authorities, for if important stakeholders do not feel their ownership of the plan, they will not contribute to its implementation. In the worst case scenario they may create competing plans or continue to operate in ways that undermine the goals of sustainable development and integrated environmental management. Not all partners, however, will be equal in the strengths and limitations they bring to the table and this must be considered in the development of partnerships. The strengths and weaknesses of potential key players are outlined by the UMP as follows (Bartone et al 1994:20–1):

- ☐ Environmental protection agencies responsible for setting environmental regulations and standards, and for monitoring and enforcement. Too often such agencies are relatively weak bodies with only coordination functions.
- ☐ Planning agencies who often have staff unfamiliar with environmental analysis and information and how to apply it to local development planning.
- ☐ Politicians, particularly at the local level, who are usually preoccupied with maintaining their power and influence and take a short-term view when allocating resources.
- ☐ Sector agencies (public and parastatal) that have little experience in cross-sectoral collaboration, and give scant consideration to the interrelationships between projects. These agencies will often promote infrastructure and development projects that lack basic environmental considerations.
- ☐ Concerned residents and community-based organisation (CBOs) whose members and leaders are acutely aware of the impacts of environmental problems at the household and neighbourhood level. Typically this group has few opportunities to participate in the preparation of urban infrastructures or industrial projects that affect them.
- ☐ Non-governmental organisations (NGOs) can be effective agents for building local awareness, for mobilising community action, and for voicing local concerns. Often, however, environmental NGOs are focused exclusively on 'green' and global issues and pay insufficient attention to 'brown' and local issues.
- ☐ Private and informal sector enterprises are generally concerned about the constraints placed on their businesses by environmental regulations and the costs such rules incur, particularly when enforcement is lax or inconsistent. Members of the business community seldom wish to be perceived as environmental villains and should be coopted into the search for solutions.
- ☐ The news media, who voice concern for the environment and report on those affected by environmental conditions. This role can be negative, however, if the tendency is to sensationalise environmental topics rather than focus on real local priorities.

☐ The scientific and engineering community, who play a pioneering role in shaping the environmental agenda. This group often sets its agenda for environmental research and monitoring based on its own scientific interests without giving due thought to the needs of vulnerable populations. Because valuable information on the environment is often published in scientific journals in technical language, the scientific community should ensure that data are communicated in a less academic form to wider audiences, including environmental policy makers, planners, managers, and the media.

☐ External support agencies are a key source of funding for large environmental projects and are important donors of technical assistance and other support. In some instances they may give high priority to the environment and poverty reduction, but many have only recently recognised the critical importance of urban areas to the overall process of national development.

8.1.3 Determining the scope of the planning exercise: defining goals and objectives

Once the planning process has identified the types of partnership required and appropriate partners to effect meaningful participation, the next step is for all the partners to define the scope of the planning exercise (ICLEI 1995:21). According to ICLEI, key questions in this phase include:

☐ What will the scope of the planning exercise be? Will it be comprehensive or will it focus on a particular geographic region or issue if the available planning resources are not adequate to review the full range of problem areas simultaneously?

☐ How will the process be organised and managed?

☐ What role will the local authority play? How will local authority departments participate and respond to the plan?

☐ How does one include or involve marginalised or under-represented groups?

☐ Is there political support for the process and if not, how will this support be developed?

☐ Who will prepare the technical plans? How will this be financed?

☐ For what period are the plans being developed? How much time can be spent on planning?

☐ How will the planning effort provide input into statutory or existing formal planning processes?

☐ How will the final plans get integrated into the municipal budgetary process?

8.1.4 Establishing the terms of reference for each planning partnership

To formalise and legitimise the partnership building process, it is necessary that terms of reference be developed to define the scope and nature of involvement of all the partners in the planning process (ICLEI 1995:21). These should include:

☐ the activities to be jointly undertaken in the planning process;

☐ the roles of the different partners in the planning process, including specific activities to be performed, information to be provided, and schedules for their contribution;

☐ agreements on the sharing of the information to be used in the process, including agreements on confidentiality;

☐ methods of decision making, including dispute resolution and review; and

☐ resources to be provided by each partner.

8.1.5 Creating an organisational framework for effectuating the partnership

Because partners are not ad hoc participants and are expected to contribute to and share responsibility for the planning process and its outcomes, their involvement must be facilitated through some kind of organisational mechanism (ICLEI 1995:21). Different organisational forms will be appropriate for different activities. Initially, these organisational groups can be established with a limited term mandate, which may be revised and renewed after initial tasks are accomplished and evaluation of the planning process is performed. However, institutionalising these groups may ultimately be desirable so that they can maintain partnerships and planning activities in an ongoing way.

8.2 Identifying environmental issues

An essential starting point in the identification and prioritisation of environmental issues is the assembly and assessment of accurate and appropriate baseline environmental data. Baseline data are essential not only for effective policy making and management, but also for the effective monitoring of the success of municipal policies and programmes. ICLEI (1995:43–4) has identified the range of methods and tools (for establishing and analysing base line data) currently used by practitioners in the fields of urban environmental planning and management:

8.2.1 Periodic monitoring reports

Monitoring programmes are a regular feature of urban management, and include, *inter alia*, the monitoring of public health, building code compliance, transportation use, water and air quality, noise levels, soil contaminants, crime rates etc. Monitoring systems are generally established to collect specific data on a periodic basis, based upon predefined standards to ensure comparability over time. The selection of data is often related to established regulations or professional standards. The result is that while the technical data collected may be of a high standard, it usually only reflects the narrow requirements of a specific regulation. The data collected may therefore not provide a user-friendly or well-rounded picture of environmental conditions in a community.

8.2.2 Geographic Information Systems (GIS)

Geographic Information Systems are computer-based data systems used for the storage, easy retrieval, manipulation, transformation, comparison, and graphic display of data. They are particularly designed for the spatial display of data and are usually established using pre-existing data from historical records and monitoring programmes. To provide an adequate picture of a particular geographic condition, further intensive data gathering is often required. Due to the time required to collect, validate, and integrate different data sets, and then input this data, GIS systems are costly to create and to maintain. However, once established, they can provide an extremely user-friendly source of data that can be used and manipulated by experts and non-experts alike. Furthermore, they can simplify the analysis and understanding of complex environmental problems resulting from the synergy created between various problems such as air and water pollution. For example, sulphur dioxide pollution will produce acid rain and the subsequent pollution of water bodies and watercourses.

8.2.3 State of the environment reporting

State of the environment reporting is a general term used to describe the review of conditions and trends of different natural resources (air, soil, water, etc) and public issues (child health, employment, training, etc) over a particular period (usually a two to five-year period). In effect, these reports contain a comprehensive compilation and review of data gathered from different monitoring programmes. State of the Environment Reports (SOERs) serve not only to collate existing data on a periodic basis, but provide analysis of this data to clarify trends in relation to some predetermined base line. In some urban areas, SOERs are done with the involvement of the public and many stakeholder institutions. This approach can increase access to data and information that is not normally made public. Additionally, it simplifies the interpretation of data by knowledgeable stakeholders during the process of data selection and analysis.

8.2.4 Rapid Urban Environmental Assessment (RUEA)

The World Bank/UNDP/UNCHS Urban Management Programme has established a specific method of state of the environment reporting called Rapid Urban Environmental Assessment (RUEA). RUEA provides a streamlined SOER framework for multi-stakeholder analysis of environmental conditions. The RUEA method uses a basic questionnaire to quickly and cost-effectively collect existing data from monitoring programmes, public records, and other formal sources. The data is used by professional staff or consultants for the development of a profile of the urban environment. This profile is then submitted to stakeholders to both validate the results of the profile and to discuss priority issues and problems identified in the profile. Analysis of data is made by both professional data collectors and the participating public. The involvement of the public offers an opportunity to gather insights about the relationships between issues, but lack of involvement of stakeholders in data collection and the preparation of the environmental profile reduces their role and influence.

8.2.5 Environmental, Social Impact Assessment and Strategic Environmental Assessment (EIA/SIA/SEA)

The most comprehensive analytical framework used for environmental data gathering is Environmental Impact Assessment (EIA) and Social Impact Assessment (SIA). Both methods have been employed internationally for many years and are supported by extensive academic, research and training networks. In South Africa, EIA and SIA are integrated into the Integrated Environmental Management

(IEM) procedure advocated by the Department of Environmental Affairs and Tourism (Department of Environment Affairs 1992). EIA/SIA use past and present data to predict the impacts of planned or future developments. Specific tools and techniques have been developed to identify the linkages between proposed activities and the different components of the natural or social environment that could be impacted, and to predict and quantify the nature of the impacts. EIA techniques are of very limited effectiveness, for three reasons (Local Government Management Board 1993:27):

☐ First, the EIA is not usually done until after the serious policy choices have already been made, and it is therefore only able to influence cosmetic and palliative mitigation measures. For this reason it has been recommended that the assessment process should be extended beyond the project level to include the development of policies, plans and programmes. This is referred to as Strategic Environmental Assessment (SEA) (Local Government Management Board 1993:27; Lee & Walsh 1992). The SEA process requires that overall objectives of the development should be stated, and that a variety of policy options to meet them considered and their relative environmental impacts assessed. Both SEA and EIA, however, need to be done early enough in the decision-making process to determine whether the programme or project should go ahead at all, and if so to influence the choice of development options.

☐ Second, many assessments concentrate on minor aesthetic issues and therefore fail to address sustainability questions adequately.

☐ Third, for many types of development proposals the 'competent authority' — the body designated by the government to oversee the quality of assessments — is so closely allied to development interests as to remove any really independent scrutiny of the process and its conclusions.

8.2.6 Service systems audit

ICLEI (1995:44) advocated a specific auditing approach for local authorities involved in the identification of issues relating to environmental service provision. This method, called service system auditing, borrows from and builds upon existing auditing methods. As well as generating base line data, service system auditing seeks to provide an analysis not only of priority environmental issues (eg the availability of accessible water resources) but of the conditions and capacities of related and affected urban service systems to sustain and distribute services on an equitable basis (eg the variation in the quality of the water reticulation systems between the poorer and richer settlement areas). It is, in effect, an EIA/SIA focused not on a project but on the urban service system to be changed or developed. The elements of a complete service system audit are:

☐ characterisation of the service system and identification of its key supporting systems, resource inputs, operational parameters, delivery mechanisms, services delivered, and impacts or side effects;

☐ evaluation of system performance both in terms of operating efficiency and success in meeting service needs; and

☐ estimation of the 'carrying capacity' of the system (the limits at which the system will fail or become dysfunctional) and the conditions for system expansion or improvement.

An essential step in this process is a community review of the audit materials. The review process gives people an opportunity to collectively reflect on audit information and to engage in information analysis and critical thinking, thereby heightening their capacity and motivation to act on the problems identified. To help this process the audit information must be prepared in a form appropriate for distribution to different communities and community groups.

8.3 Establishing priorities

Establishing priorities among the variety of environmental issues likely to be identified using any of the methods discussed previously is not a simple task because of: the multiplicity of concerned or affected parties (often with conflicting objectives, aspirations or viewpoints); the scarcity of human and financial resources with which to act; the difficulties of measurement and analysis; and the need to pursue simultaneously such diverse objectives as equity, efficiency, and sustainability (UNCHS 1994b:48). Establishing priorities is, however, essential as it is impractical for any realistic planning process to address all of the environmental issues facing a particular urban area simultaneously. There must therefore be an agreed process for the assessment and prioritisation of issues once they have been identified. The SCP, UMP and SSPF all suggest a broad-based consultation process, by which the criteria for the prioritisation of issues are worked out through a participatory process that considers both of the local impacts associated with each environmental problem and the local capacities available to respond to these problems, eg (UNCHS 1994b:48):

☐ the importance of health impacts associated with the problem;
☐ the size of urban productivity loss caused by the problem;
☐ the relative impact of the problem borne by the urban poor;
☐ the degree to which the consequences are short-term or long-term;
☐ whether or not the problem leads to an irreversible outcome;
☐ the degree of social and political consensus on the nature and severity of the problem;
☐ whether the problem can be significantly affected by local responses and actions; and
☐ the short-run limitations posed by existing institutional and other resources.

The SCP is specific regarding the form of this consultative process, and advocates a 'city consultation' approach (UNCHS 1994b:49). The City Consultation is a high profile, large-scale public meeting lasting four or five days where a wide range of participants from the public, private and community sectors are brought together to address environmental issues and possible responses in their urban area. The basic purpose of the consultation is to:

□   raise the level of awareness and understanding, locally and nationally, of the key urban environmental issues;

□   confirm the identity of stakeholders and consolidate their interest and role in the SCP process;

□   achieve a consensus on the priority issues to be tackled;

□   obtain a commitment to the SCP process, and to a general work programme, as well as a commitment to participation in that process; and

□   begin the process of establishing working groups and other working procedures and mechanisms in the overall SCP process.

According to the SCP, the City Consultation is not a simple 'general meeting'; rather it is a carefully structured and organised meeting, combining plenary and small group sessions and employing modern presentational methods and techniques of consensus building and participatory dialogue to agree on priorities for environmental action. The conclusions of the consultation are normally summarised in a 'Declaration' to which the participants commit themselves.

8.4 Development of management strategies

The formation of partnerships, the collection of base line data and the identification of priorities all lead to the next (and most important) step in the environmental planning and management process, ie the negotiating of issue-specific strategies that respond to the city's unique mix of environmental problems and priorities. Once determined these must be reconciled within the framework of an overall, coherent and coordinated urban environmental management strategy and a set of actor-specific action plans for carrying out the strategy. To be truly effective the overall strategy must not only mobilise resources through links to existing, formal planning processes such as mandated five-year plans, general plans and budgets (ICLEI 1995:60), but must also create 'synergies' by combining the efforts of different partners to achieve a common objective. This requires setting long-term environmental goals for the urban area with interim environmental objectives to guide phased investments and reforms (Bartone et al 1994:72).

Before establishing concrete strategies, targets and work plans, establishing a broad vision of the kind of future that all sectors of the urban community want to share in through a visioning process could be useful (ICLEI 1995:62). This process should ultimately identify key principles or values that all stakeholders can agree to as fundamental to their notion of sustainability. However, participants must also be willing to present their images of the ideal situation, including ideas that might normally be judged as unrealistic. A visioning process also allows common principles and values, once they are identified, to be applied to relevant theme areas — such as personal lifestyles, governance, corporate responsibility, design and management, etc — to determine what kinds of strategies and actions would be required to implement these values (ICLEI 1995:62).

The final output of the overall strategy development process (ie visioning, development of frameworks, etc) is the preparation of an urban environmental management strategy report for use by local authorities, community groups, central and regional sector agencies, the business community, and others concerned with development and environment issues. The report should be used to guide future urban planning, economic sector planning, environmental services planning, natural resource and energy planning, and investment throughout the urban area and should contain the following critical elements (Bartone et al 1994:76; UNCHS 1994b:43; ICLEI 1995:61–3):

☐ a strategic vision, developed by the stakeholders;
☐ a review of the environment and development issues pertinent to the area;
☐ a summary of the possible responses to each issue, the pros and cons of each option for various stakeholders, and the assumptions and procedures that led to agreement on the selected options (including the needed coordination with other issue-specific strategies, existing legislation, and ongoing programmes, etc);
☐ a consensus position on current problems and opportunities (including a complete description of the environmental system from which each originates, the development concerns that are affected, the stakeholders that should be involved in any future decision making, options for resolution. Ideally all these should be organised into an ongoing information system);
☐ a set of agreed long-term environmental goals for the urban region and a set of interim objectives and targets to gúide phased action;
☐ action recommendations for achieving these goals and targets;
☐ the associated policy reforms, economic and regulatory instruments, and institutional strengthening measures selected to support the implementation of the strategy;
☐ a description of key partnerships to be established for implementation, including linkages with existing planning processes; and
☐ a framework for periodic evaluation of progress ie as the environmental management strategy guides planning, decision making and sector interventions, the impacts of those decisions and intervention must be periodically evaluated and this information must be used in making incremental adjustments to the strategy as it evolves.

8.5 Development of action plans

In order to translate issue-oriented environmental management strategies into action plans, specific actions must be defined for specific actors, complete with time schedules, geographic focus, and priorities. The need is to ensure consistent actions across time, all sectors and levels of government, and geographic areas (Bartone et al 1994:76). To be successful, action plans must therefore relate to all levels where action is needéd (eg individual, neighbourhood, local, national and regional) and must be integrated into existing formal planning processes such as annual budgeting, general plan reviews, and urban development plans (ICLEI 1995:61). The establishment of action plans also requires the setting of targets. This is important because targets establish a measurable commitment to be realised within a specific time-frame. In this way they serve to focus resources, and help the selection of action options. Targets must reflect both the constraints and opportunities for action if development is to proceed in a sustainable way (ICLEI 1995:62).

In selecting action recommendations, special consideration should be given to supporting existing initiatives and to using indigenous solutions identified during the planning process. It is also suggested that it is vital to prioritise those actions that provide 'leverage points' for change, ie those actions that will have a ripple effect throughout the planning and development system. For example, by providing a more effective public transport system, a local authority will not only reduce the need for extensive road networks (thereby protecting various natural areas from destruction), but will also ensure improved urban air quality. By identifying these 'leverage points', the local authority can optimise the effectiveness and impact of any action plan.

The final output of the action plan development is the preparation of an action plan report containing the following elements (ICLEI 1995:60; Bartone et al 1994:79):

☐   a description of the strategic vision of the community, including a consensus statement on current problems and opportunities;
☐   a statement of goals;
☐   a presentation of specific targets to be achieved;
☐   a description of key partnerships to be established for implementation, including linkages with existing planning processes;
☐   action recommendations for achieving these goals and targets;
☐   describe the complementary cross-cutting actions and investment programmes agreed upon by participating stakeholders; and
☐   a framework for periodic evaluation of progress.

The success of an action plan will be significantly affected by three key factors (Bartone et al 1994:77):

8.5.1 Standards and affordability

Within a given urban area, and in a given sector, the environmental infrastructure or service to be provided to address a particular problem area can vary greatly. Technologies and service standards need not be uniform, but should be selected according to users' willingness and ability to pay. For example, some neighbourhoods may demand full, piped water supply and sewerage services, while other urban communities may be willing to pay for yard-taps and ventilated improved pit latrines.

8.5.2 Innovative institutional arrangements

Local government in most countries is fragmented and compartmentalised into traditional service-based organisations. As a result, mechanisms and procedures for ensuring cooperation across departmental and agency lines scarcely exist—and if they do, they seldom work. Yet such procedures and practices are urgently needed as complex environmental and urban development problems cannot be solved by the efforts of individual departments or sections. Any progress towards sustainable development thus requires that local government policies and actions are integrated between departments and across sectors. New institutional approaches, inter-organisational and intra-organisational collaboration will therefore be called for because of local budget constraints, the recognised operational weaknesses of many local sector agencies, and the size of existing deficits of environmental services in most developing country cities.

Local authorities can make considerable progress towards this type of policy and project integration through (Local Government Management Board 1993:19):

☐ reorganising functions to achieve integration of services affecting the environment and of corporate environmental policy and practice;
☐ setting up environmental coordination between departments and functions at both the committee and officer level;
☐ specifying environmental conditions in contracts and legal agreements; and
☐ developing an appropriate legal framework to support the implementation of sustainable development.

8.5.3 Cost-effective solutions

Options for action should be screened to determine their economic and financial soundness, and then should be ranked. A cost-benefit framework should be used whenever monetary costs and benefits can be estimated. In those instances where there is effective demand for environmental services, users' willingness to pay can be used to estimate benefits. Where only costs, but not benefits, are quantifiable, cost-effectiveness analysis can be used, based on the cost of action and the incremental contribution that it would result in regarding the long-term environmental quality goals of the strategy (such as cost per ton of waste removed).

8.6 Evaluation and feedback

Regular monitoring and evaluation are necessary for the routine assessment and adjustment of environmental management strategies and action plans. Evaluation and feedback are also necessary to maintain accountability among participants, to inform the public about progress in meeting targets, and to signal when the strategy and action plans must be adapted (ICLEI 1995:14). The feedback system should ideally employ the concept of 'triggers' — ie specified conditions that instigate further planning or action — especially in cases where established action plans fail to correct problems or satisfy prioritised needs (ICLEI 1995). Monitoring and evaluation is particularly important in rapidly developing economies where policies, institutional arrangements, and social and economic conditions are changing rapidly (Bartone et al 1994:85).

A potentially powerful tool for monitoring and evaluation is the use of indicators. Indicators employ the principle that: 'You can only manage what you measure'(Local Government Management Board 1993:24). A wide range of indicator types is relevant to the physical aspects of sustainable development. At one extreme lie indicators of the state of the physical environment and how it is changing (eg the acidity level of rainfall). Indicators of physical sustainability are also needed to measure the state of the environment and the effect of actions to preserve it and, by that, to establish convincing links between the two. At the other end of the scale lie indicators of the human contribution to or impact on the state of the environment (eg carbon dioxide or acidifying emissions from particular organisations, activities or areas) (Local Government Management Board 1993:24).

There is a need in urban areas for specific behavioural indicators that will allow individuals, families and households to measure their contribution toward achieving sustainable development, eg how much electricity is used each month. Remember that the practicability of a sustainable lifestyle will vary between different groups in society, and that indicators need to be defined and measured in ways that illuminate the links between equity and sustainability. For example, avoiding car use will often be easier for well-off residents of small towns than for people on lower incomes living in urban fringe developments without local amenities. Paradoxically, it will often be the less well-off who are least able to adopt a sustainable means of existence (Local Government Management Board 1993:25).

There is also a need for indicators highlighting the *potential* for sustainability. Examples here would include how many amenities — shops, schools, doctors, workplaces — people could get access to without a car, or the availability and affordability of environmentally less damaging products, and complete and reliable information on the environmental impacts of different products to enable people to make responsible choices. The availability or otherwise of sustainable lifestyles will determine how far 'voluntary' action towards sustainability is possible in current circumstances without unreasonable inconvenience. This will also highlight where there is a need for local government to take action to create a framework within which individuals can choose more sustainable lifestyles (Local Government Management Board 1993:25).

Finally, indicators are needed to guide and measure the success of human action to address environmental problems in urban areas. These can take a wide range of forms including (Local Government Management Board 1993:24):

☐ Environmental standards for human activities, eg the fuel efficiency of houses or cars or fertiliser inputs per hectare of crops;
☐ Whether an organisation has an environmental management system; and
☐ Activity milestones such as the production or distribution of information or guidance, introduction of incentives or regulations, by particular dates.

The use of indicators as part of the monitoring process reiterates the urgent need for the development and maintenance of detailed and updated environmental databases as a critical ancillary to the urban environmental planning and management process.

9 WHERE TO FROM HERE?

If sustainable development is the goal, and participative planning is the process to achieve it, what is the way forward for South African local authorities? The first step is acknowledging that it is no longer business as usual! A process of necessary change has already begun in South Africa's urban areas that must be fostered and built on. This transformation started with the democratisation of South African society, a factor that has made possible the re-evaluation of past planning and management practices and highlighted the inequity of environmentally unsustainable development. It has also opened a unique window of opportunity for the creation of partnerships in the pursuit of a quality environment and a sustainable future for all.

Recognising the potentially powerful unifying and stabilising force of a sustainable reconstruction and development process, the cities of Durban, Cape Town and Johannesburg have already committed themselves to the preparation of city-specific Local Agenda 21 programmes. All three cities are also participants in ICLEI's Local Agenda 21 Model Communities Programme: a three-year international research programme involving fourteen cities aimed at developing tools and models for sustainable development and participative planning that will have general applicability around the world. These early initiatives require not only the commitment of local politicians and communities, but also national level commitment if they are to succeed. National level support implies the development of a national Local Agenda 21 programme (by the Department of Environmental Affairs and Tourism) which encourages the smaller urban centres to pursue a sustainable development path and which facilitates the networking of experiences arising out of all Local Agenda 21 programmes around the country. The challenge is obvious; only time will tell how we fare.

10 REFERENCES

African National Congress. 1994. *The Reconstruction and Development Programme: A Policy Framework*. Johannesburg: Umanyano Publications.

Bartone C, J Bernstein, J Leitmann & J Eigen. 1994. *Towards Environmental Strategies for Cities: Policy Considerations for Urban Environmental Management in Developing Countries*. Washington DC: World Bank.

Department of Environment Affairs. 1992. *Integrated Environmental Management Procedure*. Pretoria: Department of Environment Affairs.

Global Forum '94. 1995. *The Manchester Report: Seeds of Change*. Manchester: Global Forum '94.

Government of National Unity. 1994. *White Paper on Reconstruction and Development*. Cape Town: CTP Book Printers.

Habitat II Secretariat. 1995. *Draft Statement of Principles and Global Plan of Action* (unpublished).

Huntley B, R Siegfried & C Sunter. 1989. *South African Environments into the 21st Century*. Cape Town: Human and Rousseau/Tafelberg.

Informal Drafting Group of the Preparatory Committee for Habitat II. 1995. *The Habitat Agenda* (unpublished).

International Council for Local Environmental Initiatives. 1995. *Local Agenda 21 Handbook*. Toronto: ICLEI.

IUCN/UNEP/WWF. 1991. *Caring for the Earth: A Strategy for Sustainable Living*. Gland, Switzerland: IUCN/UNEP/WWF.

Johnston S. 1993. *The Earth Summit: The United Nations Conference on Environment and Development (UNCED)*. London: Graham & Trotman/Martinus Nijhoff.

Lee N & F Walsh. 1992. Strategic Environmental Assessment: an overview. *Project Appraisal*. Vol 7 no 3 126–136.

Local Government Management Board. 1993. *A Framework for Sustainability*. Luton: Local Government Management Board.

Mitlin D & D Satterthwaite. 1994. *Cities and Sustainable Development*. Background paper prepared for Global Forum '94. London: IIED.

Rees WE. 1992. Ecological footprints and appropriated carrying capacity: what urban economics leaves out. *Environment and Urbanisation*. Vol 4 no 2 121–130.

United Nations Centre for Human Settlements. 1994a. *Sustainable Human Settlements Development: Implementing Agenda 21*. Nairobi: UNCHS.

United Nations Centre for Human Settlements. 1994b. *Sustainable Cities — Concepts and Application of a United Nations Programme*. Nairobi: UNCHS.

United Nations Centre for Human Settlements (undated). *A Guide to the United Nations Conference on Human Settlements (Habitat II): The City Summit*. Nairobi: UNCHS.

Urban Foundation. 1990. *Urban Debate 2010: Population Trends*. Johannesburg: The Urban Foundation.

World Commission on Environment and Development. 1987. *Our Common Future*. Oxford: Oxford University Press.

Walmsley RD & JJ Walmsley. 1995. A paradigm shift is required for environmental research in South Africa. *South African Journal of Science* 91 106–107.

— PART 5 —

Conclusion

CHAPTER 16

Beyond Local Government Transition — Towards an Agenda for Transformation

M Wallis

1 INTRODUCTION

This collection of papers on contemporary issues in South African local government cannot be regarded as complete unless some attempt is made to synthesise them. In this final chapter an attempt is made to pick out and discuss the important threads included within the work presented here. Although the papers do not all contain a high level of detail, they nevertheless can be seen as portraying a system undergoing profound change. There is apparently one overriding concern for us in this endeavour: it is what Clarke & Stewart stated when writing about England in the late 1980s — we have to 'think total' (or, as South Africans prefer, think holistically). They go on to make an observation equally applicable to South Africa today:

> 'The challenges to management in local government are deep and wide-ranging. The need is to build effective organisation capable of meeting them. To do this the various strands have to be drawn together' (Clarke & Stewart 1988:7).

The task of this chapter is to see what some of the strands are as presented by these contributors, and to try to draw them together. In doing so, an attempt is made to attach concreteness to the idea of a *transformation* that brings genuine benefit to those most disadvantaged by apartheid. Discussions of this concept often suffer from overdoses of ideology and rhetoric and an insufficient grasp of reality. Part of the problem is that the ultimate destination of such change cannot be specified. These points have been made by Singh in her analysis of the way the term came to be used in the early 1990s (Singh 1992). There are also related and important questions of *empowerment and structural reform* here (Saul 1991). Several contributions to this volume can be interpreted as attempts to give operational meaning to these notions in a local government context, some doing so in a more ideological way than others. An agenda for local government transformation may be partially developed from this modest base. At the least these essays identify and explore some key issues.

The ultimate destination, however, is not clear since the road ahead is flooded with uncertainty. It cannot be said that the present volume is a blueprint or primer for reforming the structures of local government. Nevertheless, the authors have each, in their own manner, given at least a glimpse of what is happening now and what some reasonable expectations of the future might be. Some go beyond this and bring a prescriptive element to bear, arguing for a more strategic or developmental approach.

Given the size of the problems faced in redesigning the system of local government to make it more appropriate to post-apartheid circumstances, the contributors have chosen not to bite off more than they can comfortably chew; they have worked away at aspects of the broader picture of direct interest to them, each contributing to the final, comprehensive view. The result is a collection of studies in change with some attention inevitably given to the local government system of the *ancien regime*, much concentration on the issues being confronted now, and some sense of what the future may and should hold.

2 LOCAL GOVERNMENT REFORM: DELAY AND ITS CONSEQUENCES

Since the focus is on change, it is worth re-emphasising the status quo. South Africa became a democracy at central and provincial government levels in May 1994 and on 1 November 1995 at the local level. While it is true that structures at these higher levels are still the subject of lively and even violent dispute, the fact that they are democratic cannot be seriously denied. Local government meanwhile has only managed to stagger inelegantly from racist forms to a process by which unelected councillors of assorted racial hues have assumed power within new structures and, occasionally, substructures: the transitional local councils and the transitional metropolitan councils. As this volume clearly shows, the Local Government Transition Act does not establish democracies for localities. It merely sets out a series of routes and signposts by which the goal of local democracy may ultimately be attained. As Reddy points out in his chapter on restructuring, the Act prescribes the establishment of forums and committees expected to establish the new system in phases. The constitution adds to the complexity because it too has to be taken into account in planning the way ahead; as Reddy explains, it has to be read with the Act. However, it lacks specificity on local government. What it does do, however, and this is helpful, is guarantee that there will be local government and protects it vis-à-vis other powers of government at other levels; in this respect it is better than many other constitutions that ignore the issue altogether.

The process of transition has to be understood in its legal and constitutional framework, but that is far from all. This framework permits a whole variety of interpretations as often happens with legal documents. Beyond this, however, it has opened opportunities for all sorts of political actors to influence the process by delaying or reshaping it. The additional difficulty is that the framework is itself a transitional one, likely to undergo frequent amendment. These difficulties have caused substantial delay in establishing a sustainable and democratic system of local government — the contributions to this volume are influenced by this fact.

However, being entirely negative about present uncertainties is not necessary, inconvenient though they may be. Part of the situation is that opportunities for creative intervention now exist so, for example, Sing and Moodley's ideas on alternative ways of organising local government are timely. Indeed, this volume as a whole should be seen as a contribution to an ongoing debate concerning change. Instability — because it can stimulate debate and fresh thinking — is not always undesirable as several contributions prove.

3 DEVELOPMENT PLANNING AND MANAGEMENT

Most South Africans live in conditions of poverty, both in urban and rural areas. It is because of this that several contributors argue for new ways of achieving development at the local level. The presentation by Khan is an example of this in that he believes that change can be effected by a detailed understanding of the local economic development experience of other states at differing stages of development, operating with a variety of political structures. For the same reason an attempt has been made to place local government in the context of the RDP. Wallis, in particular, tries to do this in some detail.

An underlying concern here is that new forms of planning are needed. The typical local authority sees planning as essentially a matter of assisting in the allocation of space or land for development rather than facilitating and planning development itself. Reddy, for one, argues the case for an approach to management and planning which has a far greater strategic thrust. Without such a change, overcoming existing management weaknesses and promoting a proactive, shared vision of how change should proceed will be difficult. Much greater coordination, or integration of management structures, is needed. In sum, it is vitally important to escape from the legacy of the old style local government management.

Secondly, the RDP strongly suggests a need for more effective economic and project planning, placing emphasis on skills in areas where the country as a whole has a weak legacy. These related concerns are all critical to the success of the RDP but also relate to the role local government is supposed to play within this programme. There are several factors to be noted here. One is a corollary of the need for new forms of planning in that there has to be greater emphasis on data gathering and analysis. Another is that the planning to be carried out needs to be linked to the specific concerns of the community. The final point that can be made is that many local authorities have remarkably low capacities for this type of planning and vary a great deal in the extent to which they are willing and able to take action to remedy the situation. Until this issue is effectively addressed, a significant improvement of the RDP's currently poor record and image as a development initiative is hard to envisage.

4 ENVIRONMENTAL CONCERNS

These are much more pronounced than they were ten years ago. Roberts, in her contribution to this volume, indicates several ways in which both the built and the natural environments have to be brought to centrestage regarding local government. For example, in planning development the question of the impact of investment on the environment must be considered. Echoing worldwide concerns, local authorities in South Africa face major challenges, resulting largely from the rapidity of urbanisation. This is not to ignore the rural dimension entirely, but is a reflection of how the demographic structure of South Africa is changing.

There are three issues of particular relevance, flowing from what Roberts tells us: environmental impact assessments: sustainability; and 'brown' and 'green' agendas. The three are, of course, closely related. The first — perhaps the more technical of the three — involves ensuring that the possible impacts on the environment of development projects are analysed and predicted at an early stage to prevent damage. It is essentially an environmental version of the adage that prevention is better than a cure. As Roberts points out, these approaches are well established internationally. It is important that they are taken seriously in South Africa; the indications of whether this is the case are unclear.

Sustainability represents the need for a long-term view to be taken if the environment is to be one in which the quality of life is to be enhanced. It is about natural resources such as land and water, but is also a concern that embraces urban dwellers: pollution, sanitation, etc. Roberts very usefully points out the distinction between 'green' and 'brown' agendas. In many ways this is important because the image of environmentalists in South Africa is one borrowed from the developed world. The green agenda emphasises the values of the natural habitats of game reserves, landscapes, coastlines and estuaries. The white, middle class person is much more likely to see these as vital to the quality of life than a black person living in an informal settlement. The brown agenda, on the other hand, is about the environmental needs of the less privileged. It concerns healthy cities, which are as free as possible of overcrowding and pollution, and where basic needs such as water are adequately met. These two agendas should not be seen in 'either–or' terms, but in a 'win–win' perspective in which both receive the application they deserve.

5 GLOBALISATION

Several of these chapters also stress the need to think globally about local governance. The point is made that South Africa can learn from elsewhere and is freer to do so now than it was five years ago. This finds expression in Reddy's discussion of strategic management and Maharaj and Reddy's analysis of women in local government. Globalisation goes beyond this kind of discourse, however. Membership of international bodies brings with it obligations reflected locally, for example, environmental concerns. Donor agencies make impacts in all sorts of ways and cannot be ignored in the quest for a more developmental local government. Khan & Swilling et al review aspects of the experience of other countries, some economically advanced, others very much the opposite. They do not simplistically conclude that lessons can be learnt, but see commonalities of experience and a need to be aware of the world beyond political/geographic borders in seeking solutions — a case in point is that the South African system of local government is part and parcel of an international investment marketplace. A corollary to this is that the development of a city may be inspired by the vision of local leaders but simultaneously, may be critically affected by the preferences of the international business community. This can be argued in ideological terms, of course. There is now a conventional view that the old arguments against foreign capital are not relevant in the new era. Khan, for one, gives a refreshingly insightful view, revisiting the old issues and relating them to the present dilemmas to be addressed vis-à-vis local economic development. Using the term 'global economic restructuring', he questions the validity of the views of many commentators and decision makers who assume the forces of the global market should be liberated to benefit all and sundry.

6 GOVERNANCE AND PARTICIPATION

The new South Africa has been an innovator in this area. Perhaps the pressures of the country's unique circumstances created a climate conducive to political and institutional creativity. Four examples emerge: forums; non-governmental organisations (NGOs); civic associations or community-based organisations (CBOs); and voter education. The theme of governance is discussed both empirically and conceptually in the detailed comparative chapter written by Swilling with Johnson and Monteiro. The importance of this relatively new term is reinforced by several contributors who — from differing angles — argue it is the connections and interactions between local authorities and their publics that are really of interest, and is best termed governance, as opposed to the static analysis that has been conventionally applied in studying local government.

The notion of the forum, although not the specific focus of a chapter, is a good example of innovative governance in this country. As Reddy shows in his general discussion, they have been accorded a critical role in negotiating the process of change, initially at national level and then locally through the provisions of the Transition Act now being implemented and amended. In a sense local government followed a pattern established in other fields (eg, universities, transport) where forums provided a framework for negotiation in the absence of other channels accepted as legitimate by all parties. A result of this is that a framework now exists for consultation with stakeholders on an institutionalised basis, a beneficial arrangement many other countries should envy and perhaps imitate in some respects.

Part of apartheid's legacy is shown by B Maharaj and Jaggernath to be a network of NGOs and CBOs, most of which have the long-term potential to be significant local actors. These organisations are undoubtedly undergoing a role crisis as these authors show, but to say this does not mean taking a negative view; these bodies can be as much a part of the framework for local consultation as the forum.

The death of apartheid was accompanied by the emergence of another element, organisations of both statutory and non-statutory types aimed at voter education. As Sabela and Reddy show, a vigorous process is underway by which the electorate is informed of local (or 'community') elections through various means — workshops, media, etc. This is also part of strengthening the structures by which governance can form a healthy element in South Africa's political economy. This, too, may in time come to be seen as a model for other states to emulate.

Part of governance is to note and handle society's conflicts in various ways. An ostrich-like refusal to do this cannot be a long-term solution, even if it seems useful as an immediate response. Some issues this volume discusses relate to conflict. First, and perhaps most vitally, the end of apartheid did not automatically end the city social formations created by that system. The incorporation of previously segregated areas is fraught with tension and is complicated, for example, by informal settlements affecting middle class persons, whatever their race, in many places.

Several of these contributions bring out not only this point but also its importance for local government. In rural areas there are also conflicts to be considered. McIntosh's chapter on rural institutions makes important references to conflicts surrounding chieftainship and political parties. He argues that there has been poor management of a tension often not based on principle but on personal insecurities and ignorance of what is being proposed. He also makes the point that the legislative framework is inadequate, a situation that also makes for conflict's easy emergence.

7 CENTRAL AND PROVINCIAL LEVELS OF GOVERNMENT

This is another thread running through South Africa's local government system in transition. Botha, specifically, deals with this issue but others also draw readers' attention to the fact that local government is only understandable within a framework encompassing other levels of government. Botha shows that this has to be understood in relation to provisions of the constitution giving powers to provinces. It also stipulates that government be structured at national, provincial and local levels. As local government is subordinate to the province, checks and balances are important and have yet to be firmly rooted in the system.

The danger is a real one; erosion of local government powers can arise from provinces operating under the guise of federalism just as it can from an excessively authoritarian administration at the centre. Reddy, in his chapter on reform processes, indicates the institutional arrangements that have been created in provincial government to regulate local government, and also shows the need to be aware of constitutional and legal factors affecting relationships between levels of government.

Other contributors pick up this point from different angles. For example, McIntosh sees the problem of rural local government being partly resolvable through a strong department dedicated to local government rather than a part of a broader set of issues in the Department of Constitutional and Provincial Affairs. This would, as its name implies, require a minister with a portfolio focusing on local government. It was clearly an oversight not to form such a department in 1994.

Moodley and Sing echo Croeser's view in stressing that intergovernmental relations are fundamental to the way local government finance operates and that South Africa, as elsewhere, will have to compromise between local autonomy and centralised direction and control (Croeser 1992). It can be concluded that any transformation of local government must take into account the relationships between different levels of government.

8 THE URBAN RURAL DIVIDE

A common feature of systems of local government in many countries is a sharp distinction between urban arrangements and those made for rural communities. In this sense, the system in developing countries comes to reflect a social and economic divide. In their chapter on NGOs, Maharaj and Jaggernath use the term 'urban bias' to characterise the excessive emphasis placed on urban areas in discussions of NGOs and local government itself. This term — originally coined by Lipton — is one that disguises urban poverty (Lipton 1977). However, it has considerable utility for understanding the issues emerging in South African local government, and helps ensure that the tenor of this book does not reflect an unbalanced approach in which rural issues are neglected.

Most chapters are focused on urban areas because of their importance in demographic, economic and political terms. This has not, however, excluded the rural dimension. It is addressed directly by McIntosh while Wallis, Moodley and Sing, B Maharaj and Jaggernath examine its relevance to the implementation of the RDP and to the role of NGOs in their respective chapters.

Capacity-building needs, resource scarcities, poverty and political problems are in some ways greater and more intractable in rural than in urban areas. Fundamental to this are two points.

First, in South Africa there are many rural areas that have never had local government along conventional lines (elected members, a paid staff, etc). Instead there have been traditional systems in many areas, especially in the former homelands, or a form of area management conducted by white farmers on their own land. This situation is hard to reconcile with the winds of change now blowing, and cannot be wished away. The welfare of rural people has to be given greater attention in the new era, not less.

Secondly, both the African National Congress (ANC) and the civic associations appear to reflect a phenomenon observed in West Africa many years ago; relatively well-organised in the major urban centres but weak on the periphery (Zolberg 1966:35). More than most parties in Africa, however, the ANC is an urban-based body, notwithstanding its stated desire to develop rural society through measures such as land reform and water supply. Thus, the transformational agenda for local government has to be one in which urban bias is not only eschewed, but takes seriously both the distinctiveness and importance of rural communities.

9 THE DEVELOPMENT OF RESOURCES

Two broad types of resource are to be reviewed. Both figure significantly in this volume. First, there is finance, which, although only directly discussed in one paper, Moodley and Sing's, is of definite importance. As signified by their suggestive phrase, it is a 'golden thread' running through local government. The second is, of course, people. An overview of some of the issues is provided by Penceliah while Levy and Shamina Maharaj provide a case study of human resource development in action when looking at a Durban-based affirmative action project. Pam Maharaj and Sing discuss a different issue within this broad topic; gender should not be overlooked within the agenda for transformation being suggested here.

These issues need to be seen, however, in relation to the capacity-building and empowerment needs highlighted either in general terms (particularly by Swilling et al) or in specific contexts such as development planning (Wallis), environment (Roberts) and NGOs (Maharaj & Jaggernath).

There are two broad concerns that can be mentioned here. The first is that there is a clear resource gap. Implementation of key measures like the Local Government Transition Act and the RDP cannot be expected to succeed unless resources are mobilised in a more effective way. This applies to both financial and human resources. It suggests several measures; training, restructuring of budgets and more effective placement of staff are just examples of what can be attempted.

The second point is that resource problems are legacies of apartheid that still need to be overcome. This means that resource development has to be accomplished so that the inequalities of the past are reduced even if they cannot be corrected. It is in this context that affirmative action becomes important. Through their case study, Levy and Shamina Maharaj show that genuine progress within the sphere of local government is possible. As a corollary, it can be argued that if Durban and the University of Durban-Westville can carry out such a programme, doing the same should be possible for equivalent institutions elsewhere. The question of affirmative action is too often thought to be only a matter of race. The case study of Durban does not neglect gender, however, and Pam Maharaj and Reddy's chapter contains detailed discussion to reinforce the need to act on this vital issue.

On finance, the legacy is one of marked imbalances between formerly white areas and the rest of the country. The importance of financial redress is stressed by Moodley and Sing.

10 TRANSFORMATION OR STAGNATION?

The main threads running through this volume have been outlined. They relate to the system of local government in various ways. Some are more optimistic than others but most point towards transformation and away from the stagnation feared by many. Some contributors are concerned with resources, particularly the staff and money needed to make the system deliver what is expected of it. Others are primarily concerned with the impact of local government on the wider society it is supposed to serve. The discussions of the environment and local economic development are in this category. A number of chapters concern questions of structure. Various contributors look at the existing structures and those of the past, but also to the future under the rather uncertain direction of current legislation and the interim constitution. Structural questions also include the relations between local authorities and other levels of government. The power and influence of the provincial governments need to be addressed, for example. The key issue arising is that of local government autonomy which is clearly affected by how other levels of government exercise their powers.

Another set of issues to bear in mind is the linkage between local authorities and the communities being served and represented. In the current period, much emphasis is placed on community involvement. RDP documents and political speeches are replete with references to this perceived imperative. It follows that local government has a duty to give concrete meaning to this rhetoric. Issues such as how best to involve bodies such as civics in local government development projects need to be addressed urgently. There are major problems to be faced, such as poor community organisation in many rural areas and violence in communities around the country.

The fundamental vision underlying this agenda is to build a system of local government combining local democracy with the capacity to meet at least the key needs of the communities, many of which have standards of living which cannot be accepted indefinitely in a society emerging from the evils of the past. The implied transformation agenda of this volume may not be wholly comprehensive, and it may leave some issues blurred and uncertain. However, it does indicate what has to be done, presenting vivid snapshots of current trends.

11 REFERENCES

Clarke M & J Stewart. 1988. *Managing Tomorrow*. United Kingdom: Local Government Training Board.

Croeser G. 1992. Financing of local government. In Reddy PS & M Wallis (eds) *Critical Aspects of Local Government Administration in a Post-apartheid South Africa*. Durban: University of Durban-Westville.

Lipton M. 1977. *Why Poor People Stay Poor: Urban Bias in World Development*. Cambridge: Harvard University Press.

Saul JS. 1991. South Africa: between 'barbarism' and 'structural reform'. *New Left Review*.

Singh M. 1992. Transformation Time! *Transformation* 17.

Zolberg A. 1966. *Creating Political Order*. Chicago: Rand McNally.